DATE DUE			
Jun26 '73			
~~Oct 28 '73~~			

THE RANDOLPHS OF VIRGINIA

THE RANDOLPHS
OF VIRGINIA

Jonathan Daniels

Garden City, New York

DOUBLEDAY & COMPANY, INC.

1972

ILLUSTRATION CREDITS

1. Virginia Historical Society
2. Virginia Historical Society
3. Virginia Historical Society
4. Courtesy of Angus Menzies
5. Virginia Historical Society
6. Courtesy of Mrs. Charles Baird, Jr.
7. Courtesy of Mrs. Charles Baird, Jr.
8. From the book NANCY ASTOR: *An Informal Biography* by Maurice Collis. Copyright © 1960 by Maurice Collis. Published by E. P. Dutton & Co., Inc. and used with their permission.

Library of Congress Catalog Card Number 72–76146
Copyright © 1972 by Jonathan Daniels
All Rights Reserved
Printed in the United States of America
First Edition

Contents

PART FOUR

Dispersal

THE RANDOLPHS OF VIRGINIA

THE RANDOLPHS OF VIRGINIA

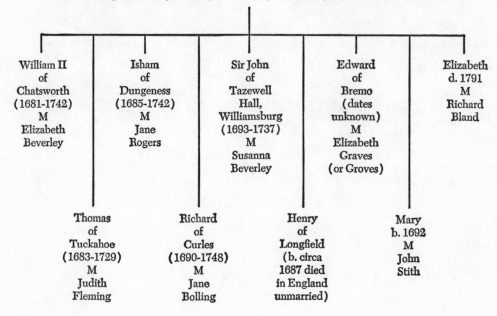

William Randolph of Turkey Island (1651?-1711)   M   Mary Isham of Bermuda Hundred

| William II of Chatsworth (1681-1742) M Elizabeth Beverley | Isham of Dungeness (1685-1742) M Jane Rogers | Sir John of Tazewell Hall, Williamsburg (1693-1737) M Susanna Beverley | Edward of Bremo (dates unknown) M Elizabeth Graves (or Groves) | Elizabeth d. 1791 M Richard Bland |

| | Thomas of Tuckahoe (1683-1729) M Judith Fleming | Richard of Curles (1690-1748) M Jane Bolling | Henry of Longfield (b. circa 1687 died in England unmarried) | Mary b. 1692 M John Stith |

CHATSWORTH

William Randolph II (1681-1742) M Elizabeth Beverley

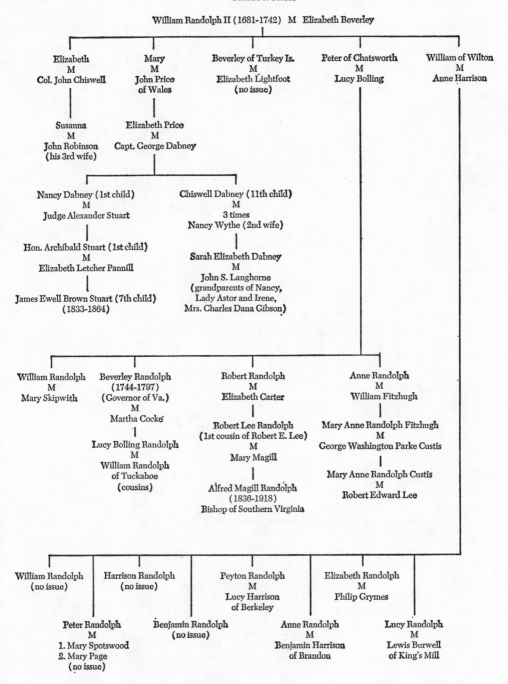

Elizabeth
M
Col. John Chiswell

Mary
M
John Price
of Wales

Beverley of Turkey Is.
M
Elizabeth Lightfoot
(no issue)

Peter of Chatsworth
M
Lucy Bolling

William of Wilton
M
Anne Harrison

Susanna
M
John Robinson
(his 3rd wife)

Elizabeth Price
M
Capt. George Dabney

Nancy Dabney (1st child)
M
Judge Alexander Stuart

Chiswell Dabney (11th child)
M
3 times
Nancy Wythe (2nd wife)

Hon. Archibald Stuart (1st child)
M
Elizabeth Letcher Pannill

Sarah Elizabeth Dabney
M
John S. Langhorne
(grandparents of Nancy,
Lady Astor and Irene,
Mrs. Charles Dana Gibson)

James Ewell Brown Stuart (7th child)
(1833-1864)

William Randolph
M
Mary Skipwith

Beverley Randolph
(1744-1797)
(Governor of Va.)
M
Martha Cocke

Robert Randolph
M
Elizabeth Carter

Anne Randolph
M
William Fitzhugh

Lucy Bolling Randolph
M
William Randolph
of Tuckahoe
(cousins)

Robert Lee Randolph
(1st cousin of Robert E. Lee)
M
Mary Magill

Mary Anne Randolph Fitzhugh
M
George Washington Parke Custis

Alfred Magill Randolph
(1836-1918)
Bishop of Southern Virginia

Mary Anne Randolph Custis
M
Robert Edward Lee

William Randolph
(no issue)

Harrison Randolph
(no issue)

Peyton Randolph
M
Lucy Harrison
of Berkeley

Elizabeth Randolph
M
Philip Grymes

Peter Randolph
M
1. Mary Spotswood
2. Mary Page
(no issue)

Benjamin Randolph
(no issue)

Anne Randolph
M
Benjamin Harrison
of Brandon

Lucy Randolph
M
Lewis Burwell
of King's Mill

TUCKAHOE

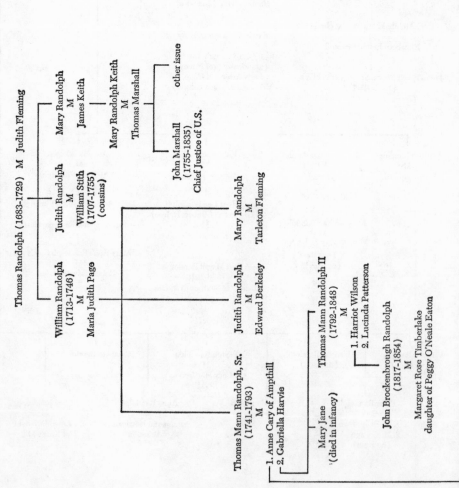

Thomas Randolph (1683-1729) M Judith Fleming

William Randolph (1713-1746) M Maria Judith Page

Judith Randolph M William Stith (1707-1755) (cousins)

Mary Randolph M James Keith

Mary Randolph Keith M Thomas Marshall

John Marshall (1755-1835) Chief Justice of U.S.

other issue

Mary Randolph M Tarleton Fleming

Judith Randolph M Edward Berkeley

Thomas Mann Randolph, Sr. (1741-1793) M 1. Anne Cary of Ampthill 2. Gabriella Harvie

Thomas Mann Randolph II (1792-1848) M 1. Harriot Wilson 2. Lucinda Patterson

Mary Jane (died in infancy)

John Brockenbrough Randolph (1817-1854) M Margaret Rose Timberlake daughter of Peggy O'Neale Eaton

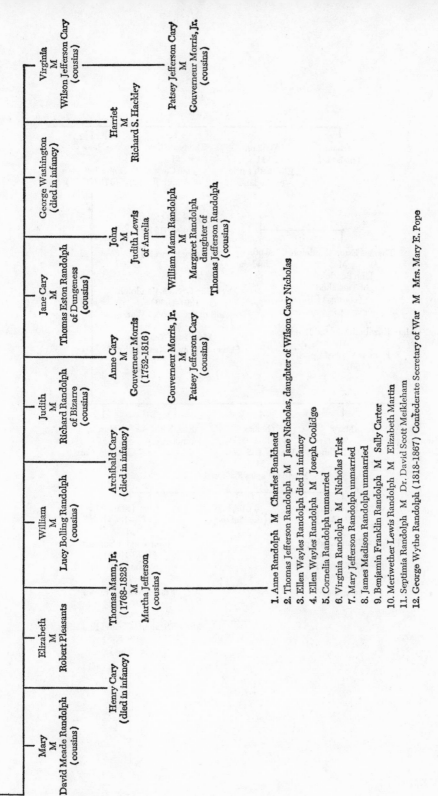

1. Anne Randolph M Charles Bankhead
2. Thomas Jefferson Randolph M Jane Nicholas, daughter of Wilson Cary Nicholas
3. Ellen Wayles Randolph died in infancy
4. Ellen Wayles Randolph M Joseph Coolidge
5. Cornelia Randolph unmarried
6. Virginia Randolph M Nicholas Trist
7. Mary Jefferson Randolph unmarried
8. James Madison Randolph unmarried
9. Benjamin Franklin Randolph M Sally Carter
10. Meriwether Lewis Randolph M Elizabeth Martin
11. Septimia Randolph M Dr. David Scott Meikleham
12. George Wythe Randolph (1818-1867) Confederate Secretary of War M Mrs. Mary E. Pope

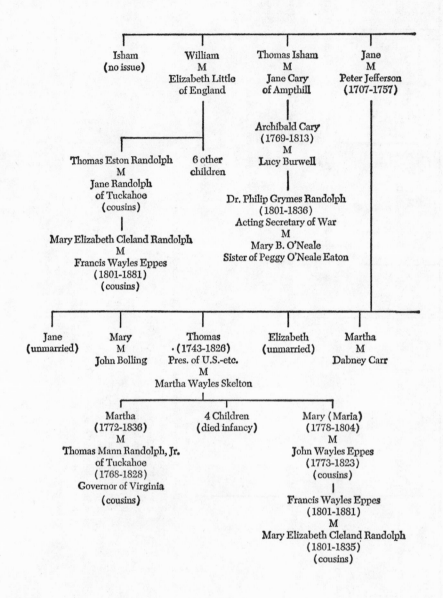

Isham
(no issue)

William
M
Elizabeth Little
of England

Thomas Isham
M
Jane Cary
of Ampthill

Jane
M
Peter Jefferson
(1707-1757)

Archibald Cary
(1769-1813)
M
Lucy Burwell

Thomas Eston Randolph
M
Jane Randolph
of Tuckahoe
(cousins)

6 other
children

Dr. Philip Grymes Randolph
(1801-1836)
Acting Secretary of War
M
Mary B. O'Neale
Sister of Peggy O'Neale Eaton

Mary Elizabeth Cleland Randolph
M
Francis Wayles Eppes
(1801-1881)
(cousins)

Jane
(unmarried)

Mary
M
John Bolling

Thomas
· (1743-1826)
Pres. of U.S.-etc.
M
Martha Wayles Skelton

Elizabeth
(unmarried)

Martha
M
Dabney Carr

Martha
(1772-1836)
M
Thomas Mann Randolph, Jr.
of Tuckahoe
(1768-1828)
Governor of Virginia
(cousins)

4 Children
(died infancy)

Mary (Maria)
(1778-1804)
M
John Wayles Eppes
(1773-1823)
(cousins)

Francis Wayles Eppes
(1801-1881)
M
Mary Elizabeth Cleland Randolph
(1801-1835)
(cousins)

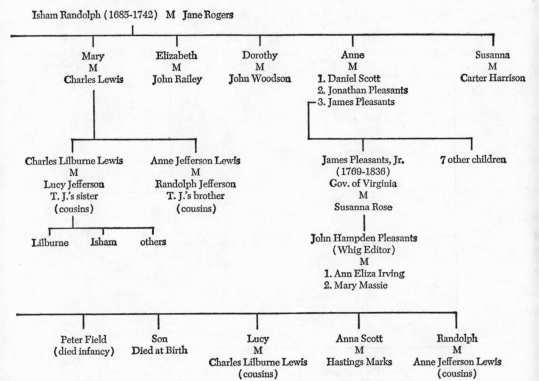

DUNGENESS

Isham Randolph (1685-1742) M Jane Rogers

Mary M Charles Lewis	Elizabeth M John Railey	Dorothy M John Woodson	Anne M 1. Daniel Scott 2. Jonathan Pleasants 3. James Pleasants	Susanna M Carter Harrison

Charles Lilburne Lewis
M
Lucy Jefferson
T. J.'s sister
(cousins)

Anne Jefferson Lewis
M
Randolph Jefferson
T. J.'s brother
(cousins)

James Pleasants, Jr.
(1769-1836)
Gov. of Virginia
M
Susanna Rose

7 other children

Lilburne   Isham   others

John Hampden Pleasants
(Whig Editor)
M
1. Ann Eliza Irving
2. Mary Massie

Peter Field (died infancy)	Son Died at Birth	Lucy M Charles Lilburne Lewis (cousins)	Anna Scott M Hastings Marks	Randolph M Anne Jefferson Lewis (cousins)

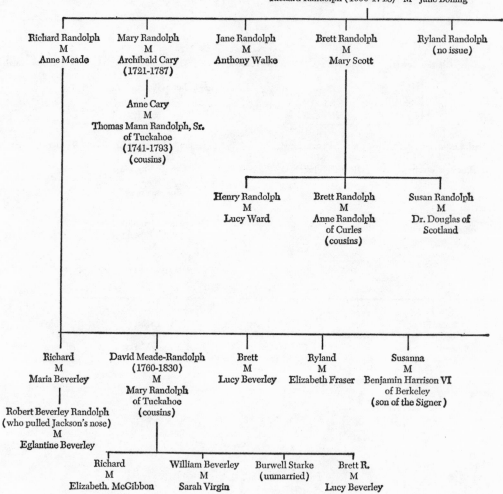

CURLES

Richard Randolph (1690-1748) M Jane Bolling

Richard Randolph
M
Anne Meade

Mary Randolph
M
Archibald Cary
(1721-1787)

Jane Randolph
M
Anthony Walke

Brett Randolph
M
Mary Scott

Ryland Randolph
(no issue)

Anne Cary
M
Thomas Mann Randolph, Sr.
of Tuckahoe
(1741-1793)
(cousins)

Henry Randolph
M
Lucy Ward

Brett Randolph
M
Anne Randolph
of Curles
(cousins)

Susan Randolph
M
Dr. Douglas of
Scotland

Richard
M
Maria Beverley

David Meade-Randolph
(1760-1830)
M
Mary Randolph
of Tuckahoe
(cousins)

Brett
M
Lucy Beverley

Ryland
M
Elizabeth Fraser

Susanna
M
Benjamin Harrison VI
of Berkeley
(son of the Signer)

Robert Beverley Randolph
(who pulled Jackson's nose)
M
Eglantine Beverley

Richard
M
Elizabeth. McGibbon

William Beverley
M
Sarah Virgin

Burwell Starke
(unmarried)

Brett R.
M
Lucy Beverley

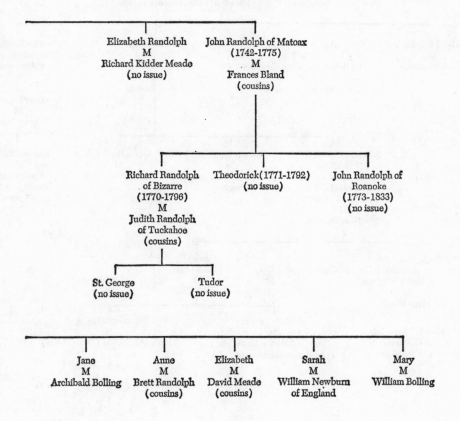

Elizabeth Randolph
M
Richard Kidder Meade
(no issue)

John Randolph of Matoax
(1742-1775)
M
Frances Bland
(cousins)

Richard Randolph
of Bizarre
(1770-1796)
M
Judith Randolph
of Tuckahoe
(cousins)

Theodorick(1771-1792)
(no issue)

John Randolph of
Roanoke
(1773-1833)
(no issue)

St. George
(no issue)

Tudor
(no issue)

Jane
M
Archibald Bolling

Anne
M
Brett Randolph
(cousins)

Elizabeth
M
David Meade
(cousins)

Sarah
M
William Newburn
of England

Mary
M
William Bolling

TAZEWELL HALL, WILLIAMSBURG

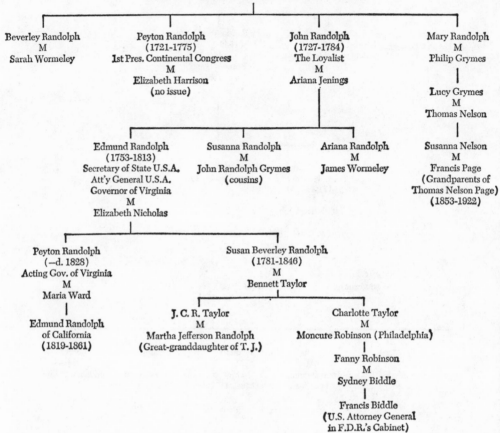

Sir John Randolph (1693-1737) M Susanna Beverley

Beverley Randolph
M
Sarah Wormeley

Peyton Randolph
(1721-1775)
1st Pres. Continental Congress
M
Elizabeth Harrison
(no issue)

John Randolph
(1727-1784)
The Loyalist
M
Ariana Jenings

Mary Randolph
M
Philip Grymes

Lucy Grymes
M
Thomas Nelson

Edmund Randolph
(1753-1813)
Secretary of State U.S.A.
Att'y General U.S.A.
Governor of Virginia
M
Elizabeth Nicholas

Susanna Randolph
M
John Randolph Grymes
(cousins)

Ariana Randolph
M
James Wormeley

Susanna Nelson
M
Francis Page
(Grandparents of
Thomas Nelson Page)
(1853-1922)

Peyton Randolph
(—d. 1828)
Acting Gov. of Virginia
M
Maria Ward

Susan Beverley Randolph
(1781-1846)
M
Bennett Taylor

Edmund Randolph
of California
(1819-1861)

J. C. R. Taylor
M
Martha Jefferson Randolph
(Great-granddaughter of T. J.)

Charlotte Taylor
M
Moncute Robinson (Philadelphia)

Fanny Robinson
M
Sydney Biddle

Francis Biddle
(U.S. Attorney General
in F.D.R.'s Cabinet)

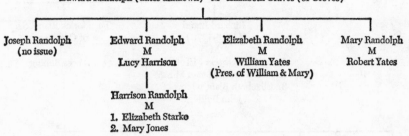

Edward Randolph (dates unknown)　M　Elizabeth Graves (or Groves)

| Joseph Randolph
(no issue) | Edward Randolph
M
Lucy Harrison | Elizabeth Randolph
M
William Yates
(Pres. of William & Mary) | Mary Randolph
M
Robert Yates |

Harrison Randolph
M
1. Elizabeth Starke
2. Mary Jones

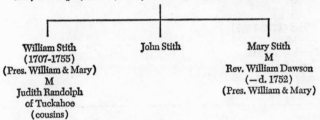

Mary Randolph (b. 1692)　M　John Stith (President of William & Mary)

| William Stith
(1707-1755)
(Pres. William & Mary)
M
Judith Randolph
of Tuckahoe
(cousins) | John Stith | Mary Stith
M
Rev. William Dawson
(— d. 1752)
(Pres. William & Mary) |

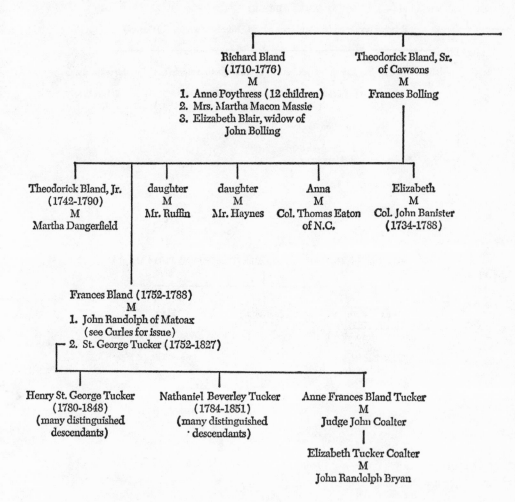

Richard Bland
(1710-1776)
M
1. Anne Poythress (12 children)
2. Mrs. Martha Macon Massie
3. Elizabeth Blair, widow of
John Bolling

Theodorick Bland, Sr.
of Cawsons
M
Frances Bolling

Theodorick Bland, Jr.
(1742-1790)
M
Martha Dangerfield

daughter
M
Mr. Ruffin

daughter
M
Mr. Haynes

Anna
M
Col. Thomas Eaton
of N.C.

Elizabeth
M
Col. John Banister
(1734-1788)

Frances Bland (1752-1788)
M
1. John Randolph of Matoax
(see Curles for issue)
2. St. George Tucker (1752-1827)

Henry St. George Tucker
(1780-1848)
(many distinguished
descendants)

Nathaniel Beverley Tucker
(1784-1851)
(many distinguished
descendants)

Anne Frances Bland Tucker
M
Judge John Coalter

Elizabeth Tucker Coalter
M
John Randolph Bryan

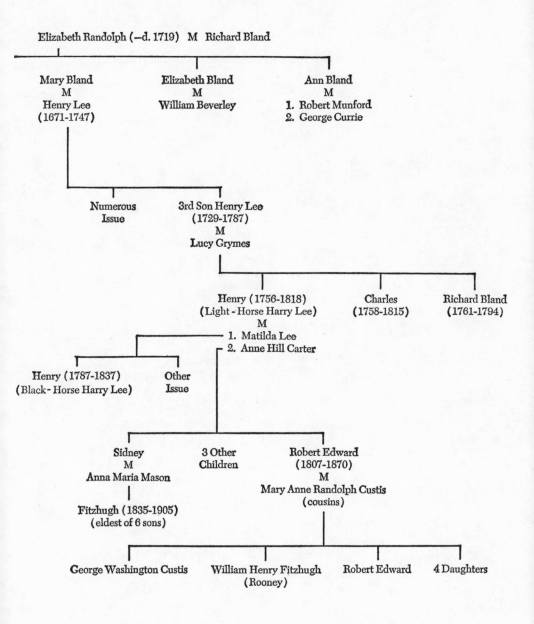

Elizabeth Randolph (—d. 1719)   M   Richard Bland

Mary Bland
M
Henry Lee
(1671-1747)

Elizabeth Bland
M
William Beverley

Ann Bland
M
1. Robert Munford
2. George Currie

Numerous
Issue

3rd Son Henry Lee
(1729-1787)
M
Lucy Grymes

Henry (1756-1818)
(Light-Horse Harry Lee)
M
1. Matilda Lee
2. Anne Hill Carter

Charles
(1758-1815)

Richard Bland
(1761-1794)

Henry (1787-1837)
(Black-Horse Harry Lee)

Other
Issue

Sidney
M
Anna Maria Mason

3 Other
Children

Robert Edward
(1807-1870)
M
Mary Anne Randolph Custis
(cousins)

Fitzhugh (1835-1905)
(eldest of 6 sons)

George Washington Custis

William Henry Fitzhugh
(Rooney)

Robert Edward

4 Daughters

PART ONE

In the Beginning

Chapter I

THE RANDOLPH STUD

ATTENDED BY THEIR slaves they came—ladies and gentlemen, young and old, at a gallop and in lumbering carriages. In caparisoned groups some shouted welcome to old friends and new summers. Others arrived at the old Virginia springs only hoping to escape aches and ills by copious consumption of the waters. All brought together gossip and anecdotes, tragic recitals, animated accounts of both great deeds and dirty tricks in the society of the Old Dominion. They made a history or a story diversely compounded of laughter and lament, battle song and hunting cry, political slogans, the wail and cackle of slaves, groan and giggle, love song and curse. And in the annual cavalcades to the springs, visiting hospitable relatives on the way, none were more omnipresent than the much intermarried Randolphs, so many of whom were greatly destined or tragically damned. Virginians who regarded them with admiration and familiarity pronounced their name as Ran'-duff.

Tall tales were told at and about the springs they frequented—fountains gushing and trickling, cool and sweet, hot and sulphurous. Romantic reports were made about these resorts and those who repaired to them, especially in the first years of the nineteenth century, for hilarity or health or, as often was the case, out of habit. These summer assemblies have been recalled in terms of beautiful women, handsome men, liveried servants, and flower-lined lovers' walks. Among the perennial visitors imported patterns of chivalry were worn like capes on the colonnaded ways from rambling hotels to the pavilioned sources of the water.

Not all descriptions of the springs were so romantic. Some visitors described them as slattern rows of cabins and barnlike hotels about the medicinal fountains which merely served as excuse for some who preferred the bars to the springs. One fastidious visitor wrote of the bar at one where "cock tails, gin slings, gum ticklers, mint juleps, phlegm cutters, and other sherberts were brewed from morn to night for the crowds of spitting and swearing, cursing and coughing, smoking and stinking *reel* gentlemen." The food was bad and the slave servants slovenly and insolent, he wrote.

Much other history suffers from such disparity of report and remembrance. The certain fact, however, is that Thomas Jefferson and George Washington, on occasion, gave the springs their praises. So did other gentle folk who hurried up from the miasmas of Tidewater Virginia, the South Carolina Low Country, and the malarial regions of other states. One such visitor in 1826 was John Randolph of Roanoke, whose life was lived, or reported, in violent extremes. He demanded, though he did not always get, decent service in the hostelries of his time. One tale is that when he was served a hot beverage at an inn he regarded it with the characteristic severity of a man who made many men laugh as well as cringe but was seldom recorded as laughing himself and as cringing never. On this occasion he said to the servant, "If this be tea, bring me coffee and if it be coffee, bring me tea."

At the springs he had the company of politicians, planters, sportsmen. Some were intimidated by him. Others were only delighted by his conversation. In all he had an audience which assured the wide repetition of any story he related. That was particularly true of anything he said about the turf and track, of horse breeding and horse racing in which, as in oratory, he had few peers. As a young man he was described as a centaur. He sat high in his saddle when he was almost too old and sick to stand on his feet.

He was no longer young at the springs in 1826. A thousand wrinkles etched his parchment skin. Now a United States Senator, Randolph as a stripling in his twenties had served as legislative leader for his cousin Thomas Jefferson. Later he had violently quarreled with the President who used his son-in-law to drive Randolph temporarily from Congress. Others hated and feared this gaunt aristocrat. Though he looked as if a slight breeze would blow him into eternity, when he spoke in his high soprano voice, which made his sexual potency suspect, the galleries filled. Even those who hated most his scorpion tongue were fascinated by his flow of words.

Some opinions attributed to him seemed fantastic. To a company of horse-lovers like himself at the springs he stated one. He announced confidently that the Waverley Novels from which Virginia gentlemen borrowed so much, including the names of their horses, had not been written by Walter Scott. The real author, he insisted, was one William Greenfield, British philologist and biblical scholar. None of the gentlemen listening to Randolph were equipped to refute his dictum with the information that Greenfield had been only fifteen years old when the Waverley Novels began to provide patterns for Virginia gentry. There was then room for speculation about the name of the novelist. Scott himself only admitted authorship of the novels in 1827, a year after Randolph talked at the springs.

His listeners, however, were not innocent about equine lore. Still apparently none of them dared contradict flatly another revision of accepted fact which Randolph made, emphasizing his booted discourse with his riding crop. Walter Scott, as the unintentional architect of Southern chivalric mythology, might be proclaimed an imposter. But this second pronouncement struck at a first faith of Virginians: the sanctity of the stud book. After a century of formalized thoroughbred horse breeding in Virginia, the Old Dominion gentry guarded, as a matter of honor, truth in horse heredity. Any divergencies were scornfully described as "Kentucky pedigrees." But now Randolph told them an amazing tale about the greatest Virginia horse of the time, Sir Archie.

He was not, said the statesman-sportsman, sired, as was generally believed by Diomed, who in 1780 had won the first Derby at Epsom. Something never told, he declared, had happened when the great blind mare Castianira had been offered to Diomed in the spring of 1804. He recalled that the mare had been in the breeding stables of his cousin, the elegant Captain Archibald Randolph of Ben Lomond in Goochland County. When she was taken to be mated to Diomed, another horse, Gabriel, a splendid English racer, had been brought into the paddock as a teaser to ready the blind Castianira for the mounting of Diomed. But impatient and powerful Gabriel declined his warm-up role and consummated his own desire instead.

Gabriel, Randolph told his scandalized listeners, was bay in color. A sire passed on his color to his get. Sir Archie was a bay, too, while his supposed sire Diomed was a chestnut. He had the story straight, the man of Roanoke said, from a white groom who had attended the mating. Possibly Randolph was spoofing some he thought deserved no better, as on occasion he did. There may have been too much in his glass as sometimes happened. The story may have been a dream induced by the opium he had begun to take to ease his painful ill health. Its telling could have been a sign of the aberration already overtaking him. Witnesses were quickly found to swear refutation of his story. Solemn statements from them appeared in Virginia newspapers, in the *American Farmer* and the *American Turf Register and Sporting Magazine*. Randolph himself later publicly retracted his own story in an advertisement that one of his stallions, Roanoke, would stand at stud for a fee of twenty-five dollars. He advertised: "Roanoke was got by Sir Archy, which was bred by Archibald Randolph, esqr., and got by Sir Charles Banbury's Diomed."

Still the story lingered on to be retold, though as mythology, a century later by another man of Randolph lineage, Fairfax Harrison, railroad president, scholar, and a student of pedigreed horses. In addition to books on his own family and other first families of Virginia, he privately published two scholarly works: *The Equine F.F.Vs.* and *The Randolph Stud*. He was curious to compare critically "essays in the genealogy of human immigrants to Virginia" with studies in the "genealogy of imported English horses." As investigator he found that "the modern practice of equine genealogy has reached a higher historical level than that of contemporary human genealogy."

He felt justified, then, he said, "in recommending the study of

Stud Books, and the really remarkable literature of scientific generalization which has been founded upon them, to those patriotic societies of America in which genealogy has become a cult."

As a Randolph, a Cary, and a Harrison, Mr. Harrison could afford to speak lightly of horses and men. Here he slyly suggested that the cult has become almost a comedy in a democracy with the multiplication of organizations of dames and daughters and sons of this and that. Mr. Jefferson saw a sinister possibility in a society based on heredity which seemed to him less concerned with patriotism than the perpetuation of privilege. Still that Society of the Cincinnati appears merely elegant in its palatial quarters on Massachusetts Avenue in Washington.

Certainly it seems almost self-effacing beside the annual teeming in the capital of the robust ladies of the D.A.R. If the Begats began in Genesis there is no end to them. Sometimes they are made merely the servants of status, occasionally deviously and sometimes desperately sought. But history does lie in the records of families, often to be more clearly seen there than in the *Congressional Record* or even Presidential Papers. Too often the families behind history are obscured by the solemnity of state papers and state-paper histories. With people, as with horses, the qualities of creatures may be better understood in terms of performance in their paddocks or home places than on the stage or the track.

Of course, in horse breeding treatises more attention is paid to the champions than to the culls as is true among the tracers of human family trees. Yet both are inescapable items in the breed. One may throw light on the other. Mr. Harrison's title, *The Randolph Stud*, could apply to the Randolph family as well as the generations of horses which they kept, primarily for breeding. If Sir Archie's heritage was momentarily touched by scandalous report, the same was also true of the Randolph line. The more important thing is that in American history and genealogy the Randolphs were and long remained a racehorse breed, outrunning all the families of their American neighbors in national contribution and in personal drama as well. This is true despite the fact that some in the breed lacked speed and stamina. Some were plugs and others could never be broken to the bit. Good and bad, they multiplied. William Cabell Bruce, biographer of Randolph of Roanoke, wrote that Randolphs "spread over Southside Virginia almost as thickly as young pines sown by the winds do over one of its broom sedge fields." Southside was only the seed-bed.

Other families have proliferated greatness. There were the Adamses early and late, and their neighbors the Cabots and Lowells presumably nearer to God. Out of the Calvinistic bed of the Reverend Jonathan Edwards and his mystic wife, Sarah Pierpont, came an amazing progeny of the great, the wicked, and the good, including as only two of its many notables Aaron Burr and J. Pierpont Morgan. Of course, there were and are other great families: Roosevelts, DuPonts, Rutledges, Pinckneys, now Rockefellers and Tafts. Still in terms of personages in power and skeletons in closets, sometimes involving the same individuals, the Randolphs are unsurpassed as a family intimately involved in the whole procession of American history from the Colonial frontier to the Chicago of Al Capone—and beyond.

They are certainly not merely "of Virginia." Indeed, as has been proudly noted by the librarian of the Boston Athenaeum, whose children are Randolphs, there have been more Randolphs in the line of Jefferson in Massachusetts than in Virginia. A proudest one of them, Thomas Jefferson Coolidge (1831–1920), indicated how long that line can stretch. At some distance from his grandfather's Declaration of Independence he wrote that he believed himself "to belong to a superior class, and that the principle that the ignorant and poor should have the same right to make laws and govern as the educated and refined was an absurdity."

Not all in the breed have been so brusquely confident of their place and powers. Yet, blood was certainly counted thicker than water in early Virginia. And Randolphs thickened it by many intermarriages. A Virginia saying was that nothing was good enough for a Randolph except another Randolph. In slight departure from that rule they bred back and forth with Carys and

Beverleys, Stiths and Lees, Blands and Harrisons, Carters and Bollings, other first families. Some of the greatest Randolphs did not bear the name. All acknowledged its blood. So intermingled did their marital relationships become that some early Virginia wit likened the family to a tangle of fishhooks so snarled together that it was impossible to pick up one without pulling three or four after it.

So strong lines were drawn together as in the twisted strands of a rope. But fault was doubled and redoubled too in bloodlines which produced strength and genius but also eccentricity, retardation, even madness. Randolphs helped put the republic together and tried mightily to tear it apart. They preached democracy and scorned it, hated slavery and depended upon it. And sometimes Randolph blood ran to murder and miscegenation. Occasionally, as in the case of Diomed and Gabriel, there was a questioning about sires. And sometimes fortune and misfortune seemed equally foaled by a blind mare.

As an insistent democrat Jefferson seemed to dismiss the ancient status of his Randolph ancestors. One tradition is that they were descended from the Earls of Moray in Scotland and connected with the family of King Robert Bruce. As an old, much beset philosopher, Jefferson wrote: "They trace their pedigree far back in England and Scotland, to which let everyone ascribe the faith and merit he chooses." This "playful fling at long pedigree," as his first important biographer Henry S. Randall described it, brought from that writer an exclamatory footnote. Jefferson, he insisted, would have been guilty of no such "questionable taste" as a "serious intention to discredit the pedigree 'traced' by his maternal relatives." He only wished, Randall wrote, to prevent "the impression that *he* attached any undue importance to the *fact just named by him.*"

Randolph of Roanoke never seemed to dismiss the importance of his ancient lineage. He was descended, he declared, from a race which was never known to forsake a friend or forgive a foe. But privately, in describing the lines from which he was sprung, he told a lady relative, "It was not necessary or even desirable that the descendants of these families should be learned or shining men, but they might have been better than mere Will Wimbles. Ah! I wish they were even no worse than humble Will. But some are what I will not stain my paper with."

This Will Wimble was no Randolph invention as a character sometimes representative of the Randolphs and other great Virginia families. If John of Roanoke had his doubts about Walter Scott, generally he knew his English literature. He lifted Will from the writings of Joseph Addison in *The Spectator,* which gentlemen had read in Virginia as well as in London coffeehouses. He expected the lady relative to whom he wrote to remember the passage from Addison and to understand its Virginia equivalent. He felt no need to repeat for her the essayist's description:

Will. Wimble is younger Brother to a Baronet, and descended of the ancient Family of the Wimbles. He is now between Forty and Fifty; but being bred to no Business and born to no Estate, he generally lives with his elder Brother as Superintendent of his Game. He hunts a Pack of Dogs better than any Man in the Country, and is very famous for finding out a Hare. He is extremely well versed in all the little Handicrafts of an idle Man: He makes a May-fly to a Miracle; and furnishes the whole Country with Angle-Rods. As he is a good-natured officious Fellow, and very much esteemed upon account of his Family, he is a welcome Guest at every House, and keeps up a good Correspondence among all the Gentlemen about him. He carried a Tulip-Root in his Pocket from one to another, or exchanges a Puppy between a couple of Friends that live perhaps in the opposite Sides of the County. Will. is a particular favorite of all the young Heirs, whom he frequently obliges with a Net that he has weaved, or a Setting-dog that he has made himself: He now and then presents a Pair of Garters of his own knitting to their Mothers or Sisters, and raises a great deal of Mirth among them, by enquiring as often as he meets them *how they wear?* These Gentleman-like Manufactures and obliging little Humors, make Will. the Darling of the Country.

There were such Randolphs. Such candor about them, often compounded with acid, could be expected from this John Randolph who added "of Roanoke" to his signature to differentiate himself from a second cousin who bore the same name. Nobody could hate a Randolph as a Randolph could and often did. The ancient motto of the family had been a phrase drawn from Horace, *Nil admirari* (Wonder at Nothing). But John of Roanoke's father, who left a will marked by extreme expressions of love and hate, had changed it on his coat of arms to *Fari quae sentias* (Say what you think). Sometimes Randolph of Roanoke in bitterness, outrage, or aberration carried this family slogan to extremes in talk about both horses and men—and women.

Mr. Jefferson, who shared the love of horseflesh and the sport of horse racing, was more moral and philosophical about the business. Once at the White House the tart diarist, Senator William Plumer of New Hampshire, listened to his Presidential conversation about crops, weather, sickness.

"From these," Plumer wrote, "he went into an effectual means to improve the breed of horses—That nineteen out of twenty of the horses that were bred for the race would not answer that purpose—that these nineteen proved excellent horses for the saddle and for the carriage, and the twentieth only answers for the turf. That all people will have their amusements—that horse racing is less injurious than playing at cards or dice as the Bostonians do. In the latter case a man is frequently ruined by a single game of cards, or throw of the dice—but not so as to horse raising (sic)—it requires several races to sweep a man's property, and that gives time for reflection."

Something similar was true of the Randolphs. Not all the colts produced would grow into Sir Archies or, down his bloodline, to such later-day horses as General Robert E. Lee's Traveller and the thoroughbred racers Man o' War, Native Dancer, War Admiral, Gallant Fox. But, though the Sage of Monticello minimized it, there was a gamble, too, in the breeding of horses and people. Not all Virginians—not all Randolphs—were men of reflection. It took Jefferson a longer time to lose his solvency than one turn of the cards, one throw of the dice "as the Bostonians do." That happened all the same.

Perhaps Virginians in many ways were different. Randolphs were special. Certainly down the track of tradition, the galloping hoofs of straining throroughbreds have made a spectacle worthy of attention, of the hurrahs of the winners, and of the loud lamentation of the losers. The Randolph Stud has produced, as Jefferson said, some horses only fit to bear the burden of riders. Some were merely fit to pull, prancing, the ladies and gentlemen of the Walter Scott kind of romantic mythology who rode in carriages, sometimes called chariots. Other high-riding Randolphs only launched their spears in romantic Southern revivals of medieval tournaments in which the successful knight crowned his queen of love and beauty. Still in a higher ratio than most breeds, the Randolph get has come as with flying manes to the power and the glory or—even in disaster—to illuminating revelation.

No sport of kings—or elegant gentry—has produced a pedigree which can be less lightly dismissed than that of the Randolph men and women. Fascination and repulsion both may attend it. The Randolph Stud still marks best the thoroughbred stock in the race to eminence over the crowded American centuries. They have excelled on the open track. They have both flashed by and faltered far behind in the national steeplechase filled with the fences, the wide water jumps, all the hurdles of history. They have been cheered and damned—and deserved both. But always with them the dramatic is bred in the bone.

Chapter II

GENESIS

IN THE SPRING of 1737 on the crushed oyster shell streets in the little village-capital of Williamsburg the position and the past of the Randolphs of Virginia was paraded in muted procession. The dogwood and redbud were just beginning to flower in the woods about the town where no Indians any longer lurked. Buds were just showing in the gardens behind prim brick and frame houses along wide, straight Duke of Gloucester Street and narrow lanes beside it. In quietness the body of Sir John Randolph, dead in his prime at forty-four, was carried to his last and ornate resting place.

The event dramatized in dignity what his father, William Randolph the immigrant, and his prolific sons and daughters had wrought since the family was established in the colony with William's arrival a little more than three score years before. In terms of noblesse oblige and pride in noble position, Sir John had planned his own obsequies, including his burial in the sandy pink brick chapel of the College of William and Mary which his father had helped found. No hearse drawn by plumed horses was required. The recently established *Virginia Gazette,* which in the prosperous and occasionally pretentious colony often indulged in lively social satire, solemnly, on March 11, told the story of the sad event and the elegant past which illuminated it:

"He was (according to his own instructions) carried from his house to the Place of Interment, by six honest, industrious, poor House-keepers of Bruton Parish; who are to have Twenty Pounds divided among them: And the Rev. Mr. Dawson, one of the

Professors of that College, pronounced a Funeral Oration in Latin. His Corps was attended by a very numerous Assembly of Gentlemen and others, who paid the last Honours to him, with great Solemnity, Decency, and Respect."

Then the *Gazette*, in terms which must have been provided and approved by the family, gave the Randolph historical background: "He was a Gentleman of one of the best Families in this country . . . yet his Family was of no mean Figure in England, before it was transplanted hither. Sir Thomas Randolph was of a Collateral Branch, which had the Honour, in several important Embassies, to serve Q. Elizabeth, one of the wisest Princes that ever sat on an English Throne, very nice and difficult, and happy, even to a Proverb, in the Choice of her Ministers. Among these, Sir Thomas made no inconsiderable Figure, and is acknowledged to have been a Man of great Parts and Ability, and every Way equal to the Employments which he bore."

Less elegiac history agrees that this Thomas was a man of parts, but the role he played for Elizabeth was often more devious than decorous. He served the Virgin Queen in her implacable feud with her cousin, the brave, beautiful, bad Mary Queen of Scots. He was ready with bribery. He was not appalled by useful murder. He was skilled in the incitement of civil war and when he made violence inevitable, wrote the Scottish man of letters Andrew Lang, he was "in high spirits as always when mischief was in hand." Elizabeth later used the talents she had discovered in him as secret agent by making him her Chancellor of the Exchequer. He served in that financial post during the years when Elizabeth was deviously seeking to avoid the break with Spain because she understood that war meant taxation and that taxation was the most probable parent of revolt. Randolph was out of the post soon after the Armada came.

In terms of pen and tankard rather than cloak and dagger, the obituary family history turned to another Randolph of the same name: "Mr. Thomas Randolph, the poet, was great Uncle to Sir John. An immature Death put a Stop to his Rising Genius and Fame; but he had gained such a Reputation among the Wits of his age, that he was exceedingly lamented; and Ben Jonson always expressed his Love and Esteem for him, calling him by no other Title, but that of Son."

This Thomas was a sweeter character than the earlier one. His education marked his family's position before his poetry endeared him to Jonson and others at the Mermaid Tavern. He was sent to Westminster, one of the most ancient and eminent public schools in England. Then at Trinity College, Cambridge, this Thomas acquired two degrees and became a major fellow of the college in 1632. In this same year a play of his was presented before King Charles I and his queen. He wrote verses and masques. One of his productions was a gay interlude burlesquing a lecture in philosophy, the whole piece being an argument to support the claims of sack against small beer. Apparently he drank his share of both. He died in his early thirties at the house of his friend William Stafford of Blatherwick. His work was of a significance justifying editions of his poems as late as 1875, 1917, and 1929. Two biographies of the poet have appeared in the twentieth century. Certainly such attention seems merited by his poem "Gratulatory to Mr. Ben Jonson for Adopting Him to Be His Son." It began:

> I was not born to Helicon, nor dare
> Presume to think myself a Muse's heir.
> I have no title to Parnassus hill,
> Nor any acre of it by the will
> Of a dead ancestor, nor could I be
> Aught but a tenant unto Poetry.
> But thy adoption quits me of all fear,
> And makes me challenge a child's portion there,
> I am akin to heroes, being thine,
> And part of my alliance is divine.

After bows to these two Thomases, the *Gazette*'s obituary history went on: "The family were high Loyalists in the Civil Wars, and being entirely broken and dispersed, Sir John's father resolved (as many other Cavaliers did) to take his Fortune in this Part of the World."

The Randolphs apparently were, indeed, as Clifford Dowdey

wrote in *The Virginia Dynasties,* members of the "armigerous gentry," or those entitled to armorial bearings. Sir John was one of the first Cavaliers in Virginia to put a coat of arms on his bookplate in one of the finest libraries in the colony. Not all escutcheoned gentlemen fought against the Cromwellian upstarts. Some peers were enlisted on the side of the Parliamentary armies, and some rabble was attached to the forces of poor, stubborn King Charles I before he lost his head. The term "Cavalier" was first flung at the King's men as an epithet. It was used to proclaim them as overbearing swashbucklers—roisterous or swaggering gallants. In similar fashion the King's opponents were indiscriminately called "Roundheads." "Cavaliers" suggested that the name derived from the grimy and sometimes obstreperous short-haired apprentices of London.

By the time of the Restoration, however, both groups accepted the epithets as designations of honor. Royalists rejoiced in the term "Cavalier." It was nowhere more tenaciously clung to than in Virginia. In some cases this was tenacious indeed. One unromantic historian, surveying the lists of emigrants in the seventeenth century, wryly suggested that the archives of Newgate Prison and Old Bailey might prove a more fruitful source of genealogical information than records in Burke's heraldic reference books.

No such blots marked the Randolph English line. Certainly Sir John's father, William the immigrant, was entitled by birth to the well-understood designation of "Gentleman." Though much obscurity attends his youth in England, he had had the education of the wellborn. His descendant and genealogist, Wassell Randolph, wrote that he could read the Greek and Latin authors. This family chronicler also wrote that he was a staunch Royalist and apparently not always above the roistering qualities Roundheads applied to such men. Early in Virginia he was a devotee of horse racing. One record shows him participating with such other sportsmen as Soanes, Eppeses, Cockes, Napiers. This definitely was the sport of gentlemen. In the period, a barber who presumed to enter a horse in such racing was sternly treated in the courts.

But it was not required that a gentleman be absolutely impeccable in behavior. At one term of court in William Randolph's early days in Virginia when a grand jury charged ninety persons with public profanity, he was one of them. These were times for hearty men. His descendant, Wassell, reported that the Virginia family founder, "like so many prominent colonists, was an indiscreet eater and drinker." He suffered much from gout. Evidently, he was active, convivial, ambitious, and acquisitive. He came to Virginia at a time when, though poverty was prevalent, large fortunes were being made. From the first, William Randolph meant to acquire one.

He certainly did not make the three-month voyage to Virginia as a Cavlier refugee. According to the varying dates of historians he came sometime between 1669 and 1674. The monarchy had been restored in 1660. Governor William Berkeley had been called the "Darling of the People" before the colony, confronted by a small Cromwellian fleet, agreed to recognize the Commonwealth. This constituted no Cavalier surrender. In fact, the colony for the first time was given the right to elect its own governor. This could have planted in some Virginia minds early ideas of their own ability to rule themselves. But the ruling class for the most part remained loyal to the monarchy. After rusticating in the interregnum on the Eastern Shore, Berkeley returned to power with the Restoration. Some then found him resentful, tyrannical, his pride in power fed by a younger, shining-eyed, spitfire wife.

Possibly behind Randolph in England, his family had been "broken and dispersed" during the Civil Wars. There had been much fighting in the Midland County of Warwickshire where his family had its seat. William's father moved with at least part of his family to Dublin in harassed and prostrated Ireland. He died there in 1671, near the time of William's departure for America.

Almost certainly William came to Virginia at the behest—or with the encouragement—of his Uncle Henry Randolph. Henry, born in 1623, had gone to Virginia in 1642, when the Civil Wars were first brewing, as a young man less than twenty years old.

He had done well there. He aligned himself with the ruling coterie when he married Judith, daughter of Henry Soane, speaker of the House of Burgesses. His position in the colony was measured by his political advance at a time when offices, as a matter of course, went to the gentry. He became clerk of court in Henrico County in about 1656, a position in which William was to succeed him by his influence or in a sort of system of office inheritance which prevailed in the Old Dominion. In addition Henry was clerk to the House of Burgesses from 1660 to his death. He was obviously the Randolph referred to in the will of Miles Cary, proved in June 1667, in which this early member of a tribe with which the Randolphs would intermarry directed the sale of "the housing at Towne (which I bought of Mr. Randolph and have paid him for)." Evidently possessed of properties, this older Randolph, after twenty-seven years in the colony, returned to England on a visit in 1669. William's decision to settle in America coincided with his uncle's trip home.

Dying in 1673, Henry lived only briefly after his return to Virginia. He had prepared the Randolph way. Though he left progeny he is not counted as the founder of the famous family. William took that place. He was no pioneer. The "starving time" was far behind settled Virginia. By 1670 the colony's population had grown to 40,000 people (including 6,000 indentured servants and 2,000 Negro slaves). Settlement spread up the shores of the Tidewater rivers. The truly westward movement was yet to come. But already the Indians had been pushed back from the shore. Land-hungry Englishmen were pushing them deeper into the hills.

William was in his first twenties, a big man with a hawk nose, when he arrived in Jamestown, the still malarial capital of the colony. Fact and legend are mixed in his story. Charles Campbell, in his generally authoritative history of Virginia published in 1860, wrote of his arrival, "poor, it was said." He was described as arriving with only the tools of a carpenter with which as an "undertaker" or contractor he built houses, even barns. The biographer of his great grandson, Edmund Randolph, sniffed at this. He wrote that the statement that he had "built" houses for himself and his sons "led some literalist to suppose him a carpenter."

Whatever was his position or financial status, in 1674 he had money enough to pay the passage of twelve indentured servants whose headrights let him purchase a property of 500-odd acres on Swift Creek, less desirable than the James River shore. He was only beginning to acquire his landholdings. Still, by 1676, he had built a house and furnished it for—or in preparation for—a wife. This was a crucial year for Virginia and for Randolph.

The year before had been marked by omens, "prodigies" as they were called, which alarmed the superstitious. A large comet was seen nightly "like a giant horse's tail across the sky." Then came the flights of pigeons "in breadth nigh to a quarter of the mid-hemisphere, and of their length there was no visible end." When they roosted their weight broke the limbs from trees. Thousands were killed with the guns which still made the whites supermen compared with the arrow-armed Indians on the pushed-back frontier. But old settlers, regarding the "prodigies," remembered that "the like was seen in the year 1640 when the Indians committed the last massacre." The final ominous portent was the arrival of a vast swarm of flies which seemed to erupt from the earth. These insects were about an inch long and the thickness of the tip of a man's little finger. Afterwards these three happenings were regarded as "ominous presages" of Bacon's Rebellion.

There was nothing obscure about the background of Nathaniel Bacon, Jr. Both he and Randolph were young—Bacon, at twenty-nine, four years the elder. But Bacon was a cousin of Governor Berkeley, though he came with a somewhat tattered reputation to Virginia in 1674. His father had withdrawn him from Cambridge University because he had "broken into some extravagancies." His tutor found him a young gentleman of "very good parts, and a quick wit," but "impatient of labour, and indeed his temper will not admit long study." Such was his reputation that when he married Elizabeth Duke, daughter of Sir Edward Duke of Benhall, her father disinherited her and never spoke to her again.

Finally, though he had a "genteel competency," Bacon was involved in a scheme to cheat a young associate of part of his inheritance. With his patience exhausted, his father gave him 1,800 pounds and sent him on a tobacco ship to Virginia. There his faults were unknown or overlooked. He was welcomed by his cousin the Governor and by another elder cousin also named Nathaniel Bacon, a member of the prestigious Council of the colony. Berkeley helped him acquire lands, licensed him to trade with the Indians, and less than a year after his arrival paid him the extraordinary honor of appointment to the Council.

A place upon that body was the peak of the official hierarchy. Members were in a favorable position to secure large grants of land, which they did not hesitate to use. Good family helped to put a man on the Council and membership helped a man improve the family position. Men from a small number of families related by blood or marriage were in general chosen. Though a newcomer, young Bacon seemed to fit into the pattern of the conservative coterie. Within a year, however, the young man was embarked upon the course which led to the statement that William Randolph rose on Nathaniel Bacon's ruin.

Discontent was widespread in Virginia in 1676. Restored Governor Berkeley seemed querulously distrustful of the people and many of them were angrily distrustful of him. British trade laws had reduced the markets for tobacco and cut its price. Carolina and Maryland were competing in the growth of the crop and adding to overproduction. Taxes had been raised for defenses against the Indians who in futility still struck back at the pressures upon them and their lands. People murmured that Berkeley's taxes burdened them without really defending them. He was even charged with pampering the red men with whom, it was said, he profited in the fur trade. Even nature seemed intent upon impoverishing the people. Berkeley could not be blamed for the inordinately dry weather which made it hardly worthwhile for men to tend their planting. Indian sorceries, related to the "prodigies," could be blamed and related to sporadic Indian attacks. One redskin foray had resulted in the death of an overseer on young Bacon's frontier land. Near him, idle, angry men gathered with their arms.

"If wee make ¼ Cropps this year," wrote one planter, "Ile swear it must be by miracle, haveing the Dryest year, added to the maddest that ever I think the world saw."

Accused, angry, and beset, Governor Berkeley exclaimed, "How miserable that man is that Governes a People wher six parts of seaven at least are Poore, Endebted Discontented and Armed."

Not all the discontented were poor and indebted. While the ordinary folk murmured, four gentlemen were drinking together on the north bank of the James River near its junction with the Appomattox. One was William Byrd, son of a London goldsmith of moderate means, who was building a great fortune as land speculator, planter, merchant, Indian trader. He and Bacon had been partners in Indian trade. Faced with their demands for more vigorous anti-Indian action, Berkeley had cut off their trading rights. Byrd was twenty-four, five years younger than Bacon. Drinking with them was an older man, James Crews (spelled also as Crewes and Cruse). He was to be called "Bacon's parasyte." The fourth gentleman in the company, Henry Isham, was then or later closer to William Randolph.

Over their drinks that afternoon the gentlemen were "making the Sadnesse of the times their discourse, and the Fear they all lived in, because of the Susquahanocks who had settled a little above the Fall of James River, and Comitted many murders upon them, among whom Bacon's overseer happen'd to be one. . . ." While they talked, they observed a mixed body of armed gentlemen and frontiersmen on the other side of the river at Jordan's Point. It was proposed, apparently by Crews, that they visit the assemblage, and carry a quantity of rum for the armed men to drink. This they did, said investigators of the rebellion soon afterwards, "and (as Crews etc. had before laid the Plot with the Soldiers) they all at once in field shouted and cry'd out, a Bacon a Bacon! w'ch taking Fire with his ambition and Spirit of Faction and Popularity, easily prevail'd on him to Resolve to head them. . . ."

Bacon became a figure around whom endless debate has gone

on. 1676 was made a patriotic prelude to 1776. One biographer of the Lee family described young Nathaniel as the combined Patrick Henry, George Washington, and Thomas Jefferson of this earlier revolt. Today an impressive memorial in the Virginia Capitol at Richmond describes him as "A great Patriot Leader of the Virginia People who died while defending their rights, October 26, 1676. Victrix Causa deis placuit, sed victa Catoni." The argument about his role was marked within the Randolph family. Jefferson early helped build Bacon's image as that of an aristocratic young evangel of democracy but Edmund Randolph in his history of Virginia described him as a "penetrating demagogue" of "nefarious ambition." Only in the 1950s did Wilcomb E. Washburn discover among the papers of Henry Coventry at Longleat, the Wiltshire estate of the Marquis of Bath in the West Country of England, documents which belatedly gave Edmund Randolph the better part in the argument. Washburn's report was only colored by his evident feeling that the Indians were largely the innocents in the "defense" against them.

Bacon's legend will not soon be dismissed. Argument will continue about the events which followed his acceptance of the leadership of the angry men on Jordan's Point. They were determined to strike at the Indians with or without the Governor's permission. Enthusiastic historians and novelists have written of the retaliation on the menacing Indians (or the slaughter of innocent ones). In fact or fiction the story of Bacon's revolt races from the flight of Berkeley to the Eastern Shore once more, to Bacon's first submission, then on by gunfire, the incendiary torch, cry and countercry, to the politics of force. The oratorical leader of revolt and the outraged official of the crown both make dramatic figures on the stage of this angry year. But the lighting of the event is more incandescent than illuminating. Bacon won a majority of the House of Burgesses for democratic or demagogic reform. But Bacon and Bacon's men lost in their high-stakes gamble when the young leader suddenly died of exhaustion, camp filth, or malaria. Berkeley exultantly tied his hangman's knots.

Dialogue put into Bacon's mouth has helped make him seem

the hero: "Come on my hearts of gold! He that dies in the field, lies in the bed of honour." In high tragedy it is remembered that when he died his body was forever secreted to prevent its being drawn and quartered for post-mortem display by the victorious Governor. Berkeley in victory was made to seem a bloody tyrant. Other rebels were hanged in such numbers that King Charles II has been repeatedly reported to have said of Berkeley: "The old fool has killed more people in that naked country than I have done for the murder of my father."

William Randolph played no romantic role in this disturbance. Dowdey states categorically in *The Virginia Dynasties* that William was "a neutral during the rebellion." Still, possibly he was too close to Berkeley's ravening suspicions for comfort. His acquaintance, Crews, was one of those who swung from the gallows. Byrd, who afterwards became Randolph's close friend, made his peace with Berkeley long before the hanging season began. So apparently also did Henry Isham. That last was particularly important to young Randolph.

Henry Isham had long been established on the south side of the James on his plantation Bermuda Hundred. In that sparsely settled area, according to one Virginia historian, he was "something of the social arbiter." Randolph became the older man's friend and suitor for the hand of his daughter Mary. She was described as a "much courted belle" who played a lutelike musical instrument called a cittern. One writer felt, possibly in error, that her portrait showed "a long solemn face bearing a certain indication of suppression." She brought to William important colonial connections. Also she came as the principal heiress of her father.

William is generally reported to have married Mary Isham in 1680. However a document before this time showed her waiving her dower rights in one of his many land transactions. Perhaps the approximate date of their marriage is indicated in a document which must have been of considerable importance to William at the time it was drawn. In effect it undertook to prove that he had not been merely neutral in the rebellion but one of its victims. It purported to show that he was much plundered by Bacon's men. Whether the document stated the facts or was designed as an alibi, it indicated much as to Randolph's status. Evidently in the few years he had been in Virginia, his possessions had become impressive. Also the paper indicated that he had a wife—or one in prospect—to share them.

A later member of the Randolph family, Bishop William Meade, in writing of the "great folly in erecting . . . immense and costly houses," declared that William in his lifetime lived in "a house of moderate dimensions." Dowdey wrote of a dwelling he built as "an unpretentious one-and-one-half story house with a gabled roof and enormous outside chimneys." Randolph did not describe, in 1677, his losses in the rebellion as those of a moderately furnished household. Some of the items mentioned are described in archaic language. They make clear, however, that in the rebels' relentless foraging for food and dress, they had taken much. Obviously they had not only stripped Randolph's house and plantation of furnishings and cattle. Also what Randolph said they took suggests that Randolph was living at a higher than frontier level. Some of the things listed in his plea for reparations are surprising. Evidently he was living in a house where petticoats were worn and tablecloths were used. His own dress was indicated by the loss of a fine broadcloth coat and breeches to the foragers.

Whatever else it showed, this declaration of 1677 apparently settled any question about his loyalty to the Governor. Furthermore, Wassell Randolph wrote that he was the warm friend of Sir William and Lady Berkeley. He "was taken by Governor Berkeley to his heart, was a particular favorite of Lady Berkeley." Randolph's statement of losses was calculated to evoke the sympathies of both the Governor and his lady. Their own spreading brick mansion on their Green Spring Plantation, the first manor house in Virginia, had been both looted and greatly damaged by the rebels. Such a friendship would have brought young Randolph into the "Green Spring coterie" composed of Berkeley favorites who were said to be loaded with grants and honors. However, if Randolph was favored by such lofty affection it must have preceded the rebellion. The Berkeleys' days in

Virginia ended the year after the revolt had been sternly repressed.

Randolph had other excellent connections. Early he had taken the position occupied by his uncle as Henrico County clerk. His marriage brought him other valuable ties. Gradually he was elected to the offices, always in Virginia assigned to the gentry, of justice of the peace, coroner, sheriff, member of the House of Burgesses, and finally speaker of that body. He became a lieutenant colonel in the militia. Perhaps most significantly, he was escheator general for much of the colony. That was an office whose holder was in a place strategic for the acquisition of lands. Randolph tenaciously held it to his death. Then his friend and neighbor, the even more acquisitive William Byrd II eagerly sought it. It had special value at a time when the lands of Bacon and his followers had been forfeited to the crown.

If Randolph had come poor, he began to acquire lands early. He not only took the lands which he was entitled to purchase for his importation of indentured servants as new settlers. In 1674 he had bought his Swift Creek lands. In 1678 he had land to spare, selling 591 acres of this property in Henrico County, "on N. side Appomattox River & on N. side of Swift Creek," to one William Robins for 4,000 pounds of tobacco. The willing Mary waived her dower rights in this transaction. It was about this time that his acquisitive eyes regarded the properties of both James Crews and Bacon.

Others were looking at such lands. Benjamin Harrison (1673–1710) acquired the Berkeley Hundred property which had been occupied by Giles Bland before he took the route by rebellion to the gallows. The Harrisons and the Blands were to be neighbors who much intermarried with the Randolphs. Nearby were the properties of Byrd which he had saved by making his peace with the Governor. Randolph regarded other properties of Bacon and Crews on the north bank of the James. In 1684, he acquired, from the escheated estate of Colonel Crews, property on Turkey Island which became his family seat. And in 1698 (apparently the processes of confiscation moved slowly), he acquired the plantations of Curles, formerly Longfield, and Slashes. They had been "late in the seizen and inheritance of Nathaniel Bacon, jun., deced., and found to escheat to his most sacred Majesty by the attainder of Nathaniel Bacon, Junr., of high treason." For the Bacon properties Randolph paid only a hundred and fifty pounds.

If Randolph profited by his office that apparently was the accepted fashion. The Governors who followed Berkeley were not averse to using their power to fatten their pocketbooks. Robert Beverley, the historian whose people had played a conspicuous part in quelling Bacon's Rebellion, wrote of this in his *History and Present State of Virginia*, published in 1705. Of Thomas, Lord Colepepper (Culpepper), who became Governor soon after Governor Berkeley's departure, he said: "The Noble Lord was skilful in all the Ways of getting Money, and never let slip any Opportunity of doing it." Of Francis, Lord Howard of Effingham, who succeeded Culpepper, the historian declared: "This Noble Lord had as great an Affection for Money as his Predecessor, and made it his Business to equip himself with as much of it as he could, without Respect either to the Laws of the Plantation, or the Dignity of his office. His Lordship condescended to share with his Clerk, the Meaner Profits of Ministerial Offices."

Such Governors did not introduce greed and graft as alien things from England. Thomas J. Wertenbaker in his *Patrician and Plebeian in Virginia* wrote that the Council members were the boldest of all in dishonesty. If some Governors robbed the colony, some Council members even robbed the King. Quitrents, a tax on land the proceeds of which went to the King, were usually paid in tobacco. It was often convenient to sell the tobacco before shipping it to England. At the sales, conducted by their colleague the Treasurer, Councilors often bought the tobacco at far less than the prevailing price. Intimidation was used to keep outsiders from bidding. Also, wrote Wertenbaker, wealthy planters outrageously lied about their holdings: "Collectors and sheriffs in the various counties found it convenient not to question their statements of the extent of their property, while none would dare to prosecute them even when glaring cases of fraud came to light."

Beyond the Bacon bargain, there is no evidence that William Randolph engaged in sharing the corruptions of power. During the governorship of Sir Edmund Andros, who never turned his authority to personal profit, the ascending Cavalier was made the King's Attorney—a position which became almost a family possession. The only complaint against Randolph in that office was that he was not a trained attorney though he is said to have studied law privately.

He wanted opportunity for others to study in more formal fashion. He was an early supporter of the plan to establish a college in Virginia. In this he worked with Commissary James Blair and Governor Francis Nicholson who both collaborated and quarreled. Nicholson was as hot headed as he was honest. Randolph may have felt with Blair the violent temper the zealous Nicholson often displayed. Possibly he approved when the Commissary read the Governor a lecture on conduct. Randolph certainly was of the gentry which was appalled when Nicholson, after a belle of the Burwell family rejected him, threatened to cut the throats of her bridegroom, the clergyman, and the justice giving the license. No significant collision, however, marked Randolph's work as burgess and speaker with Nicholson. They worked together in the affairs of William and Mary College which was chartered on February 8, 1693. William was one of its trustees and founders.

Six of his seven sons became students at the college with which by blood and marriage so many of William's descendants were to be related—two as presidents. Some like Sir John, whose body was welcomed to its crypt, were eminent scholars there and some only dabbled and danced in its shaded environs.

Lawyer or not, William Randolph was almost everything else: official, soldier, planter, land speculator, merchant. His own ship sailed between his Turkey Island wharf and Bristol, England—carrying out tobacco, bringing back luxuries. From incoming vessels he purchased more and more black slaves. Such black cargoes accelerated the growth of the fixed Virginia aristocracy in which he was an increasingly important figure. Men able to acquire vast acreages and farm them profitably with slaves prospered, where poor men, with lesser holdings, quickly exhausted their soils by overcultivation of tobacco, and either confronted failure or moved on westward. It took a longer time for the slave culture of tobacco to deplete the big plantations of the rich. For them the problem was postponed for their sons. In William's last and richest years the swift increase in servile blacks had already begun which would carry their number in Virginia from 6,000 in 1700 to 30,000 in 1730, before Sir John was laid to rest.

From his plantations and his wharves William carried on an elaborate business through his agent Micajah Perry, to whom, like other planters, he sometimes found himself surprisingly indebted. Many shared the view expressed by Governor Berkeley, in London speaking as a Virginian before he was beset by Bacon, that "we cannot but resent, that forty thousand people should be impoverish'd to enrich little more than forty Merchants, who being the only buyers of our *Tobacco*, give us what they please for it, and after it is here, sell it how they please; and indeed have forty thousand servants in us at cheaper rates, than any other men have slaves. . . ."

No people appeared less servile than the new Virginia gentry. Despite the hazards of tobacco prices in London and overproduction in the colonies, which brought a kind of plant-cutting rebellion in 1682, William Randolph was no longer in danger of impoverishment. Apparently in his later years, despite Bishop Meade's report of his modesty in building, he joined in the first stages of mansion building. Moncure Daniel Conway, in his life of William's great-grandson Edmund Randolph, wrote that on William's vessel plying between Virginia and Bristol he brought English brick with which was "built the grand mansion with lofty dome." Its ruins, he said, remained as late as 1888. Undoubtedly, Randolph needed more room than the small house Bishop Meade described for the growing family with which Mary Isham presented him. She had less time now for the cittern than the cradle.

The boys came first and fast. A second William was born in 1681. Then came Thomas (perhaps named for one of the two Thomases mentioned in Sir John's obituary). Isham took his name from the family name of his mother. In swift succession came Richard, John, Edward, Henry. Two girls added to the family were Mary and Elizabeth. Genealogists have provided the statistics of their arrival. But the best picture of the family is provided in *The Secret Diary of William Byrd II of Westover 1709-1712*, who added the flesh of friendship to his reports about its members. The relationship of the Randolphs with the richer Byrd was particularly close. This was indicated when the diarist's father, William Byrd I, who had come so close to involvement in Bacon's Rebellion, was dying at his Westover plantation in December 1704. Historian John Spencer Bassett wrote: "He sent a boat for Lieutenant-Colonel William Randolph, who came at once, though the weather was bad. To him Byrd gave some instructions in regard to his will, and early the next morning he died." Such intimacy was continued when the younger William Byrd (1674-1744) succeeded to his father's vast estate and high position in the colony. He was made a member of the Council in 1704, taking the seat of his father. In his secret shorthand journal, he made many mentions of his friends the Randolphs.

One of the first such entries was about Isham, then in his twenties. Colonel Randolph, fifty-eight and unaware that death waited him three years later, came to talk with Byrd about a ship for that young man who was already looking to the sea. Byrd's next entry two months later was about Edward, Little Ned Randolph, who had come to visit at the Byrd place in order to be nearer school. In homesickness he outraged Byrd by spreading a tale that he was being starved. When rebuked, he ran away. His father joined Byrd in dire threat of punishment if he did such things again. Little Johnny Randolph, afterwards to become Sir John, Byrd found to be a much more promising pupil. Indeed, later, when John was nineteen, his rich neighbor was piqued when college authorities declined to make the young man an usher in recognition of his scholastic performance.

The brothers, Will and Tom, were old enough to play billiards with the master of Westover. Richard in his teens came over to talk with Byrd. So did Henry. Their father handled some of Byrd's business. He was the lawyer of the elegant diarist in a suit against a man who had carried off sixty of Byrd's apple trees. The elder Randolph did not lose Byrd's faith or friendship when he got only one shilling in damages for his client.

In August 1709, Byrd met the wife of young William Randolph II, Elizabeth Beverley of Gloucester County, "a good humored woman and is handsome." The elder William sent Byrd a sturgeon and shortly afterwards came to talk about their joint agent in London, Micajah Perry, whose close contacts with the Board of Trade seemed often better to serve him than his Virginia clients. Byrd must have been sympathetic since he was receiving ten letters from Perry "with a sad account of tobacco."

In connection with this matter, the suggestion drawn from Mary Isham Randolph's portrait that she was "suppressed" seemed not borne out. Byrd evidently regarded her as a wife seriously concerned in her husband's affairs. He noted that he had discussed with Mrs. Randolph "the debt which the Colonel owes to Mr. Perry." Apparently she was also already worried about the Colonel whose increasing tendency to gout the diarist noted.

Not all the Randolph visits to Westover were of such business-like nature. Byrd played a practical joke on Isham by luring him onto thin ice with a two-bit bet. Isham dropped into the cold water to his mid-leg. Still Byrd seemed to have a special interest in Isham. He invited him to stay with him and study French. He talked with Colonel Randolph about getting a ship for the young man. A little later Byrd noted that the death at sea from smallpox of a young ship captain "makes way for Isham to command Colonel Hill's ship for which he shall have my recommendation." Nobody in early Virginia scorned "trade," from ocean commerce to selling pots and pans—sometimes guns and whisky—to both Indians and their neighbors. The only tradesmen scorned were Yankee merchants who presumed to undersell big planters on Virginia rivers.

Command of a Virginia ship assured a man of both profit and a social position of consequence. However, Byrd not only helped but on occasion criticized the Randolph boys. Early in 1711 he spoke sharply to young Will, as budding lawyer, saying that the Governor was displeased with him "for not making more haste with the laws," which the young lawyer had been employed to transcribe or codify.

Worse news than a young lawyer's carelessness was in prospect. On March 17, 1711, Tom Randolph came to dinner. He settled the accounts of his father with the master of Westover. Also then, Tom told Byrd that his father "had the gout very much." News of the old complaint did not seem disturbing. But on April 4, Byrd learned that Colonel Randolph was very sick. On April 10, John Randolph "told me his father was very sick and desired a bottle of sack, which I sent him." Apparently, however, the family was not alarmed. John Randolph stopped at Westover on his way to Williamsburg. But on April 20, while Byrd was dining on roast mutton with the Governor, "the Doctor returned from his journey and told me all were well at Westover and that Colonel Randolph was extremely sick and in great danger."

The Colonel died at Turkey Island the following afternoon at five o'clock. The next day the sad but practical Byrd decided to seek Randolph's place as escheator "and then returned to Williamsburg where I made a visit to Mrs. Bland to console the death of her father." Elizabeth Randolph had married Richard Bland of Jordan's Point as his second wife. Richard was the cousin of Giles Bland, "the rebel," but lost neither his neck nor his lands in Bacon's revolt. Their child Mary was to be an ancestor of many of Virginia's famous Lees.

Wassell Randolph wrote that Colonel Randolph suffered from melancholia in connection with his final illness but that he had retained his mental faculties "through his declining years as evidenced by his execution of the lengthy will of March 6, 1709." He left debts to Micajah Perry which were to result in litigation. There was no question, however, about his wealth. Despite the house-building humility ascribed to Randolph, William Cabell

Bruce, in his biography of William's great-grandson John Randolph of Roanoke, had a very different report to make. Bruce wrote that Randolph "erected a splendid mansion at Turkey Island. . . . While the lofty dome of the mansion lasted, it was one of the conspicuous beacons by which the James River navigator directed his course, and its structure was so elaborate that we are even asked to believe that a man served out the entire term of his apprenticeship to the trade of carpenter in one of its rooms." Blair Niles, in *The James—From the Iron Gate to the Sea*, quoting an early authority, wrote that the first William built "a goodly house, with a portico on three sides, surmounted by a dome visible a great way off to the navigators of the James River, the whole surmounted by an aerial structure called the 'bird cage because many birds do hover and sing about it.'"

There is no question as to the wide dimensions of the landed estate William left. Before he died his lands extended in all parts of settled Virginia and in the west as well. He held 10,000 acres in Henrico County alone. He provided well for his daughters. He had seen them well married—Mary to Captain John Stith. Their son became president of William and Mary. His seven sons William established on estates of their own. They became the nearest American equivalent to lords of manors, masters of wide plantations and many slaves: William of Chatsworth; Thomas of Tuckahoe; Isham of Dungeness; Sir John of Tazewell Hall, Williamsburg, with lands in York County; Richard of Curles; Henry of Longfield; and Edward of Bremo.

A landed dynasty was established. It was later well described by a visiting Englishman overwhelmed by Randolph hospitality which he had little reason to expect. Whatever may have been the merit of the reported Randolph pedigree running back to jousting, combat, chivalry in early England and Scotland, the line ran to almost feudal position in Virginia. Thomas Anburey, in his journal of travels in Virginia, gave it classic description. He wrote: ". . . it may not be necessary to observe that the Randolphs are descended from one of the first settlers in this province of that name, and are so numerous, that they are obliged, like the clans of Scotland, to be distinguished by their places of residence."

In lands and slaves, money and progeny, lavish hospitality and high place, William's life seemed richly fulfilled. Only one item was lacking in the Randolph Virginia position. The family founder's name was repeatedly listed by Royal Governors as that of a person suitable for appointment to the lordly Council of the colony. He was never elevated to that privileged group. He did not require its inside opportunities for advance.

PART TWO

The March to Power

Chapter III

THE FINER CLOAK

YOUNG JOHN CARTER, law student at one of the Inns of Court, seemed much at home in the house of Captain Isham Randolph in London. He appeared as a familiar guest on August 5, 1718, when he dropped in after dinner and drank arrack punch with Sea Captain Isham and his wife, "a pretty sort of woman." Other Virginians gathered at this Randolph board. Isham was then not only making the long voyages back and forth between England and Virginia. He was also "merchant in Shakespeare's walk." Prior to this time he had been made an agent of Virginia in London though he was only twenty-seven. The company in his house was so congenial that it seems strange that three years later Jack Carter drew from his father, the great, rich Robert ("King") Carter, an almost furiously unfriendly Randolph portrait.

Jack Carter was no mere dandy corrupted, as so many rich young colonials were, by the pleasures of the city. Still, in July 1720, his tailor's bill outraged his father whose acres never spread so wide that he did not demand a penny's worth for his penny. Young Carter defended his expenditures. He wrote of a Randolph who had done him some disservice possibly by tattling to his father. And this Randolph, he said, was wearing finer clothes than he. Evidently he felt that this would touch his haughty father's pride. It produced an explosion.

"Mr. Randolph," the elder Carter replied, never had said anything to him to Jack's disadvantage, "so if he is under any obligation to you, he is, for what I know, clear of the sin of ingratitude." But "King" Carter cleared this unspecified Randolph of few other things.

"As for his wearing finer linen or finer clothes than you, he never appeared in any such here that I have seen. My acquaintance with him is very slender—only now and then casually at dinner. His principles and mine are of a very different nature: a rank Tory, a proud, humble parasite, a fawning sycophant to his patron, with all the other requisites to a servile courtier. These are as much reverse to my nature as white is to black; besides, though he was my tenant for a year and I gave him a retaining fee at his first coming in, he hath been, in all causes that I have had, against me. From whence you may conclude there is very little familiarity between us."

Possibly, as the editor of Carter's letters has suggested, this blast showed Carter's qualities better than those of the Randolphs. It may be that "King" Carter, whose boiling point was always low, was in a particularly irascible mood at this time. He was irritated with young John Randolph, who, as precocious advocate, had appeared with a "Mr. Beverley"—probably his brother-in-law—in a cause which Carter opposed. He wrote in scorn of a Cary, then or soon to be a Randolph marital connection, who was seeking, Carter thought, an unconscionable profit in a land deal. Also Carter's gout, from which so many Virginia grandees suffered, was troubling him.

But beyond personal irritations the times seemed out of joint. The financial world was entering the period rocked by the gyrations of the South Sea Company in England and the Mississippi Company in France. Carter's London agent had invested some of his money in the speculations. His great trading activities were threatened by pirates operating off the Virginia capes. Though the price of tobacco had shown some improvement, planters feared the opposite dangers of overproduction and poor harvests because of worm infestation. The "King" was in a mood to damn Randolphs, Beverleys, Carys with whom—possibly to his amazement in heaven toward which he was certain he was headed—his bloodlines would be joined.

Certainly his picture of parasitic, sycophant, upstart Randolphs was not the one presented in the planter society along the James River this summer. Their place seemed easy and secure, warm and welcome there. The eating, drinking, dancing, horse racing society Byrd described in his diary seemed almost a catalogue of Randolph friends and neighbors. Most of them were joined or would be joined in the "web of kinship" which underlay the growing oligarchy of prestige and power. Noted, in Byrd's account of the informal visiting back and forth, the dining, the exchange of gifts of fruit, fish, beverages, were the second generation Randolphs, William, Henry, and Thomas. They shared good living with Harrisons, Bollings, Burwells, Stiths, Ludwells, Hills, Cockes, Lightfoots, Eppeses, others. In this summer of Carter's explosion, young John Randolph of Williamsburg made an especially impressive entry into such company, from which he had been separated for years as student abroad.

On August 9, Governor Alexander Spotswood, with whom Byrd and others had quarreled over proposed changes in the method of collecting the quitrents and the powers of the Council, made a formal visitation to residents along the James River shore. Elaborate preparations were made to receive him. Byrd "got everything in great order" and went to meet the executive and his entourage at the "outer gate." There, prominent in the Governor's company, was young John Randolph. From Byrd's house the Governor's party went to Colonel Hill's. "After dinner we went to Colonel Randolph's in his boat." In the evening the Governor walked to "visit old Mrs. Randolph."

This gubernatorial promenade certainly seemed to make clear the Randolph position in the governing gentry. Yet another event soon made it apparent that Randolph advancement in the governmental hierarchy of Virginia was not yet aristocratically automatic. On August 30, Byrd, who became almost the Boswell of the Randolphs in this period, described an election for the Burgesses from the "upper county" of Henrico. Will and Tom, as he called the Randolph candidates, "won the greatest number of votes by their great industry." Already, however, they could depend upon more than their own electioneering labors.

In his diary Byrd mentioned "two Blands" and John Bolling as evidently helping the Randolphs. The Blands were almost certainly Richard, who had married their sister Elizabeth, and one of his two brothers, Theodorick or John. Theodorick Bland had married a Bolling as had Will's and Tom's brother, Richard of Curles. The identity of one person at the voting in the court-house is not clear. Rather oddly in that day of limited masculine suffrage, "Mrs. Randolph" was present. She could have been Candidate Will's wife Elizabeth of the powerful Beverley tribe. She might have been Candidate Tom's wife, Judith, of the richly landed Flemings. She may have been the honored ma-triarch Mary Isham Randolph still concerned as a widow with the advance of her brood.

Apparently the only Randolph not present in Virginia this summer was the sea captain Isham. He did not marry into the Virginia "web of kinship." Possibly he brought a leavening element into it. The Virginia and Randolph preference for Cavalier ancestry was already a part of the plantation parade. But Isham brought an almost perfect Roundhead or radical heritage into the family. Dumas Malone, in his biography of Isham's grandson, Jefferson, wrote that little is known about the Jane Rogers to whom Isham was married in the "parish of White Chapel" in London about 1717. Malone casually men-tioned that she was a "distant relative" of John ("Freeborn John") Lilburne. Remote as the relationship may have been, Randolph kin in Virginia preserved the surname Lilburne as a first name for generations.

In the days when Randolphs and others were said to be turning to Virginia as Cavalier refugees from Puritan revolution at home, "Freeborn John" Lilburne definitely qualified as a Roundhead. As the younger son of a good family apprenticed to a clothier, he probably wore his hair short like other young men in that status. Certainly he quickly acquired the political meaning of the term. His enemies later said that he early became addicted to "contention, novelties, opposition to govern-ment, and violent and bitter expressions." Even one of his radical friends said that "if the world was emptied of all but

John Lilburne, Lilburne would quarrel with John and John with Lilburne."

In his time he was much like some of the later British figures whom Jane Rogers Randolph's grandson, Jefferson, much admired. Lilburne got into trouble with the authorities early and was flogged and imprisoned for importing publications offensive to the bishops. Cromwell himself defended him in Parliament. But, as a soldier in the parliamentary army, he was too radical for his leaders. He turned on them writing under the Commonwealth about "England's New Chains." Brought to trial time and again, he was acquitted "to the great joy of London." He was too violent to tolerate and too popular to punish. "For the peace of the nation" he was confined in the Tower and a succession of other places. At last, coming under Quaker influence, he agreed to be done with "carnal sword fighting and fleshly bustlings and contests." A quieter man, he died at forty-three. He was not the lone deviate from a conventional Lilburne line. His brother, Colonel Charles Lilburne, member of Parliament for the East Riding of Yorkshire, was one of those who signed the death warrant of Charles I. At the Restoration, he was sentenced to life imprisonment.

There is no indication that Isham's Jane shared any radical ideas though it has been suggested that some Randolph eccentricity might have stemmed from her genes. In London she seemed only a pretty housewife to Virginians (including Jack Carter) to whom she served Virginia ham and arrack punch. Isham's acquaintanceship as sea captain and merchant was by no means restricted to colonials. Among those with whom he became acquainted was Peter Collinson, a Quaker, variously described as an apothecary and a plantsman. Actually, though much neglected by history (his name is not mentioned in the Encyclopaedia Britannica), he was an amazing international link between the new scientists and naturalists of his time. He was one of the principal correspondents of Carolus Linnaeus, the Swedish botanist who first brought system to naming of plants and animals. Collinson was also the man who first turned young Benjamin Franklin's interest to experiments in electricity. Other such persons of eminence and curiosity shared in London the hospitality which Isham and Jane dispensed to Jack Carter and other Virginians.

Isham's presence in Virginia in the summer of 1720 was not essential to the Randolph progress. He contributed more to it, however, than his brothers Edward and Henry. Edward, who was present in Virginia at this time and entertained at merry parties on his ship in the James, withdrew to England even more than Isham. He married an heiress in Bristol who, it was said, so hated slavery that Virginia was repugnant to her. Some of their descendants returned to the Old Dominion. Henry died unmarried in England. But before the election which Byrd reported, the Randolph brothers at home were building the family dynasty.

Long before his father's death, William II had in 1702 been named, at twenty-one, to the remunerative and influential office of clerk of the House of Burgesses. In 1710, he was appointed clerk of Henrico County, a position which both his father and his uncle had held before him. He acquired from brothers, probably Henry and Edward, some of their inherited lands. Also, he bought up the estates of deceased colonists which had been inherited by their kin in England. He seemed both shrewd and occasionally indiscreet. He repeated a remark of Byrd's about a request of Governor Spotswood for 20,000 pounds to finance Indian war in the west. No Governor should be trusted with 20,000 pounds, said Byrd. In the tight society of little Williamsburg, Spotswood heard Randolph's repetition of this remark. Byrd felt the Governor's ire but his friendship with the Randolphs was not broken. Both evidently were pleased by the reconciliation marked by Spotswood's visitation.

From 1713 forward, Thomas of Tuckahoe was one of the justices of Henrico in these days when the justices of the peace, largely drawn from the leading families, constituted positions of power and honor. Less politically inclined than William, however, he devoted himself largely to his plantations. Something of his wealth and position, before he was elected to the House of Burgesses, was shown by the still-preserved H-shaped house which he built in 1712 at his Tuckahoe Plantation. So, following his father, the builder Thomas demonstrated the architectural interests which marked the family. This house with its high chimneys without and elaborate carved paneling within was possibly improved after its first construction. It provided early a stage set for Randolph prominence as it stood high above the river with great trees and labyrinths of green box beside it. It would shelter scandal and promise and triumph, too, in the oligarchy of family relationships.

Richard of Curles, who married Jane Bolling, was a member of the House of Burgesses before Tom and Will were elected to it. By his marriage he not only brought Pocahontas as an ancestress into the family. He also, some thought later, brought a weak strain marked in its mildest form by a Bolling tendency to deafness. Richard was noted both for the support of the Anglican Church and his acquisition of land. Before 1720, he was already acquiring land in the valleys of the James, the Appomattox, and Roanoke rivers which would at last amount to 40,000 acres.

Young John, when he appeared with Governor Spotswood at Westover and Turkey Island in 1720, was already the pride of the family. Before he went abroad to study and before he was twenty-one, he had been appointed by Governor Spotswood to represent the crown in the courts of Charles City, Henrico, and Prince George counties. Now returning, he was said to be—possibly by his family—the best educated Virginian of his time. This may have been a slight exaggeration as Jack Carter had received his pre-law college education at Cambridge while John, as a Randolph, naturally went to William and Mary.

In the decade and a half after 1720 the family story seemed much on his shoulders. Soon after his return to the colony he married Susanna Beverley, sister of his brother William's wife. He became, as another Randolph, clerk of the House of Burgesses. Briefly he served as King's Attorney to stamp the office as almost an exclusive Randolph possession. Following his father in that office he would be succeeded in it by two of his sons. His grandson would hold a similar position as first

Attorney General of the State of Virginia and of the United States, too.

A man of less vigorous health than his brothers, he lived not on his inherited plantation but in Williamsburg. There, in 1725, he built a comfortable dwelling later to be called the Randolph-Peachy House which was long afterwards to be deemed worthy of inclusion in the Rockefeller restoration of the colonial capital. Later, as his legal earnings mounted, he would build the greater, splendidly paneled Tazewell Hall. Both houses, each with room for his growing library (said to be the best in the colony), and his collection of historical manuscripts, indicated his position as barrister, diplomat, and scholar.

He was only thirty-four in 1727 when William Gooch arrived as Governor to inaugurate what was to be called Virginia's "golden age." John was one of its principal ornaments. It began auspiciously when the Virginia Assembly, with Randolphs in in its membership, in effect spoke to Gooch in an address to the new King, George II. It declared: "It is the peculiar happiness of this country that we are more than any other of the American [colonies] united in the religion of the Church of England, and our civil rights and liberties are secured to us by the same excellent laws which have been the boast of the English nation, and have made them greater than any other people."

Governor Gooch responded to that address with such good will and good sense that he became the most popular Royal Governor Virginia ever had. The colony was not quite so united as the Assembly, composed largely of the Tidewater gentry, suggested. Governor Gooch indicated the kind of people with whom he was surrounded by his statement that "the gentlemen and ladies here are perfectly well bred, not an ill dancer in my government."

Not all were dancing in Virginia. Small farmers were more and more being crushed out beside the great plantations flourishing from the labor of many slaves. So profitable did the larger planters find the use of blacks that by a dozen years after Gooch arrived Negroes outnumbered the whites in the population of the colony. Already, however, a stream of migration composed of

Irish, Germans, Scots—many of them dissenters—were pouring into western Virginia. Hardly aware of it, Tidewater gentry were already threatened by the democracy of the west, by debts to English agents, and by the depletion of the land from which they produced more and more and more tobacco.

Tobacco was dancing, riding, feasting, fine clothes, or it was hard times, debt, anger, and insolvency. Ever since Nathaniel Bacon's time, however, tobacco had been the basic problem as well as the golden treasure. Now, particularly in terms of it, Governor Gooch made himself the Governor of Virginia as well as the Governor of the King and the powerful British merchants. And in this John Randolph became his chief collaborator.

The year after the Governor's arrival in a cause which had his first support, John Randolph was dispatched to England by the Assembly. Probably William Randolph, who this year became a member of the Council to which his father had aspired but had never attained, had something to do with John's choice. Other Randolphs sat in the House of Burgesses which dispatched him. While the tobacco problem was paramount, his mission was threefold. It was hoped that the sea voyage would improve his delicate health. For Randolphs and other tobacco planters, he was sent to seek the repeal of an act of Parliament which prohibited the shipping of tobacco stripped from the stalk. This regulation had added to shipping costs which cut tobacco income.

John's third concern demonstrated the close ties of the Randolphs with William and Mary College of which their father had been a founding trustee. The college sent him to ask the Archbishop of Canterbury to sanction the use of certain funds, which had been provided for the education of Indians, for the purchase of books. John, as scholar as well as lawyer, was to select the volumes. He was successful in all the purposes of the voyage to England with the possible exception of improvement in his health. The obnoxious tobacco act was repealed. A grateful Assembly voted him a thousand pounds for his efforts. The trip bound the Randolphs closer than ever to William and Mary. Beyond wealth this relationship to the colony's intellectual aspirations added to their distinction. Like clothes, acres, mansions, and slaves, relationship to learning added to status. Philip Fithian, as a tutor later in the great house of the Carters, told his successor that "having finished with Credit a Course of studies at Nassau-Hall" would add 10,000 pounds to his valuation in Virginia.

No family was so long so close to William and Mary. Evidently, as many did not, they got along well with Reverend James Blair. This pugnacious founder and president of the college was also, as Commissary, the resident head of the Anglican Church in the colony. Governors might come and go (often at his insistence); Blair remained despite the opposition of some rich and powerful persons. He had married a lady as tart as himself, Sarah Harrison, daughter of Councilor Benjamin Harrison II. While others did Blair's bidding (or else!), this lady at this early date declined to agree to the word "obey" in the wedding ceremony. Still, the web of kinship was shaping in this marriage, too. John Randolph's son Peyton would marry a Harrison. So would William II's son, William of Wilton.

The Randolphs seemed almost wedded to the college. At least four Randolphs were to represent it in the House of Burgesses. Randolph sister Mary became almost the lady of the college due undoubtedly to the efforts of William, Isham, Thomas, Richard, and John. She had married Captain John Stith, "sometime sheriff of Charles City County and member of the House of Burgesses." Soon she was left a widow with promising children. Looking out for their own, the Randolphs secured her appointment as housekeeper to board and lodge the masters and scholars. As a witness of her work, Reverend Hugh Jones, in his *The Present State of Virginia,* published in 1724, wrote: "This office is at present performed in the neatest and most regular and plentiful manner, by Mrs. Mary Stith, a gentlewoman of great worth and discretion, in good favor with the gentry, and great esteem and respect with the common people." Obviously she was no drab housekeeper. Visiting the college Byrd recorded in his diary that he had lost "two bits" to her in a card game. The stakes apparently were not high but no Puritan ideas barred the minor vices, against which dissenters and even some Anglicans were beginning to inveigh. Graduates of William and Mary were expected to learn not only Greek and Latin but fencing, dancing, and riding. As to the last, little instruction was required. Many scholars arrived mounted and riding at the planter's pace which approximated a gallop.

The Randolph connection with the college was to continue long after Mary served so plentiful a fare. Her son, William Stith, who in Randolph fashion married his first cousin, Judith, daughter of Thomas of Tuckahoe, became president of the college. This was only the beginning of the Randolph blood connection with the institution. William Stith's sister Mary married Reverend William Dawson, who became president, too. He was succeeded by his brother, Thomas Dawson, who perhaps had special need of Randolph connections. Before the board of visitors he confessed to habitual drunkenness. He was given a second chance. As said by the Governor at the time, who often joined Randolphs at the race track, "he had been teased by contrariety [sic] of opinions between him and the clergy into the loss of his spirits, and it was no wonder that he should apply for consolation to spirituous liquors." Only death ended Thomas Dawson's drinking. His successor, William Yates, "one of the family which abounded in ministers," almost as a qualification married Elizabeth, daughter of Edward Randolph of Bremo. To cap the connections this Yates's brother, Reverend Robert Yates, married Mary Randolph, the sister of his brother's wife. Evidently in much of this period the Randolphs, as in the case of their housekeeping sister Mary, carried on nepotism in "the neatest and most regular and plentiful manner."

Some mystery both at home and abroad attended the year 1732, when John undertook a second mission to England. He was sent again by the Assembly in connection with perennial tobacco problems. He was to urge upon the British government a plan for an excise collected through a bonded warehouse system in place of existing import duties on tobacco. This time John failed to get what he sought. Still the trip was a triumph for him. The Burgesses rewarded his efforts with double his previous remuneration. Also, though he failed to convince the British government, he must have pleased it. He was knighted, "presumably in 1732," in recognition of his legal and diplomatic skill. Two centuries later, however, his descendant, U. S. Attorney-General Francis Biddle was still wondering "what was the nature of his service to the King" which warranted the honor. Whatever it was, he was the only Virginian so honored in the colonial period. Robert Carter might be "King" by a popular nickname. The Randolphs had Sir John attested in the College of Arms.

This visit to England added to his fortune as well as his fame. According to Washington's biographer Freeman, he was not only dispatched by the Assembly but also sent "across the Atlantic" by the rich and irascible John Custis, whose son was the first husband of Martha Washington. Custis needed John as the most distinguished member of the Virginia bar in connection with prolonged litigation involving the estate of his father-in-law, aristocratic, arrogant, profligate Daniel Parke. Custis had married Parke's daughter Frances; William Byrd II, his daughter Lucy. As British Governor of the Leeward Islands in the West Indies, Parke's rakish career ended in 1710 with his murder by an angry mob in Antigua. He left a complicated will and heirs including not only his daughters in Virginia but also bastard progeny in the islands. Also he left debts and properties in Virginia, the islands, and in England. One who turned up among his creditors was Micajah Perry, British merchant, to whom everybody in Virginia, including Randolphs, seemed to owe money.

Custis must have been a difficult client though he expressed confidence in John's "prudent management" of the litigation. Custis and his wife hated each other in a classic case of conjugal antagonism. Once in anger with his wife he drove his carriage from his place in Arlington on the Eastern Shore into Chesapeake Bay. His wife Frances demanded where he was going. "To Hell, Madame," he cried. Imperturbably she said, "Drive on. Any place is better than Arlington."

John evidently handled the case with skill and his client with tact. How large a fee he collected in this case is not clear. Certainly such private practice improved Randolph's personal prosperity. And he shared with Sir William Gooch the plaudits for the planter prosperity based on reforms in tobacco marketing in England and at home. The romantic picture of colonial Virginia began to be drawn. The notion grew that it would always be high tide in Tidewater. Even a plantation like Tuckahoe constructed "after the Virginia manner of building" no longer sufficed. Neither did the old plantation breed of horses. Mansions in the English tradition, called Georgian after the contemporary Kings, were erected. English racing thoroughbreds were imported.

As a genealogist of both horses and men, Fairfax Harrison wrote that the gentry began to "import and use 'chariots' for occasions of ceremony; to drink madeira instead of bumbo; to ride formally to hounds; and to keep horses for racing only." The gentry had long matched "speedy riding nags" and had claimed a caste privilege in doing so, but now advertisements began to appear for organized subscription race meets. On fast horses the gentlemen were booted and spurred. It seemed incredible as tobacco money poured in that gentlemen might be riding to a fall worse than any stumble in steeplechase racing.

Not all was happiness in the Randolph family, however, in the year Sir John was knighted. His brother Thomas of Tuckahoe had died before he reached fifty in 1730. And in 1732 while Sir John was making his arguments and earning his honors in England, Byrd, on a visit to his iron mines in the west, stopped on the way at Tuckahoe. Thomas had left 8,300 acres of land on both sides of the James, but Byrd found the household poorly stocked with drinkables. As a diarist he was provided with plenty for his pen.

"The widow smiled graciously upon me," he reported, "and entertained me very handsomely." She had, however, a tale of trouble to tell. Byrd recorded it:

"Here I learned all the tragical story of her daughter's humble marriage with her uncle's overseer. Besides the meanness of this mortal's aspect, the man has not one visible qualification, except impudence, to recommend him to a female's inclinations. But there is sometimes such a charm in that Hibernian endowment, that frail woman can't withstand it, though it stand alone without any other recommendation. Had she run away with a gentleman or a pretty fellow, there might have been some excuse for her, though he were of inferior fortune: but to stoop to a dirty plebian, without any kind of merit, is the lowest prostitution. I found the family justly enraged at it; and though I had more good nature than to join in her condemnation, yet I could devise no excuse for so senseless a prank as this young gentlewoman had played."

In that passage lies the only contemporary record of this Randolph humiliation. Gossip then and later, however, expanded the story. Pious historians have undertaken to dismiss it. Albert J. Beveridge, in his *Life of John Marshall,* gave only a footnote to this story of the Randolph girl who was to become the grandmother of his hero. In small print he stated that "tradition" had dealt with her "most unkindly and in highly colored pictures."

Beveridge gave his authority for the "tradition" about Mary Randolph as William M. Paxton's book, *The Marshall Family, or a Genealogical Chart of the Descendants of John Marshall and Elizabeth Markham* (Cincinnati—1885). Paxton wrote: "Stories are told of this lady that need confirmation." However, he presented what he called the "Legend of the Randolphs." It related:

The story is told that when Mary Isham Randolph was blooming into womanhood, she was induced by the bailiff upon the estate of Tuckahoe to elope with him. There was great excitement among the family and neighbors, and threats were freely made by the brothers. . . . The search for the fugitive for a time was fruitless. At length their retreat was discovered on Elk Island, in James River. The angry brothers came upon them at night, murdered the bailiff and the child, and brought their sister home. The deed of blood and cruelty so affected the wife and mother that she became deranged. But care was taken that no allusion should be made to the harrowing scenes she had witnessed, and her reason was at length restored.

Years passed. Mary Randolph married Parson James Keith. A family of children had grown up around them. The tragedy at Elk Island had been forgotten. The bailiff was supposed to be dead. But, one day Mrs. Keith received a letter, and, on opening it, found that it purported to be from the bailiff. It stated that he still lived; that he was left as dead, had revived, had changed his name, and had fled to foreign countries; after years of wandering had returned to look upon his lawful wife; had found her married and happy; that he would not afflict her by claiming her as his own, but advised her to be happy and forget him, who had more than died for her love, for she should hear no more from him. This letter was perhaps written by some evil-disposed person, or may have been only a practical joke. However that may be, it unhinged the mind of Mrs. Keith. She vainly sought for him, and throughout the remnant of her days the insanity manifested itself by a quiet melancholy, varied by some sudden freak of folly. Mrs. Colston lived with her for many years, and she, and all who met her in her widowhood, testify that she was a lunatic.

Much mystery attends this tale. Mrs. Colston cited as a source was evidently Mrs. Rawleigh Colston who was Elizabeth Marshall, Mary's granddaughter and sister of Chief Justice Marshall. She would certainly have been a qualified witness to her grandmother's insanity and perhaps as to its cause. But Mary Randolph had no "brothers" who could have murdered the despised husband of their sister. The only brother she had was the Tuckahoe heir William Randolph, described by Byrd as a "pretty" boy of nineteen. Still, gossipy as the famous diarist was, it seems impossible to believe that he fabricated the tale. The grisly story of Elk Island (later owned by Jefferson) was full grown before Byrd's diary was published. Whatever the truth was, this story seems to have had no effect on rising Randolph prestige.

Death in the family would emphasize its position. Sir John's health had not been improved by his sea voyages. Perhaps the labors which built his eminence overtaxed his strength. Two years after he was knighted, he gave up his lucrative clerkship of the House of Burgesses and accepted a seat in that body as the representative of William and Mary. Three days later he was chosen Speaker. He was almost universally honored though he was one of the first of the Randolphs to be suspected by the clergy of unorthodox religious views. Actually he was a vestryman of Bruton Parish and in his will expressed his Christian faith, though also his distaste for theological wrangles.

With so many clerical relations, some of these may have seemed like quarrels in the family. Randolphs, "with few exceptions," wrote the Randolph connection Bishop William Meade of Virginia, were "steadfast" to *the* Church. Some early Randolphs who were devout were also critical of the clergy. William II's son, Beverley, who died young, requested that his body be interred in a plain decent manner "without the hypocritical farce of mourning and without the praise of minister in a sermon whose approbation of the lives of men I have long since despised seeing that they give it all indiscriminately." Certainly there seemed true discrimination when, after Sir John's death on March 2, 1737, the Anglican college of William and Mary regarded him as one worthy to lie in its crypt. The Latin phrases in his praise were delivered by one of those Reverends Dawson of the Randolph connection.

Byrd wrote, "Sir John Randolph is dead, and unless his brother Isham returns to his element the sea, I fear he will not survive him many years."

Isham, at fifty-one, made his last voyage that year. He brought home no such tangible honors as his dead brother had received. He had been less successful as an agent of the colonies in England. Still, on his ship, in the Virginia Coffeehouse, and now on his plantation Dungeness, he must have been a more colorful if less erudite and impeccable character than Sir John. He was frankly in trade (as most Virginia planters of the time were) including dealing in black slaves. Yet he was no mere trader. He was curious about the earth, the sea, and "all that in them is." He had the respect of a generation of men freshly concerned with plants and animals, all natural phenomena. From his lands and from the sea he had acquired all the resources necessary to lavish hospitality when he settled at last on his Dungeness plantation. It was said that a hundred of his slaves were required as the servants of his establishment.

Sea captain turned planter again, Isham was not devoting all his time to discussions of natural philosophy. He had hardly left the sea before Virginia called upon his abilities at home. He was elected a member of the House of Burgesses, probably with the

expenditure of less "industry" than had been required of Will and
Tom in the election sixteen years before. The Council, in ap-
pointing him adjutant general of the colony, described him as a
gentleman "well known and universally accepted" in the country.
In an absence of the Governor he commanded all the militia of
Virginia.

He approved the sometimes savage punishments which prevailed. As a justice he joined several other such officials in the
trial of some Negroes charged with murder. Since three of the
slaves on trial belonged to his brother William he might have
excused himself. Still he agreed in the judgment that two convicted slaves not only be hanged but that their bodies be dis-
membered and that the heads and quarters be displayed on
poles in various parts of the county. This was no more ferocious
justice than Bacon's followers feared when they hid Bacon's
body from Berkeley. The decorative society in which Isham lived
could be a harsh one, too, sometimes both together. But the
easygoing underside of that society was well described by Byrd
who had slaves whipped and then gave them a bottle of rum:
"they had a fiddle and danced and I walked in the garden."

Perhaps from London Peter Collinson described Isham best
in a letter which he gave to the young Quaker, John Bartram,
whom Linnaeus described as the greatest natural botanist of his
generation. To Bartram, Collinson wrote:

". . . when thee proceeds home, I know no person will make
thee more welcome than Isham Randolph. He lives thirty or
forty miles above the falls of James river in Goochland, . . and
above the other settlements. Now, I take his house to be a very
suitable place to make a settlement at, . . for to take several
days' excursions all around, and to return at night."

But Collinson added a warning reminiscent of Carter-Randolph
contentions over fine clothes. Plain Quaker though he was, he
wrote: "One thing I must desire of thee, and do insist that thee
oblige me therein; that you make up drugget clothes, to go to
Virginia in, and not appear to disgrace thyself or me; for though
I should not esteem thee the less,—come to me in what dress thou
will,—yet the Virginians are a very gentle, well-dressed people—

and look, perhaps, more at a man's outside than his inside. For these and other reasons, pray go very clean, neat, and handsomely dressed to Virginia. Never mind thy clothes: I will send thee more another year."

Bartram found items of interest on his visit to Randolph. He wrote particularly of a tree near his place which would add beauty to a garden. His host was modest, confessing "the want of a penetrating genius in the curious beauties of nature." Isham was, of course, only an amateur in science like many including his grandson Thomas Jefferson. His hospitality to scientists and ideas, however, was shown by Bartram's letters to Collinson later. The botanist wrote of "Our friend Isham Randolph (a generous, good-natured gentleman, and well respected by most who are acquainted with him)." They had agreed, he said, "to have a correspondence together," meaning apparently some sort of joint exploration. But "can't tell well which way to carry it on—whether back of the mountains by way of Shenandoah, or below the mountains, we can't tell yet."

Apparently no such "correspondence" ever took place. Isham was too busy with public affairs and tending to his acres and slaves. Evidently also he felt some responsibility for the family of his dead brother Thomas of Tuckahoe—and perhaps some guilt about it since, before he retired from the sea, it may have been Isham's overseer who carried off temporarily the daughter Mary of that house. Certainly he seems to have been close to his nephew William of Tuckahoe. William introduced another significant visitor to his Uncle Isham—a rugged giant of a man named Peter Jefferson.

At the time when Byrd listened to the story of the humiliation of the Tuckahoe house, he had described young William with little charity. Perhaps Byrd was in no charitable mood as he found good drink scarce at Tuckahoe, "the family being reduced to the last bottle of wine." Of young William he wrote: "The heir of the family did not come home till late in the evening. He is a pretty young man, but had the misfortune to become his own master too soon. This puts a young fellow upon wrong pursuits, before they have sense to judge rightly for themselves. Though at the same time they have a strange conceit of their own sufficiency when they grow near twenty years old, especially if they happen to have a small smattering of learning. 'Tis then they fancy themselves wiser than all their tutors and governors, which makes them headstrong to all advice, and above all reproof and admonition."

Byrd, fifty-eight then, was unduly pessimistic about the young man. William attended William and Mary College. He farmed his 3,256-acre share of the lands on both sides of the James which his father had left. In addition, between 1730 and 1736, he patented 8,800 adjoining acres. Also, he became leader in the county. He was prominent in the establishment of Albemarle County which was formed from Goochland County in 1744. One of his friends there was Peter Jefferson. The Jefferson position has sometimes been minimized in comparison with that of the Randolphs. Though serious citizens, the friendship of William and Peter was attended by humor. Once William Randolph sold Jefferson a tract of land for a single "biggest bowl" of the famous arrack punch mixed by Henry Wetherburn (or Weatherbourne) in his tavern in Williamsburg. A biographer of William Randolph's grandson wrote that probably the purchaser of the land helped the seller consume it after the trade. They were more serious in their trading when together they patented large tracts of land in the west. Both made marriages important to the Randolphs.

Certainly a greater occasion than that about the bowl of punch in the tavern was the marriage of William to Maria Judith Page. Her father, Mann Page, left a rich orphan when he was sixteen, was sent abroad to Eton, then to St. John's College, Oxford. On his return to the colony Page was made, in his early twenties, a member of the Council. Precociously prominent as he was, he advanced his position socially and economically by his marriages. Maria Judith was his child by Judith Wormeley, whose father, Ralph Wormeley, was the secretary of the colony. She was only a very little girl, however, when Page took as his second wife, Judith Carter, daughter of the rich and irascible "King." This stepmother was much praised for her mental powers, unexpected in a woman, her love of books, her intellectual curiosity, qualities which were reflected in the child's upbringing.

Though Maria Judith was to be the progenitor of many Randolphs, she grew up in dazzling company in the family of "King" Carter who had drawn a Randolph portrait in scorn. Her father was evidently "King" Carter's favorite son-in-law. Carter pulled Page into his great affairs in land ownership and copper mining. Page acquired wide acres in eight of the colony's counties. He became, according to tradition, the second largest landowner in Virginia, and probably second only to his father-in-law.

In 1725, a decade before his daughter's marriage to William Randolph, Page began the building of Virginia's greatest private house, "Rosewell," on the York River in Gloucester County. A structure with a frontage of 232 feet, containing thirty-five rooms, it was built of brick, three stories high with marble casements. Under its lead roof, the house had beautifully carved mahogany furnishings. The mansion was barely completed when Page died in 1730. Probably William Randolph and Maria Judith Page were married in its halls. Carters, Pages, Wormeleys, Harrisons, Braxtons, Fitzhughs, Hills, Nicholases, and Randolphs in the web of kinship blessed the alliance.

Peter Jefferson brought to Isham Randolph's daughter Jane no evidence of opulence. Beyond their marriage bond, signed October 3, 1739, little is recorded about their wedding. Isham, still alive then, must have given the bride away as a satisfied father. Though in history Peter Jefferson has been generally described as a man of much plainer stock than his wife's family, he was no johnny-come-lately in Virginia. Marie Kimball, in her study of Thomas Jefferson's background, described his father as "a very eligible young man." His people were solid folk. He himself was a surveyor and an enterprising small planter. He conducted important surveying operations for the colony.

Jane was the more shadowy figure in this marriage. Her son never made much mention of her qualities. Perhaps, as Dumas Malone wrote, this "may be attributed to his characteristic reticence about the women of his family." Malone suggested that Jane got the better of the bargain in her marriage to Jefferson. He wrote: "There was instability in this branch of the Randolphs and, beginning with Peter, the Jeffersons served to offset it." Actually at this point, unless it was the elopement of the girl at Tuckahoe, there had been no evidence of any instability in the Randolph family in Virginia. And this errant Mary was to be the matriarch of one of the strongest Randolph lines. The first real Randolph instability was shown in the generation which included Peter Jefferson's children.

Certainly Isham Randolph had shown no sign of instability. His portrait showed him as "a gentleman in conventional costume, wearing a wig, and with ruffles at his wrists." Malone only detected signs of good living in his face. Possibly that good living was responsible for the line in his will directing that his debts be paid to his "great creditor, John Hanbury, of London, merchant." This Hanbury became the world's greatest tobacco merchant. Other Randolphs were to be troubled by debts to his heirs. Hanbury, a Quaker born in 1700, was the brother of Capel and Osgood Hanbury. Their firm in 1774 became known as Hanbury and Lloyd, fiscal ancestor of the great financial organization of Lloyd's.

When Isham died, in November 1742, three years after the marriage of his daughter, he was buried in the graveyard on the Turkey Island estate which his brother William had inherited. Prepared undoubtedly in filial affection, his epitaph spoke of his great qualities as a gentleman and a man of good nature. It added: "By an easy compliance and obliging deportment he knew no enemy, but gained many friends, thus in his life meriting an universal esteem."

His brother William had died a month before. Richard of Curles still lived. Records are obscure about the deaths of the other Randolph brothers and sisters. But the second generation was passing. Even the third generation was touched by death at this time. Perhaps the "golden age," imperceptibly, was dying, too, almost as it began. To the great regret of Virginians, Governor Gooch, now Sir William, was soon to resign his office because of ill health. And he could say with much truth to his brother that "I have ruled without so much as a murmur of discontent in my administration." Randolphs and others blessed him and lifted their glasses toward him in salute to their King.

Death did not take a holiday in the "golden age." Peter Jefferson's friend William Randolph, son of Thomas of Tuckahoe, was left a widower with two daughters and a son at the age of thirty. And, in 1745, he died prematurely. In his will, made earlier, he had named his brother-in-law William Stith and Peter Jefferson his executors. The document did not give him the assurances he wanted for his two little girls and his four-year-old son, Thomas Mann Randolph, bearing the first names of his two grandfathers. So, to his will, as he approached his end, he added a codicil requesting that his "dear and loving" friend Jefferson move with his family to Tuckahoe as guardian in residence. Jefferson moved with his family, now including three daughters and his two-year-old son, Thomas, to the big Randolph plantation around the house by the river.

The seven little children in the Randolph line at Tuckahoe were already members not only of a family but of a tribe which would wear many names but remember always the Randolph blood. The seven sons and two daughters of William and Mary Isham Randolph, who would sometimes be called the Adam and Eve of Virginia, had produced forty-two children.

Already they moved plumed in the "golden age" of the colonial dominion. Sometimes they seemed beside other Virginians as Virginia felt of itself among the other colonies. Hugh Jones had described that feeling as early as 1724. He wrote then as the Randolphs were splendidly rising: "If New England be called a receptacle of dissenters, and an Amsterdam of religion, Pennsylvania the nursery of Quakers, Maryland the retirement of Roman Catholicks, North Carolina the refuge of run-aways, and South Carolina the delight of buccaneers and pirates, Virginia may be justly esteemed the happy retreat of true Britons and true churchmen for the most part; neither soaring too high nor drooping too low, consequently should merit the greater esteem and encouragement."

Some felt Randolphs dressed their merits too well. Even some Randolphs, early and late, sharply questioned their virtues beside their faults. As a man aware of both, Fairfax Harrison, two centuries and a half after their arrival in America, urged the Virginia historian and antiquarian, William Glover Stanard, to write a history of the Randolphs. Correctly he wrote that Stanard was the man with the knowledge and perspective to undertake it. Stanard never did. Perhaps he was deterred by a paragraph in Harrison's letter:

"I have grown up among Randolphs and I never knew one to be *loved!* Respected yes; sometimes admired, but never loved. On the other hand, a kinsman at my house the other day, looking at the portrait of old William R. of Turkey Island said unexpectedly and passionately: 'If God had been the God of Virginia, he would have blasted that man with sterility.'"

By the time Tom Jefferson and Tom Randolph began to go to school with their cousins, it was clear that God had other plans. It was also clear that there would be Randolphs to love, to follow, to fight, to hate. Their destiny was never to be disregarded. Yet, even their differences were sometimes disguised behind the appearance they presented to the world. They did, as young Jack Carter said, dress with an elegance which sometimes aroused envy. They did not differ from their equals, however, in the dress according to the latest English mode which they wore. They moved impeccably in silk knee breeches and stockings, colored coats, richly ornamented waistcoats, in fine linen with lace at their wrists, buckled shoes—all the accouterments of fashion which Governor Gooch had left behind in London and was delighted to find duplicated in Virginia where only good dancers served his government.

Chapter IV

COLONIAL COLUMN

PEYTON AND JOHN were boys when their father Sir John Randolph had been nominated for Speaker of the Assembly. This was a time when Williamsburg, crowded momentarily with Burgesses, their ladies and others, put on its periodic airs as a small city, even, as some said, a little London. The best clothes that tobacco could buy were worn. This was true also of their liveried slaves. Horses and chariots stirred the dust on wide Duke of Gloucester Street. Gentlemen wet their whistles in the Raleigh Tavern. Some wiped their lips with lacy sleeves. As the boys watched in pride, the glory of plantation Virginia paraded before them.

Suddenly in the capital, however, Randolphs were surprised and chagrined when luminous John Robinson, then only in his middle thirties, was also proposed as speaker. Perhaps there was no danger that the much honored Sir John would suffer the indignity of defeat. But Robinson was no mere upstart. His father had been president of the Council. His family had inherited the sizable estate of a Bishop of London. A cousin of his became Commissary of Virginia and, in effect, head of the Established Church in the colony.

Still, his opposition to Sir John was incredible. Robinson's mother was a member of the Beverley family into which Sir John and his brother William married. The relationship was even more complicated. Robinson was to marry the daughter of Colonel John Chiswell, proprietor of the Raleigh Tavern, who himself had married Elizabeth, daughter of William Randolph and Elizabeth Beverley. The presentation of his name made a tense moment, shared by Sir John's young sons, in the aristocratic oligarchy which in uninterrupted power prided itself on the honorable service its members gave to Virginia.

"But," said the record, "Mr. Robinson standing up in his place, declared, That he did not expect to be made a Competitor with the Gentleman that had been named; that he was no ways qualified; and prayed that Sir John Randolph might be chosen without opposition."

This was done. And when Sir John died soon afterwards Robinson had no more devoted advocates than the Randolph boys or more loyal supporters when they came to maturity. As Speaker, then as Treasurer of the Colony also, Robinson met their loyalty with his own. Indeed, as time went on, in broadcloth and lace they formed the colony's aristocratic political machine. Dumas Malone labeled it the "Robinson-Randolph group." It contained members of other interconnected "Cavalier" families. It was arrayed not merely in sessions and caucuses. It appeared more impressively in the formal and convivial gatherings of Tidewater society. Though stuffy chroniclers have seemed to make its members participants in a pageant, they were no starchy company. Many of its sons were educated in England, and the daughters wore the finest and latest fashions tobacco could bring from England. But young and old enjoyed country dancing, lively fiddling, full glasses and loaded tables, flirtation, gossip, and song. Christmas celebration ran from its eve to Twelfth Night. Weddings meant days, even weeks, of festivities.

The marriages of the Randolphs were such events. Soon after Peyton returned from London he married Elizabeth Harrison at old Berkeley, a warm red brick house at the head of low gardens above the James. Her brother Benjamin, Peyton's friend, would be "the Signer." Nearby in time and place Mary, daughter of Richard Randolph of Curles, became the bride of Archibald Cary, vociferous planter, miner, manufacturer, and politician. Oddly both of these wedding scenes had come into their serene possession by Harrisons and Randolphs from confiscations in Bacon's Rebellion now more than half a century before. Randolphs moved en masse to the wedding of Peyton's brother

John to Ariana Jenings, child of the Attorney General of Maryland. Ariana was of distinguished Virginia ancestry and she
was fertile as Elizabeth Harrison was not. That made a difference
in a society proud of progeny.

The clients of Peyton and John lived in the parade of fine
houses along the James, the York, and other rivers. Such places
marked the prosperity Sir John had helped to make by his
tobacco missions. They required the labor of many slaves who
had to be fed in good tobacco years and bad ones. Display
did not disappear when profits did. Appearances were permanent if nothing else was. Wealth—or its evidences—which
in retrospect seemed to have come easily could not be let go
quickly. Men who had gambled on tobacco prices in rigged
markets were early concerned in land speculations.

As population increased and Tidewater lands were occupied
or exhausted, grandees and others saw the possibility of profit
in the green, limitless west, with its wide fertile river bottoms.
In them might be wealth or a ready hedge to the growing
debts to their tobacco agents abroad. If the planters seemed
extravagant, there was loud complaint from William Randolph I's
time forward that British merchants like the Hanburys and
the Perrys were extortionate. Some Virginians had a greedy
grasp. Also there was a feeling that like horse racing land
speculation should be reserved for the elite. On May 15, 1741,
at a meeting of the Council, the petition of one Alexander
Stinson for 12,000 acres was rejected "as the petitioner is not
known to any of the Board and therefore thought too much
for so obscure a person."

There was nothing obscure about Robinson-Randolphs. William
of Tuckahoe and Peter Jefferson were only two of those early
seeking large grants. Robinson and his friends had long been
interested in western lands. In 1745, he had secured one grant
for 100,000 acres on the Greenbrier River in what is now West
Virginia. He became interested in a lead mine near the present
Tennessee line discovered by his close connection Chiswell. He
had as a partner in land development around the mine his
protégé Edmund Pendleton, the great gentleman and jurist who

had begun his career as an apprentice boy. Reports circulated in Virginia that Chiswell might be able to turn lead into silver. Some other plans were chimerical. Some others seemed to be made fantastic by conflicts.

In 1748 the Ohio Company was formed under the leadership of Thomas Lee, rich planter and father of famous sons, one of whom was Richard Henry Lee. This company had secured its charter and a grant of vast acreage in the Ohio country from the British ministry with the aid of the rich and powerful Duke of Bedford. Then or later the Hanbury family to which Virginia planters owed thousands of pounds became involved in it.

The Robinson-Randolph group was aroused. Now in competition, though in a separate area, Robinson *et al.*, organized the Loyal Land Company. Some mystery exists as to the significance of the word "loyal" in its name. Questions of loyalty to the King and the empire had not yet arisen. Certainly at this point Loyal Robinson felt no subservience to energetic and belligerent Governor Robert Dinwiddie. Dinwiddie became a partner in the Ohio Company and its strongest supporter. Thomas Perkins Abernethy, in his study of the development of the western lands, put it mildly when he wrote that Robinson's "influence was not used in its [the Ohio Company's] favor."

In 1750 the Loyal Company dispatched Dr. Thomas Walker, physician, explorer, and speculator, to survey its lands. Walker was Peter Jefferson's friend and became a guardian of his boy, Thomas. But when the Ohio Company sought the required certification as a public surveyor for its similar agent, William and Mary, the licensing authority declined to grant it. Randolph kin—Dawson, Stith, Yates—were heading the college in this period which may have made a difference. In every possible way the Ohio Company retaliated. Apparently Dinwiddie's pistole fee order, issued soon after his arrival in the colony late in 1751, was regarded by the powers in the Burgesses as a part of this retaliation, though it must have hit both of the great land companies.

It had long been the practice of large land speculators to secure an order for a certain number of acres and to occupy them for years before securing instruments of conveyance, called patents. This was one of the ways in which they escaped the payment of quitrents. But now Dinwiddie ordered that patents be taken out immediately and that a fee of a pistole be paid for signing the patent and the use of the seal. The pistole was the quarter doubloon of Spain, used in Virginia where little specie circulated. Its value was said to be about four dollars but can better be fixed as the value of a fine pair of silk stockings advertised in the *Virginia Gazette* at the time.

The Burgesses voiced their colonial indignation in terms which sounded almost like the cries of their patriot successors two decades later. They labeled the order an invasion of ancient liberties by the Royal Governor: "The rights of the subjects are so secured by law that they cannot be deprived of the least of their property but by their own consent."

In this matter Robinson promptly turned to Randolphs. Peyton and John had both been rapidly advanced after they came home from their legal studies in London. Big Peyton, who developed a double chin by the time his portrait was being painted, had many virtues according to his cousin, Thomas Jefferson. But: ". . . Being heavy and inert in body, he was rather too indolent and careless for business, which occasioned him to get a smaller proportion of it at the bar than his abilities would otherwise have commanded." Certainly the eminence he attained in both Virginia and the nation made this judgment of laziness at least questionable.

John was smaller, less ponderous. Laziness was not attributed to him but he gave much interest to more concerns than law. Unlike the childless Peyton, he had three children to whom he was much devoted. He was a bookish man. He loved to work in the gardens about his Tazewell Hall and the 1,700 acres adjoining it. Indeed, while some of his writing was to win him disapproval, he wrote a much reprinted *Treatise on Gardening by a Virginia Gentleman.* He had the patience required by plants and the stubbornness needed in confronting the elements. Most of all, apparently, as a sensitive and introspective man, he loved his music. He brought home from his legal studies abroad a splendid violin, much coveted by his young cousin Jefferson. His music a little later brought him into the intimate company of Francis Fauquier who was to follow Dinwiddie as Governor. Fauquier, whose only vice was an obsessive addiction to gambling, was a gracious, amiable man and an accomplished musician.

John not only played in the Governor's musical coterie. Also, bringing along his cousin Jefferson, he was a frequent guest at the Governor's table in the palace. About it gathered such select and selected men as the Englishman William Small, great teacher of the then emerging and exciting sciences at William and Mary, and George Wythe, already regarded as a Solomon of legal learning. In that company John was described as much as Governor Fauquier and the others were in a statement made later by Jefferson that at this table he heard "more good sense, more rational and philosophic conversation" than on any other occasions in his life.

Such amenities had not attended the earlier rule of Governor Dinwiddie, particularly after he issued his pistole order. Yet Peyton and John had even then become important figures in the government over which he presided. They had been swiftly advanced. Before he was thirty Peyton became King's Attorney, the office which by this time had become almost a Randolph prerogative. John secured, as so many other Randolphs did, the lucrative and influential position of clerk of the House of Burgesses. Now in the pistole controversy with Dinwiddie, Robinson, who held both the offices of Speaker and Treasurer of the colony, turned to Peyton to serve as his advocate though he was King's Attorney.

So, in 1754, Peyton sailed for England without saying by your leave to his superior. His mission was unlike those his father had undertaken. He needed no sea voyage for his health. There was no certainly unified colony behind him. He faced more dangers at sea. Already the hostilities which would become the French and Indian War in America and the Seven Years' War in the world had begun in French and British colonial collisions on the lands in which rival Virginians speculated.

Apparently Peyton had little trouble in London, though behind him the angry Dinwiddie had removed him as King's Attorney. He was much at home where he and his brother had studied law. Something of the Randolph wealth and position had recently been indicated in the city where a less well-known brother, Beverley, lost £500 in cash in the burning of his lodgings. This Beverley was married to a Miss Wormeley, of a great family later strong in its Tory sentiments. Some Virginia Randolphs still preferred residence in Britain.

Peyton was well received and effective before the Board of Trade. That body not only directed that no pistole fee be charged on patents of land west of the mountains, or upon lands surveyed before April 22, 1752. Also the board strongly suggested or directed that Dinwiddie reinstate Randolph as King's Attorney. That was easily accomplished since the close Randolph friend, George Wythe, who had been put in Peyton's place, promptly resigned on Peyton's return. Possibly Dinwiddie's agreement to the readjustment was made easy by Peyton's graceful statement that perhaps he had been wrong in undertaking the mission without the Governor's approval. Jefferson, who wrote of Peyton's laziness, also said of him that he could be "of attic pleasantry in conversation, always good humored and conciliatory."

Peyton, evidently, however, was not penitent. He accepted a reward of £2,500 from the Burgesses. The nature of that reward indicated the sharp division in the colony between the Governor and the Burgesses and also between the rival land speculators. The Assembly met to consider a plea from Dinwiddie for more funds to aid forces under George Washington to contest French advance to the Ohio. The Burgesses voted £20,000 from a poll tax. But, as Douglas Southall Freeman wrote in his biography of Washington, they "insisted that the sum of £2,500 of this be used to reimburse the Speaker and several other gentlemen who had advanced that sum to pay the expenses of Peyton Randolph, Attorney General, when he had been sent to England to present the Colony's side of the controversy with Dinwiddie over the pistole fee."

Pistole or no pistole, apparently no speculative Virginia land companies were secure. General Edward Braddock was mauled by the French and Indians in the summer of 1755, despite the efforts of young Washington. Even Peyton organized a company of Williamsburg lawyers to assist the regular forces. Fortunately, it turned out that no great sacrifices by the barristers in arms were required. By Christmas 1759, Quebec had fallen. It was clear that the French were being defeated by a combination of British sea power and American frontier fighters. Tranquillity was at hand. Celebration in Williamsburg and the plantations about it seemed certainly in order. Another event justifying rejoicing may have been the death the year before of Hanbury, though his heirs remained to plague indebted planters.

Christmas in 1759, the last year of the reign of George II, was, wrote Julian P. Boyd, the editor of the definitive edition of Jefferson's papers, "no ordinary Christmas, not even for that golden age of plantation Christmases." Yet the best description by a Randolph of this Christmas was written in a petulant vein. Years later Jefferson described the season as background for his first meeting with Patrick Henry. Both were guests for "perhaps a fortnight" on the plantation of Colonel Nathaniel West Dandridge on the upper reaches of the Pamunkey River in Hanover County. To modern readers Dandridge's position may seem best indicated by the fact that his niece, the rich young widow Custis, had married George Washington the year before. Actually the Dandridges then were more prominent than the Washingtons. Jefferson was by birth entitled to the society of such gentry. He explained the presence of Henry at the Christmas festivities by saying that he was "a near neighbor." He went on to say that Henry's manners "had something of the coarseness of the society he had frequented." Even in this fastidious feeling which he expressed much later, some evidence of jealousy lingered. As he coveted John Randolph's violin, he envied Henry's ease in winning attention and affection. He wrote, ". . . his passion was fiddling, dancing and pleasantry. He excelled in the last, and it attached every one to him."

This combination of scorn and admiration left much unsaid

about the two men at the time of this meeting. Henry was not present merely because he lived in proximity to the Dandridge plantation. He was to be Colonel Dandridge's lawyer in important matters, and later personally much closer to him. Henry at this time was no such uncouth fellow as Jefferson suggested. Though born on the fringe of the frontier, he was the son of educated and cultivated parents. Jefferson's presence is the greater mystery. He was the male head of the family of his widowed mother at Shadwell in Albemarle County. Five sisters and a younger brother would normally have expected his company at Christmas. And Shadwell was no dull place. Within a month after this Christmas, Jefferson wrote his kinsman Colonel Peter Randolph of Chatsworth that one reason he wanted to go to William and Mary College in Williamsburg was that there was "so much company" at Shadwell that his studies were interrupted.

Soon afterwards Jefferson entered college, almost like a student prince on money advanced him by his guardian Dr. Thomas Walker. Henry followed, as Randolphs (notably Jefferson) scornfully caricatured him, like a presumptuous bumpkin. Never a student at the college, on the basis, it was said, of only a few weeks' study he wanted a law license. Various versions come down as to the examination and the examiners. The central figure, however, was John Randolph. The eminent Robert Carter Nicholas was reported to have withheld his signature from Henry's application but gave it "on repeated importunities and promises of future reading." Edmund Pendleton signed after much entreaty. George Wythe refused to sign. It was said of Wythe that no one expressed more courtesy in a bow and he bowed Henry out. John Randolph was reluctant to give the examination and only consented after he learned that two members of the board had agreed to the application. Peyton shared his brother's doubts. The quiz was not easy and the answers were not always correct. Yet Henry himself quoted John as saying after the examination: "I will never trust to appearances again. Mr. Henry, if your industry be only half equal to your genius, I augur that you will do well, and become an ornament and an honor to your profession."

Jefferson was in no such hurry. He studied. He made music with John and others. He escaped college disciplines which caught up with Jack Walker, his lifelong friend and son of his guardian. He fell, as he believed, hopelessly in love with the "fair Belinda" with whom he danced in the Apollo Room of the Raleigh Tavern where later were held solemn meetings of patriots. He wrote the gossip about his cousins Betsy Yates and Anne Randolph, called Nancy Wilton as the child of William of that estate. He recorded the news of Jack Walker's betrothal to Betsy Moore, a young lady Jefferson later regarded as more passionately desirable even than Belinda.

Indeed, his heart seemed to put him in no haste about Belinda who was Rebecca Burwell of a prominent family soon to be connected with his own. She could wait—though she didn't. He was prepared at Christmas in 1762 to "hoist sail and away. I shall visit particularly England, Holland, France, Spain, Italy (where I could buy me a good fiddle), and Egypt, and return through the British provinces to the Northward home." He seemed, as it turned out, more loyal to the fiddle than to Rebecca, though he never sailed away. In a letter this Christmas he turned from the playful to dark almost Gothic romancing. Again away from home, this time in his sister's house, he described that dwelling as almost like a later Virginian's House of Usher. Rats abounded and the rain came through a leaky roof.

Rats were not everywhere apparent. Not all roofs leaked on the polished floors. Extravagant frolic could hide gaps and reasons for fears in this supposed golden plantation age. Still the times snatched at good news. But the rejoicing at the end of the French and Indian War turned out to be a little premature. If the war had been costly to England, it had also loaded Virginia with debt. The colony of about 150,000 white men had spent £500,000—a vast sum at that place and time. This public debt was added to and above the private debts, which, from the time of William Randolph I, the tobacco planters had been piling up with such British merchants as the Hanburys and the Perrys. Later it turned out that John Randolph of Matoax, son of Richard of Curles, owed the British firm of Capel and Osgood Hanbury £11,000. Colonel Cary was in debt to the Hanburys for £11,000 and more to Jones and Farrell. Jefferson's debts to Kappen and Company, of Glasgow, and Jones and Farrell, of London, had not yet been piled to the £10,000 he would owe British merchants. Such debts were on men's backs and minds. Now with the debts—and new taxes—being pressed across the Atlantic, a blow to hopes of Virginia solvency was delivered beyond the mountains.

By the Treaty of Paris, signed February 10, 1763, the British were given possession of all the lands east of the Mississippi. But to the dismay of both frontiersmen and planter speculators, George III, more intent upon pacifying Indians than guaranteeing the profits of land companies, forbade, by his Proclamation of 1763, settlers to move beyond the line of the watershed in the Appalachian Mountains. So far as the mass of little men moving into the west was concerned, this was a sort of King Canute command. But it struck hard at the formal, big operations of the contending land companies.

Hard times were knocking at the mansion doors. Possibly the Tidewater planters could only blame themselves for past extravagance and careless bookkeeping. As historian of the Lee family, Burton J. Hendrick wrote that the planters were "a fast living lot, devoting more of their hours to unproductive pleasure. Their chief purpose in life was no longer the maintenance of their estates and service to the community, but a continuous excitement." There had been a procession in the building of great houses. Fast English thoroughbreds had been imported. Randolphs began to build the name of their stud. Portraits and silver plate, books and furniture added to the grace or the excitement of living. Still "fast living" was hardly an adequate phrase for the class of Virginians soon to contribute so much to their country. There were wastrels as well as wise, good men among the elite. Yet for all, wrote Hendrick, "the glory of the Virginia planter must be maintained." Those who had loyally supported Robinson expected loyal support from him.

Robinson seemed the inviolable leader. As Speaker and Treasurer he was only slightly surpassed by the Governor in power and dignity—and that not always admitted. Sir John Randolph's grandson Edmund, in his unfinished history of Virginia, described this leader of the "Robinson-Randolph group." He wrote: "His reputation was great for sound political knowledge and an acquaintanceship with sound parliamentary forms,—a benevolence which created friends and a sincerity which never lost one. When he presided the decorum of the House outshone that of the British House of Commons. . . . When he propounded a question his comprehension and perspicacity brought it equally to the most humble and the most polished understanding. . . . In the sphere of colonial politics he was a column. The thousand little flattering attentions which can be scattered from the chair, operated as a delicious incense." Jefferson, who knew Robinson, described him as "an excellent man, liberal, friendly, and rich." One of his close friends was George Washington.

Certainly Robinson was rich. The Robinsons seemed to have the Midas touch. Speaker John's brother, Beverley Robinson, had moved to New York where he had married a daughter of the vastly wealthy Frederick Philipse. Philipse had been accused of dealing with Captain William Kidd, the pirate. Later, as a greater crime in the eyes of patriots, he became a Loyalist leader with his Robinson son-in-law in his fighting train. In this earlier Virginia, John by his own rights was "loyal" to his friends but, as it turned out, not quite rich enough.

It seemed impossible that such a "column" should fall. Certainly it was an impertinence rudely to raise any question about John Robinson. Yet in 1765, the frontier figure Henry, whom John Randolph had reluctantly licensed, appeared in the Assembly ready to do just that. And not merely the column but the edifice of the Tidewater oligarchy over which Robinson presided was threatened before the members knew it. The long disregarded Piedmont and west had not only grown mightily with the inflow of immigrants, many of them dissenters from the Anglican faith of the aristocrats. Also the upcountry men in native homespun, with buckskin shirts and coonskin hats, were increasingly aware not only of their numbers but the prowess they had shown in fighting the French and the Indians.

Suddenly their growing number of representatives in the Assembly found a leader in Patrick Henry who had been in the Assembly less than two weeks. With him stood Richard Henry Lee, an aristocrat of the aristocrats whose family had been founders of the Ohio Company. Some felt that he took his role in opposition to the Robinson-Randolph group because he felt he had been denied honors he deserved. Some conservative planters regarded him as an unblushing opportunist. Others saw in his opposition the old contentions of the Ohio and the Loyal Land companies. One minor figure behind them was Thomas Marshall whose wife was the granddaughter of Thomas Randolph of Tuckahoe's supposedly errant child Mary.

In simplest terms, as each side saw the situation in scorn, the division was one between upstarts and stuffed shirts. Men from both sections were greatly disturbed by British plans to tax the colonists to help pay for the war. Randolphs had been among the first to protest. In October 1764, scholarly Richard Bland, grandson of William Randolph the family founder, had helped draft an address to the King, a memorial to the Lords and a Remonstrance to the Commons, protesting the taxation of Virginia by any other power than its Assembly. This Richard could hardly be regarded as a conservative. He had taken the lead in a move to strictly regulate the pay of the Anglican clergy in relation to the prices planters got for their tobacco. Still as one who revered the past he became known as the "Virginia Antiquary" for his work in saving historic papers from fires, housecleanings, rats, and insects. His cousin Peyton Randolph also in 1764 had sent a moderately worded protest against the Stamp Act to the King for the House of Burgesses. But as loyal gentlemen both were shocked by what seemed the intemperance of an almost intruder.

The explosion came suddenly. Nine days after Patrick Henry had taken his seat as a Burgess he sent forward his violent resolutions against the Stamp Act and the British powers behind it. As full of effrontery as the resolutions seemed, Henry's speech which accompanied them was regarded as worse in both taste and tactics. It ended with the often quoted interrupted line: "Caesar had his Brutus—Charles the First his Cromwell—and George the Third—"

Cries of "Treason," some reported, rose from the rostrum and the benches. Henry, like the great actor he might have been in another day, deftly stepped aside with his closing phrase—"may profit by their example."

Possibly, as has been often said, the Robinson-Randolph group feared a threat to their power as well as apostasy to the crown. Two of Henry's five (or seven) resolutions were defeated or withheld on the day of his speech. At the end of what young Jefferson called a "bloody debate" one was passed by a single vote. The student spectator heard his cousin Peyton growl as he passed him in the lobby, "By God, I would have given 500 guineas for a single vote."

That would have left Speaker Robinson to break the tie. There was no doubt about how he would have voted against the upstart Henry and the renegade Lee. Next morning Jefferson saw his cousin Peter Randolph, current family occupant of the office of Clerk of the Burgesses, seeking precedents by which the resolution might be expunged from the journal. The damage had been done or the signal given. All of Henry's resolutions, passed or not, had been broadcast to the press and to the world.

In this same angry year Henry and Lee hit the Robinson-Randolph group in its tenderest spot. In his high post Robinson moved in public dignity which hid his private fears. In the hard times following the war when the glories of the golden age had to be maintained, he and his friends found a way. The Speaker remained well-off. He lent money from his private purse to help aristocratic associates who enjoyed the "delicious incense" of his eminence. Evidently his own means did not suffice, so he devised a plan. Treasury notes issued in the war passed as currency. Those due were annually presented to the Treasurer for cancellation in flames. Instead Robinson quietly handed them over to those who otherwise might have been the insolvent gentry. Possibly he salved his conscience by the knowledge of his own wealth and faith in his friends' purpose to redeem them. But the business got out of hand. Whispers grew about what was going on. Suspicions were the topic of cynical conversations in the Raleigh Tavern. Then, in 1765, Robinson found himself in too tight a place.

Members of the proud oligarchy proposed that a public loan office be set up. That would make it possible for those who had received money from Robinson or the Treasury to transfer their debts to the new instituion, taking the Speaker off the hook. Jefferson, who was in Williamsburg at the time, put the matter mildy: "It had been urged that, from certain unhappy circumstances of the colony, men of substantial property had contracted debts, which if exacted suddenly, must ruin them and their families, but with a little indulgence of time might be paid with ease."

But Patrick Henry exploded. Evidently addressing himself directly to the Speaker he cried: "What, sir, is it proposed then to reclaim the Spendthrift from his dissipation and extravagance by filling his pockets with money?"

The Tidewater powers nevertheless pushed the measure through the House of Burgesses. Peyton Randolph, along with his in-laws Benjamin Harrison and Archibald Cary, was among the managers who presented the bill to the Council. It was killed by that body. Still at Lee's insistence an investigation of the Treasury was ordered. Cary coolly reported its findings. His report was in the nature of a rebuke. Nothing was wrong in the Treasury. There had been no defalcations. Virginia's money had been put to no improper use. Lee seemed more than ever a traitor to his class. He was abused and Robinson applauded.

No whitewash was possible, however, when Robinson died the next year. At his death his accounts were found to be short by £102,000. The beneficiaries of Robinson's illegal largess were long carefully shielded. Thomas Perkins Abernethy, in his story of the scandal, wrote that "such action as was taken was carried on in a quiet manner." One who could "definitely" be listed among those who got the money, however, Abernethy said, was Colonel Cary. Malone wrote that "some prominent planters have been strongly suspected." And he added: "The fact that Colonel Peter Randolph and Edmund Pendleton were among the executors of Robinson's will need not imply that they were personally involved but it does suggest where their political sympathies lay."

Not until 1952 was much of the mystery removed by David John Mays, who discovered long neglected sources which he used in writing a biography of Edmund Pendleton. There he listed those Robinson had favored with loans. Among Randolphs and their relations were Richard Bland, Archibald Cary, Ryland, Peyton, John, Peter, and Richard Randolph. Only the energetic whitewasher Cary, however, owed a large sum: £3475:-16:10. The largest debt owed by one of Randolph name was that of John Randolph who loved his music and planted his garden. He owed nearly a thousand pounds. His brother Peyton's debt was little more than ten pounds.

Mays, whose research uncovered this information, doubted that the purpose of the proposed loan office was to save Robinson and those he had favored. Nothing was likely to save them now though it was to take decades to squeeze payments out of some of the indebted. There was an initial reluctance apparently among some named to serve as executors. Old Peter Randolph of Chatsworth, the son of William II who was the eldest son of William I, expressed an almost frantic sense about the matter in a letter to Pendleton. Peter, a member of the Council, had talked with Robinson's distressed and beset widow. He feared the destruction of the family of Robinson "whose humanity and good nature have been the only inducements to his acting in a manner that must inevitably reflect on him." "Quite inactive" himself, he could not undertake the administration of the estate so he pleaded with Pendleton, "For gods sake refuse not."

Outside the Assembly patience with patricians was growing thin. Murder pointed that. Colonel Chiswell, who was Robinson's father-in-law and a Randolph son-in-law, took the lurid center of the Virginia scene. Not only did Chiswell's connections indicate he was no ordinary innkeeper. Also, his father had built in Hanover County a country place called Scotchtown which Patrick Henry acquired. Later it was the house in which Dolley Madison spent her childhood. Antecedents and connections notwithstanding, Chiswell was a tough, quick-tempered man. On a summer evening in the Effingham Tavern at Cumberland he killed a man. Evidence at the time was that his victim, one Robert Routledge, was drunk and unarmed. Chiswell was "under the influence of nothing but his passions."

As enthusiastic promoter Chiswell had been describing to the guests at the inn his lead mine by the New River. Routledge questioned his rosy statements. In the quarrel that ensued, Chiswell, calling Routledge a "fugitive rebel and a Presbyterian fellow," sent for his sword. When it was brought, he ran the man through.

In the hearing which followed, three rich and aristocratic judges all Chiswell's friends—William Byrd III, Pressley Thornton, and John Blair—admitted Chiswell to bail. Vociferous complaint quickly came from writers of letters to the *Virginia Gazette* to the effect that in the class dominated colony such a man as Chiswell apparently could not be sternly called to account for his crimes. Peyton Randolph, though still Attorney General, absented himself from the county. The embarrassing situation was ended by Chiswell's sudden death. His doctor testified that his death was the result of "nervous fits, caused by constant uneasiness of mind." The almost universal popular verdict was that he killed himself. Portentously the scene of the episode was the same as that where supposedly untouchable Randolphs were to be tried for even darker crime.

The oligarchy was not overthrown. The column stood. Proximity to neither corruption nor homicide marred the Randolph image. As Abernethy wrote of Robinson, "Virginia has made every effort to forget him." Chiswell escaped both his guilt and his debts. But Peyton and John were promoted. When the offices of Speaker and Treasurer were separated after Robinson's death, Peyton was chosen as Speaker though he was opposed by Richard Henry Lee who had smelled the scandal in the Treasury. John, though he had been "quite unpopular since the Stamp Act controversy," was put into the position of King's Attorney which Peyton vacated as he advanced. This post seemed one which should always be occupied by a Randolph. That pattern would not soon be broken. Even when families were divided, a Randolph would follow a Randolph in the office, a father in exile by a son still armed by his name for early eminence at home.

Chapter V

LOYALTIES AND LIBERTIES

ALMOST as father and son, Dr. Walker and young Thomas Jefferson went to Williamsburg to represent Albemarle County in the House of Burgesses in 1769. Such service was no new experience for the physician-explorer who had been a dominant figure in the Loyal Land Company. He had made his first appearance in the Burgesses when his friend and neighbor Peter Jefferson was alive. Since Peter's death he had from his nearby estate at Castle Hill given the Jeffersons at Shadwell much the same kind of guidance Peter had provided for the family of William Randolph at Tuckahoe. Walker naturally took a special interest in Thomas, the close lifetime friend, schoolmate, and college classmate of his boy Jack. He could regard even Thomas's known faults with some forthright amusement.

Early in his college career Jefferson had been penitent about his extravagances, as he often was without ever being able to curb them in his whole life. He had indulged, according to his first biographer Randall, "in a little too showy style of living— particularly in the article of fine horses." So he wrote Walker asking him to charge the entire amount of his expenses to his own separate share of his father's estate.

"No," Walker replied, "if you have sowed your wild oats thus, the estate can well afford to pay the bill."

Whatever were his wild oats then, Dr. Walker probably never knew of the wild weeds Jefferson sowed in the few years afterwards. Indeed, he was such a dependable seeming young man that when Dr. Walker, with his son Jack as his clerk, went off for four months in 1768 to an important treaty-making meeting with the Indians at Fort Stanwix in New York, Jack not only left his pretty young wife and baby in Jefferson's care but also named him first among his executors in his will. Then, as Malone put it, the twenty-five-year-old Jefferson "made a mistake." Jack only learned long afterwards that while he was gone Jefferson began to make and afterwards continued to make improper proposals to his wife Betsy Moore. She kept secret these "base transactions," she said, for fear disclosure might lead to an encounter fatal to her husband.

Certainly it must have been a lacquered silence. Jack and Thomas remained close friends. Said Jack of Thomas in his later grief: "We loved (at least I did sincerely) each other." The two men met often in Betsy's presence. Jefferson was frequently in the Walker home. The Walkers visited at Shadwell. While Jefferson was beginning his literary leadership of the Revolution, he also prepared and slipped into Betsy's sleeve cuff, she said, a paper tending to convince her of the innocence of promiscuous love. This, according to her story, she on first glance tore to pieces (certainly a loss to the papers of Thomas Jefferson). Her story, which Jack later put together in a document of aggrievement, might have been the fabrication of a woman angry about something else. Some felt that it was exaggerated because of political disagreements later between the men. But Jefferson verified at least the essence of the affair when gossip about it was put into print by his enemies. "You will perceive," he wrote one of his defenders, "that I plead guilty to one of their charges, that when young and single I offered love to a handsome lady. I acknowledge its incorrectness. It is the only one founded in truth among all their allegations against me." The handsome lady was, of course, Betsy Moore Walker.

Malone in his standard biography of Jefferson quoted one of his friends as saying that there was no whisper in the neighborhood at the time about the affair. Malone wrote that it was a natural assumption "that the lady did not regard the offense as grave." The biographer also said that later Jefferson "relieved Walker's mind in a time of embarrassing publicity by exculpating the lady from all blame." What actually occurred in the extremes between Jefferson's admission that he offered love to this handsome lady and Walker's depiction of Jefferson in the lady's chamber clad only in his shirt "ready to seize her" can never be known. The only certainty is that Jefferson acted in ardor and the lady was handsome. History seems lacking the facts. But no more than Jack Walker was when, as he said, the "base transactions" were occurring between 1768 and 1779. As to the continuance of the affair until as late as 1779, it must be remembered that this date rests only upon the authority of Walker as an old, aggrieved, possibly mentally failing man in 1805.

Two years after Jefferson and Dr. Walker went to the Assembly together, Dr. Walker stood aside and Jack became Jefferson's colleague from Albemarle. Both young men identified themselves with the more ardent colonials in the argument with Britain, but at the outset they served in the "dull monotony of colonial subservience." Revolution seemed improbable. In Albemarle, Jack, possibly also Betsy, watched the first steps Jefferson took in the building of Monticello. He moved there as a bachelor, occupying a first erected outbuilding, before he began to pay court to a young widow in Charles City County. Despite Jack Walker's statement later, Malone greatly discounted the report that Jefferson's attentions to Betsy Walker continued into the days of his courtship and marriage.

Certainly his friendship with Jack Walker continued. They worked together with other ardent spirits in 1773 when the news came that Britain had closed the turbulent port of Boston. Using a modern sounding phrase for propagandistic operations, Jefferson wrote that he and some of his radical friends "cooked up" a plan to arouse the people of Virginia. It was the calling for a "Fast Day" to mourn the British repression in Massachusetts.

In later days when the relationship of Church and State altered, Jefferson condemned such Fast Days as providing a sort of proscription of some "in public opinion" and as "intermeddling in religious institutions." Now, however, he was anxious to give a "grave and religious character" to the cause. That was accomplished by persuading the pious and conservative Robert Carter Nicholas to offer the resolution they had drafted calling for the mass mourning. The day served to set apart under a slowly mounting stigma those who did not participate. One such was John Randolph, King's Attorney. He was suspected of writing a pamphlet criticizing the action and upholding the British policy which was published anonymously at the time.

Thomas and Jack were re-elected as the representatives of Albemarle in July 1774. Jefferson, however, was stricken with dysentery and unable to attend. So he sent, probably by Walker, resolutions he had drawn which he hoped might be adopted as instructions to Virginia's delegates in the Continental Congress in Philadelphia. One went to Patrick Henry, the other to Peyton Randolph. Nothing resulted from the copy to Henry, but his cousin had his copy read before a large company at his house, where it was applauded but somewhat questioned by conservatives. The paper was never acted upon officially but it was published without his name in Williamsburg as *A Summary View of the Rights of British America*. Soon it was reprinted in Philadelphia and appeared twice in England. The authorship of the work was no secret. In effect the highly respected Peyton had put Jefferson forward as the penman of the Revolution.

In this time of great affairs and altering and changing loyalties, personal details have seemed unimportant in history. Some seem better forgotten. The story of Jefferson's covetousness for his cousin John's violin, however, is better and more pleasantly documented even than that of his lust for his friend Jack's wife. Certainly as a man becoming better and better known for his ability to write resounding prose, Jefferson seemed no cloaked profligate. In terms of the times, however, at twenty-eight he was a belated bridegroom. But he followed the illustrious example of George Washington in choosing a rich widow, Martha Wayles Skelton, daughter of a wealthy planter-lawyer and slave dealer, John Wayles.

Much of the story of his marriage to Martha Wayles Skelton is as shadowy as that of his relations with Betsy Moore. While there is every reason to believe that it was an idyllically happy one, little more is known of it than tradition and the vital statistics that Martha had six children in the ten years of their lives together, only two of whom lived to maturity. Their first child, Martha, was born in 1772. Another daughter, Jane, born in 1774 lived less than two years. Malone suggested that there were miscarriages as well. Beyond the records of their progeny the one thing most definitely reported about Thomas and Martha was their common love for music. She played on the harpsichord and the pianoforte, he on the violin and the cello.

Well authenticated is the fact that Jefferson tried to get a better violin for himself than the one he had used in Fauquier's musical coterie. He is said to have carried a small fiddle on his travels in these days. He bought one instrument at Williamsburg for five pounds. Desire for a better one marked his continuing affection for his cousin the troubled Attorney General John Randolph. Already the arrival of brusque, arrogant John Murray, Earl of Dunmore, as Governor in 1771 promised sharpening lines in loyalty when John and Jefferson made a contract in that year. Evidently John's loyalty to the colony was not angrily in question when the cousins made this agreement which must have been playfully prepared as well as serious in intent. It read:

It is agreed between John Randolph, Esqr. of the City of Williamsburg and Thomas Jefferson, of the county of Albemarle, that in case the said John shall survive the said Thomas, that the Exr's. or Adminirs of the said Thomas shall deliver to the said John 800 pounds sterling of the books of the said Thomas, to be chosen by the said John, or if not books sufficient, the deficiency to be made up in money: And in case the said Thomas should survive the said John, that the Executors of the said John shall deliver to the said Thomas the violin which the said John brought with him into Virginia, together with all his music composed for the violin, or in lieu thereof, if destroyed by any accident, 60 pounds sterling worth of books of the said John, to be chosen by the said Thomas. In witness whereof the said John and

Thomas have hereunto subscribed their names and affixed their seals the day and year above written.

John Randolph (L.S.)
Thomas Jefferson (L.S.)

Sealed and delivered in the presence of

G. Wythe
Thomas Everard
P. Henry, Jr.
Richard Starke
Wm Johnson
Ja. Steptoe

Virginia s.s.

At a general court held at the capitol on the 12th day of April, 1771, this agreement was acknowledged by John Randolph and Thomas Jefferson, parties thereto, and ordered to be recorded.

Teste.
Ben. Waller, c.c. cur.

The probability is that at least a bowl of arrack punch was consumed by amiable gentlemen at the signing of this agreement. George Wythe gave the document judicial prestige. Certainly Patrick Henry's name was a patriotic ornament on the document. James Steptoe was a gentleman of Middlesex County whose son married a daughter of Christopher Robinson and Sarah Wormeley of the strong Tory family. The others were evidently planters of prominence in Virginia. Benjamin Waller, clerk at this time of the Virginia General Court, had had a role in exposing the Robinson scandal.

Despite sharpening differences of opinion, evidently business in violins and other commodities was continuing. Two years before this time ardent colonials had signed non-importation agreements in retaliation against British taxation plans. The first name on the 1769 agreement was that of Peyton Randolph. Other Randolphs, including Jefferson and Richard II of Curles, signed along with Patrick Henry, Richard Bland, Archibald Cary, Carter Braxton, Thomas Nelson, Jr., Dr. Walker, Lees, Carters, others.

One name missing was that of John Randolph. A new name added to a similar agreement in June 1770 was that of Jefferson's cousin and boyhood friend Thomas Mann Randolph. This Thomas was sacrificing his interest in the importation of British thoroughbred horses. He had become one of the leading horse breeders in the colony. His stallion Shakespeare was provided with a specially built stable which contained sleeping quarters for his Negro groom. Tuckahoe horses were noted on the track. In a meet at Petersburg in 1766 one bay from its stables won a race in which "the course was run swifter than ever before." Now, however, Thomas Mann Randolph and other patriotic turfmen so cut their importations that only three British thoroughbreds were brought to Virginia in the period.

As a non-British item, one important commodity, however, apparently was imported as usual. An advertisement in the *Virginia Gazette*, on October 8, 1772, was signed by Jefferson's father-in-law, John Wayles, and his cousin Richard Randolph II of Curles. It announced: "Just arrived from Africa, the Ship Prince of Wales, James Bivins, Commander, with about four hundred fine healthy slaves: the sale of which will begin at Bermuda Hundred on Thursday the 8th of October, and continue until all are sold." Wayles, however, told his son-in-law Jefferson, who was to sternly blame the King for the slave trade, that business in this line was not good.

Randolphs were having other troubles. The brothers, Peyton and John, were drifting and being pushed apart. In 1773, Peyton was named chairman of the Virginia Committee of Correspondence working with other resentful colonies. In 1774, and again in 1775, he presided over Virginia revolutionary conventions. John, in 1774 and 1775, as the candidate of Governor Dunmore, secured election as Burgess for William and Mary College. Then the Governor sought his Attorney General's election as a member of the board of visitors of the college. This was a position which normally would have properly and easily gone to a Randolph. But objection was raised to his election by a member of the Council, John Page, whose cousin had married William Randolph of Tuckahoe. He opposed Randolph "as not possessing the disposition and character, moral and religious, which the charter and the statutes of the college required." Perhaps John was unorthodox in his religious views. So also were other honored men of the times, including his cousin Jefferson. More important, however, John was a doubtful patriot. Nathaniel Burwell, relation if not kinsman, was elected in his stead. While John was denied this relatively humble post, Peyton was the first on the list of the seven delegates elected by Virginia to the First Continental Congress in Philadelphia. He was chosen as president of that body in 1774 and 1775, in effect becoming the first to preside over the nascent American nation.

Neither Peyton nor his young protégé Jefferson were devoting all their interests and energies to the quarrel with Britain. Even as tensions mounted they and others had ideas that life might go on in productive ways in the colony. As late as 1774 Randolphs had joined with others in plans to introduce the culture of grapes, olives, and other such fruits to Virginia. In the company organized behind the Italian enthusiast Philip Mazzei, who would be remembered for other things than horticulture, were Jefferson and the Randolphs: Peyton, Thomas Mann, Peter, Richard, and Ryland, representing the lines of four of the sons of the family founder. Once again John Randolph's name was missing.

Still, early in 1775, Peyton and John were working together or in concert as oddly different conservatives to prevent violence in Virginia. In March, Patrick Henry, urging the arming of the colony, had made his famous "liberty or death" speech at a convention in the little village of Richmond. Then, on April 20, Governor Dunmore aroused the colony by removing the powder in the arsenal at Williamsburg to a British ship in the river. Henry at the head of gathering colonials prepared to march on the capital. Now probably for the last time, Peyton and John joined in their aims.

They worked with such other Virginians as Robert Carter Nicholas, Edmund Pendleton, and Carter Braxton in the effort to save Williamsburg from destruction which might ensue from the collision of Henry and Dunmore. Most Virginians at the time had greater faith in Peyton than any other man—even Henry. John was one of the few Virginians still close to the Governor. Together the brothers and others shaped an agreement whereby Dunmore paid for the powder and the threatened march was suspended. The powder at Williamsburg was not replaced with the £330 of the King's revenues which Dunmore remitted. According to Bruce in his life of Randolph of Roanoke, money for new powder was provided by another John Randolph of Matoax, his father-in-law Theodorick Bland, Sr., and his brother-in-law Theodorick Bland, Jr. They sold forty slaves to raise the money. Such gentlemen were readier to make such a transaction because Dunmore added to his crimes by inciting slaves to desert their masters and join his forces.

Peyton's services as colonial leader were in demand both in Philadelphia and Virginia. So Jefferson was elected to serve in the Continental Congress in case Peyton was required at home. Jefferson sat in that body during the summer and autumn of 1775. But in this summer also he and John had come to the conclusion expressed by the younger man that John was "not eligible" to remain in Virginia. So in August of that year the violin-book bargain of 1771 between them was terminated at the instance of Randolph. The correspondence of the two men suggests that, as rich as some Randolphs might be, John was in need of funds as he contemplated exile. Jefferson delivered to Carter Braxton an order for £13 in favor of John for the much-desired instrument. Also he offered to buy such of Randolph's books as the exile might wish to dispose of. Braxton was apparently only a messenger in the affair. He owned lands on which he grew tobacco in Albemarle. As merchant he supplied Jefferson with some of his needs. Apparently he acted only as a matter of courtesy on one of his trips between Albemarle and Williamsburg.

The letters of the cousins were friendly. Jefferson hoped that Randolph would write him "as often as you are disposed to think of things here." Randolph wrote: "Tho we *may politically* differ in Sentiments, yet I see no Reason why *privately* we may not cherish the same Esteem for each other which formerly I believe subsisted between us. Should any coolness happen between us, I'll take Care not to be the first mover of it." He added later, however, that the insults he had received gave him some uneasiness, "But the unmanly and illiberal treatment which the more delicate part of my family met with, I confess filled me with bitter resentment."

Not all the differences among the Randolphs came to dramatic termination when John with his wife and two lovely daughters sailed away. They left behind their young son Edmund who joined the patriot cause. Soon afterwards, on October 31, 1775, Archibald Cary wrote to Jefferson in Philadelphia. Cary had doleful news to relate of other younger members of the complexly intermarried Randolph tribe. He had just come from the deathbed of his brother-in-law John Randolph of Matoax and Curles, who recently had helped provide the money to replace the powder Dunmore had taken. Cary had married this John's sister Mary, daughter of Richard of Curles. John had married his second cousin Frances Bland, granddaughter of Elizabeth Randolph, the family founder's child. Both John and Frances were also descended from Bollings. Their children were also to marry cousins. John had taken cold by riding in the night to see his ill cousin Thomas Randolph, Jefferson's uncle, who had married his cousin Jane Cary. Thomas survived but John died on October 28, 1775, leaving a fated brood. But Archibald Cary in his letter had more shocking news to tell of a younger Peyton Randolph and his kin. He wrote:

"A dispute arose at Dinner at Chatsworth between Payton (sic) Randolph and his Brother Lewis Burwell, who gave the other Lye, on which Payton Struck him, Burwell Snatch'd a knife and stuck him in the side, but fortunately a Rib prevented its proving Mortal. He was prevented by the Ladys from making a Second Stroke. You'l judge what Poor Mrs. Randolph must suffer on this Unhappy Affair, but she is become Familiar with Misfortune. Payton is well and no Notice is Taken of The Affair, As I can see by Either. They dined at my House the day After I got Home."

The cast of characters in what Julian Boyd called this "grim affair" is fairly clear. "Poor Mrs. Randolph" was, as the mistress of Chatsworth, Lucy Bolling widow of Peter Randolph. He had held among other offices that of "Surveyor General of Customs for the Middle District of America." With his brother William of Wilton and Speaker Peyton Randolph he had undertaken to "encourage Arts and Manufactures in the colony by giving bounties to be raised by popular subscriptions for inventions, Etc." After his death in 1767, Braxton and William Randolph sold his house in Williamsburg. It was "elegantly papered and handsomely situated," said their advertisement in the *Virginia Gazette*. It included "a good kitchen, a servant's house of the same dimensions, two new stables, each sufficient for six horses."

The antagonistic members of "Poor Mrs. Randolph's" family company at Chatsworth were her nephew and her niece's husband. This younger Peyton was the son of William of Wilton and Anne Harrison, sister of Benjamin Harrison then in Philadelphia as a delegate to the Congress. Lewis Burwell who snatched the knife had married Peyton's sister Lucy. He was kin to Jefferson's youthful flame Rebecca Burwell. One Burwell had been president of the Council. Two other Lewis Burwells were prominent at this time, one of whom would be the appraiser of the great Peyton Randolph's estate.

Cary gave no indication as to what the quarrel was about. These were quarrelsome times. The whole affair was kept out of the newspapers but gossip about it spread across Virginia. To his letter, Cary added a line about the great Peyton which gave an even more doleful cast to his news.

"If the Speaker and his Lady have not been acquainted with this Matter, say nothing of it to them."

Speaker Peyton would never know about this. Suddenly in Philadelphia on October 22, more than a week before Cary wrote, he died of apoplexy. He left his large estate, including 105 slaves, to his wife for life and after her death to his nephew Edmund Randolph who had taken the patriot side when his father had chosen exile. Jefferson's cousin Richard Bland, at sixty-five, had declined to serve longer as a delegate in the Continental Congress. Though related by close ties to Benjamin Harrison, Carter Braxton, and Thomas Nelson, Jr., Jefferson at thirty-two was the leader of the Randolphs in the movement to Revolution.

His colleagues certainly did not indicate that the aristocracy had been overthrown after the debates and disclosures of 1765. Richard Henry Lee as a delegate was also an aristocrat. Patrick Henry alone represented, as one of them, the rustic people of the up-country. Evidently even in revolution the frontier had not overthrown the plantations.

Though revolutionary events were moving rapidly, Jefferson was absent from Philadelphia from December 28, 1775, to May 14, 1776. He stayed much at Monticello which he had begun to build half a dozen years before. His early biographer Randall suggested that his stay in Virginia was in a sense a mission from Philadelphia in mobilizing public opinion and organizing public support. This is supposition only. He planted trees; he shaped his landscaped hill. One item of business did concern him. Though he had given up the practice of law, he handled some legal matters in the family. One such concerned his mother's brother William who with his brother Isham had long before chosen England as their place of residence. Like all Randolphs, he was concerned about the land. This William's mother, Jane Rogers Randolph, had by will bequeathed her estate of Dungeness, where her husband had maintained his great establishment, to her eldest son, Isham. But if Isham died without issue, the estate was to pass to William. Isham did die childless. But in Virginia their younger brother Thomas remained at Dungeness and became male head of this branch of the family in Virginia. Now William wanted the rental rights due him.

Jefferson did not answer his uncle's query until after he returned to Philadelphia in May 1776. Though the colonies behind some delegations lagged, the Congress was ready for bold action. Less than a month after Jefferson arrived, the Congress adopted a Virginia resolution offered by Richard Henry Lee: "That these colonies are, and of a right ought to be, free and independent states." On the following day, June 10, a committee was named to draw a document which would provide a justification of the decision already made to cut the tie with Britain and to provide a warm appeal to all men to support that decision. Contrary to usual procedure Lee was not named chairman of this committee—nor even a member of it. Among the reasons given was that he departed for Virginia to be with his sick wife. Not all accepted this reason.

All agreed that young Jefferson had a more masterly pen. But John Adams in after years declared that one basic reason was that when Lee "was very young, and when he first came into the House of Burgesses, [he] moved and urged on an inquiry into the state of the treasury" which was found deficient in large sums, which had been lent by the Treasurer to "many of the most influential families of the country, who found themselves exposed, and had never forgiven Mr. Lee."

There seems little doubt that, as Abernethy wrote, the rival interests of the Ohio Company group and "the Albemarle-Valley membership in the Loyal and Greenbrier Companies . . . created a cleavage which may be traced down the years in Virginia politics." Yet Lee must have seemed to have given up little when he left before his resolve for independence was put into eloquent terms. That would be only elaboration of the decision already made at his instance. It would be ratification of it only as it invited members to sign and so stand up to be counted. Lee could not have contemplated—he could not have created—the magnificent poetry for the world which Jefferson wrote and his associates only slightly modified.

It did not suffer because, as rough and unjust, a section was deleted holding George III personally responsible for the continuing brutalities of the slave trade. George III, Jefferson had written, "waged cruel war against human nature itself, violating its most sacred rights of life and liberty in the persons of distant people, who never offended him, captivating and carrying them into slavery in another hemisphere, or to incur miserable death in their transportation thither."

His rhetoric in denunciation was as resounding as that he had used in the expression of aspirations for mankind. He arraigned the monarch: "Determined to keep open a market where men should be bought and sold, he has prostituted his negative for suppressing every legislative attempt to prohibit or to restrain the execrable commerce; and that this assemblage of horrors might want no fact of distinguished dye, he is now exciting these very people to rise in arms among us, and to purchase that liberty of which he has deprived them by murdering the people upon whom he also obtruded them; thus paying off former crimes committed against the liberties of one people, with crimes which he urges them to commit against the lives of another."

Mr. Jefferson always deplored the whole black business from African shore to plantation labor. But his kin and father-in-law were involved in the malodorous trade. Some slaves fled from his own estate to British promise of freedom. He kept slaves till he died. Some delegates at Philadelphia not only opposed abolition of the trade; also some doubted that they, as innocent accusers, could damn George. It was enough to hold that all men were created equal—and that only with reservations.

As finally adopted no more masterly document was ever produced. Yet as Jefferson wrote, he embodied in it ideas he had long been shaping, phrases which had been long growing in his mind. Possibly the letter to his uncle which he drafted at the same time was emotionally a more difficult composition for him. His Uncle William was a shadowy figure in the distance. His Uncle Thomas was a neighbor close at hand. Though Uncle Thomas lived not far from Monticello, Jefferson had not taken the matter up with him. He told his English uncle that his brother Thomas, who the fall before had survived the illness about which his in-law Archibald Cary had written, was "good and just" but ill and "much displeased." He had, he wrote, not even been able to see him.

Independence intervened between British owners and American rents as it did between American debtors and their English creditors. Some Americans were ready for both revolution and debt repudiation, the first made more appealing by the latter. Uncle William would have to wait and hope as would the Hanburys and Perrys of London. In 1779, while war went on, Dungeness was confiscated under the act pertaining to British property in Virginia. Apparently, however, possibly with Jefferson's help, the property was allowed to remain in the possession of the ailing brother Thomas. Ultimately the estate passed to his nephew, Thomas Eston Randolph, eldest son of the expatriate William.

How well William Randolph, the long-time expatriate, got along in England without his Dungeness rents is not known. There is more information about John Randolph. There are varying reports about the experience of the loyalist exiles whom John joined. Bishop William Meade, whose aunt married the second Richard of Curles, in his *Old Churches, Ministers and Families of Virginia* (1857), gave a pleasant picture of their residence in England as refugees. He wrote: "While in London the American loyalists seem to have had a merry time of it, dining and supping together at various inns, and having more private lodgings. Those who approved their principles and conduct were not wanting in hospitality to them,—especially Lord Dunmore, who either lived in London or was often there." Not all accounts were so rose tinted. John Randolph was reduced to living on a meager pension from the crown.

Apparently, however, he was not troubled by his apostasy. He maintained his correspondence with Jefferson trying to convince him that the colonies should seek reconciliation rather than independence which would never be granted. Once when it was feared that the French might supplement aid in America by an invasion of England he offered his military services to the King. He also proposed a plan for reconciliation to the War Office. Less honorable activities were attributed to him. He was accused of producing and circulating forged letters in which Washington as American commander was made to speak as one late and reluctant in the break with Britain.

The forged letters, wrote Freeman, were "the somewhat skillful work of a person who knew the main facts concerning Washington's family and way of living but erred amusingly on the smaller, more intimate details of Washington's life during the months the contest was developing." Washington himself suspected that John Randolph was the man responsible for them. H. J. Eckenrode, as Randolph historian, wrote that "The weight of evidence appears to point to him but it is not conclusive."

In the furies of the time almost any crime could be imputed to the Loyalists.

John Randolph was often "disposed to think of things" in America. Virginians in England clung together. John's daughters married other Virginians in exile. The Old Dominion was still home. As John lay dying, in hardship and homesickness, he expressed the hope that he might be buried in the chapel of William and Mary where his father, Sir John, and his brother, Peyton, lay. When his lovely daughter Ariana, now Mrs. James Wormeley, returned to Virginia after the war she brought his remains. There was a place for him in the chapel. A Randolph might stray from the path of Virginia, but he could never cease to be one of her own.

Chapter VI

ARMS IN ALBEMARLE

SEVENTEEN SEVENTY-SIX was, of course, a very significant year—for America, for Virginia, and for Randolphs.

In June, before his cousin Jefferson composed the Declaration of Independence, tall, handsome Theodorick Bland, Jr. (the name was pronounced Thee-*odd*-orick in Virginia), moved, mounted, to help make that independence possible. These two gentlemen of the fourth Randolph generation in the New World did not then seem fated as soldier and civilian to come so close together in the war ahead. History has little marked their proximity to each other. But time and change touched both. Jefferson and Bland were men in their middle thirties. Virginia was 169 years old. Also, 1776 was the centennial of Bacon's Rebellion which Jefferson insistently regarded as the prelude to independence. In remembering that, it was no longer necessary to recall that a Bland then died on the gallows as a rebel and the first Randolph carefully avoided even the suspicion that he was involved in the revolt.

Despite the picture shaped in history, the year was hardly one of jubilant fife and drum corps music for the Americans. The times were such, as Tom Paine wrote then, as tried men's souls. Theodorick, Jr.'s uncle Richard Bland, "the Virginia Antiquary," who had been one of the first to speak clearly in the colonial cause, was brought home for burial on his Jordan's Point plantation in October. In this same month Washington told Congress that its army was "upon the eve of political dissolution." Theodorick Bland, Sr., who had been early and eager in efforts to arouse the Virginia countryside, was growing old on his adjoining plantation, Cawsons, at the broad confluence of the James and Appomattox rivers. Yet in this autumn Mr. Jefferson could as a philosopher look beyond the disturbing present to prospects of a more perfect Virginia.

In this October he was back in Virginia, never to return to Philadelphia until the war was over. For public and private reasons he was eager to be home. Immediately after his return Martha became pregnant with her third child. He took her with him to Williamsburg where they accepted the hospitality of the house of George Wythe who remained in Philadelphia. Jefferson framed bills for religious freedom and to put an end to the laws of entail and primogeniture which many regarded as the basis of the Virginia social and political hierarchy. More immediately accomplished was the removal of the capital to Richmond, a move which took government away from possible subservience to Tidewater aristocracy. Jefferson could not neglect these activities, which he always regarded as paramount in the contributions of his career. At the time, however, he moved to reform in Virginia before it was at all certain that a free Virginia would exist to be reformed.

The bad news from the North continued. On the eve of Christmas, while Jefferson was at Monticello, the Assembly received the news that Washington had been forced to let go his hold on the Hudson and had crossed into the Jerseys. Then the King's Army was in the valley of the Delaware, heading South. Panic produced the fact—or the tradition to some extent vouched for by Jefferson—that Governor Patrick Henry was ready to be made Dictator. And the tradition relates that Jefferson's great friend Archibald Cary, "Old Iron" as he was called for his foundries or his personality, put a swift end to that by sending a message to Henry.

"Tell him from me that the day of his appointment shall be the day of his death—for he shall feel my dagger in his heart before the sunset of that day."

Jefferson was not ready to play Brutus to any Virginia Caesar. He seemed remote from the harsh realities of the war front, devot-

ing himself idealistically to securing revisions of old laws, which
seemed to him essential to true liberty in Virginia. Though as lieutenant of Albermarle he had been commander of its militia, he
now seemed almost quixotically absent from arms. The younger
Theodorick Bland in completely different fashion was to seem
even more quixotic. Indeed, despite his gothic name, he brought
comedy as well as ardor to the Patriot cause. He left a scene he
loved as much as Jefferson loved Monticello when he went to war.
He was happy on his own plantation, Kippax, which had come
to him down his mother's Bolling line. Also his heartiness seemed
required at Cawsons where his well-loved sister, Frances Randolph, with her three fatherless boys, spent much of her time
with her father. There she was safer from the loneliness of her
own place, Matoax, where her husband John Randolph had died
the year before. With other properties he had left it to her in a
will marked by his great love for her and the violence of which
he was capable toward others. Though Frances's Bolling line did
not come down from Pocahontas, as her husband's had, she
was so dark that her brother Theodorick playfully called her
his "tawny sister." He agreed with those who said she could
charm a bird out of a tree with the music of her tongue. She
made music now only for her three fatherless boys, Richard,
another Theodorick, and John, cherubs whom none suspected
could be damned.

Her tall brother taught the boys to ride. The young Randolph
boys, sometimes with their cousins John and Patsy Banister,
watched in tumultuous admiration the horsemanship of their
uncle and his brother-in-law, John Banister, of nearby Battersea.
Banister, grandson of the famous Virginia botanist of the same
name, had married a decade and a half before Theodorick's
sister, Elizabeth. The two gentlemen thundered past the children
on some of the thoroughbreds from the splendid stud of Theodorick Bland, Sr. Theodorick, Jr., loved not only the fine horses
from his family's stables but also the wide land under their hoofs
in the adjoining plantations of his father and uncle. He loved
the world very much, too, but was perhaps not quite so intense
about the land as his sister Frances who passed her feeling to

her youngest boy, John Randolph, who later added "of Roanoke" to his name.

Riding with the boy over vast Randolph estates down on the Roanoke River she spread her arms to encompass the land. She told him: "When you get to be a man you must not sell your land; it is the first step to ruin for a boy to part with his father's home. Be sure to keep it as long as you live. Keep your land and your land will keep you."

The Blands and other Randolphs put almost equal faith in the land, the saddle, and the book. Undoubtedly on the estates of Cawsons, Jordan's Point, Kippax, Bizarre, Roanoke, other properties, slave grooms had put Theodorick, the cavalryman to be, astride great horses in the green paddocks when he was little more than a toddler. They did not laugh as the boy became almost one with the horse. Still, at eleven he was sent abroad to school in Wakefield, Yorkshire. He went on to receive his M.D. degree at the University of Edinburgh when he was twenty-one years old. As a rich colonist with a black slave valet, he could have been no ordinary college student in this period. After graduating in proper style, he traveled and studied in London, Paris, and Leyden, then at the peak of its glory as a seat of medical education. The subject of his thesis, *De Concoctione Alimentorium in Ventriculo,* sounds more impressive in Latin than in its English equivalent, "Concerning the Digestion of Food in the Stomach."

Much was expected of him when he came home after eleven years absence to practice as country doctor in Prince George County. Yet, considering the heroic therapies which he prescribed for his patients—including bleeding, purging, sweating, puking— possibly the general health in Prince George County was improved when he decided, as a man worn out by work that he did not like, to give up practice five years later, in 1771, when he was twenty-nine.

Tensions with the mother country were mounting. He was ready with strong medicine for the British. Before he rode to war, he wrote, under the signature of Cassius, some bitter letters against Governor Dunmore in the *Virginia Gazette.* He already had some reputation as the writer of verses. Now more militant, he was ever ready to defend his cause, it was said, with a "fluent and correct" pen which, "if sometimes too florid and diffuse" was "wanting neither in energy of thought nor elegance of diction." Patriotically declining to deal with a British mercantile house, he wrote that the actions of the mother country "induce us to exert every nerve to imitate the silk worm and spin from our own bowels, although the web should be our winding sheet."

So prepared for death or glory, he became one of the first of the Virginia gentry who, as hereditary horsemen, provided a first, fine basis for the cavalry Washington desperately needed. One version of his entry into arms is that he "was appointed captain of the first troop of Virginia Cavalry." Elsewhere that organization has been described as "Theodorick Bland's regiment of Virginia Cavalry." Worn as he may have been when he gave up his practice five years before, now, at thirty-four, he rode with dash and style.

Others gathered to his standard. One in dramatic particular was his young cousin Henry Lee then aged nineteen. Certainly when Theodorick's aunt, Mary Randolph Bland, married this young Lee's grandfather, also a Henry Lee, an extraordinary union was made. The Blands and the Lees were early described as "both in fortune and understanding inferior to none in the colony." Certainly the Lee family founder Richard's place in early Virginia had been at least equal to that of William Randolph of Turkey Island. Indeed, this first Lee became a member of the Council to which William Randolph was never appointed. Now Lees were thick in the forefront in Virginia. Two of Henry's brothers were destined for eminence. Their cousins in this period (not in the Randolph line but indicative of what Lee blood brought into it) were the four famous brothers, Arthur, Richard Henry, Francis Lightfoot, and William, all of whom played prominent roles in the move to independence. Two of these Lees signed the Declaration.

Henry Lee, the young cavalryman in Theodorick's force (later to be known as Light-Horse Harry), was born in 1756 at Leesylvania in Prince William County, below Alexandria on the Potomac

River. Tradition among the gentry there said that his mother, Lucy Grymes, whose family much intermarried with the Randolphs, had been one of the early sweethearts of Washington. Growing up in such a society, he went as a precocious boy to the College of New Jersey (Princeton), then under John Witherspoon who later was a signer of the Declaration. It was a college in intellectual ferment while William and Mary had come upon a period in its existence described as "dissolute and unenviable." In the same college generation James Madison turned to Princeton, too. Others among Lee's college mates were Aaron Burr and Philip Freneau, the poet of the Revolution. Joining in the patriotic and national sentiments aroused in the college at the time, Lee graduated in 1773 at the age of seventeen. Madison did not get his degree until he was twenty-two.

At any other time Lee would doubtless have carried out his plans to study law in England where he had been accepted at the Middle Temple. These were special times, however, and young Henry, almost born in the saddle, happily accepted a lieutenancy in the cavalry of his cousin Theodorick. He decorated it. Blond and blue-eyed with a strong chin, he wore his hair powdered and slicked back to a neat queue. As uniform he wore a bright green jacket, tight leather breeches and highly polished boots. A horsehair plume rose above his leather cap. A body servant attended him in camp. Even in the field he drank from a silver cup.

Theodorick's command did not remain long in Virginia. In April 1777, his superbly mounted cavalry joined Washington's army. Lee and Bland were to have widely different amounts of the General's confidence. Lee turned down an invitation to become one of the General's aides which would have meant a promotion but activity on the staff instead of in the field.

"I am wedded to my sword," he said, "and my secondary object in the present war is military reputation."

At least as eager for glory, Theodorick early earned ridicule instead. On July 9, 1777, Major Benjamin Tallmadge of Connecticut, later a member of Congress, wrote to Jeremiah Wadsworth, who had just been chosen deputy commissary-general of purchases. He described one of Bland's exploits. Though he wrote in satire, Tallmadge was evidently not amused. He told Wadsworth:

Colo. Bland on the 25ult. determined with about 260 horse to take Strawberry Hill, near Amboy . . . notwithstanding there were more than 10,000 Regular Troops drawn up on it in full view. We had but about 300 infantry to support us, and were then more than 9 miles advanced from our army; Notwithstanding these trifles the Heroe determined to gain some laurels, and so we moved on till we came within long musket shot and then drew up precisely at that distance where the King's arms could do execution & our carbines could do none. After we had tarried here long enough, to lose a few men and horses, it was wisely resolved that it was best to take ourselves away as soon as possible, inasmuch as we had to pass through thickets, which by this time were filled with the enemies advanced parties which gauled us in our retiring (for it is not suffered to be called a retreat.) However, to crown all & compensate for all losses & trouble we blundered over *one* Hessian & brought off the poor dog, with shouts of joy for victory was now ours. . . . I wish and so does every Officer of the Horse in the Army that Colo. B was safely landed in Heaven for so noble an Exploit.

Then in the Battle of Brandywine Creek on September 11, 1777, young Lee distinguished himself but Bland apparently was guilty of another blooper. His action as a mounted intelligence officer on this occasion was followed later by a censorious comment even from his subordinate Lee. The younger man wrote: "Col. Bland was noble, sensible, honorable and amiable, but never intended for the department of intelligence." His bumbling in that department was said to have had much to do with the British success along this Pennsylvania stream.

Lee's military behavior was in dramatic contrast. A week after the battle Washington dispatched Lee with young Lieutenant Colonel Alexander Hamilton on a hazardous mission to destroy supplies left behind which the General did not wish to fall into the hands of the British. With a small force they galloped off to burn the supplies stored in mills on the shores of the

Schuylkill. They were able to apply their torches but almost lost their lives when they were surprised by a superior British force. Indeed, each sadly reported the death of the other, though as it turned out, Lee got away by horse and Hamilton escaped in a small boat under enemy fire. Their courage helped to endear both to the General. They became his equally devoted soldiers in war and supporters in politics later.

In January 1778, now a boyish major, Lee was given command of a somewhat irregular force composed of three troops of cavalry and three companies of infantry. This was "Lee's Legion," the skill and audacity of which soon became evident. In it Lee had as courageous subordinate another cousin, stalwart John Marshall. Possibly the Marshall kinship was not so much stressed then as later. Indeed, Edward S. Corwin, as a Marshall biographer, wrote that early writers about him scarcely noted his Randolph connections because of doubts as to the validity of the marriage of his grandmother, Mary Isham Randolph, to his grandfather the Reverend James Keith, after her earlier elopement with an overseer. Young Marshall himself at this time was no such embodiment of the aristocracy as Lee and Bland. His background was close to the frontier, not the plantation.

His qualities were not overlooked, however. He had come into service at twenty-two, along with his father, strong, advancing Thomas Marshall. After participating in some skirmishes in Virginia, the younger Marshall was, on July 30, 1776, mustered into the Continental service in the 3rd Virginia Regiment as lieutenant. From it he was selected as one qualified for Lee's elite corps. As Lee had been imbued with a sense of American nationalism at Princeton, Marshall later said that in arms under Washington, "I was confirmed in the habit of considering America as my country and Congress as my government." Possibly this brought both Lee and Marshall into a philosophic view in contrast with that of their cousin Jefferson who spoke of Virginia as "my country" then and later.

Whatever may have been the philosophy of these two young Virginians, both welcomed dangerous assignments. The first significant one was in doing the scouting and preparing the way for "Mad" Anthony Wayne's bold assault on Stony Point, the northernmost British post on the Hudson, on July 16, 1779. Washington himself had planned this move. Wayne's hope of success depended upon surprise. Before the date set for the attack Major Lee had been scouting the whole country about the post. Then as "Mad" Anthony readied for the attack he met Lee who assured him that the country about the post was quiet and unalarmed. So assured, Wayne moved in. The surprise was as complete as Lee had reported it would be. The British force of over 600 crack troops was overwhelmed. Lee and Marshall in lesser measure shared with Wayne the acclaim of the country.

A little more than a month later Lee, again with Marshall in his band, duplicated Wayne's victory at Stony Point. This time, again under cover of night, Lee's Legion surprised a supposedly impregnable post at Paulus Hook, across the river from New York where Jersey City later spread. He did not depend this time wholly upon stealth and darkness. He sent in eight or ten of his stalwarts, disguised as countrymen with produce to sell, who got the gate opened and held it until their companions rushed in. The legion captured 160 prisoners with very slight American loss. The immediate result was not acclaim, however. Jealous officers, evidently other Virginians, charged both that Lee had by falsification gained command of the expedition and that in command he had withdrawn too quickly leaving some of the enemy safe in a redoubt which "might so easily have been destroyed." In anger Lee considered resigning. But a court dismissed the charges. Washington stood by him. As he felt he had earned it he debonairly wore the nickname "Light-Horse Harry" Lee then and forever after. Even some Virginians, however (notably Edmund Pendleton), thought that though acquitted he had been "too highly puffed by some Family Partisans." Pendleton hoped "Our countrymen his accusers" would not suffer "in their reputation by his Acquittal."

Washington needed the young man in another field. In October 1780, he sent Lee to give General Nathanael Greene in the South the cavalry support he required. Lee's name was known before him. But his appearance and that of his legion of several hundred men, horse and foot, lifted the morale of the troops he joined, many of them irregulars, poorly clad and armed. Lee's men were newly equipped in Virginia. In plumed leather helmets, green jackets, white breeches and knee boots, they matched the elan of the men of the British cavalry led by brilliant Banastre Tarleton. They matched them in skill and courage, too. Also, from the stables of Virginia, Lee had secured the best horses while the British had been reduced to poor tackies. Lee was as dashing in prose when he later wrote his memoirs of the Southern campaigns. Some of his story Jefferson described as a "historical novel." It did not lack historical drama.

No glory gathered about the name of Theodorick Bland. He was made colonel of the 1st Continental Dragoons but his duties were less and less related to combat. He spent some time in Virginia (where many were reluctant to risk their best horses) seeking mounts for other riders, possibly for Lee and his men. Then, evidently regarded as dispensable, he was assigned to escort to Virginia and to guard there 4,000 British and Hessian troops who had surrendered at the Battle of Saratoga. These "Convention Troops," when they arrived in January 1779, seemed far from any scenes of war. Charlottesville, where barracks were prepared for them, had only become a town seventeen years before on lands purchased from the second Richard Randolph of Curles.

While keeping his rank, Colonel Bland was definitely rusticated to this backcountry area which had only the partly built Monticello as its monument. With Jefferson in residence it was a monument, indeed. In it he was guarding and enjoying his domestic felicity. The child Martha was bearing when he began to shape reforms in Virginia laws had lived only briefly. Another child, Mary, destined to attain maturity, was born in August 1778. Five months later Colonel Bland led his prisoners to Albemarle.

The war had gone on longer than Mr. Jefferson had expected. Soon after the adoption of the Declaration he had written a Virginia friend from Philadelphia that the general opinion was that the conflict would be severe for only a few months.

By the summer before the prisoners arrived he was confident that the aid of the French removed all doubt as to the outcome. He could be philosophic in his withdrawal on his hill. He was much engaged in the continued construction of his great house. In the midst of war he ordered three stone columns and noted that 90,000 good bricks had been made. He planted his garden. He kept his meteorological data. Yet the unfinished house on the hill was not entirely serene. It must have been crowded with his own family of Martha and two children. In addition his sister Martha, widow of his great friend Dabney Carr, was living there with her six children. Tragedy had touched the household. Jane Randolph Jefferson, the matriarch, died suddenly early in 1776. She had been saddened by the death of her confused, if not deranged, daughter, Elizabeth, whose body had been found where she had wandered off to die two years before. Now, as the prisoners arrived, Jefferson's dull or retarded brother, Randolph, was marrying his cousin Anne Jefferson Lewis. Her brother, Charles Lilburne Lewis, had already married the Jefferson brothers' sister Lucy in a marriage which was to show the possible poison of inbreeding.

Guarding his wife and building his estate Jefferson evidently missed cultural associations. Particularly he missed music which he wrote was in a barbaric state in America. He described to a gentleman in France his longing for a band of domestic musicians attached to his estate. He could not quite afford that. But he wondered if this gentleman could not find in Paris artisans, willing to come to Virginia, who in addition to their crafts could play the French horn, the clarinet, the hautboy or the bassoon. Perhaps this was only a vague wish put into correspondence. But almost like an answer to it Colonel Bland brought him his band plus a vocalist in the person of the stout and handsome wife of the Hessian commander, Baron von Riedesel. The lady in her riding boots seemed both an Amazon and an imprisoned prima donna.

The Baroness not only sang so sweetly that she reported her singing won the hearts of the most crusty Patriots. She also kept a journal. She wrote of early hardships, of little food and spoiled meat, of intense heat, of thunderstorms and rattlesnakes, of lower class Virginians who had been almost overindoctrinated in their hate of the enemy. Among the country folk around the camp she observed two incidents of overt incest. She left an unpleasant portrait of Mazzei, whose place Colle she and her family occupied. He was stingy and hostile, she wrote. Possibly the Italian foresaw that after he was gone the Hessians' horses would trample his vineyard ending forever Randolph plans for vine culture in Virginia. The Baroness, however, enjoyed the hospitality of the Virginia gentry—particularly Jefferson, but including other Randolphs. In his turn Jefferson intervened when some of his neighbors wanted the prisoners removed as unwelcome consumers of food who might create a famine.

The Hessians particularly fed Jefferson's need for music. The Baroness sang arias in Italian. A young German captain accompanied the master of Monticello in a violin duet. Another was a master with the guitar. Other players made music in Monticello. One young German wrote of Mrs. Jefferson that she "touches very skillfully the harpsichord." Others conversed with Jefferson about philosophy. One gave him a painting. The captives in the midst of war helped make Monticello a center of the arts. After this amiable interlude ended, Jefferson wrote to the Baron how much he regretted "the loss of the agreeable society . . . of which Madme. de Riedesel and yourself were an important part."

More about such amenities in wartime, particularly involving other Randolphs and Randolph kin, was written by a British officer among the prisoners. Thomas Anburey, in his *Travels Through the Interior Parts of America,* told of visits on parole to a kind Colonel Carye (sic), a rich Mrs. Bowling (sic) and of her relationship to Pocahunta (sic). Particularly he wrote of a stay of several days at the Tuckahoe plantation of Colonel Thomas Mann Randolph. The Colonel, he said, "possesses that fondness for horses, which I observed was peculiar to the Virginians of all stations, sparing no trouble, pains or expense in importing the best stock and improving the breed." The prisoner-visitors were presented to Colonel Randolph's pride Shakespeare, a huge dappled gray so pampered and fat that it seemed incredible that his small thin legs could support him. Like music, horse talk eased the relations of aristocratic Virginians and their well-bred foreign guests. But, said Anburey, war politics was taboo, "though sometimes in the presence of the ladies there was good natured talk about the prisoners situation." And that could lead to a regrettable lapse in the amenities.

There were many ladies at Tuckahoe, several of them young girls. At this time, however, Mary (or Molly), the eldest was only about seventeen. Her sister Elizabeth was fifteen. The other girls, Judith and Nancy (who were to be involved in scandal later), Jane, Harriet, and Virginia were children. Apparently Molly's young curiosity created the incident Anburey reported: "Colonel Randolph every year made a present of two hogsheads of tobacco to his daughter as a venture to purchase dresses and ornaments, and the ships had always been so unfortunate as to be captured. As several officers were sitting with the ladies, the conversation ran upon politics, when Miss Randolph innocently asked, 'How we came to be prisoners?' the officer with some warmth replied, 'Just as your tobacco was, by a superior force.'"

Anburey seemed to exaggerate when he wrote that by this comment the officer "forfeited all claim to the hospitality of Tuckahoe." But at this time exaggerations and suspicions grew quickly in Virginia, particularly among the plainer people. Aroused by their betters to hatred of Britain, they could not understand the urbane entertainment of enemy officers by the gentry. They almost overunderstood, Anburey thought, the doctrines of equality Jefferson had enunciated in the Declaration.

Anburey described a visit of three ordinary farmers of Goochland County to Tuckahoe while he was there. Entering the parlor and ignoring the British guests, he wrote, they "took themselves chairs, drew near the fire, began spitting, pulling off their country boots all over mud, and then opened their business." He quoted Randolph's bitter, perhaps plaintive, comment after the men departed: "No doubt each of those men conceives himself in every respect my equal."

Indeed, some such men quickly and angrily asserted their

confident superiority in patriotism. Muttering about Randolph's hospitality to enemy prisoners, they threatened to burn down his mill. Randolph met the menacing whispers with an aristocratic outburst. He appeared at the county seat on court day and made "a very animated speech" to the gathered citizens. Firmly he declared that no one had a right to scrutinize into his private concerns, that his public character was well known, and that no one could with more zeal and perseverance support the cause of the Americans than he had done. He offered a reward for "the discovery of those who had made use of those threats."

The mill was not burned and the reward was never collected. Such an incident, however, indicated the difficulties faced by Colonel Bland as both Virginia gentleman and as a guard and guardian of the prisoners. Despite the complaints of Baroness de Riedesel about the food and the fears of some Virginians that the prisoners might eat them out of house and home, the supplies he secured seemed sometimes even more than adequate. Indeed, once he wrote the commissary department that it had sent him ten "muttons" when he already had six or eight more than he knew what to do with. His own needs seemed less well met. He wrote plaintively, "I really wish you would supply me with the butter you have so long promised me, having been without butter now a week, you will be pleased to engage me a Quarter Cask of Good wine, as that I brought up with me is almost gone. If you could procure me some black-eyed peas, I should be much obliged to you." Two days later he added, "In addition to my former requests to procure me some wine, I would farther desire that you procure twenty or thirty pounds of Loaf Sugar. The butter you mentioned I should be glad to receive."

Evidently at this period the Colonel was a man who would be obliged for black-eyed peas though his desires soared to loaf sugar. Obviously, he was entertaining, too. Dinners were given by some of the higher officers among the prisoners. Friends could always count on Theodorick's hospitality. One who was undoubtedly at his table in Charlottesville was his old friend

and fellow horseman John Banister. Anburey wrote of Bland as
a man determined to maintain his dignity in an unheroic
position. When he had been appointed to this post he had
told Virginia's government that "he must either decline it, or be
supported in such a way as would keep up that respect which
was essential to his command; without, at the same time, ruining
his private fortune." So Jefferson later told Washington. Bland's
nephew, John Randolph of Roanoke, later stated that his uncle's
command of the prison camp nearly ruined him "for he was
proud and magnificent." Anburey saw the Colonel as more
amusing than magnificent. His description of the ragged American troops Bland commanded in Albemarle reads almost like
a comic counterpart to chilling pictures of men at Valley Forge
where Henry Lee, John Marshall, and other Randolphs were
then sharing the hardships of Washington's winter camp.

Anburey wrote of the Colonel's men: "some hoseless with their
feet peeping out of their shoes, others with breeches that put
decency to the blush; some in short jackets, some in long coats,
but all have fine dragoon caps and long swords swung around
them; some with holsters, some without, but gad-a-mercy pistols;
for they have not a brace and a half among them; but they are
tolerably well mounted, and that is the only thing you can
advance in their favor. The Colonel is so fond of his dragoons
that he reviews and maneuvers them every morning, and,
when he rides out, has two with swords drawn before and two
behind."

Colonel Bland showed great politeness and consideration to
Anburey and other British officers. However, said the prisoner,
"I could not help smiling at the pomposity and the great importance he assumed to make himself appear to us consequential;
called to a negro he had purchased from one of the French
language, having mounted his horse without his sword, he
called to a negro he had purchased from one of the French
West Indian Islands to bring it to him; which the fellow did
without the scabbard; when the Colonel in great anger, said
to him: *donney moi, donney moi,* and, after great hesitation,
donney moi mon scabbard."

Very possibly the Colonel, who once had written a scientific thesis in Latin, was aware of the smiles even of his prisoners at his French and his position. He indicated to Jefferson a desire to rise high above the place in which he found himself. When on a second ballot by a vote of 67 to 61 the greater Virginian was elected Governor on June 1, 1779, Bland wrote him promptly:

"Having been inform'd that since your Excellency's Appointment to the Government of this Commonwealth your residence will be chiefly if not entirely at the seat of Government, you will pardon me if (tempted by the perpetual view of your delightful seat from my lowly and I may say Dirty Cottage) I should venture to ask a preference should you be disposed to permit any other than your family to Occupy it. Mrs. Bland who is and has been for some time with me Joins me in Congratulation and in paying her respects to your Excellency and Mrs. Jefferson and in wishing you both all possible earthly felicity. . . ."

Nothing came of the request. Perhaps Jefferson shared the view of his friend Madison that Bland was eccentric. And as it turned out the Colonel would not long have needed the mansion. In November he received permission to retire from his post. The next year his popularity was shown and his pride was served by his election as a delegate to the Continental Congress. The Blands were certainly no longer persons to be packed off to prison camp duty in Virginia. "Dear Patsy," as Bland called his wife, wrote her sister of many visits to Washington's headquarters. She described his charming aides as "polite, sociable gentlemen who make the day pass with a great deal of satisfaction to the visitors." But she reported that the great hour was that of the riding parties after dinner. Usually Washington went along when the day's report brought no bad news and then, said the ebullient Mrs. Bland, the General "throws off the hero and takes on the chatty, agreeable companion—and he can be downright impudent sometimes—such impudence, Fanny, as you and I like." Certainly this was a sort of earthly felicity.

Possibly her husband, the Colonel, could have saved Jefferson some of the earthly felicity he had wished him if he had stayed in Albemarle with his much drilled though ragamuffin troops. Indeed, something of their possible need had been suggested to the Colonel before he departed. His sister Frances was no longer the "unhappy widow" she had described herself in a note in her prayerbook. On September 23, 1778, still beautiful at twenty-six, she had married on the eve of her birthday St. George Tucker, who had come from Bermuda to become brave soldier and able jurist in Virginia. As Jefferson became Governor in 1779, succeeding Henry, Tucker wrote his new brother-in-law Bland referring to a minor British incursion in the month before.

"I wish his Excellency's activity may be equal to the abilities he possesses in so eminent a degree. In that case we may boast of having the greatest man on the continent at the helm. But if he should tread in the steps of his predecessor, there is not much to be expected from the highest talents. Did the enemy know how very defenseless we are at present, a very small addition to their late force would be sufficient to commit the greatest ravages throughout the country. It is a melancholy fact that there were not arms enough to put into the hands of the few militia who were called down on the late occasion; of those which were to be had a great number were not fit for use. Nor was there by any means a sufficiency of ammunition or camp utensils of any kind. In short, never was a country in a more shabby situation; for our fortifications and marine, on which more than a million have been thrown away, are in no capacity to render any service to us; nor have we any standing force to give the smallest check to an approaching enemy."

Governor Jefferson was apparently not so disturbed. Bland must have been in transition from military to civilian service when Jefferson wrote his father, Theodorick, Sr., at Petersburg near his Cawsons plantation in January 1780. Even "the most timid" were satisfied, the confident Governor said, that "the enemy will not pay us a visit." British forces had left New York "about the 27th of December, so they must have gone somewhere else." That sense of safety was to linger though the King's troops moved briefly into the Chesapeake area in October 1780. Then, Benedict Arnold, in December 1780, struck in a marauding raid that reached the capital at Richmond from which the Governor and others hastily departed. Finally, with a juncture of British forces under Cornwallis in the early summer of 1781, the Assembly, which had convened briefly in Charlottesville, was put to flight; some members were captured and Jefferson himself escaped only, reported Tarleton who had been sent to Albemarle to capture him, because "he provided for his personal safety by a precipitate retreat."

No retreat has been more profusely and more diversely reported. Jefferson was certainly not the only great Virginian involved in it. Patrick Henry and Benjamin Harrison, with other legislators, were soundly scolded for their "cowardice" by an old woman at whose house they stopped for much needed refreshment. The most lively contemporary report was made in letters to a friend by Betsy Jaquelin Ambler, daughter of Jefferson's old flame "Belinda" Burwell. Betsy's father as a member of the Council was also one in flight. Some significance later was added to young Betsy's report by the fact that her sister married Jefferson's cousin and later antagonist, now the fighting Marshall. Betsy wrote her friend in the midst of the summer's excitement:

"At the moment I was writing you, we had too certain confirmation of the British having landed and being actually on their way to town. Not a moment was to be lost and we were off in a twinkling. I would have almost wished you could get a view of them in your snug little retreat,—and where I should hope that you are perfectly secure;—but my father seemed to think we had not a moment to lose. Such terror and confusion you have no idea. Governor, Council, everybody scampering. . . .

"Your account of your neighbor S——'s escape just as the enemy entered the town made even my poor mother smile. What a gallant fellow he was, to look back and bid them come on, when he was a full mile ahead, with a swift horse that had borne him off many a day before! But this is not more laughable than the accounts we have of our illustrious Governor, who, they say, took neither rest nor food for man or horse till he reached C—[arte]—r's Mountain." (A small mount beyond Charlottesville.)

Jefferson could never see anything funny about the humiliating situation in which he was involved. Ever afterward he was sensitive about mention of it. He did not flee in cowardice, as was later charged, but in good sense from the British at Monticello. But real questions were raised as to his preparations for Virginia's defense. Then certainly he was precipitate in retiring from the awkward situation in which he found himself. As he put it, he "resigned" the Governorship, on the grounds that his term continued only one year and not until his successor qualified. Whatever the facts, his administration, as Malone wrote, did come "to an unheroic end."

His personal losses in the raid were considerable. Monticello was spared the torch. However, he wrote later that at his Elkhill Plantation the British destroyed all his growing crops of corn and tobacco, burned his barns and carried off cattle and horses, leaving "an absolute waste." Thirty of his slaves "fled to the enemy." As sensitive slave owner he preferred to say that Cornwallis "carried off also about 30 slaves." He added: "Had this been to give them freedom he would have done right, but it was to consign them to inevitable death from the small pox and putrid fever then raging in his camp."

Jefferson was particularly incensed later by the writing of Henry Lee as a military historian. That young soldier had not been on the Charlottesville scene but had the luck to be in Yorktown at the time of the surrender of Cornwallis a few months later, in October 1781. He wrote, however, of the official flight in Virginia. He said that Jefferson "readily saved himself by taking shelter in an adjacent spur of the mountains." He spoke of the occasion as one of "gloom, of disorder, and of peril." He added, however, that twenty of the convention prisoners Theodorick had been guarding joined Tarleton in the few hours he was in Charlottesville. Some may have still been there but the great bulk of the prisoners had left in October

1780. Jefferson's sharp questioning of this secondhand report from his young cousin came later. Now he had other critics to answer.

Worse than his property losses, he wrote his young friend James Monroe, was his hurt pride. He "stood arraigned for treason of the heart and not merely the weakness of the head." This was a sensitive overstatement of the fact. However, a resolution was quickly presented in the shaken Assembly, meeting in the safety of Staunton, proposing that at the next session of the Assembly "an inquiry be made into the conduct of the Executive of this State for the last twelve months." Jefferson said that his eloquent predecessor Henry was secretly behind the resolution. Indeed, the historian William E. Dodd wrote that "Henry joined in the hue and cry against Jefferson and thus laid the foundation for a feud which lasted as long as either of them lived." The inquiry was proposed, however, by George Nicholas, a young man of military experience who was just entering politics. He was the son of Robert Carter Nicholas who Jefferson had secured as sponsor for his Fast Day Patriot propaganda move a few years before. Young Nicholas and his brothers later became friends and ardent supporters of Jefferson.

With Henry maintaining silence, the case against Governor Jefferson was considered in a tight Virginia society, almost within the web of kinship. Rough Archibald Cary, who had been ready with his dagger for any dictator, apparently first wrote Jefferson about the proposed inquiry. As Speaker of the State Senate, he was sure that any investigation would only do the former Governor honor. Cary was obviously surprised that the resolution had been introduced by his nephew whose sister became the wife of Edmund Randolph. While the matter was pending Benjamin Harrison, the Signer, whose sister was the widow of Peyton Randolph, became Governor, rising from the position of Speaker of the House.

Jefferson took the matter very seriously, then and later. Though announcing his purpose to reject every other proffer of public office, he got himself elected to the Assembly. There he presented elaborate answers to every question raised about his

conduct. Nicholas, who was on the committee named to consider his charges, absented himself. The report of the committee
was made on December 12, 1781, two months after the surrender
of Cornwallis at Yorktown had brought a welcome sense of
relief. Past dangers could be forgotten.

The document, clearing Jefferson from all fault, was presented
to the Assembly by Banister of Battersea. From the riding
fields at Cawsons he had gone, like Theodorick, into the cavalry. George Washington in an intimate letter from Valley Forge
indicated his high regard for his service. His wife, Theodorick's
sister, had died, while he served, in 1777. Now he was married
to Anne Blair, of the rich and powerful colonial family. His ties
with the Blands and the Randolphs were still close. Close, too,
were his relations with Jefferson. They had served together in
the Assembly from 1769 to 1771, and in the Virginia Convention
of 1776. More important, as Thomas Tileston Waterman related
in *The Mansions of Virginia 1706–1776*, "the architectural evidence indicates that Thomas Jefferson was the designer" of Banister's house, Battersea, near Petersburg. They remained friends.
From Paris later Jefferson wrote him as "your affectionate friend."
Indeed, he wrote that he held his acquaintance with Banister as
"among the most precious of those he has ever made."

Now Banister offered a resolution of thanks for his services
as Governor "to obviate and remove all unmerited censure."
Slightly amended by the Senate, to remove a long reference to
popular rumors, it was unanimously adopted by the Assembly.
That was that. Jefferson's friends felt it should have ended the
resentment which seemed behind his announced purpose to
retire forever from public life. Yet he was, as he showed then
and later, a wounded man. No sign of chagrin or bitterness
appeared, however, in one of the best descriptions of him ever
made which was written only four months later. It was composed by the Marquis de Chastellux, a member of the French
Academy and a major general in the Army of the Comte de
Rochambeau who had had his headquarters in the Peyton
Randolph house in Williamsburg during the siege of Yorktown.
The Marquis had already seen Colonel Bland before he came

to Monticello to which the cavalryman had looked up with
so much envy or aspiration. Of the Colonel the Marquis wrote:
"He is said to be a good soldier but at present serves his
country and serves it well in Congress." Certainly at this time
if Jefferson had lost prestige in Virginia, this French visitor
did not reflect it. In one enthusiastic, mammoth sentence, he
portrayed the master of Monticello in April 1782.

"Let me then describe to you a man, not yet forty, tall, and
with a mild and pleasing countenance, but whose mind and
attainments could serve in lieu of all outward graces; an
American, who, without ever having quitted his own country,
is Musician, Draftsman, Surveyor, Astronomer, Natural Philosopher, Jurist, and Statesman; a Senator of America, who sat for
two years in that famous Congress which brought about the
Revolution and which is never spoken of here without respect
—though with respect unfortunately mingled with too many
misgivings; a Governor of Virginia, who filled this difficult
station during the invasions of Arnold, Phillips, and Cornwallis;
and finally a Philosopher, retired from the world and public
business, because he loves the world only insofar as he can feel
that he is useful, and because the temper of his fellow citizens
is not as yet prepared either to face the truth or to suffer
contradiction."

He summed up in a shorter sentence:

"A gentle and amiable wife, charming children whose education is his special care, a house to embellish, extensive estates
to improve, the arts and sciences to cultivate—these are what
remain to Mr. Jefferson after having played a distinguished role
on the stage of the New World, and what he has preferred to
the honorable commission of Minister Plenipotentiary in Europe."

The entranced Frenchman reported animated conversations on
weather observations, about droughts and baleful winds caused
by the cutting down of trees, with regard to the Natural Bridge
which Jefferson had acquired, concerning the difference between
European and American deer. They shared an exciting evening
beside a punch bowl in mutual admiration of the "sublime"
poems of Ossian, which neither of them recognized as a literary

hoax. Apparently both the philosopher and the Frenchman said goodbye with regret. Jefferson, the Marquis wrote, would have accompanied him on his further Virginia travels "but his wife was expecting her confinement at any moment, and he is as good a husband as he is philosopher and citizen."

De Chastellux left Monticello on April 17, 1782. Martha Jefferson's last child was born three weeks later (and lived for two years). She was only thirty-three, but her life was early and finally exhausted. On September 6, 1782, the meticulous and grief-stricken Jefferson recorded in his Account Book, "My wife died this day at 11:45 a.m." His friends and his daughters left records of the wild grief they watched him suffer. Yet evidently he aroused to duty. In "October or November," he took his children to Ampthill, the home of Archibald Cary on the south shore of the James below Richmond for the still hazardous operation of innoculation against smallpox. It was while he was there that a letter arrived asking him once again to serve as American diplomat in Paris. There at Ampthill, toward the end of November, he accepted the appointment.

Earlier the Marquis de Chastellux as a visitor had described this scene of Jefferson's decision. Soon after his visit to Monticello the Marquis had noted that he and companions, missing their way to Richmond, "skirted the James River to a charming place called Warwick. A group of several pretty houses forms a sort of village here; but some really superb ones may be seen in the neighborhood, among others that of Colonel Cary, on the right [south] bank of the river, and Mr. Randolph's on the opposite shore." Apparently de Chastellux did not note the destruction of the shipyards, the ropery, the iron mills, warehouses done by Benedict Arnold's forces to Colonel Cary's properties there. Destroying properties of war potential, the British had spared his great house Ampthill. They had also left undamaged "Mr. Randolph's house on the opposite shore." This was Wilton, built in 1753 by William Randolph III, husband of Anne Carter Harrison, sister of Benjamin Harrison the Signer, now Governor of Virginia.

Certainly more than Monticello this was a Randolph scene.

Nearby were the Cawsons and Jordan's Point plantations of the Blands, and Colonel Theodorick's Kippax. Close by, too, was Matoax, from whence during the British invasion Frances Randolph Tucker fled to another Randolph plantation, Bizarre, near Farmville and as far west as Charlottesville. Nearby, too, was Banister's Battersea. The British had destroyed its furnishings and mutilated its structure but the Marquis hardly noticed the damage. Instead he wrote that "Mr. Banister's handsome country-house . . . is really worth seeing. It is decorated rather in the Italian, than the English or American style, having three porticoes at the three principal entries. . . ."

Down the James shore was Turkey Island where William, the founder, built his estate and the Curles lands which he took after Bacon's fall. Here was the Randolph seedland. There, too, was Berkeley, home of the related Harrisons, and Westover, which had been owned by Blands before it became the seat of the Byrds. De Chastellux contemplated the family from this area: "When traveling in Virginia," he wrote almost like a warning, "you must be prepared to hear the name of Randolph frequently mentioned. This is one of the first families of the country, since a Randolph was among the first settlers, but it is also one of the most numerous and wealthiest. It is divided into seven or eight branches, and I am not afraid of exaggerating when I say that this family possesses an income of upwards of a million livres."

Obviously he was talking about the gold livre of France which had been almost as much welcomed in Revolutionary paper-currency Virginia as the French Army and the French fleet. Certainly in their array of great houses on river shores, the Randolphs looked rich even after war and invasion. Some Randolphs were rich. Jefferson was going to be able to afford a palace in Paris and remodel it in more splendid terms than it had been when built for a King's mistress. Thomas Mann Randolph of Tuckahoe had been able to back his father-in-law Cary to the extent of £20,000 which the much indebted Cary had needed. But long before war Cary had been in financial trouble. As early as 1768, on a £5,000 debt to Capel and

Osgood Hanbury of London, he had given a mortgage of approximately 11,000 acres, all the personal property on those lands and numerous slaves. Also, though he had given assurances to the Assembly that the Treasury was in fine shape, he had owed Robinson's estate nearly £4,000 when the Treasurer's defalcations were disclosed at his death. Peter and William Randolph had tried to help him with endorsements. He had managed to pay with depreciated paper money much debt including that owed to British merchants. But even when Jefferson and his children were his guests, creditors were not far from Ampthill's door.

Perhaps at the time of the Jefferson visit the two men were sadly congenial since Cary's wife, Mary Randolph, daughter of Richard of Curles, had died just the year before. The family of Mary's brother, dead John Randolph of Matoax, was at this time fearful that British creditors would descend upon all their property, too. Young John Randolph of Roanoke, then a boy of nine, long cherished a grudge against his uncle Ryland Randolph. To save Ryland after he had "squandered" his estate, John Randolph of Matoax had given a mortgage on his entire property (except his favorite body servant Syphax) to the Hanburys of London. Now young John's stepfather, Tucker, feared that peace with Britain might mean also the legal seizure of this Randolph property to satisfy Hanbury debts.

Evidently the Blands at Cawsons and Jordan's Point were still secure. This must have been the time of young John's boyhood memory of Cawsons as "the seat of plenty and cheerfulness." He was nine when Jefferson visited nearby. Colonel Bland was evidently safe from creditors on his plantation, Kippax or Farmingdale. He had grown fat but hope of glory still stirred in him. Active in public affairs, he had ideas that he might become Governor. He was defeated by his cousin Edmund Randolph, who at least seemed well off as the heir of his Uncle Peyton.

Jefferson's host, Cary, embodied dangers which de Chastellux could not see. Cary was no Randolph but the son-in-law of one—Richard of Curles who had left an estate of 40,000 acres.

He was also the father-in-law of two other Randolphs—Thomas Mann of Tuckahoe, and Thomas of Dungeness who had clung to the estate which rightfully belonged to his expatriate brother, William. They could not hold off the wolves at Cary's door.

Cary died in 1787, while Jefferson was still in France. He was then the ostensible owner of 14,172 acres of land and 266 slaves. But his debts were greater. By 1781 he had patriotically advanced to the state £58,000 in depreciated currency. He paid his British debts—at least £10,000—in the same paper. But other creditors still clamored. Under Virginia law then, according to Francis Earle Lutz in *Chesterfield—An Old Virginia County*, a creditor not only might imprison a debtor, but he could also even attach the body of a dead one. "One story," Lutz wrote, is that Cary was secretly buried in the basement of Ampthill. Another was that his body was committed to the James River in the night. Perhaps better authenticated is the version that he was buried at a place called "Ceeleys" in Warwick County, though no stone in the burial ground there marks his grave.

The Randolphs remembered him. A certain immortality was to be added to his name when a younger Randolph gave it to the greatest race horse of Virginia and a special symbol of the Randolph stud.

Chapter VII

ENVENOMED MAZE

THE CONVENTION danced. It wagered, drank, ate heartily, and made love while it debated the merit or the folly of ratifying the proposed Constitution for a United States. Some attributed the presence of a quorum on the day set for the Virginia convention to the festive fact that it coincided in this June of 1788 with the annual races of the Richmond Jockey Club. The debates were recorded for history though sometimes Patrick Henry's anti-Constitution eloquence poured forth in a profusion that overwhelmed the stenographers. The record of the races was neatly kept, though dismissed as irrelevant to studbook data were the cheers that roared up from the fences and the stands. At the track the favorites did not always win. And in the convention the final decision was startling to many.

Edmund Randolph, the brilliant, handsome young Governor, appeared as hero or traitor, depending upon the politics of those who described him. He had helped draft the Constitution at Philadelphia but had refused to sign the finished document as inadequately republican and needing amendments to guarantee liberties. Now in what seemed an amazing somersault he led in urging ratification rather than lose the hope of any union. Behind him, untroubled by any debate within themselves, were his cousins, Light-Horse Harry Lee and John Marshall. Lee had come into politics, as he would into land speculations, like a man leading a cavalry charge. The shrewd, convivial Marshall stood as firmly as he had in Lee's elite corps. Edmund helped carry the day though he was called a young "Ar [nol] d" by those who were insisting on guarantees of rights as well as assurances of union.

Edmund's inconsistency was clear, even if it actually amounted to conversion by such friends as Washington and Madison. What seemed like wavering was the habit of mind of a man who had had to consider both sides between his Patriot Uncle Peyton and his Loyalist father. Those who cheered or condemned him in the debates of the day knew nothing of the fears he shared with his wife by night—and by day, too—that she had a cancer in her mouth. Hope for its treatment lay only, he confided to Madison, in Philadelphia or in Europe. But slaves and lands could not be easily turned into sterling to finance such a trip.

Such personal troubles were never flaunted by Randolphs. They seemed invulnerable in Virginia. Their prestige was not dimmed by the absence of Jefferson. The three Governors of the state in his absence were all Randolphs—Edmund, Light-Horse Harry, and Beverley whose bravery had been demonstrated in the Revolution. Regard for Beverley was not reduced because, as John Randolph (later of Roanoke) wrote, his every other word was an oath and he considered religion as "the imposture of the priestcraft."

More things than the Constitution were ratified in Richmond this summer. Amid the gaiety of the racing season and the drama of the debate, young lovers plighted their troths. One such tender episode involved the household of the great, rich Philadelphian, Robert Morris, financier of the Revolution. Humbly born Morris was present with his brilliant, aristocratic aide, Gouverneur Morris, no kin though of the same name. Son of the manor house of Morrisania in New York, Gouverneur was adept in both finances and flirtations. His wooden leg never seemed to reduce his charm with the ladies at home or abroad. The two Morrises had business in Virginia in connection with the monopoly of the tobacco trade with France which the elder Morris possessed. Also, they were suspected, as ardent supporters of the Constitution, of coming to try to influence Virginia's decision. Possibly to give a social coloration to the visit, Robert Morris had brought along his family. He complained of the "great depredations on my purse" which the visit of his ladies entailed. Still, he retained John Marshall as his attorney with a payment of only four pounds, four shillings. A more personal Morris-Marshall connection was begun then which would culminate in the marriage of Hester Morris to Marshall's younger brother, James.

The Marshalls had seemed a poorer branch of the Randolphs. Their line to the first Thomas of Tuckahoe by his youthfully errant daughter Mary seemed less elegantly erect. Thomas Marshall who had married this Mary's daughter by her second preacher husband was more a man of the frontier than of Tidewater. Though he acquired large properties, Tom Marshall seemed to have much the status fastidious genealogists have given to Peter Jefferson at the time of his marriage to Jane, daughter of the lordly Isham Randolph of Dungeness. Actually, like Peter Jefferson, Thomas Marshall was a substantial propertied citizen. He was a close friend of George Washington, bequeathing his devotion to that great Virginian to his sons. Much like his father, John Marshall was as indisputably a Randolph as his cousin Thomas Jefferson.

The marriage of John's younger brother, James, to the heiress Hester Morris put the fortune of America's greatest land speculator behind the acquisitive Marshall heritage which their father had begun. The Marshalls of this generation married well. John's wife was the daughter of the "fair Belinda," the lost darling of Jefferson's youth. She was more aristocratic than rich. But her cousin John Ambler, who was "one of the richest men in the state of Virginia," married Lucy, the sister of John and James Marshall.

Robert Morris had reason to be satisfied with the marriage of his daughter. As one who had begun his career as an immigrant engaged in a small way in tobacco exporting, his social ambitions expanded like the vast acreages he had acquired. He himself had married the sister of Bishop William White, venerated figure in the American Episcopal Church. Already he was planning the great mansion in Philadelphia he would have L'Enfant design for him. The marriage of his daughter to a Virginia Randolph was as tangible a social asset as a marble palace on Chestnut Street.

Of course, in the small Virginia capital the Morrises met other Randolphs. The present master of Tuckahoe, Colonel Thomas Mann Randolph, as an enthusiastic breeder of horses was certainly on hand for the races. Present with him were members of his family, including his fifteen-year-old daughter Judith. As the horses ran and the Constitutional debaters poured forth their words, in her case a more familiar pattern in Randolph marriages came into prospect. Amid the festivities she gave her heart to her cousin, Richard Randolph of Matoax and Bizarre.

In the complex family genealogy he was a double Randolph. His mother was the great-granddaughter of William I of Turkey Island through his daughter Elizabeth who married Richard Bland of Berkeley and Jordan's Point. His father was the grandson of William I in the line of Richard of Curles. Both his mother and father were descended from Bollings but only his father was a descendant of Pocahontas in the Bolling line. Now, though only eighteen, Richard Randolph was described as an almost knightly young man, the epitome of the Cavalier at his best. His appearance equaled his virtues. Not least in his inheritance was his ancient precious slave valet Syphax who (or which) alone among his properties his father John Randolph had declined to pledge in his mortgage to English creditors. So tended, his dress was always elegant but simple. In the North where he had studied he was one of the young men the famous hostess, beautiful Mrs. William Bingham (born Anne Willing), wanted at her parties which Robert Morris envied. She was the wife of *the* richest man in America. In Virginia, Richard's cousin Martha Jefferson Randolph would write that her opinion of him was "most exalted." Still, for all his looks and promise, at this point Richard's prospects seemed dim.

His uncle, Colonel Theodorick Bland, had fought ratification as a chief aide to Patrick Henry and perhaps with better grounded fears than those about tyranny and loss of liberties which Henry proclaimed. Now St. George Tucker, Richard's stepfather and guardian since the death of his mother the winter before, put those fears into words of distress. He wrote to his wards, Richard, his reputedly pleasure-loving brother Theodorick, and the youngest one, the complex, hard-riding, fiercely poetic, and sometimes sardonic John. Tucker told them:

"You will have heard that the Constitution has been adopted by this state. That event, my dear children, affects your interest more nearly than that of many others. The recovery of the British debts can no longer be postponed and there seems now to be moral certainty that your patrimony will all go to satisfy the unjust debts from your papa to the Hanburys. The consequence, my dear boys, must be obvious to you. Your sole dependence must be on your personal abilities and exertions."

Other Randolphs were similarly involved. Gouverneur Morris rode out to visit at Tuckahoe apparently before Tucker wrote his stepsons. Under the great shade trees there, he enjoyed the company of Thomas Mann Randolph's big household, his wife who had been rough old Archibald's daughter Anne Cary, and their nine children. It seems doubtful that on this occasion Morris, as a man of the world at thirty-six, would look at one of the daughters, a plantation child of thirteen, and fix then an image of grace and charm in his mind that would last to meet his need for serenity a score of years later. So it seems improbable that Gouverneur Morris then paid much mind to Anne Cary (Nancy) Randolph. Nancy then generally gave only polite attention to the so many older visitors of her father. While her elders talked she was often precociously reading such a book as Fielding's *Tom Jones,* which amused men like Morris and shocked many of her other elders. More likely, across the fields and in the lanes, she was riding as boldly as the boys who eagerly galloped at her heels.

Possibly Gouverneur's eyes wandered after her as he listened to her father, a sociable, kindly, lavish man, now troubled. For him Morris wrote an attorney in New York that "a friend of mine in this country, Mr. Thomas Mann Randolph, a gentleman possessing one of the best fortunes in this country and clear of any debt of his own has become unfortunately involved by being security for another." At forty-seven and the father of nine dependent children, Randolph had already paid ten or twelve thousand pounds sterling. Part of this at least had been on the guaran-

tee he had given for his Cary father-in-law. More was due in
Britain but still in Virginia "the law is against British creditors."
His lady, Morris wrote, was "not in much good health . . . and he
is in the benevolent intention of taking her to New York." But the
Virginian was anxious to know whether legal actions in New
York might put him under more immediate pressures. Morris
wrote his New York correspondent that he could answer in care
of Benjamin Harrison, Jr.

Unconsciously the outsider Morris made almost a design of
family troubles in coupling his correspondence for his friends at
Tuckahoe to Benjamin Harrison, Jr. This sixth of the name in the
Harrison line was no Randolph, but his aunts Anne and Elizabeth
had married William Randolph of Wilton and Peyton Randolph,
the Speaker. He himself was also to marry a Randolph. Indeed,
Clifford Dowdey, the Virginia historian, wrote that a visitor to
Tidewater regarding the family combinations, might have suspected that "he had stumbled into some sort of grandiosely
incestuous group."

Like the Randolphs of Tuckahoe, the Harrisons, whose family
seat was Berkeley on the James, had troubles. The great Benjamin, the Signer, aged-seeming in his early sixties, was disturbed
that he could not go along with his friend Washington in support
of the Constitution. He was a Virginian first and last. And in
writing Washington he made what seemed afterwards the prophetic statement that "if the Constitution is carried into effect,
the States south of the Potomac will be little more than append-
ages of those to the northward of it." He did not, however, have
to look into the future for troubles. They were at hand in his
dilapidated fortunes, and perhaps, worst of all, in the character
of his eldest son whose name Morris gave as his address.

Benjamin and his brothers in the new Randolph generation had
lost the will to rebuild the war-depleted plantations. Separation
from Britain brought new problems for tobacco. Sometimes slaves
seemed consuming more than they produced. One of the Harrison
boys was to depart from Virginia altogether and become President of the United States. But he was only a child in the Signer's

last days. Benjamin, Jr., then played a dark role in an ugly situation which the involved families could not quite hide.

This Benjamin had been trained in the Philadelphia establishment of Thomas Willing, father of the famous Mrs. Bingham.
He had learned there some personally profitable tricks in dealing,
as paymaster of the forces in Virginia, with the public finances
in collaboration with the national money chief Robert Morris.
He had little financial success after the war. And at the time
when Gouverneur used his address he was still involved in
an emotional furore with his second wife, Susanna Randolph,
and her parents, Richard and Anne Meade Randolph of Curles.
He had married her a few weeks after his first wife had died in
childbirth in August 1787. Soon after this marriage Susanna with
the first wife's child chose the protection of her parents at Curles.
Not long after in a state of aberration or drunkenness Harrison
wrote a scrawled document in the form of a will in which he
mentioned the break with Susanna but spoke with more affection
of his dead wife, of Susanna's sister Betsy Randolph and of Abby
Willing of Philadelphia. Harrison's eccentricity seems clear. But
gossip gave Susanna a share of the blame. Genealogists differed
as to Susanna's part, one declaring that to say Susanna was erratic was to cast "a slur upon the entire 'Curles' branch" of the
family. That branch in this period included Richard, Theodorick,
and John, whose grandfather Richard of Curles was Susanna's
grandfather, too.

Such marital troubles in the family were, of course, known at
Tuckahoe. Mrs. Thomas Mann Randolph, born Anne Cary, was
not only ill but much troubled about her children. Her Judith
was evidently a girl of much appeal. This summer as an indication of her husband's wealth, John Leslie, humbly born scholar
who was to become the famous Scottish mathematician and
physicist, was brought across the Atlantic to tutor the Tuckahoe
children. The youngest, Virginia, had then not reached her teens.
Leslie had become acquainted with Thomas Mann Randolph,
Jr., and his brother William when their father had mortgaged a
plantation to send them to the University of Edinburgh. Only

twenty-two when he came to Virginia, young Leslie was soon writing disillusioned letters about his stay at Tuckahoe.

"I must confess that Virginia has fallen below my expectations," he wrote. "I reckon Mr. Randolph's the best family and Tuckahoe the best land. My republican notions are completely sobered."

Leslie's disillusionment apparently began when he fell in love with Judith. He later told his friend young Thomas Mann that he felt "a burning affection tinctured with tender melancholy" for his sister. Possibly as a poor Scot he was pretentious in thinking of marriage to the rich Virginia girl. Maybe she would have been happier if she had married him. But her affections were already given to Richard. Even this marriage of Randolph to Randolph, however, did not seem entirely desirable to Judith's mother.

On September 23, 1788, she wrote to Tucker who was worried about the solvency of Richard and his other stepsons. Though she herself had married at sixteen—perhaps because of that—she told him, "It has been my wish to keep my Daughters single 'till they were old enough to form a proper judgment of Mankind; well knowing that a Woman's happiness depends entirely on the husband she is united to; it is a step that requires more deliberation than girls generally take, or even Mothers seem to think necessary; the risk *tho* always great, is doubled when they marry very young; it is impossible for them to know each other's disposition; for at sixteen and nineteen we think everybody perfect that we take a fancy; the Lady expects nothing but condescention, and the Gentleman thinks his Mistress an Angel."

Death in March 1789 relieved Mrs. Randolph of this and other worries. Soon after her funeral her tall, dark son Thomas Mann, Jr., set out for New York as a place well suited to one who wanted "to be in the way of politics." Other Randolphs were there. In enthusiasm young John Randolph described the first inauguration of Washington. Also, his brothers Theodorick and Richard visited and studied there. All Randolphs were proud of the appointment of Edmund as Attorney General of the new nation, marking the climax of the Randolph procession as Attorneys General in the colony and state of Virginia and now in the capital of the nation Virginia had helped make. Edmund himself had had some misgivings about accepting the position. He wrote to his friend Madison, to whom he had earlier confided his fears about his wife, that he expected a "load of calumny" to be poured upon him for accepting the office as if it were a payoff for his support of the Constitution. Washington personally owed him more than that since Edmund had long been handling without fee the complicated legal matters relating to Washington's wide land holdings. The job was no bonanza. The salary of the Attorney General then was only $1,500 a year, though it was presumed that he might augment it by private practice on the side.

Tall, swarthy young Thomas Mann came home in the fall of 1789 in no mellow mood. He quarreled with his father for some obscure cause and again left home "in a hurry & in bad weather." His frustrated father wrote his sensitive, turbulent son placatingly in December declaring that apparently the young man was "disgusted not only with the world, but, I fear, with your father." Possibly peace reigned at Tuckahoe in the festive season from Christmas to New Year's Eve when Judith and Richard were married. Certainly young Thomas's mood brightened in the new year. Possibly, though not probably, among the wedding guests at the Tuckahoe wedding were Jefferson and his daughters Martha and Mary who had returned with him from France late in November. They had stopped at Tuckahoe, December 10, on the way home. They reached Monticello on Christmas Eve. On the way, as Malone wrote, Jefferson "picked up numerous items of personal information, such as deaths and marriages among the Virginia gentry." Certainly he learned more from young Thomas Mann who was soon afterwards at Monticello. Before January ended—before Richard and Judith were settled at his Bizarre plantation—dark Thomas and blond Martha were betrothed.

Their wedding quickly followed. Jefferson, having reluctantly accepted appointment as Secretary of State, needed to be off to his post. Both fathers, as childhood companions, were delighted with the match, though the elder Thomas Mann doubted his ability to attend the ceremony because he was suffering with the gout. Both parents gave them land and slaves. The marriage which took place on February 23, 1790, was, according to the editors of Jefferson's family letters, "a small affair, with only the immediate family in attendance." Even if Colonel Randolph's gout kept him away the immediate family constituted a considerable company. Though Martha had only one sister, she had Jefferson and Wayles aunts and uncles, their spouses and their children. Thomas Mann, Jr., had nine living brothers and sisters. Three of them, Judith, Molly, and Jane, were married to Randolphs. He had Randolph aunts and Cary aunts and uncles. One of them, Jane Cary, after a family fashion, had married Thomas Randolph of the Dungeness line. Her son Archibald and her sister Mrs. Carter Page (born Mary Cary), of the Fork, certainly would have had to be counted as immediate family.

Following this wedding the young Randolphs made a round of visits to their mutual relatives along the lower James. One place which they certainly visited was the Presqu'ile plantation of David Meade Randolph, son of Richard Randolph of Curles and his wife Anne, daughter of David Meade. David Meade Randolph was a brother of Susanna Randolph Harrison. He had married Thomas Mann, Jr.'s, sister Mary (or Molly) about 1782. David at this time was on excellent terms with the Monticello family, sometimes carrying letters or parcels to and from Philadelphia. Other members of the family frequently visited Presqu'ile where David ably operated his plantation even after he was named by President Washington U. S. Marshal of Virginia.

Perhaps all went merry as a marriage bell. But another such bell began to clang ominously when the widower Colonel Randolph himself took a new wife. Gabriella Harvie was less than half the Colonel's age, indeed, as a biographer of the Colonel's son and namesake said, she was "still in her teens." She was the granddaughter of John Harvie, who had been one of Jefferson's guardians. Possibly more important, she was the granddaughter of Gabriel Jones, powerful lawyer of the valley country. Jones had been adviser and executor of the vastly landed Lord Fairfax at whose lands the Marshalls, with Morris behind them, were already looking. Described as a "peppery old gentleman," his outbursts of temper became a part of the Valley's tradition. One tale was that the county court had threatened to jail a man if he "did not quit worrying Mr. Jones and making him curse and swear so." Though John Randolph later thought that Gabriella had "manners that a queen might envy," some felt that she got not only her name but her disposition from the old tempestuous Gabriel Jones.

Martha Jefferson Randolph was worried about her father-in-law's marriage even before it took place. She was apparently not reassured by her father's statement that the marriage was to be expected as the Colonel's amusements depended upon society. She could, he told her benignly, regard any roughness in the Colonel's new lady's disposition as no more than "one bad stop in your harpsichord," which she could avoid touching. Yet soon there were new difficulties between the Randolphs, father and son, over some Randolph property which young Thomas Mann wanted but which the Colonel announced he planned as patrimony for children he meant to have by his new marriage. Undoubtedly the son "took fire" easily. The father was hurt again by the attitude of his son. Justice in these difficulties is not easy to determine. Obviously, however, a difficult situation existed at Tuckahoe with its new mistress.

Mr. Jefferson's letters home hardly reflected a more abrasive situation growing about him in New York. He found society there amazingly undemocratic even "monarchial." Still he had the companionship of Madison and his devoted cousin Edmund Randolph, though apparently in one dramatic incident he suggested he was not adequately warned by them. Edmund was absent much of the time because of the illness of his wife, who despite her desire for better doctors than were available in Virginia was still there. The new Secretary of State wrote home more like a philosophic father than the "innocent" politician he described himself as being.

Within the same month in which he advised Martha to be forebearing, he afterwards felt that he had been too amenable to suggestions of his colleague, the brilliant, decorative Secretary of the Treasury Alexander Hamilton. Jefferson wrote Martha casually on June 27, 1790, that "I think it probable that Congress will pass a bill for removing to Philadelphia for ten years, and then to Georgetown." He did not mention the fact that this was part of a bargain, into which he said later he was innocently led, by which Virginia got the permanent capital on its border in exchange for votes to put over Hamilton's plan for Federal assumption of state debts.

Jefferson later described the Federal assumption of depreciated state securities as the basis of a Hamilton plan for the corruption of the government for his anti-Republican purposes. Some members of Congress did purchase, on the basis of inside information, the securities they had voted to enhance in value under Hamilton's plan. That endeared him politically to such public profiteers. But Jefferson's later combination of repentance and resentment about the capital site and assumption bargain followed furious repudiation of the business in a states' rights protest by the Virginia Legislature. Jefferson had known in advance that assumption would be a bitter pill for Virginia, but the rebuke was not sweetened by Patrick Henry's leadership in the matter.

Actually, Jefferson may have been given too much of both blame and credit for the bargain. He apparently arranged for the two Virginia votes Hamilton needed. Yet, the fact is that the Congressmen who cast them were more Hamiltonian than Jeffersonian in their sentiments. Alexander White, though a lieutenant of Madison in the ratification of the Constitution, was in 1793 defeated for re-election by the faction—not quite the party—Jefferson was to head. The other was Richard Bland Lee, carrying the Randolph relationship in his middle name. Soon he was a vigorous anti-Jeffersonian, along with his brother Light-Horse Harry Lee.

Another incident this year provided materials for the growing hostility of Light-Horse Harry to his cousin Jefferson. Jefferson's old boyhood friend John Walker was replaced in the Senate by Jefferson's protégé, James Monroe. Malone related this to Walker's bitterness toward Jefferson for Jefferson's behavior toward his wife. The Secretary of State at this time heard that Hamilton, involved in a scandal with a less impeccable lady than Mrs. Walker, knew this story and might publicize it. It was Lee who instigated such publicity later after he had taken as his second wife Ann Hill Carter, the niece of Mrs. Walker.

Other Randolph collisions and abrasions were to receive attention. William Cabell Bruce, in his life of John Randolph of Roanoke, wrote of an "internecine feud" in the family. A quarrelsome quality seemed bred in the breed. Randolphs, whose marriages often suggested that they could love only Randolphs, sometimes seemed to hate each other more than they could other folk. Political philosophy rather than personal animus was now shaping the great Jefferson-Marshall antagonism. But differences led to deep dislikes. Soon Jefferson would be writing Madison that Marshall was being plied with flattery by Hamilton who was urging him to run for Congress as a Virginian with nationalist or Federalist anti-Jefferson political opinions. Jefferson suggested slyly that the popular Marshall might well be diverted from the differences in the nation by a judgeship on the state bench—or the shelf.

No such high level difference or deviousness was involved in the feud to which Bruce referred. This was an intimate, bitter conflict of men and women, cousins, brothers, sisters in almost household proximity to each other. Certainly aided by scandal it was to continue to a time when Martha Jefferson Randolph wrote that "the divisions of the family increase daily. There is no knowing where they will end. The old gentleman has plunged into the thickest of them governed by the most childish passions. He lends the little weight his imprudence has left him to widen the breaches it should be his duty to close."

That would seem to put too much blame on old Colonel Thomas Mann Randolph. Certainly, however, after his remarriage bitterness did grow in his household. Apparently it was sharpest between his young wife and Nancy, his oldest daughter remaining at home. Though only in her teens, she was not much younger than her stepmother. Martha wrote of Nancy's visits to Monticello, sometimes with her younger sister Virginia (Jenny) who became a permanent resident in the Jefferson mansion and was later married there. Also, Nancy visited her sister Molly, Mrs. David Meade Randolph, at Presqu'ile and later set the scene there for an almost incredible story of the malignancy of a brother against a brother. Unfortunately, history is left with completely contradictory reports made by Nancy and John Randolph of Roanoke, brother of her sister Judith's husband. Indeed, an envenomed maze is left of the story of Nancy and the three brothers, Richard, Theodorick, and John. The truth may be as lost as a stranger might be in the elaborate boxwood labyrinth in the gardens at Tuckahoe where Nancy sometimes ran never quite lost as a child.

Chapter VIII

THE BIZARRE STORY

THE STORY Nancy Randolph told about herself and the Randolph brothers of Bizarre was evidently dated as of warm weather in 1791 when she was visiting her sister Molly at Presqu'ile. She presented herself as a bewildered girl of sixteen then and John Randolph as an eighteen-year-old torturer ready to break her heart if he could not have her for his own.

John (she called him "Jack" then and laughed scornfully later when he added "of Roanoke" to his name) was a man about whom the truth was not always told but one who often indulged in fabrications about others. Even at this early age he was accustomed to mastery from an upbringing beside horses and slaves. His education had been varied and spasmodic, reflecting voracious reading but little discipline. He and his brother Theodorick had briefly attended Princeton where John later said President John Witherspoon misappropriated his funds. Also with Theodorick, he studied for a short time at Columbia in New York. He began but never finished reading law under Edmund Randolph in Philadelphia. Edmund, according to John's story, also embezzled his funds. Such charges seemed almost standard with him, at last applying them even to his stepfather. Then he went to William and Mary where his stay was terminated by a duel, apparently over no more than the proper pronunciation of a word. In February 1791, before the scene Nancy described, he had written his friend Henry Rutledge of South Carolina that he had led a life of debauchery for "the last three months." This may have been boyish exaggeration. However, in

August 1791, his guardian St. George Tucker sent him $268 for his gambling debts along with the hope that "this, my dear boy, will be the last demand of this kind you will ever have to pay and I rely upon your promise that it shall." Such facts surround Nancy's later angry report of the scene she wrote took place at Presqu'ile.

"Be pleased to remember," she told John in a furious letter later, "that in my sister Mary's house, you led me to the portico, and, leaning against one of the pillars, expressed your surprise at having heard from your brother Richard that I was engaged to marry his brother, Theodorick."

In terms of the portico, the pillars, the house by the James River of so much tradition, Nancy made her recital at least a true Randolph scene. She wrote on:

"That you hoped it was not true, for he was unworthy of me. To establish this opinion, you made many assertions derogatory to his reputation—some of which I knew to be false. . . . The defamations of your brother whom I loved, your stormy passions, your mean selfishness, your wretched appearance, rendered your attentions disagreeable."

Nancy's anger in recollection colored her description of Jack. He would be put forward in politics soon by sober neighbors including his cousin Jefferson. Though his face may have been marked by the recent dissipation he claimed, possibly romanticized portraits of him about this time showed him as an almost pretty young man in sharp contrast to the appearance of a furious wraith he made later. But Nancy went on:

"Your brother, Richard, a model of truth and honor, knew how much I was annoyed by them. He knew of the letters with which you pestered me from Philadelphia. It was your troublesome attentions which induced Richard to inform you of my engagement. At that time my father had other views. Your property, as well as that of your brothers, was hampered by a British debt. My father, therefore, preferred for my husband a person of clear and considerable estate."

The Colonel's feelings about Randolph finances had real basis in fact then. His own troubles were not entirely resolved. Others

had money troubles. In the summer of 1791 Jefferson in Philadelphia, where as was customary with him he remodeled a house
to his expensive tastes, was embarrassed about his possible in-
ability to pay money due on his debts to Farrell & Jones of
Bristol, England. So far as his letters home indicate this worried
him much more than the embarrassment caused him by political
furore created by his supposedly unwitting endorsement of Tom
Paine's book, *The Rights of Man,* which struck at the "heresies"
of Adams and Hamilton. Fortunately Jefferson's money troubles
of the moment were relieved when he found that he would have
the tobacco which made it possible for him to meet his obligation.

Certainly at this time, as Tucker had foretold, the Randolph
brothers were financially doubtful as prospective husbands. This
was true even though the Colonel had agreed to Judith's marriage to Richard. Ironically, John's addiction to the race track
later helped solve his and his brothers' problem as debtors to
British creditors. As one lover of racing he met another in John
Wickham, New York-born lawyer who became a famous Virginia
attorney. As lawyer and agent for the British creditors who held
the mortgages on the Randolph estates Wickham made a new
arrangement under which the payment of the debt was provided
for upon terms much more indulgent to the brothers.

There must have been more questions about Nancy's marriage
to Theodorick than the objections of her father. For "nearly a
year," according to John, Theodorick had been very ill. John
wrote later that in this period Theodorick was "reduced to a
mere skeleton; that he was unable to walk; and that his bones
were worn through his skin." Possibly this was exaggeration to
serve John's own story. However, Theodorick himself had written
in August 1789 that he had "been very sick for sometime past."
Possibly his illness was due to dissipation as John always suggested. Theodorick may have been a lazy boy who brought in
rowdy companions to interfere with John's studies. To the end of
his life John, in the language of pious affection, described his
brother Theodorick's bad character even in their childhood. In
1830, when Theodorick had been nearly forty years dead, John
wrote his nephew: "I remember getting severly thrashed by my

poor brother Theodorick in attempting to rescue from his tor-
ments a black kitten, to which he was acting the part of Jack
Ketch." This cruelty, resembling that of the notorious British ex-
ecutioner, seemed a strange thing to recall in supposedly sympathetic recollection. It carried the implication that Theodorick
might be cruel in more important relationships than that one
with a tortured kitten. Yet the evidences left by and about
Theodorick are by no means all of evil complexion. Bruce
thought his letters as a boy brought him back into memory in
"a more attractive way." He was ambitious for a medical education in Philadelphia. And his promise was such that as late as
January 1790 it was the intention of Tucker, his guardian, to
send him to Edinburgh to study medicine there. Undoubtedly,
however, Theodorick came home to Bizarre in 1791 as a sick
man. Apparently, though John suggested that his brother died of
dissipation, he was ill with tuberculosis. He died on February
14, 1792.

Strangely, Martha Jefferson Randolph, returning to Monticello
after an absence, wrote her father on February 20, 1792, saying
that she had received his letters at Dick Randolph's. But she made
no mention of Theodorick's illness or death. She did write of a
dark time coming home: "We have had a most disagreeable
journey traveling [the] greatest part of the way thro a deep
snow and dismal weather generally raining or hailing. I never
saw the end of anything with more pleasure in my life."

The Bizarre behind her must have been a melancholy place.
One report was that Nancy went into hysterics at the mention of
Theodorick's name. She was often unwell and much depressed.
Apparently, however, she showed no wish for seclusion. She rode
much about the countryside. Judith seemed entitled to more
consideration. On May 7, 1792, Martha Jefferson wrote her father
from Monticello that Nancy was coming with her brother Thomas
Mann, Jr., to Monticello. In the same letter she wrote that Judith
"has a fine son." This was St. George, named after Richard's
stepfather, who turned out to be deaf and dumb.

Only afterwards was it publicly stated that soon after this time
some suspicions were directed at Nancy—and at Richard. Some

visitors said that they thought that their displays of affection exceeded that to be expected between a man and his sister-in-law. But the person most sniffing at a possible scandal, as she herself later indicated, was Nancy's Aunt Polly, Mrs. Carter Page. Possibly she presumed a sort of guardianship as the sister of Nancy's dead mother. Strangely she seemed almost eager for scandal involving her sister's child. Evidently she had inherited some of the domineering qualities of her father who, as long as he lived, kept his youngest daughter Elizabeth from marrying the man she loved.

Polly Cary Page herself was only twenty-six when she came to visit at Bizarre in the early summer of 1792. She was not an impressive dowager, but an officious, inquisitive, young woman. Her suspicions, she said, were aroused by a supposed thickening in Nancy's young figure. Apparently she asked her niece to let her examine her and was indignantly refused. With unsatisfied curiosity, she peeped through a crack in Nancy's door when Nancy's Negro maid was undressing her. Polly's husband, Carter Page, later backed his wife, saying that he had noticed a change in Nancy's shape in May.

During this period John Randolph was in Philadelphia supposedly studying law under his cousin Attorney General Edmund Randolph. He and his fellow student, Joseph Bryan of Georgia, in this summer gave up the law and, he said, "commenced men of pleasure, plunging into the gaiety that fills the mouth with blasphemy; the heart with ——!" Then, he related, his money gave out and he returned to Virginia. In Richmond on the way to the home of his stepfather in Williamsburg, he was taken with scarlet fever "and brought to the brink of the grave." Possibly it was from this illness that the fact or the suspicions of his impotency dated. Legend about it grew into a confident report that this crippling of his manhood was a certainty. This was supported by his voice which in oratory and conversation grew ever more shrill. It was related in harsh Virginia gossip to his later rejection by another girl, Maria Ward, who preferred his cousin, Peyton, son of the Attorney General. Recovering sufficiently for travel he went to Williamsburg. There, he said later, he was coldly received in the house of his step-father who had, he wrote, married a shrew and a vixen. This slur, his biographer Bruce thought, was as unjust as his accusation against Edmund Randolph. But from there he set out for Bizarre, and "was once more restored to the society of the fondest of brothers."

Certainly this suggests a happy atmosphere in that brother's house. Yet not long afterwards it was stated that in September Nancy overheard Judith talking with Martha Jefferson Randolph who spoke of gum guaiacum as good medicine for certain ills but dangerous because it induced abortions. A few days later, it was also afterwards said, Nancy asked her prying aunt, Mrs. Page, for some of the drug. Eckenrode wrote that she obtained it. Considering the reports of her earlier resentment at her aunt's prying, this seems hardly likely. Perhaps talk of drugs with Martha at this time was not strange as her little daughter, Anne, was sick and she was delivered of a son, Thomas Jefferson Randolph, on September 12.

Her father was at Monticello then. Because of his own tragic experience he was much concerned about the deliveries of his daughters. Yet he spoke of child bearing as woman's trade. He was much interested in birth processes. He had encouraged his son-in-law in making a study of the birth processes of the opossum. Thomas Mann had trouble securing proper specimens for his investigation. However, in the same scientific spirit he had captured a wolf and, noting that the creature was "extremely fond of being caressed," tried to breed it to a dog.

With the lines being sharply drawn between his followers who would be called Republicans and Hamilton's Federalists, Jefferson could not devote himself to such studies of natural history which he said he preferred to politics. On September 27, he left Monticello for Philadelphia. On the way he stopped at Mount Vernon where Washington expressed great regret at the quarrel in his Cabinet. The President scoffed at Jefferson's idea that his antagonists wanted to create a monarchy. Probably both knew the quarrel had advanced too far for simple solution. Before they talked Hamilton, writing under a pseudonym of

Catullus, described his Cabinet colleague as an epicurean masked as a stoic and a concealed voluptuary. Among the chief of Jefferson's defenders Aristides, identified as Edmund Randolph, described Hamilton-Catullus as a "calumniator" and a "cowardly assassin."

While Jefferson was at Mount Vernon or on his way to or beyond it, other Virginians were traveling. On Monday, October 1, in a sort of cavalcade of the young gentry, Randolphs rode to the still unfinished house, Glenlyvar, of Randolph Harrison in Cumberland County, not far from Bizarre. It was a fecund family group. Mrs. Randolph Harrison then had a baby little more than a month old. Her cousin Judith had left her four-month-old child, St. George, at Bizarre. Parents and children represented amazing inbreeding. Randolph Harrison had married his first cousin Mary Randolph. She was close kin to her visitors, Judith and Nancy, through both the Randolphs and the Carys. Others among the Glenlyvar visitors were Richard Randolph, of the great Curles-Bolling line, and Archibald Randolph, the brother of the hostess. He was another suitor for the hand of his cousin, Nancy. Also in the company, according to Bruce, was a Mrs. John Randolph whose identity seems to have eluded genealogists. Apparently slaves accompanied them, including Nancy's fifteen-year-old maid and a seven-year-old Negro child.

It was a party of very young people. The oldest among them, Randolph Harrison and Archie Randolph, were only twenty-three. Richard Randolph was twenty-two. Mary Harrison and Judith Randolph were each nineteen. Nancy was only seventeen. Long afterwards Nancy wrote to John Randolph of Roanoke, who had apparently stayed behind at Bizarre, of the months behind her then and of Theodorick who was dead: "I was left at Bizarre, a girl, not seventeen, with the man she loved. I was betrothed to him, and considered him as my husband in the presence of that God whose name you presume to invoke on occasions the most trivial and for purposes the most malevolent. We should have been married, if Death had not snatched him away a few days after the scene which began the history of my sorrows."

It was cold in the unfinished house at Glenlyvar in this autumn of 1792. Outside big brown leaves fell into the piles of building debris still left about it. Nancy did not feel well. After the early afternoon dinner, she went upstairs and did not come down again that day. There was a great frost in this part of Virginia that night. John, left behind at Bizarre, made a note of it in his diary.

All seemed serene at Bizarre when Martha Jefferson Randolph took her little girl and her new baby there little more than a month after her cousins had returned from their visit to Glenlyvar. From this Randolph plantation, on November 18, she wrote her father. Perhaps she was too preoccupied about her children to note any troubles of others in the household. Her baby was lively but little Anne was sick. Undoubtedly Judith, nursing her own six-month-old son St. George, offered advice and suggested remedies. So did Jefferson in far-off Philadelphia. Also perhaps to divert her, he told her of news about a European friend of hers, Lady Elizabeth Tufton, who had married "some very rich person . . . whose name could not be recalled by Mr. Hammond, my informer." George Hammond, the British Minister then, was evidently chitchatting with the Secretary of State. However, he was, as Jefferson knew, much more intimate personally and officially with Hamilton whose British sympathies were in contrast to the Virginian's affections for France.

Jefferson did not mention to his daughter the fierce attacks upon him by Hamilton and his associates in this autumn. Indeed, as he insisted, he did not deign to put pen to paper in answer to them even when it was said of him that "the *externals* of pure Democracy afford but a flimsy veil to the *internal* evidences of aristocratic splendor, sensuality and Epicreanism." Madison, Monroe, and Edmund Randolph joined in his defense.

Such conflict seemed far away from Bizarre. Indeed, the plantation was apparently secluded even from sinister reports circulating in Virginia about its young residents. Yet rumors spread quickly after the visit to Glenlyvar. Evidently when Richard, Judith, and Nancy returned they told John Randolph nothing untoward that had happened there. But before October was over at Battersea on the James he was told of growing gossip by his devoted cousin John Banister. The stories had begun apparently in the slave quarters at Glenlyvar. Peyton, the brother of Randolph Harrison, was told, he stated later, by a slave that a fetus or the remains of a new-born child had been found in a pile of shingles near the unfinished house. He said that he felt bound by his friendship for Archie Randolph to inform him. It seemed strange that Archie, who was present, had to be informed of what had happened on the first night of October.

The word which had spread from slave to slave moved from aristocrat to aristocrat. Nancy later suggested that among the chief bearers of the tales were her stepmother, Gabriella, her sister Mary, Mrs. David Meade Randolph, and the wife of Peyton to whom the slave had talked. Certainly another was Mrs. Carter Page. Richard listed as one of the most venomous talkers William Randolph, whom Bruce identified as one of the brothers of Nancy and Judith. This seems amazing, if correct. In the same letter in which Richard pointed his indignation at this William, he said that, being unable to provoke this William into a duel, he had urged "Col. Tom" to bring an action of slander against him. Colonel Tom would have been this William's brother or father. Of such a possible suit, however, Richard said, "This will bring the whole affair once more before the eyes of everyone, the circumstances, from beginning to end, of the persons accusing and accused will be seen at once, and the villainy of my traducers exposed. When this is done I shall once more know the blessing of a tranquil mind! . . ."

To Randolphs this must have seemed the season of slander. In the sharpening quarrel of the Republicans and Federalists in Philadelphia, Jefferson admitted to Martha, in January 1793, that he had "for some time past been under an agitation of mind which I scarcely ever experienced before." He had been firmly determined to retire, he wrote, when the attacks upon him in the papers so intensified that his friends, undoubtedly including

Edmund, urged him to remain longer. They "urged that my retiring just when I had been attacked in the public papers, would injure me in the eyes of the public, who would suppose I either withdrew from investigation, or because I had not the tone of mind sufficient to meet slander."

Richard's dilemma was a more bitter one. If he remained silent, while the tale spread that he and Nancy had destroyed the child of an incestuous affair, that might be taken as admission of guilt. To bring it into the open would present a dirty story for all to hear. He seemed, as late as March 14, 1793, uncertain. He had, he told his stepfather, promised Judith, "my beloved wife . . . not to say anything more, or make any further inquiry into the abominable story." At this time he even wrote that he meant "to spend the summer in one of the Northern States." While gone, the suit for slander, he suggested, could go on. And he added, "Again, Nancy's situation would yet be worse than mine from the same causes, on account of the delicacy of her sex and sentiments. For this reason, she will go with us, and, while the most important inquiry that could take place is going on, we shall be out of the way of that observation, which could do nothing but wound our feelings."

It did not turn out that way. Evidently Richard himself threw the matter into the courts and the papers. On April 28, 1793, Jefferson wrote Martha a letter which has often been quoted as evidence of his gentle tolerance. He told her: "A paper which I some time ago saw in the Richmond gazette under the signature R.R. proved to me the existence of a rumor, which I had otherwise heard of with less certainty."

Then he added: "It has given me great uneasiness because I know it must have made so many others unhappy, and among these Mr. Randolph [his son-in-law] and yourself. Whatever the case may be, the world is become too rational to extend to one person the acts of another. Every one at present stands on the merit or demerit of their own conduct. I am in hopes therefore that neither of you feel any uneasiness but for the pitiful victim, whether it be of error or slander. In either case I see guilt in but one person, and not in her. For her it is the

moment of trying the affection of her friends, when their com-
miseration and comfort become balm to her wounds. I hope
you will deal them out to her in full measure, regardless of
what the trifling or malignant may think or say. Never throw
off the best affections of nature in the moment when they become
most precious to their object; nor fear to extend your hand to
save another, less you should sink yourself. You are on firm
ground. Your kindness will help her and count in your own
favor also. I shall be made very happy if you are the instruments
not only of supporting the spirits of your afflicted friend under
the weight bearing on them, but of preserving her in the peace,
and love of her friends. I hope you have already taken this
resolution if it were necessary; and I have no doubt you have;
yet I wished it too much to omit mentioning it to you."

That attitude was not universal even in the Randolph family.
Martha did not fully share it. As the rumors grew she had not
mentioned them to her father. How long he had known of the
"error or slander" before he wrote this letter is not clear. Eight
days before, however, on April 21, 1793, Judith, without her
husband's knowledge, wrote a letter to St. George Tucker at
his request and sent it to him by John. She wrote, Bruce said,
"in the vain hope that it might put an end to the ugly rumors
about Richard then abroad." It amounted to a categorical denial
that any child could have been born or miscarriage taken place
and the remains carried out that night at Glenlyvar. Later this
letter was made public by Tucker. But the case was not to be
tried in the newspapers.

"God," once said a Virginian of such a high-bred individual
as Richard Randolph, "would think twice before damning one
of that quality."

Yet in April Richard was held in jail without bond on a charge
of feloniously murdering a child, said to be born of Nancy
Randolph. It is not clear whether Nancy was also jailed. It is
very clear that Richard, recognizing the seriousness of the
capital crime with which he stood charged, sought the best
counsel for his and Nancy's defense. He asked the advice not
only of his stepfather but also of his cousin, John Marshall, who

as he became more and more Federalist in his politics was less and less charitably regarded by Jefferson. Marshall agreed to appear for the defense. Then perhaps at his suggestion, Richard sent a message offering Patrick Henry a fee of 250 guineas to defend him. Henry protested that he was not well; it was a long journey to Cumberland Court House. Richard raised the offer to 500 guineas and Henry, who, Jefferson said, loved money even more than fame, agreed. To this distinguished pair was added Alexander Campbell, a leading Richmond lawyer who had appeared with the other two as attorney for Virginia debtors against their British creditors.

The trial was held on April 29 before sixteen "Gentlemen Justices." Their names seemed almost a roster of the gentry. No accounts of the trial take notice of the prosecutor or prosecutors in the case. Witnesses, however, undertook to show a night of tumult and mystery at Glenlyvar. There were reports of Nancy's screams, of the administration of laudanum to her for "hysterics"—or the pangs of childbirth. Richard was described as going up and down the stairs in the night. One strange item was the testimony that a sixteen-year-old Negro girl and a small Negro child were in Nancy's room during her reported ordeal. The most hostile witness to the defendants was Nancy's aunt Mrs. Carter Page, who told of seeing an apparently pregnant Nancy in the summer before by peeping through a crack in her door. Henry, as skilled actor in cross examination, deflated the lady and demolished her testimony by demanding, "Which eye did you peep with?" The courtroom roared. Probably even some of the "Gentlemen Justices" grinned.

More important for the defense, Judith denied that anything like the circumstances charged could have happened. Nancy had only a little stomach upset. There was no ingress or egress from her room except beside Judith's bed. Nothing had happened. They had gone home from Glenlyvar in good spirits. Nancy in good health rode her horse as usual at Bizarre. Even without Judith's testimony in defense, it is hard to see how any case could have been made for the prosecution. The slaves who supposedly found the fetus or body were under Virginia law then incompetent to testify. Some Randolphs present at the time had carefully not looked for the bloody mass slaves said they had found. Indeed, the mystery for history was heightened by the fact that apparently no corpus delicti was displayed or described. That might not have proved guilt of crime. But if only a fetus had been found Richard would have been more suspect. If the remains were those of a fully formed child, the dead Theodorick could well have been the father.

Richard and Nancy were found not guilty of any crime, and, Nancy later wrote, so found to loud cheers in the courtroom. Her own attorney Marshall in his notes on the trial put the matter of guilt or innocence more soberly.

"The friends of Miss Randolph," he wrote in connection with his notes of the trial, "cannot deny that there is some foundation on which suspicion may build; nor can it be denied by her [Nancy's] enemies but that every circumstance may be accounted for without imputing guilt to her. In this situation, candor will not condemn, or exclude from society, a person who may be only unfortunate."

Martha Jefferson, despite her father's charitable counsel, was not so judicial in her personal verdict. She had received her father's letter of advice about the matter after the trial was over. She would have answered it immediately, she said, "but that the house was full of company at the time," and no doubt full of Randolphs and of conversation.

"The subject of it," she wrote, "has been one of infinite anxiety both to Mr. Randolph and my self for many months and tho I am too sensible of the iliberality of extending to one person the infamy of another, to fear one moment that it can reflect any real disgrace upon me in the eyes of people of sense yet the generality of mankind are weak enough to think otherwise and it is painful to an excess to be obliged to blush for so near a connection. I know it by fatal experience."

Then she rendered her verdict: "As for the poor deluded victim I believe all feel much more for her than she does for herself. The villain having been no less successful in corrupting her mind than he has in destroying her reputation. Amidst the distress of her family she alone is tranquil and seems proof against every other misfortune on earth but that of a separation from her vile seducer. They have been *tried* and acquitted tho I am sorry to say his Lawers (sic) gained more honour by it than they did as but a small part of the world and those the most inconsiderable people in it were influenced in there (sic) opinion by the decision of the court. In following the dictates of my own heart I was so happy as to stumble upon the very conduct you advised me to, before I knew your opinion. I have continued to behave with affection to her which her errors have not been able to eradicate from my heart and could I suppose her penitent I would redouble my attentions to her though I am one of the few who have allways *doubted* the truth of the report. As the opinion I had of R.R. was most exalted would to heaven my hopes were equal to my fears but the latter often to often presides. The divisions of the family increase daily."

Martha had more things to worry about than the guilt or innocence of her cousins. Her father-in-law, old Colonel Thomas Mann Randolph, Sr., died in Richmond on November 20, 1793. The estate he left was much burdened with debts. Already in prospect were suits against the estate by three British firms. These suits, notwithstanding the efforts of John Marshall who, despite his politics, appeared as the family's lawyer, would bring on the calamity which the Colonel had feared when he talked to Gouverneur Morris five years before. Young Thomas Mann was ill with a disease doctors could not diagnose and visits to spas with Martha could not cure.

The courts declined to recognize the validity of payments made earlier by the Colonel in Revolutionary paper money and ordered Thomas Mann, his brother William, and the estate of their father to pay $65,000 to John Lidderdale of London, Farrell & Jones of Bristol, and John Bowman of Glasgow. Still Thomas enjoyed a recovery of health as mysterious as his illness had been. Perhaps the cure lay in writings of philosophers to whom he turned. He took from Francis Bacon the prescription that "tranquility is better than jollity to avoid or appease pain." Brilliant, erratic, supersensitive, he had little of either.

He hated the Federalists and the British, worried about the hysteria being aroused against the French. But among the gentry in Albemarle facing democratic upstarts, he was not clear in the faith that all men were created equal. He was eager at home to be a soldier; ready to be a statesman. But sometimes he looked from Virginia to the West to which his cousins, Brett and Ryland Randolph, were proposing to move.

They were not only the first cousins of Richard at Bizarre but close friends also whom Richard had named as executors in his will. The mother of Brett's wife, Lucy Beverley of Blandfield, was the daughter of Colonel Theodorick Bland, Sr., of Cawsons. Lucy's sister, Maria, had married Brett's brother, another Richard. The genetic circle came around like children holding hands in a ring. This last Richard's brother, David Meade Randolph of Presqu'ile, had taken as wife Molly Randolph of Tuckahoe, whose sister Judith had married Richard of Bizarre.

The simile of Randolph genealogy like a tangle of fishhooks was complete.

Chapter IX

HUE OF THE CHAMELEON

WHATEVER might be the scorn in the great houses and the smirks in the smoky rooms of taverns, the trial of the Randolphs of Bizarre did not bring all Randolphs under a shadow. Indeed, at the time of the trial's termination, probably the most glamorous figure in Virginia was Light-Horse Harry Lee of the Bland branch of the family. Rich, eloquent, literate, at thirty-three he was honored in his position as Governor of Virginia. As widower of his cousin Matilda Lee, he held, though the ownership was in his small son Henry, the great fortress-like mansion of Stratford. As his young wife's death indicated it was not safe from tragedy. The great brick steps which led up to it from its gardens above the Potomac were not only impressive. Also they recalled the death of an earlier Lee child who tumbled down them. Even Lees could fall.

Now as Governor who wore his Revolutionary fame like a cloak on broad shoulders, Light-Horse was engaged with his cousins John and James Marshall in negotiating for the purchase of a hundred and sixty thousand acres of the best land in Virginia, the remnant of the millions of acres in the Northern Neck long before granted to Lord Fairfax. The lure of land speculation appealed much to Lee. But military glory still beckoned this young man of whom it was said that he was a warrior from his mother's womb. The tender had been made to him of the rank of major general in the army of France. The temptation to accept it suggests that at this point he was not, as he would soon be, a charging leader in anti-French Federalism. That would make him a general a year later when, at the behest of his wartime friend Alexander Hamilton, he led the forces against Pennsylvania farmers in the Whisky Rebellion. His cousin Jefferson described this Federalist foray as bringing an "armament against people at their ploughs."

Now in 1793, he gave up ideas of military glory abroad to marry, on June 18, young Anne Hill Carter of Shirley on the James. That great house of tawny brick, built early in the century, had been owned by Colonel Edward Hill, whom William Byrd had long before persuaded to give the captaincy of one of his ships to Isham Randolph. The estate, within easy horse or boat distance of several Randolph plantations, had been inherited by Elizabeth Hill, who had, in 1723, added wealth to wealth and aristocracy to aristocracy in her marriage to John Carter, eldest son of "King" Carter. Anne Carter, who was to be best remembered as the mother of a boy christened Robert Edward, was seventeen years younger than her handsome husband. In this second of two marriages Harry Lee brought to his resources the estates of two of the richest and greatest families in the Old Dominion. Nobody dreamed that would not be enough despite the style of living he required.

Such wealth, of course, was not necessary to Randolph eminence. Lacking the romantic aura which attended Harry, Edmund Randolph, only three years older, was as much or more respected. Now Attorney General in Washington's government, he lived in no such grand style as Lee required. Possibly much of the plainness of Edmund's establishment was due to his wife Betsy Nicholas. She was, according to Edmund's devoted biographer, Moncure Daniel Conway, "a homely woman in all senses; she was also, it may be suspected, straight-laced." Conway noted that when Jefferson and George Wythe came to Edmund's house to play chess on Sunday her disapproval was so apparent that no such play ever recurred. Also she was an ill woman or one who imagined herself to be. Yet, in Washington's court she played her part though in muted fashion in Philadelphia where the Binghams and the Morrises led a society unrestrained by any patterns of republican simplicity. Jefferson noted that she was one of the ladies who first called on his younger child Polly when he brought her to Philadelphia for her schooling.

Apparently Edmund Randolph was land-and-slave poor. In a listing of the properties of one hundred first Virginia families in 1780, he was shown to own 7,463 acres in James City, Charlotte, Albemarle, and Henrico counties. He owned—and his conscience was troubled by their possession—101 slaves. He kept nineteen horses and grazed 127 cattle. Much of this which had come to him by inheritance was also, however, attended by debts. He was eminent as a lawyer; Jefferson turned over important law cases to him when he went to France. Perhaps he was too generous with his legal talents. He had declined to accept any fee from his friend and his Uncle Peyton's friend Washington for handling his often complicated business affairs.

Evidently in Philadelphia he eked out his income as Attorney General by taking in such law students as John Randolph and Joseph Bryan. He had little time for the private practice customary then. His wife's medical expenses may have been high. Evidently he had to depend much on his salary of $1,500. Jefferson, who received $3,000 a year as Secretary of State, spent $5,240.03, as he carefully noted in his Account Book. Randolph's outside sources of income were more limited. And Jefferson never seemed to be worried enough about his debts to curb his extravagances in house construction and hospitality. Edmund Randolph evidently lacked that art.

They had much else in common. The two would seem to have been, for every reason of kinship and companionship in ideas, bound most closely together among the men around Washington. Edmund had much aided Jefferson in the fight for religious liberty. When Jefferson was charged with incompetence and cowardice as war Governor, Edmund had been one of his champions. Living close to Monticello at Colle, formerly the plantation of Mazzei, he had consoled his older cousin after his wife's death and helped persuade him to give up his withdrawal from public affairs by accepting the mission to France.

Conway wrote that he kept Jefferson's name before the public in his absence. When Jefferson returned he organized the official welcome home demonstration for him.

While in the Cabinet Jefferson made repeated entries in his diary, or *Anas*, about Edmund's friendly reports to him. Then suddenly the Secretary of State began to write confidential letters home condemning Edmund for lapses in his republicanism, for his inconsistencies, for his ambition, and for his failure to join Jefferson in his conviction that his political enemies were taking over Washington and his administration.

Conway, in his study of the mounting irritability and hostility Jefferson expressed secretly toward Randolph, stated that from Jefferson's entry into the Cabinet to the end of 1793, there were about nineteen significant divisions in the Cabinet on "party" lines. On sixteen of these, he wrote, Randolph voted with Jefferson. In one or two cases he proposed slight modifications, "but on every important question of practical action, especially in foreign affairs, Randolph voted with Jefferson." Yet, on May 12, 1793, Jefferson began to damn Randolph as undependable to their mutual friends though maintaining the surface of their friendship.

A question had come up about enforcing the administration's policy of neutrality in the conflict of the British and French which threatened to involve America on one side or the other. Jefferson was suspicious that Hamilton's proposal that his customs inspectors be used was a plan to set up a Hamiltonian system of espionage. Randolph shared these fears but regarded the customs inspectors, being those closest to the scene of possible violations, as the most suitable informants. He got Hamilton to agree that they would report not to the Treasury but to the district attorneys. Jefferson was far from satisfied. He wrote Madison, on May 12, 1793, that everything in the differences in the council hung on the vote of a single person [Randolph], "and that the most indecisive one I ever had to do business with. He always contrives to agree in principle with one but in conclusion with the other." Oddly Jefferson made no note of this in his *Anas* at the time, though he did note that this month for the first time a decision in the council was made by a majority vote, including the President's own.

Jefferson wrote this letter at the beginning of a summer full of difficulties. He enthusiastically hailed the arrival in the United States of young Edmond Genêt, the new French Minister. On April 28, he was sure that this enthusiastic young Frenchman's arrival "would furnish occasion for the people to testify their affections [for France] without respect to the cold caution of their government." That government, of course, was Washington's administration in which Jefferson was Secretary of State. But increasingly he had begun to regard it as the political mechanism opposed to his own republican beliefs. As Randolph did not share that idea about the "government" as enemy, Jefferson, Schachner wrote, "perpetually poured the vials of his wrath on that unfortunate Virginian's head."

When Randolph went home for a vacation in the early summer, Jefferson sent his animadversions before him. He urged Madison in a letter, on June 9, 1793, to bring the views of ardent Republicans to bear upon him. He particularly wanted Randolph to be indoctrinated in Virginia by his brother-in-law William Cary Nicholas who, like Jefferson, was enthusiastically sympathetic with the Revolutionary French. Madison was to impress on Nicholas "The necessity of giving him a strong & perfect understanding of the public mind." So perhaps, he went on, the trip "may strengthen his nerves, and dispose him more favorably to the propositions of a treaty between the two republics" such as Genêt was proposing.

By July, however, the Secretary of State was embarrassed by the Gallic impetuosity of Genêt. He told Madison, "Never in my opinion was so calamitous an appointment made, as that of the present Minister of France here. Hot headed, all imagination, no judgment, passionate, disrespectful and even indecent toward the P. in his written as well as his verbal communications. . . . He renders my position immensely difficult." At the same time his position with the President was made embarrassing by Washington's furious outbursts against the criticism of the caustic Philip Freneau whom Jefferson and others had set up as editor

of the *National Gazette* in opposition to Hamilton's editor John
Fenno of the *Gazette of the United States*. It was at the end of
such a harassed summer that the great Virginian wrote another
letter about his cousin and associate the Attorney General whose
personal ties were as close to the President as to Jefferson. The
fight between Jefferson and Hamilton, the pro-French and the
pro-British, the Republicans and the Federalists had reached
new intensity in the Cabinet. Jefferson was ready to abandon
Genêt as a political liability. But Hamilton and his stooge Secretary of War Henry Knox wanted not only that but to make
the Genêt case the basis for an appeal to the people in such a way
as would, Jefferson thought, serve their political purposes. He
opposed this "totally," he said, "told the President plainly in
their presence, that the intention was to dismount him from
being the head of the nation, & make him the head of a party;
that this would be the effect of making him in an appeal to the
people declare war against the Republican party."

So angrily the lines were drawn. Then Randolph intervened.
Jefferson reported: "R[andolph] according to his half-way system between wrong & right urged the *putting off* of the appeal."
Washington approved Randolph's suggestion. In effect the political plan of the Federalists was dismissed. But Jefferson was
far from appeased.

In this letter to Madison, on August 11, 1793, drawing the
lines between the parties and outlining the political strategy of
his own, he abandoned Randolph almost as completely as he had
abandoned Genêt.

"I can by this confidential conveyance speak more freely of
R[andolph]. He is the poorest cameleon (sic) I ever saw having no colour of his own, & reflecting that nearest him. When he
is with me he is a whig, when with H[amilton] he is a tory,
when with the P[resident] he is that he thinks will please him.
The last is his strongest hue, tho' the 2d. tinges him very
strongly. The first is what I think he would prefer in his heart if
he were in the woods where he could see nobody, or in a society
of all *whigs*."

Conway gave a longer version of this letter, which he complained had been generally suppressed by historians. Apparently Jefferson had enclosed a "paper" in this communication which "in some degree lessened my apprehensions of the estimation in which the Pr. held him [Randolph]: still it is not the less true that his opinion always makes the majority, and that the President acquiesces *always* in the majority; consequently that the government is now solely directed by him."

Jefferson continued: "As he [Randolph] is not yet openly thrown off by the Whig party, it gives to the public a false security that fair play is given to the whiggism of the Pr[esident] by an equal division of whig and tory among his counselors."

Then in a somewhat obscure passage Jefferson spoke of both his personal relations and personal resentment toward his fellow Virginian: "I have kept on terms of strict friendship with him hitherto, that I might have some good out of him, and because he has really some good private qualities; but he is in a station infinitely too important for his understanding, his firmness or his circumstances. I mentioned to you that we had convened the judges to consult them on the questions which have arisen on the law of nations. They declined being consulted. In England, you know, such questions are referred regularly to the Judge of Admiralty. I asked E.R. if we could not prepare a bill for Congress to appoint a board or some other body of advice for the Executive on such questions. He said he should propose to annex it to his own office. In plain language, this would be to make him the sole arbiter of the line of conduct for the U.S. towards foreign nations."

This Jeffersonian expression was clearly one of resentment at what seemed to him Randolph's pushing into the field of his prerogatives. A part of his resentment against Hamilton had been such intrusion into matters of foreign affairs. Conway in his biography of Randolph perhaps overemphasized Jefferson's personal feelings as opposed to his political ones. He wrote: "One would be glad to suppose that his long-continued private defamation of Randolph arose from even unjust considerations of public policy, rather than from a desire to lower an eloquent and popular rival in the affections of the South, strong in the confidence of Washington. Whatever judgment may be formed of his motives, the fact remains that by that skillful hand Randolph's portrait has been given to the world as he was not, and endures to this day."

Not until many years later when Jefferson's *Anas* was posthumously published was his report of a conversation with Washington about Randolph available to citizens and students. It contained the Secretary of State's narrative of a visit to him in his house on the Schuylkill River by the President. This visit occurred on August 6, 1793, just before Jefferson wrote his scathing letter about Randolph to Madison. Washington had driven out to try to persuade Jefferson to give up his intention of leaving the Cabinet from which, the President said, Hamilton was also departing soon. Expressing his repugnance to having to move in the Federalist Philadelphia society which hated him, Jefferson held to his intention to retire. They discussed a possible successor to him as Secretary of State. One and another were mentioned and set aside. Then wrote Jefferson, "I asked him whether some person could not take my office *par interim,* till he should make an appointment, as Mr. Randolph, for instance. Yes, said he, but there you would raise the expectation of keeping it, and I do not know that he is fit for it, nor what is thought of Mr. Randolph."

This seems an odd expression from Washington who had known Randolph all his life, who trusted him with all his personal legal affairs, had sent hearty congratulations when Virginia chose him as its Governor, and finally had chosen him as his legal adviser as President. This may have been one of those calm revisals which Jefferson said he made in his *Anas* long afterwards.

Jefferson wrote: "I avoided noticing the last observation, and he put the question to me directly. I then told him, I went into society so little as to be unable to answer it: I knew that the embarrassments in his [Randolph's] private affairs had obliged him to use expedients, which had injured him with the merchants and shop-keepers, and affected his character of independence;

that these embarrassments were serious, and not likely to cease soon."

As retiring Secretary of State Jefferson left Philadelphia on January 5, 1794. Three days earlier without any hesitation which might have been indicated by an interim appointment, Washington named Randolph Secretary of State. Conway perhaps showed partisanship when he wrote that "A small deposit of mistrust in the President's mind, and a large mass of unanswered mail—especially of such as involved Committal on French questions—were Jefferson's bequests to his successor." Certainly Randolph could not have known then about Jefferson's undercutting letters to Virginia or Jefferson's lack of confidence that he could ever rehabilitate himself with dunning shopkeepers. Unquestionably Jefferson left him great unsolved questions of foreign affairs and foreign politics. And the very certain thing is that Randolph accepted on important occasion—and to his injury—the very firmness in opposition to Federalists about which Jefferson had accused him of indecisiveness, of being, indeed, "a trimmer."

As Secretary of State, Randolph had been almost ignored by Hamilton and John Jay, Minister to England, while Jay negotiated the Jay Treaty which might better have borne Hamilton's name. The disclosure of its terms raised a national fury. Democrats regarded it as subservience to Britain and a slap at France. To Federalists it became almost a flag in their crusade against Jefferson and Jacobinism. Beveridge in his laudatory biography of its defender, Marshall, called it "the most humiliating compact into which America ever entered." He added by this treaty, the United States "yielded everything and gained little not already ours. But we secured peace; we were saved from war." Almost, however, it split the young nation.

Randolph committed the ultimate sin in Federalist eyes when he tried to persuade Washington to withhold his signature to the treaty's ratification until the British should revoke a recent order to seize American vessels carrying provisions to France. Apparently Washington was ready to follow Randolph's advice, instructing him to tell British Minister Hammond that he would not sign while this order was in effect.

In a certainly neat coincidence at this juncture Hammond gave to the Federalist Secretary of the Treasury, Oliver Wolcott, Jr., an intercepted letter from the French Minister, Joseph Fauchet, to his government which seemed to implicate Randolph in an attempt to obtain money from the French. Wolcott carried it to his Federalist associate Secretary of War Timothy Pickering, Knox's successor in that post. Pickering took it to the President saying that it showed Randolph to be a traitor. At a Cabinet meeting, on August 12, 1795, Pickering declared the opposition to the treaty was a "nefarious conspiracy" and to Randolph's amazement the President said that he would sign it.

Randolph had a greater surprise awaiting him. When, on August 19, 1795, he went as customary to report to the President in the morning, he was kept waiting for an hour and a half. When admitted he found Pickering and Wolcott with the President. Without preliminary the President rose and handed him a translation (not a good one) of the captured dispatch.

"Mr. Randolph, here is a letter which I desire you to read, and make such explanations as you choose."

Randolph read the letter with composure, commenting on it as he went along, denying in toto any implication that he had asked or received any money. To his amazement it was suggested that Pickering and Wolcott interrogate him. But it was agreed that he retain the letter and prepare an explanation. But when he got home he was appalled at the manner in which he had been treated by the President who conferred with the two Federalists before giving him the smallest intimation of this outrageous charge against his honor. He promptly resigned. He concluded his letter: "Your confidence in me, sir, has been unlimited; and I can truly affirm, unabused. My sensations then cannot be concealed, when I find that confidence so immediately withdrawn without a word or distant hint being previously dropped to me!"

Randolph quickly followed Fauchet to Newport where the Minister was preparing to sail for France. Fauchet wrote a statement denying he had made any such charge or implication. Actually, as an adequate translation of the letter indicated, the most serious charge that could be squeezed from the letter was that Randolph had suggested to the French Minister that his country pay promptly what it owed to American provisioners to free them from pressure by their English creditors. Evidently, however, the letter was made to serve as an instrument in a British-Federalist purpose to get rid of the troublesome Secretary of State. Young John Quincy Adams, on his way to his post as Minister to the Netherlands, made notes in his diary which support the probability that the British provided the material and the Federalists the push to get rid of Randolph as Secretary of State. Adams saw Hammond in London who told him that if Randolph denied his guilt he could produce other proofs. Also the Briton talked about "the Virginians, the Southern people, the Democrats" in such a way that young Adams felt prompted to tell him that he considered "them all in no other light than as Americans."

Those Virginians, however, were not ready to see Randolph damned by friends of the Jay Treaty even including their own Washington, who apparently, in this case, let his mounting irritations with Republican criticism lead him into cruel credulity. Even the powerful John Marshall made little headway in defending the treaty in the President's own state. When Randolph arrived back home in Richmond on November 20, he was received with a public demonstration of faith. While he had had to borrow money from his brother-in-law Wilson Cary Nicholas for his return, he immediately took a prominent and lucrative position at the Virginia bar. No formal charge of treason, bribery, or any kind of malfeasance in office was ever brought against him.

Still as an angry man, he was mistaken in the bitterness about Washington which he put into the "Vindication of Mr. Randolph's Resignation" which he wrote. Even those most opposed to the treaty could not accept his attack on Washington in which Randolph accused the President of engaging in a "plot" with the Federalists to destroy the Republicans. Some idea of his resentment against his old hero, however, was shown in a letter he wrote at this time to Madison in which he said: "I feel happy at my emancipation from an attachment to a man who has practiced upon me the profound hypocrisy of a Tiberius, and the injustice of an assassin."

Washington left no comment on Randolph's strictures upon him. His reaction came secondhand from Pickering who along with Wolcott was described by Madison's biographer, Irving Brant, as "two of the most malevolent men who ever decorated a Presidential Cabinet." To his participation in the political destruction of Edmund Randolph he added later an interview which he said he had with the President about the "Vindication" pamphlet. Washington chose him, Pickering wrote, in his need to unburden himself on the subject.

Recalling the death of Peyton Randolph, "my dearest friend," Washington told Pickering, "In an hour of affectionate and solemn communion, in which he had expressed an expectation that before long he would thus be removed, he begged me to be a friend to his nephew and adopted son Edmund. I promised that I would be to him as a father: that promise has been sacredly kept. If in any instance, I have been swayed by personal and private feelings, in the exercise of political influence or of official patronage and power, it has been in this."

Washington went on, according to Pickering, reciting the role he played in every step in Edmund's advance. Then in culmination: "In 1794 I made him Secretary of State, placing him at the head of my official council: in my Cabinet, from the beginning he has been admitted to my utmost confidence. I have held with him a daily intimacy. He occupied the chief seat among the guests at my table."

Then, said Pickering, his voice rose like a gathering storm: "While at the head of my Cabinet he has been secretly, but actively, plotting with the opponents of my administration, consulting and contriving with them for the defeat of its measures. . . ."

This, of course, was what Federalists said Jefferson was doing in the days when he complained that Randolph did not stand decisively beside him.

The recital of the President's anger went on: ". . . he, the Secretary of State, to whose trust the foreign relations of the country are confided, has been conducting an intrigue with the ambassador of a foreign government to promote the designs of that government, which were to overthrow the administration of which he Randolph was a trusted member, receiving from the ambassador money to aid in accomplishing that object; soliciting from him more for the same purpose,—all this time I have had entire faith in him, and been led by that faith to pay deference to his representations, to delay the ratification of the British treaty, thereby exposing myself to imputation of having been intimidated by party clamor from the discharge of a public duty, an imputation contrary to the truth, a thought abhorrent to my feelings and my nature, and now he has written and published this."

Pickering added: "As he uttered these last words, he threw the pamphlet down, and gave way to a terrific burst of denunciation in unrestrained expressions. He then calmly resumed his seat. The storm was over. With perfect serenity other business was entered upon, and the name or thought of Edmund Randolph was never again suffered to disturb his temper."

While Randolph suffered in this cruel climax of the acrimonious conflict which he had inherited from Jefferson, that statesman was rusticating at Monticello. He was insisting that he never read newspapers or gave any attention to politics. He wrote this fall to Edward Rutledge of South Carolina, that he was "in a retirement I doat on, living like an Antediluvian patriarch among my children & grand children."

Still on his hill he received a copy of Randolph's Vindication from his strong political supporter Congressman William B. Giles, who had served under him in the fight with the Federalists. "I thank you much for the pamphlet," he wrote. "His narrative is so straight and plain, that even those who did not know him will acquit him of the charge of bribery. Those who knew him had done it from the first."

Yet, even when he saw Randolph unjustly humiliated by Federalist enemies, Jefferson, certain of his cousin's honor, sneered at his supposed inconsistency. In the same letter to Giles he wrote: "The fact is that he [Randolph] has generally given his principles to the one party & his practice to the other; the oyster to the one, the shell to the other. Unfortunately the shell was generally the lot of his friends the French and republicans & the oyster to their antagonists. Had he been firm to the principles he professes in the year 1793, the President would have been kept from a habitual concert with the British & Anti-republican party. But at that time I do not know which R. feared most a British fleet, or French disorganizers . . . Where the principle of difference is as substantial and as strongly pronounced as between the republicans & the Monocrats of our country I hold it as honorable to take a firm & decided part, and as immoral to pursue a middle line, as between the parties of Honest men, & Rogues, into which every country is divided."

Randolph was never so quickly able as Jefferson was to draw the line between himself and "the Rogues" whose crime was that they disagreed with him. Perhaps Randolph paid doubly for that. Jefferson damned him as ambitious and inconsistent. And Pickering, when he succeeded to Randolph's old place as Secretary of State, ran up a big account against his predecessor of $49,154.89 for "moneys placed in his hands to defray the expenses of foreign intercourse." At that time the Secretary of State was held responsible for all such moneys including money lost in a captured ship or in a bankrupt bank. Of the funds charged against Randolph, $9,000 was lost in the failure of a bank in Amsterdam. There were other such losses, many of them obviously piled upon his accounts in animus. No adjustments of this malevolent manipulation was made under the following Jefferson-dominated Republican administrations. Indeed, not until 1889 was the "criminal carelessness" of this accounting revealed in a report made to the U. S. Senate. Also, though Conway wrote in 1888, not until 1950 was Randolph's innocence in all particulars proved beyond a vestige of a doubt by Irving Brant, biographer of Madison.

Edmund Randolph did not go back to Virginia repining. Despite the charges against his name and his accounts, his biogra-

pher wrote that his return was a "passing from poverty to wealth."
His wife's health was improved by the move. He offered freedom to his house slaves but at least one of them burned the
papers granting her freedom. In Virginia, while he wrote his
Vindication, he was more than ever opposed to the Jay Treaty
in the fight in the House of Representatives over funds to im-
plement it. And in that he found himself at home in the midst of
a roaring Randolph fight.

John Marshall's biographer wrote that in Virginia Randolph "in
disgrace, was then sweating venom from every pore." Marshall's
defense of Washington and the treaty in the Virginia legislature
drew angry censure from the recluse at Monticello, who was receiving reports from his son-in-law Thomas Mann Randolph,
Jr., also a member of the Assembly. Jefferson wrote: "Though
Marshall will be able to embarras (sic) the republican party in
the assembly a good deal, Yet upon the whole his having gone
into it will be of service. He has been hitherto, able to do more
mischief acting under the mask of Republicanism than he will
be able to do after throwing it plainly off. His lax lounging manners have made him popular with the bulk of the people of
Richmond; & a profound hypocrisy, with many thinking men
of our country. But having gone forth in the plenitude of his
English principles the latter will see that it is high time to make
him known."

Actually Marshall's Federalism had been no secret. Several of
his relatives had been rewarded with administration patronage.
His brother-in-law, Edward Carrington, was Washington's chief
and often too optimistic informer on the political situation. But
if ever masked, Marshall threw it off as the political fight advanced in Virginia. He organized mass meetings for the treaty
and at one spoke eloquently in opposition to Alexander Campbell, who had been his associate in the trial of Richard and
Nancy Randolph. Beveridge wrote that Washington would have
named Marshall to succeed Edmund Randolph as Secretary of
State if he had thought he would accept. Carrington reported
that Charles Lee was aiding Marshall in support of the treaty.
This Lee of Randolph blood was rewarded by appointment as

Attorney General in Washington's now solidly Federalist Cabinet. Strenuously active too in Federalist anti-Jefferson politics was his brother, Light-Horse Harry, already venomous in his anti-Republicanism and hatred of his Monticello cousin.

One Randolph, later to rise like a meteor in American politics, was little concerned in this fight. John Randolph of Bizarre and later "of Roanoke" became of age on June 2, 1794—a year and two months after the trial of his brother and his sister-in-law, and less than a month after Jefferson began his confidential criticism of his cousin Edmund Randolph. At the advice of his brother Richard, John had sold his plantation Matoax and moved permanently to Bizarre. He was often absent, however. In this period he was more devoted to the track than the forum. Apparently, at least upon the surface, all things went on smoothly in the Randolph household though in one diary entry John wrote of "Quarrels of the women." Yet, on July 31, 1795, Jefferson at Monticello wrote to his daughter Martha that Dr. James Currie of Richmond had spoken to him of the "homeless situation of Nancy Randolph." This conflicts with most versions of the story of Nancy's life which have her living continuously at Bizarre during this period despite the shadow of the unforgotten scandal which hung over Richard, Judith, and herself. Jefferson in this letter to Martha added, "I do not know whether she is on such footing with Mr. Randolph and yourself as that her company would be desirable or otherwise to you. If the former, invite her here freely to stay with you. But if disagreeable, do not do it; my object in mentioning it being to place you both at your perfect ease on that subject." Nancy did not come to Monticello.

John Randolph was often gone from Bizarre on rides which would have taxed the strength of ordinary men and ordinary horses. Certainly, in February 1796, he was in Charleston where he visited his friend Henry Rutledge and won a famous horse race with a visiting English nobleman. On this occasion his description seemed approaching that which was regularly given him thereafter. One who saw him in a bookshop remembered him as "a tall, gawky looking flaxen haired stripling, apparently of the age from 16 to 18, with a complexion of a good parchment color, beardless chin, and as much self-consequence as any two-footed animal I ever saw."

From Charleston John went on to Savannah to visit his friend Joseph Bryan. There he found Georgia convulsed with indignation over the Yazoo Fraud, the sale of vast lands of uncertain title by a corrupt legislature to corrupting land speculators. An aroused state and new assembly was repealing the land granting legislation passed by the former session under which parcels had been sold all over the United States and particularly in New England. Almost in a rite of indignation the old laws were burned, with the aid of a magnifying glass, by fire from heaven. John Randolph shared and retained the righteous wrath which he observed.

His trip home was a measure of the endurance of the man— and sadly of his horse, named Jacobin in reflection of the rider's enthusiastic Gallic sentiments at the time. Crossing the "deserts of Carolina" in midwinter, often sleeping on the ground in his bearskin, he reached Bizarre at the end of a galloping trip of 1,800 miles. But Jacobin died at the journey's end, perhaps of the "Carolina distemper" as John wrote his stepfather, more probably of exhaustion.

Riding from track to track, plantation to plantation, town to town, John was in Petersburg in June 1796. He was probably at the home of his brilliant, fated friend, John Thomson, who at twenty was already recognized as a brilliant supporter of Jefferson and opponent of Marshall. Randolph was ill, he wrote, of "bilious fever" which like the "Carolina distemper" of which he said his horse died may have been another name for exhaustion. While he lay ill there, his brother Richard came from Bizarre to see him and left him convalescent, though a relapse soon occurred. This was the last time the brothers saw each other. Richard, John wrote later, "was in the most strange and mysterious manner snatched away from me about a week after he had reached his own house." It was never suggested that Richard may have picked up John's illness at his bedside.

Fortunately and fortuitously many of the circumstances surrounding that mystery were reported by a remarkable witness.

A young artist and architect, Benjamin Latrobe, was wandering much about Virginia at this time. After a successful career in England, his life was thrown into disarray in 1793 by the death of his wife. In Virginia, while he practiced his profession, he was not above such tasks as tuning a harpsichord for one lady and scribbling doggerel for another. In June 1796, he lost his way in a storm and found refuge and hospitality at the household of a sick man and distraught women at Bizarre. The weather he described was as depressing as the situation which he found. Traveling in heavy rains with the woods full of thunder and lightning, he missed directions which had been given him by Colonel Beverley Randolph and found himself in early afternoon at the gate of Richard Randolph's place. He had lost a bundle of his clothes and drawing materials. The gate was too high to jump. His architect's eye found nothing bizarre about the house. The name he learned had been applied properly to an earlier house on the same site.

Writing there, on June 12, 1796, he noted: "My misfortunes have followed me to this house. . . . My philosophy was nearly worn out before, but it quite forsook me now, and I stood at the gate, absent and uncertain what to do, for a quarter of an hour, to the great astonishment of those who observed me from the house, till a heavy shower reminded me of my horse and the neighboring shelter, and I rode on to the house. I soon forgot my personal loss at finding Mr. Randolph very dangerously ill of an inflammatory fever. He induced me, however, to stay, and immediately sent a trusty servant to seek my bundle, who in a couple of hours returned with it, safe but wet. . . . From the moment of my arrival to eight this morning it has thundered, lightened, and rained incessantly. The river, however, remains just within its banks. Mr. Randolph is much worse. His family, however, has shown me every attention and kindness in their power."

Latrobe rode on to Petersburg and there resumed his story: "Mr. Randolph was visited about noon by a medical practitioner in the neighborhood, Dr. Smith. He appeared a man of good sense. His opinion was against the probability of Mr. Randolph's recovery, though masked by a long string of hopes and technical phrases. I dined with the melancholy family of my host, and immediately set off. . . ."

Latrobe suspected nothing sinister in the situation. Fevers, as he noted earlier in his diary, were prevalent in the region. The doctor seemed competent and unsuspicious. Certainly nothing Latrobe observed gave basis to a rumor which later grew into a bitter accusation that a poison or a fatal overdose of medicine may have been given to Richard by a woman's hand. Some did say later sympathetically that Richard's will to live had been reduced by the burden of humiliation he carried despite the acquittal in the case.

One significant thing Latrobe did not mention and historians apparently have taken little note of it since. Possibly it only adds mystery to the story of the man and the two sisters in the house. The fact is, however, that at the time of Latrobe's visit and Richard's death, Judith was either pregnant or had recently borne a child. Genealogists have only recorded that Theodorick Tudor Randolph, always called by his second name, was born in 1796 without giving the day of his birth. In his relatively brief life, he was to show himself precocious or deluded and in either case play a role as child monster in the Randolph story.

Though Latrobe gave no indication of it, the young architect must have been aware of the scandal which hung over the house at Bizarre. Tongues still wagged in Virginia when he traveled in it, listening and observing. He counted other Randolphs, notably Edmund and his wife, among his friends. The fine house with octagonal ends which they built a few years later in Richmond showed, some thought, his influence. Latrobe commented on the extraordinary number of cousin marriages among Randolphs and other Virginia gentry. He saw no danger in them on genetic grounds but from the development of closely organized and selfish cliques. Evidently he was not quite aware of the sharper divisions between intermarried kin which could develop.

On this melancholy visit Latrobe was fascinated with Nancy and made a sketch of her. His biographer, Talbot Hamlin, felt there was a disturbing quality in this picture in which her face is partially concealed by a bonnet with only her classic nose and strongly sculptured profile appearing. Fifteen years later the architect wrote that few circumstances would give him more pleasure than to see her again. At this time Latrobe was not always finding pleasure but sometimes exasperation in his dealings with another Randolph who had brought him into the building of the national capital. Thomas Jefferson was acutely sensitive about disagreements with him in the field of architecture—more even, some believed, than in politics. He could be relentless with any who differed from his design in either field.

1. *William Randolph I of Turkey Island*

2. *Mary Isham Randolph*

3. *Susanna Beverley Randolph, Lady Randolph, wife of Sir John*

4. *Anne Cary (Nancy) Randolph (Mrs. Gouverneur Morris)*

5. *Lucy Randolph Burwell (Mrs. Lewis Burwell)*

6. *Hetty Cary (Widow of General John Pegram)*

7. *Constance Cary (Mrs. Burton Harrison)*

8. *Nancy Witcher Langhorne (Lady Astor)*

PART THREE

Decadence and Destiny

Chapter X

FOAM OF THE PYTHONESS

ORDINARY LANGUAGE did not suffice Virginia historians in describing the acts, good and evil, of the Randolphs. So one wrote of the preamble to the will of Richard Randolph, probated in 1797 in Prince Edward County, as foaming "like the lips of a Pythoness with an abomination of slavery that mounts up almost to a sort of ecstasy." As one reviled in life himself, Richard of Bizarre made his testament an expression of the guilt of Virginians in which, this time, he almost embraced participation.

"To make retribution, as far as I am able," he wrote in contemplation of death, "to an unfortunate race of bondsmen, over whom my ancestors have usurped and exercised the most lawless and monstrous tyranny, and in whom my countrymen (by their iniquitous laws, in contradiction of their own declaration of rights, and in violation of every sacred law of nature . . .) . . . I do hereby declare that it is my will and desire, nay most anxious wish that my negroes, all of them be liberated, and I do declare them by this writing free and emancipated to all intents and purposes whatsoever."

His widow Judith carried out her husband's wishes. Two hundred slaves were freed and established on four hundred acres of land at a nearby place called Israel Hill. Later Virginians, fearful of freed blacks as well as many enslaved ones, said it quickly became "a mere nest for lazzorini." Still consciences were not cleared at Bizarre by the manumission. John Randolph, who became the often absent man of the house there, described it as a place disciplined almost to the point of fanaticism. He wrote that "the house from cellar to garret, and in every part [was] as clean as hands could make it. . . . The chamber pots were as clean and sweet as teacups, being constantly washed and sunned, and the necessary was as clean as the parlor."

Apparently Negroes remained. Fences of sawn plank about the house, John wrote, kept out dirty children, white and Negro. Servants were not allowed beyond the fence at night, "although every one of them was in sound of the lady's bell." Once when he pronounced some lamb brought to the table to be spoiled, Judith indignantly denied such a possibility and ate some to hide her anger at the lapse. As dependent sister Nancy described her role in the rigid household: "I was continually occupied with my needle or other work for the house, obeying to the best of my knowledge, the orders I received, differing from any other servant only in this: I received no wages, but was permitted to sit at table, where I did not presume to enter into conversation or taste of wine, and very seldom of the tea or coffee."

Certainly this was not the general Randolph style of living at the time. Even at Bizarre John was the personification of freedom and indulgence in maintenance of fine horses to carry him where he wished to towns and tracks. Still, while living in greater show of affluence, the more prominent Randolph cousins, Jefferson and Marshall, were not free from financial problems. Both lamented slavery and owned slaves—Jefferson two hundred when he went to become Secretary of State. In the winter before Richard Randolph died, the master of Monticello had freed by indenture James Hemings of the handsome mixed blooded family he had inherited from his wife. But Jefferson and Marshall at this time seemed to differ on the virtue of land holdings.

Soon Jefferson was to express the feeling that "the unprofitable condition of Virginia estates in general leaves it now next to impossible for the holder of one to avoid ruin." Marshall and his brother, evidently less pessimistic, were, with the aid of Robert Morris, acquiring the vast acreage of the remnant of the Fairfax estate. In his ever-building of Monticello, however, Jefferson indicated no will to escape the ruin he predicted. As early as 1789 Marshall had built a fine square brick house in Richmond.

Jefferson planted, built, and collected. On October 13, 1797, he watched with great approval the marriage of his pretty younger daughter Polly to her cousin John Wayles Eppes, whose mother was the half sister of his bride's mother. Much pleased Jefferson wrote: "I now see our fireside formed into a groupe, no one member of which can ever produce any jarring or jealousies among us. No irregular passions, no dangerous bias, which may render problematical the future fortunes & happiness of our descendants." He proposed to give the newly weds the plantation on Pantops, a lower hill close to Monticello.

Marshall's household also seemed serene. He lived well, comfortably caring for his wife, Mary Ambler, who early after her marriage had become "a prey to an extreme nervous affliction which more or less embittered her comfort thro' life." This did not prevent her from bearing ten children. Marshall had money for play. He listed in his accounts the loss of £19 at whist.

The two men seemed very similar in their desire to stay in Virginia and out of public life. Jefferson at this time, however, had some misgivings about this. Of the period of his retirement after he resigned as Secretary of State, he wrote later, "I remained closely at home, saw none but those who came there, and at length became very sensible of the ill effects it had upon my mind, and its direct and irresistible tendency to render me unfit for society, and uneasy when necessarily engaged in it. I felt enough of the effect of withdrawing from the world then, to see that it led to an antisocial and misanthropic state of mind, which severely punishes him who gives into it."

Marshall expressed no such psychological uneasiness. It was because of financial necessity related to his speculation in the Fairfax properties that he felt it necessary to stick to his lucrative law practice and repeatedly to decline the importunities of Washington that he enter public service in Philadelphia. In August 1795, he excused himself when Washington urged him to become Secretary of State but despaired of his acceptance. In July 1796, shortly after the death of Richard Randolph, he politely said "no" to the President's proposal that he become Minister to France.

To some Jefferson did not seem so reluctant, as he said he

was, about participation in public affairs. He welcomed political visitors to Monticello. Even some of his neighbors regarded his high house as "the very headquarters of Jacobinism." Reports of his activities, apparently to Washington by Light-Horse Harry Lee, among others, brought from him a letter of protest late in 1795. Jefferson wrote the soon-to-retire President denying statements that he was "still engaged in the battle of politics and in turbulence and intrigue against the government." Anybody who said that was "a miserable tergiversator."

Yet, he had already written, on April 24, 1796, a letter which became famous or infamous (when it was published in January 1797) to his old Italian friend Mazzei. In it Jefferson wrote of apostates "who were Sampsons in the field & Solomons in the council, but who have had their heads shorn by the harlot England." Federalists loudly insisted that among others he was specifically referring to Washington. Jefferson declined to get into the newspaper row about it. He had then already been elected Vice-President of the United States. Washington at Mount Vernon declined then to believe that Jefferson could or would mean to assail him. But as other incidents piled up, some of them trivial seeming, Washington's faith in Jefferson's friendship was finally broken.

Jefferson had seemed in no antisocial and misanthropic state before he left to take his oath as second official of the republic. Neither did he seem to be disturbed by his debts. Early in 1796, he had begun the demolition of Monticello for its almost endless remodeling. Sometimes he felt it necessary to warn his visitors about this. One such was Constantin François Chasseboeuf, Comte de Volney, French Revolutionary philosopher. Jefferson was not troubled by Federalist suspicions that he was a French secret agent. He welcomed Volney as fellow intellectual though he warned him as he came that "the noise, confusion and discomfort of the scene will require all philosophy and patience." Volney was equal to it and stayed three weeks in June.

Better remembered in the Monticello story is the visit in the same month of François Alexandre Frédéric, Duc de La Rochefoucauld-Liancourt. He not only wrote that the remodeled

house when finished would "certainly deserve to be ranked with
the most pleasant mansions in France and England." Also he
described the farming methods and techniques of the master of
Monticello. Although he found Jefferson in the heat of the Virginia summer in the harvest fields, he concluded that his host
was "little accustomed to agricultural pursuits" and "has drawn
the principles of culture either from works which treat on the
subject or from conversation."

Before Rochefoucauld came to Monticello he had visited David
Meade Randolph's place at Presqu'ile on the James. It was, as
Jefferson had warned his daughters who visited there, an unhealthy place. When the Frenchman visited it "young and amiable" Molly Randolph had "not enjoyed one month of good
health since she first came to live on this plantation." Still, with
only 350 acres of his 750 under cultivation, Randolph was making $3,500 a year. The visitor found him "fully entitled to the
reputation he enjoys of being the best farmer in the whole country." Yet wishing to leave on account of the climate, Randolph
was not able to get the $20,000 which he thought the place was
worth. "This fact," Rochefoucauld wrote, "furnished a proper
idea of the low price of land in Virginia." At about $25 an acre,
however, the Presqu'ile lands, as the Frenchman reported, were
five times the acre value he found to prevail in Albemarle.

Rochefoucauld saw other Randolphs. He wrote that Thomas
Mann Randolph, Jr., seemed more Jefferson's son than his son-
in-law. Though financially unsuccessful, Thomas Mann claimed
to be the originator of the practice of transverse rather than
horizontal plowing on hillsides to reduce erosion in the red slopes
of Albemarle. Like other planters Thomas Mann was showing
interest in politics as well as plowing at the time. In both he
seemed plodding by his cousin John of Bizarre who was much
away from the field at the breeding paddocks and race tracks of
Virginia. As John rode vigorously about he was enthusiastically
showing strong pro-French feelings. He called himself Citizen
Randolph and so addressed his Republican friends. With Jefferson he had little patience with the pro-British Federalism of their
cousin Marshall. That tall attorney, though he had inherited

lands in Fauquier County from his father, showed more interest in buying land than farming it. But he was in landed trouble now.

So in 1797, as one of his biographer's put it, Marshall was "finally induced to accept appointment" by President John Adams as one of three emissaries sent to deal with threatening Republican France. Actually, at this time Marshall needed the post and the emoluments it promised. His great backer, Robert Morris, beleaguered by his creditors was now hiding from them in the country near Philadelphia. Morris was now referring to the great residence he had started in Philadelphia as "that unfortunate building on Chestnut Street." Soon he would be in "Prune Street," the debtors prison. As a result Marshall was in danger of losing his Fairfax lands.

So with his fellow commissioners, Charles C. Pinckney and Elbridge Gerry, Marshall departed for France. There where suspicions of American friendship had been stiffened by the Jay Treaty, they found no welcome. In the spring of 1798, indeed, the XYZ story—that French agents had demanded bribes from the commissioners for peace—was learned in Philadelphia. This country was in an uproar at the insult. The phrase, "Millions for defense but not one cent for tribute," rose from the mouths of orators across the land. Supporters fell away from Jefferson's pro-French Republican party. Its members, even including Vice-President Jefferson, were damned as menaces to national safety. And Marshall returned the hero of the hour.

As important to the returning envoy, he was the beneficiary of what Jefferson called "the greatest God-send that could ever have befallen a man." Pickering, who was delighted with the anti-French and anti-Republican furore Marshall had created, promptly arranged to pay what was due him. The total amount he received for his eleven months' absence upon the French mission was, Beveridge wrote, $19,963.97. This, allowing $5,000 for his expenses ("a generous estimate," his biographer said) was considerably more than three times as much as Marshall's annual income from his law practice. It was a huge sum, considering the pay of public officials at that period—"not much less than the annual salaries of the President and his entire Cabinet; more than the total amount annually paid the justices of the Supreme Court. Thus, for the time being, the Fairfax estate was saved."

Jefferson's political losses, Marshall's biographer thought, were greater than Marshall's financial gains in the XYZ explosion. The Vice-President saw his party going to pieces and his prospects of pushing Adams from the Presidential chair in 1800 "jeopardized if not made hopeless." All this he laid to Marshall and "from the moment of his fellow Virginian's arrival from France, this captain of the popular cause began that open and malignant warfare upon Marshall which ended only with Jefferson's last breath." Other historians could not be certain who began and who continued the warfare.

Fortunately for Jefferson the self-righteous zeal of the Federalists exceeded their wisdom. In the anti-French war frenzy of the time, the Federalist Congress with Adams's approval, in June and July 1798, passed the Alien and Sedition Laws. The Alien Act gave the President the power to seize and deport any aliens he thought dangerous. The Sedition Act was intended and interpreted to provide criminal actions against practically all critics of the government and its officials. As enforced even ridicule became treason.

The Republicans now had an issue under which they could reassemble their forces. Across the nation rang the phrases "liberty of the press," "freedom of speech," "trial by jury." And in the Randolph background of Virginia in the late summer protest meetings were held in a number of counties including Albemarle. Then in secrecy Jefferson and Madison framed the Virginia and Kentucky resolutions. As finally passed, Madison's Virginia Resolution emerged as a rather mild protest. The tougher Kentucky Resolution which Jefferson drafted was softened also from his original language that such arrogation of powers by the Federal government would, "unless arrested at the threshold, necessarily drive these states into revolution and blood."

Certainly this language carried a threat of possible secession as well as a warning of tyranny. Long afterwards President Adams's grandson, the historian Henry Adams, in his tartly prejudiced life of John Randolph of Roanoke, undertook to prove that Jefferson's Virginia was preparing, if necessary to support its protests, to destoy the union. He wrote that Jefferson and Madison not only induced Virginia and Kentucky to attack the Alien and Sedition Laws but "were privy to the preparations making in Virginia for armed resistance; or if they were not, it was because they chose to be ignorant."

Henry Adams quoted later statements by John Randolph, who was certainly ardent in opposition to these laws to support this secession report. In a speech in Congress in 1817 the then gaunt John of Roanoke said: "There is no longer any cause for concealing the fact that the grand armory at Richmond was built to enable the State of Virginia to resist by force the encroachments of the then administration upon her inalienable rights." Adams also quoted John as saying: "I was asked if I justified the establishment of the armory for the purpose of opposing Mr. Adams's administration. I said I did; that I could not conceive any case in which the people could not be entrusted with arms; and that the use of them to oppose oppressive measures was in principle the same, whether those of the administration of Lord North or that of Mr. Adams."

Other reasons existed for the building of the armory. Virginians not only regarded settlements of freed Negroes as possible nests of lazzaroni. They were aware of black mutterings even in the towns. Even Jefferson expressed fears. Early in 1799, while the Alien and Sedition controversy raged, he expressed some to Madison. A bill had been introduced in the Federalist Congress which was ready to make any move against France. It proposed the recognition of Toussaint L'Ouverture and support for Haitian independence from France. Under the bill the President was authorized to admit Haitian blacks to free commerce with American ports. Jefferson wrote in alarm: "We may expect therefore black crews & supercargoes & missionaries thence into the southern states; & when the leven begins to work, I would gladly compound with a great part of our northern country, if it would honestly stand neuter. If this combustion can be introduced among us under any veil whatever, we have to fear it."

Whatever may have been his fears about black "combustion"

at home, he had extreme views as to what might happen to white liberties under the repressive Federalist laws. He wrote about this to Stevens Thomson Mason, U. S. Senator from Virginia. In his letter he said: "For my own part, I consider those laws as merely an experiment on the American mind, to see how far it will bear an avowed violation of the constitution. If this goes down we shall immediately see attempted another act of Congress, declaring that the President shall continue in office during life, reserving to another occasion the transfer of the succession to his heirs, and the establishment of the Senate for life."

Others felt as strongly the danger and threat of a wild democracy. Washington who now distrusted Jefferson distrusted the people he led. So he pressed Marshall to run for Congress. Both Washington and Adams believed that the Jeffersonian opposition to the Alien and Sedition Laws was not defense of the liberties of the press and the people but a political readiness to invite chaos, weaken the nation in the face of foreign danger and even to destroy the nation by secession. Indeed, Marshall's devoted biographer wrote as a fact that "the philosophy of secession" was implanted in Jefferson's mind.

However much the issues were exaggerated on both sides, the race for the Virginia seats in the Sixth Congress has been described by historians as the most stirring in the history of the state. Perhaps it brought first into open conflict the two men who made one of the greatest antagonisms in history. Jefferson, of course, was no candidate in the Congressional elections but neither was he sitting idle in the Vice-Presidential chair or in a then famous revolving chair which he had invented at Monticello.

Marshall entered the race in the district containing Richmond against John Clopton, an ardent Jeffersonian, who had served two previous terms in the House of Representatives. So rough was the going in the aroused state that Marshall, to the chagrin of some Federalists elsewhere, disavowed the Alien and Sedition Laws, declaring that had he been in Congress he "certainly would have opposed them." Even so, he barely squeaked through to election with the aid of an endorsement by Jefferson's bête noire, aging Patrick Henry. Marshall won by 108 votes. He only served part of his term, going on to higher public offices, and in the next Congress Clopton came back to remain until his death in 1816.

One other Federalist of Randolph blood was chosen in this election—Light-Horse Harry Lee, who would hold his seat only for a single term. But so far as Congressional service was concerned the greatest new figure who would appear in the Sixth Congress was John Randolph, still of Bizarre. Historians have preserved the impression that this dramatic Randolph appeared, as Bruce wrote, "simply as a restless young devotee of the stubble-field and the race track." The candidate himself, still months short of the age of twenty-five required of members of Congress, admitted his inexperience, particularly under the circumstances of his debut. He told his friend Francis Scott Key, "The first time I ever dreamed of speaking in public was on the eve of my election in March 1799, when I opposed myself (fearful odds) to Patrick Henry." They were fearful odds even though the great old orator had only three more months to live. The old man and the young one met at Charlotte Court House before a large crowd of candidates and voters. Many gathered to hear the great old forensic actor. Much mythology has gathered about the occasion of this swan song of Henry and the first speech of Randolph. They were not opposing candidates. Henry, to defend the Federalists also at the behest of Washington, was running for the Virginia Senate.

Randolph had two opponents. The Federalists had put up Colonel Clement Carrington, against whom as a neighbor the Randolphs maintained an intermittent grudge across at least two generations, involving land, roads, and straying dogs. Also another Republican was opposing Randolph. The description of this opponent's appearance matches the show of arrogance Randolph himself often seemed to make. H. A. Garland, in his life of Randolph, described this gentleman, Powhatan Bolling, a relation of Randolph's, as appearing in the courthouse crowd "dressed in his scarlet coat—tall, proud in his bearing, and a fair representative of the old aristocracy, fast melting away under the sub-divisions of the law that had abolished the system of primogeniture." He bristled under the bantering of Randolph's friends. Randolph himself seemed so boyish that the story is told that when later he presented his credentials as Representative, Speaker Theodore Sedgwick, fierce Connecticut Federalist, asked him whether he was old enough to be eligible.

"Go ask my constituents," was the reported Randolph retort.

The certain fact is that Randolph did not run impetuously for Congress. His sponsor was Creed Taylor, of "Needham" in Cumberland County, close to the Bizarre plantation. Taylor was rather unpleasantly described by Bruce on the occasion of the meeting of Henry and Randolph as "such a bigoted Democrat that he did not scruple, during the delivery of Henry's speech, to keep up . . . a strain of caustic comment on it, even to declare that the old man was in his dotage." Taylor was, however, a man of education and prominence later unanimously deemed worthy by the Virginia Assembly to succeed George Wythe as Chancellor.

Of Randolph, Taylor said as the speaking proceeded, "He can take care of himself."

Evidently he had been chosen as the Jeffersonian candidate with care, probably with Jefferson's participation. Certainly soon after Randolph took his seat in Congress Jefferson wrote his daughter Polly Eppes as if both knew the young man well.

"J. Randolph," he wrote, "has entered into debate with great splendor and approbation. He used an unguarded word in his first speech, applying the word raggamuffin to the common souldiery (sic). He took it back of his own accord and very handsomely the next day, when he had occasion to reply. Still in the evening of the 2d. day he was jostled and his coat pulled at the theatre by two officers of the Navy who repeated the word raggamuffin. His friends present supported him spiritedly so that nothing further followed. Conceiving, and, as I think justly, that the H. of Representatives (not having passed a law on the subject) could not punish the offenders, he wrote a letter to the President, who laid it before the house, where it is still depending. He has conducted himself with great propriety, and I have no doubt will come out with increase of reputation. . . ."

Not all agreed with Jefferson. Randolph had spoken in a debate over a proposal to cut the size of the military establishment which the Federalists had built as a part of preparations against France. During the debate it was reported that some resentful military officers wanted their fellows to call him repeatedly to the dueling field until he was killed. Federalists charged him with impertinence in addressing the President about the matter. The episode was important only as it indicated the extent to which the inter-party abrasions had gone. Bruce reported that Randolph emerged from the incident "as buoyant and unharmed as a cork from the splash of a waterfall." Certainly he emerged advanced in Jefferson's approval.

One position which John took in his first days as Representative appeared to put him in a position with regard to slavery in striking contrast to the passionate declarations about the wickedness of that system which his brother Richard had made in his will. Some free men of color, backed by Philadelphia Quakers, brought a petition to Congress asking among other things for "the adoption of such measures as shall in due course emancipate the whole of their brethren from their present situation." Randolph hoped that the House would so act as to deter anyone from ever afterwards bringing any such petitions. Under the Constitution the House had no power to act and this, he said, should be the last occasion when the interest and feelings of the Southern states should be subjected to such petitioning.

This occasion may have served as a basis for another of the taunts Nancy Randolph in fury later directed at him. She wrote: "There are many who remember, while your slaves were under mortgage for the British debt, your philanthropic assertion that you would make them free and provide tutors for them. With this project you wearied all who would listen. When, by the sale of some of them, a part of the debt was discharged, and an agreement made to pay the rest by installments you changed your mind. This was not inexcusable, but when you set up for representation in Congress, and the plan to liberate your slaves was objected to in your District, you published to the astonishment of numbers, who had heard you descant on your liberal intentions that you *never* had any such idea. Thus your first step in public life was marked by falsehood."

Bruce, in noting Nancy Randolph's taunt, wrote that while it was true that Randolph did not often give public expression to his disapproval of slavery, his life was marked by "aversion to the institution of negro slavery. The slave traffic he simply abhorred; and there is little room for doubt that, if he could have freed all the negro slaves of Virginia under proper conditions he would have freed them." He was, however, eternally opposed to Federal interference with slavery which he regarded as a state matter or a state's right.

One great Virginian was absent at the beginning of this session of Congress which began on December 2, 1799. Vice-President Jefferson only left Monticello on December 21. Already in Virginia he must have heard of the death of Washington since report of it reached Philadelphia three days before. Malone thought that, if he had wished, he would have had time to reach Philadelphia in time for the official mourning ceremonies: "But in view of all that had been said in recent years about his relations with his old chief, this exceedingly sensitive man may have concluded that he would find these ceremonies embarrassing. If he had been there, some Federalist spokesman would almost certainly have described him as a hypocrite, and no doubt he was glad of a good excuse to be away."

He was traveling on "a pleasant journey of fine weather and good roads" when two of his Federalist kinsmen in Philadelphia took the most prominent part in those mournful ceremonies. Marshall officially notified the House of Washington's death, says the *Annals of Congress*, "in a voice that bespoke the anguish of his mind, and a countenance expressive of deepest regret." The next day Marshall addressed the House in eulogy and offered resolutions of national grief. Only later was it known that the singing phrases in the resolution of mourning were written by Marshall's cousin and colleague Light-Horse Harry

Lee. Those words, "first in war, first in peace, and first in the hearts of his countrymen," marked the apogee of Harry's life.

Jefferson made no public statement about the great man's death. He did not mention the event in his letters home. Even in private he was reticent about it. He had, however, earlier predicted that the "resuscitation" of the "Republican spirit" would be hastened when the great name of Washington could no longer be used as a banner by anti-Republicans. Certainly the Republicans were determined to be "resuscitated."

On January 11, 1800, less than a month after the death of Washington, a meeting of over a hundred Virginia Republicans was held in Richmond to promote Jefferson's election to the Presidency in the approaching elections. That victory was practically assured in April when Republicans in New York, led by Aaron Burr, routing Hamilton made certain that the state's Presidential electoral votes would be cast for the Republicans. Federalist chagrin was compounded within their own party when Adams boldly, without consulting his Cabinet which was more loyal to Hamilton than to him, sent a new Minister to seek peace with France. Federalists were furious but Marshall, who might have taken the new overtures to France as a repudiation of his own mission there, stood by the President. Hamilton made divisions among Federalists complete when he circulated a letter sharply critical of the President. Adams suddenly dismissed Hamilton's stooges, Pickering and McHenry. Reluctantly Marshall accepted the vacated post of Secretary of State in June 1800.

That was a dark summer for Federalists—and for Virginians, too. While white men still argued over liberties, in Virginia black revolt was brewing. On August 30, 1800, two slaves told their master a fantastic story. That night more than a thousand Negroes were to assemble at the head of Old Brook Swamp and march the six miles to Richmond. They planned to seize the arms there, kill all who resisted "except the French inhabitants." Then they would crown their leader, a free Richmond Negro named Gabriel Prosser, "King of Virginia." One odd item reported that Gabriel "declared that he would save Mrs. David

Meade Randolph and make her his Queen because she knew so much about cooking."

Some Virginians thought God intervened. Instead of an uprising, "the most furious tempest known in Virginia burst upon the land that day." The turmoil which followed in Richmond was like a tempest, too. Hundreds of slaves were rounded up. Jefferson's then journalistic protégé, James Thomson Callender, in jail under sentence by Judge Samuel Chase under the Sedition Act, wrote Jefferson from the Richmond jail about the racial furies and fears. He composed his letter, he said, while listening to "the bellowing of the Bandetti downstairs." The leaders were captured, Gabriel going to the gallows defying all interrogation. At last the hangings were ended, a contemporary writer said, "owing to the immense number who are interested in the plot, whose death . . . will nearly produce the annihilation of the blacks in this part of the country." Virginia did not soon lower its guard. It was armed and ready for any defense its safety and rights might require.

The autumn came on, its leaves as bright as the confident elation of the Republicans but containing winds as cold as Federalist fears. Then suddenly, at one of the most crucial points in American history, Marshall was in a position of unique power as the one man trusted by all the Federalist factions from Adams to Hamilton. The fortunes of politics placed him where he might make a vital decision as to the Presidency. In the national victory, in those days when separate votes were not cast for President and Vice-President, Jefferson and Burr were tied with 73 votes each. The Federalist House of Representatives, voting by states, had the authority under the Constitution to resolve the tie. Some Federalists even suggested that, the election having been thrown into the Federalist-controlled House, that body might reject both Republican candidates and put a Federalist into power until the next election.

The circulation of a report that Marshall said that this could be done—and seemed to suggest even that the man chosen might be himself—stirred the threat of civil war. False as this report might have been, Virginians were certainly now ready to march in arms. They made no mystery about Virginia's arming then as in the days of the Alien and Sedition Laws. In the new capital at Washington, Jefferson wrote of the "great dismay and gloom of Republican gentlemen here and equal exultation on the Federalists who openly declare they will prevent an election." This, he wrote, "opens upon us an abyss at which every sincere patriot must shudder."

Despite the fact that Federalist papers sneered that the Virginia militia was armed only with cornstalks, Jefferson believed that the threat of arms made the Federalists draw back from the choice of any one of their own. Instead they turned against the hated Jefferson to the inscrutable Burr.

Everything in Burr's background as soldier, statesman, politician made him seem to the Federalists preferable to Jefferson. The Virginian had not only seemed to damn Washington in his Mazzei letter. He had described all Federalists as "an Anglican, monarchial & aristocratical party." He spoke of them as "timid men who prefer the calm of despotism to the boisterous sea of liberty." In resentment they cast their votes at the beginning of a prolonged deadlock; eight states for Jefferson, four for Burr—nine states necessary to election. Though Jeffersonians afterwards accused him of connivance, Burr early and publicly declined the role which he said would be that of a "usurper."

The possibility of Burr as President threw Alexander Hamilton into a panic. He hated and opposed Jefferson. But Burr was his enemy in his own bailiwick whose exposure of Hamilton's improper political movements even against Adams had destroyed much of the Federalist New Yorker's influence in his own party in his own state and in the nation as well. It is doubtful that he could or did change a Federalist vote in this impasse. But he knew that Marshall might. So he turned to the Secretary of State.

Marshall was not moved by Hamilton's appeal. If what Hamilton said of Burr were true, he wrote, his election might be a "greater danger than even from Mr. Jefferson may be apprehended." But Marshall evidently did not believe that any such possible great danger justified the choice of Jefferson as an alternative.

"To Mr. Jefferson," he wrote Hamilton, "whose political character is better known than that of Mr. Burr, I have felt almost insuperable objections. His foreign prejudices seem to me totally to unfit him for the chief magistracy of a nation which cannot indulge those prejudices without sustaining deep and permanent injury.

"In addition to this solid and immovable objection, Mr. Jefferson appears to me to be a man, who will embody himself with the House of Representatives. By weakening the office of President, he will increase his personal power. He will diminish his responsibility, sap the fundamental principles of the government, and become the leader of that party which is about to constitute the majority of the legislature. The morals of the author of the letter to Mazzei cannot be pure. . . ."

Beveridge thought that Marshall would have preferred the election of Burr to that of his Virginia cousin, but believed he did not turn his hand to break the tie. To have done so might have proved a suspicion that he hoped to continue as Secretary of State under the New Yorker. Instead, he stood aloof. Federalists insisted they permitted the election of Jefferson only when they secured assurances satisfactory to themselves from him with regard to neutrality, the finances, the Navy, and job tenure. Jefferson endlessly denied this but he was deeply embarrassed about it to the end of his days. Evidently if a deal was not made some such agreement was reached.

Marshall was certainly prepared to minimize if possible the Jeffersonian danger. No Republican was a member of the national judiciary. Plans were made to keep things this way. Marshall wrote President Adams's message to the lame-duck Federalist Congress on December 3, 1800, when the Republican executive and legislative triumph was already apparent. In it he strongly urged the "extension" of the national judiciary. Soon thereafter legislation to that effect was introduced. After the next vacancy upon the Supreme Court it was to be reduced to five members. This would prevent the appointment of a

Republican to the high court. But many new judgeships were created. There was nothing secret about the Federalist purpose to hold the fort of the judiciary in the American government. But Republicans even charged that items in the bill would reduce the threat to Marshall and his associates of claims against the precious Fairfax estate. Beveridge noted that in the "Annals, 6th Cong., 1st Sess., page 897" an insinuation which nobody made on the floor was added in a "curious entry.": "[It is understood that the present assignees of the claims of Lord Fairfax, are General Marshall, General Lee, and a third individual and that they maintain their claims under the British Treaty.]" Insinuations were commonplace in the politics of both parties in the period.

In the midst of rumors and insinuations, suddenly the fact was that Marshall was nominated by Adams as Chief Justice of the United States on January 20, 1801. He was promptly confirmed by the Federalist Senate. As chief of the judiciary he was influential in naming other judges appointed under the bill. And that process went on into the night before Jefferson's inauguration, with the Federalist Senate staying in session to confirm them. Democrats called the appointees "midnight judges." A legend grew that Marshall only stopped signing and sealing commissions when Jefferson sent a messenger to say that by his watch March 4th had come.

Next morning Marshall proffered the Bible and Jefferson swore the oath. In the crowded, half-circle Senate chamber with its arched ceiling, other Randolphs listened as Jefferson delivered his inaugural address in an almost inaudible voice. Probably among them were John Randolph, Harry Lee, Lee's brother Charles, retiring Attorney General who had been one of the "midnight judges" named. Possibly present was David Meade Randolph who was anxious to know whether he would keep his place as marshal under the new administration. They heard the new President's almost whispered words, "We are all Republicans, we are all Federalists."

Some men in the packed chamber heard that sentence in surprise. Some reacted sardonically to it. Some of the victorious

Republicans, eager for the spoils, heard the balanced statement with vague feelings of dismay, remembering rumors of a Presidential deal.

Much was uncertain at the beginning of what Jefferson liked to consider a "Second American Revolution." Certainly, however, there was no uncertainty about the Randolph place in history then, though in division. With the President and the Chief Justice in the room and in power, John Randolph would soon, at less than thirty, become the Republican leader of the House of Representatives and the President's sharpest blade there. The trio was tangible and unique as the nation moved forward in the new century already filled with promise and anger, the love of liberty and the fear of anarchy. In one thing the three Randolphs were agreed. None of them shared any sense of fault. Each was sure he offered what the republic required. Despite contemporary ideas even the good, dead Richard Randolph, when he left his will damning slavery, was absolutely sure that he was right. That characteristic seemed central in the Randolph genetics. It was never to be more apparent than now.

Chapter XI

SHARK AND TIGER

FOUR DAYS after his inauguration Jefferson completed his plans to fire David Meade Randolph as U. S. Marshal in Virginia. Soon thereafter, in not entirely pleasant ablutions, he washed his hands of the journalist James Thomson Callender, whose hatchet work on the personalities of Federalist leaders he had approved and paid for before. Whatever, if any, agreement about office holders he may have made with Federalists before his election in the House, it was apparent that he meant to raze the fortifications Marshall had put around Federalist control of the judiciary.

The President's Federalist cousins had much to lose. Under the Marshall-Adams program for the perpetuation of a wholly Federalist judiciary, John Marshall's brother James had been named assistant judge of the Territory (District) of Columbia. John's brother-in-law, George Keith Taylor, had been made U. S. Judge for the Fourth District. Another Marshall brother, William, had received the post of clerk of the U. S. Court at Richmond. Finally, Joseph Hamilton Daveiss, who had adopted his middle name from love of the great Federalist leader Alexander Hamilton, was U. S. Attorney for the District of Kentucky. And Daveiss was then courting Marshall's sister Ann. Even so, he was to seem prehensile in his Kentucky post to Jeffersonians.

Also apprehensive and resentful were Randolph cousins and collaborators the Lee brothers of Leesylvania, on the Potomac. Richard Bland Lee had years before seemed to serve Jefferson in his bargain with Hamilton as to Federal debt assumption and the site of the national capital. Actually his leanings were already Federalistic then. Light-Horse Harry Lee, out of Congress after a single term, seemed to hate Jefferson more as his own financial problems increased. He was, wrote Jefferson biographer Merrill D. Peterson, stirring up the old Walker affair "out of malice" toward Jefferson. He was not, however, as Peterson said, "a political turncoat." His Federalism was as long-fixed as it was ferocious. Charles Lee, Marshall's close friend, was aware that Jefferson would try to pull from under him the bench upon which he had been placed in the last-minute maneuvers of Marshall and President Adams.

So, on December 21, 1801, Charles Lee, who had been Attorney General under Adams, initiated the case of Marbury vs Madison. He asked the Supreme Court for a mandamus to the Secretary of State requiring him to deliver commissions to William Marbury and other "midnight appointees" to the office of Justice of the Peace in the District of Columbia. Though signed and sealed the commissions had not been delivered in the last-minute rush of the Adams administration.

Anyone who stood in the shadow of a Randolph was apt to be rendered invisible. That has certainly been the fate of William Marbury. Legal scholars have written thousands of words about this case but most of them have not even given Marbury a first name. Clearly the assumption has been that this really was the case of Lee vs Jefferson brought before Marshall.

Marbury was no nonentity. Shortly before the "revolution of 1800," as Jefferson liked to call his election, Marbury had purchased the house of "massive dignity" on M Street in Georgetown, which General Uriah Forrest, friend of Washington, had built thirteen years before. He was not only rich enough to buy the big Forrest house. Also the regretful report of architectural historians is that he had money enough to add a third story, a heavy overhanging cornice and probably a wing to the house. Federalists were fearful that Jefferson might make equally unfortunate changes in the structure of the republic.

Certainly to Federalists the President seemed to be doing

that when, with John Randolph in brusque command, the Judiciary Act, passed in the closing days of the Adams administration, was repealed. In this Randolph cousin at least the President had then an ardent and powerful supporter. Always he seemed both booted and spurred for mastery. His entrances into the House were dramatic. Wearing a blue riding coat and buckskin breeches, he was accompanied by the jingle of silver spurs and the padded footsteps of a slinking hound which he often brought to the floor. He strode down the aisle with a whip in his hand. And his voice became a whip which stung when he spoke against "the pretension of rendering the judiciary an hospital for decayed politicians."

Equally vigorous Federalist language had been spoken in opposition to the repeal. But Congress in the repealing act prohibited any immediate judicial expressions as to the constitutionality of the new act by postponing in this legislation the next term of the Supreme Court until February 1803. That meant no interim of anti-Jefferson pronouncements, particularly in Virginia.

Old ties had been torn there. Tempestuous Gabriel Jones was a good example of that. He had been a first client of young Jefferson in 1767. His daughter married John Harvie, the younger, whose father had been one of Jefferson's guardians. Old Gabriel's granddaughter, Gabriella, as the second and some said unhappy wife of Thomas Mann Randolph, Sr., had added children to the Randolph clan. But now in his seventies, old Jones, who had sponsored Washington's entrance into public life as a Burgess, attacked the new President. One of Jefferson's friends, signing himself as "Veritas," replied in what a biographer of Jones described as a "vicious attack on the character and practices of Jones." The old man came back in one of the sharpest of the caustic political pamphlets of the angry time. His biographer called it "a gem." It must not have seemed so to Jefferson. This exchange pointed an old charge that Jefferson had acted with less than generosity in settling a debt with his first client. Malone wrote that this debt was "unquestionably discharged."

As Jones's blast indicated, however, other Virginians felt that they had debts to settle and were determined to pay Jefferson what they thought was his due. Among the most bitter though most forgotten of Jefferson's family enemies were David Meade and Mary (Molly) Randolph, who brought together the lines of the first Thomas of Tuckahoe and the original Richard Randolph of Curles. David had first attracted attention as a young student at William and Mary early in the Revolution. He led in a proposal for a ball celebrating Washington's "birth-night." Governor Patrick Henry damned the idea. David quoted him in his diary: "He could not think of any kind of rejoicing when our country was engaged in war, with such gloomy prospects." Others of the elders also opposed the plan. The ball, nevertheless, was held at the Raleigh Tavern. Then almost from the sound of its music David and his brother William rode off to join Theodorick Bland's Dragoons. David was probably still in uniform, sharing the plaudits due heroes, when he came back to Tuckahoe to marry pretty Molly about 1782.

He kept his bearing as a soldier. In 1791, when Washington passed on his Southern Tour, David commanded a cavalry escort which turned out in the President's honor. Washington appreciated the courtesy but did not care for the clouds of dust the horses kicked up around his carriage on the Virginia roads. David was already then about to serve under Washington, this time as a civilian. Jefferson, though apparently with some show of reluctance, put his cousin's name forward for appointment as marshal. In March 1790, immediately after his arrival in New York as Secretary of State, he wrote: "I have recommended Mr. D[avid] R[andolph] to the President for the office he desired. . . ." Three weeks later he reported that he had spoken again to the President "on the subject of Mr. D. Randolph, and I believe you may assure Mr. Randolph that he will probably have the appointment." Washington, however, first gave the position to John Marshall's brother-in-law, Edward Carrington. David did not get it until more than a year later when Carrington was promoted to the position of Virginia Collector of Internal Revenue. The President reappointed him, however, to a four-year term in December 1795. And John Adams, looking out for good Federalists, in December 1799 gave him another four-year term. That would have made him secure in office until 1803 if Jefferson had not intervened with dismissal.

If Jefferson was hesitant about pushing David for the job in 1790, certainly the relations between Monticello and Presqu'ile seemed warm at this period. Young Mary (Polly) Jefferson was visiting David and Molly at their plantation early in this summer. David visited Monticello as autumn approached. As he served he seemed entitled to respect. When Rochefoucauld saw him in 1796 he was as marshal, planter, and man of business clearly an advancing Randolph.

The efficiency with which he handled his few slaves and the ingenuity with which he added to his income by catching and salting sturgeon, shad, and herring from the James indicated drive toward wealth. His connections were excellent. His brother William, with whom he rode off to war, had married his cousin Maria Beverley of the great house of Blandfield. David himself was connected in an inventive and advisory capacity with the Blackheth coal mining operations near Richmond in which, along with Harry Heth, his cousin Beverley Randolph was a partner. It provided other labor than tobacco for Virginia's ever-growing slave population. David later made a proposal that low-grade coal be turned into coke, a suggestion which a Virginia historian thought indicated that he was "a number of years ahead of his times." Another student of the economic life of the state listed him as one of the "considerable inventors: in Virginia prior to 1825." Indeed, he must be set down as one of the greatest inventors Virginia ever produced. An authoritative article on shoes in the classic 1911 edition of the Encyclopaedia Britannica stated: "In 1809 David Meade Randolph obtained a patent for fastening the soles and heels to the inner soles by means of little nails, brads, sprigs or tacks. . . . This invention may be said to have laid the foundation of machine boot-making."

Evidently isolation at malarial Presqu'ile did not satisfy David and Molly. About 1798 they built a "very commodious, finely situated, two-story Brick Dwelling House at the corner of Fifth and Main Streets" in Richmond. Edmund Wilcox Rootes, a Richmond wit who had "a propensity for . . . conferring names," called the house of Molly and David "Moldavia," and on the basis of their hospitality in it dubbed Molly "the Queen." It was constructed in "a square of four lots" on the south side of Main Street, with offices attached.

Something of their prestige and cultural interests was indicated this year. Newport, Rhode Island, then was a resort much frequented by rich and aristocratic Southerners. (A few years later John C. Calhoun of South Carolina met his Low Country heiress wife, Floride Bonneau Calhoun, there.) What the Randolphs found was a tutor for their children whose later eminence testified to their good judgment. William Ellery Channing, afterwards famous as a Unitarian minister and social reformer, was employed by them to come South in the fall of 1798 to teach their children.

Though a very solemn and sententious young man, Channing, who had graduated first in his class at Harvard, left an illuminating picture of the Randolph household. In the stiffening political divisions in Virginia it had become a center of Federalist society. He admired the Virginians he met through the Randolphs as a courageous and articulate people with many virtues offset only by "their sensuality and their slaves." He was troubled, too, by avowals of infidelity which he said he heard from intelligent men. But he felt deeply "the charm of the cordial and elegant courtesy" which everywhere greeted him. Particularly, among the many who came to the hospitable house, he was impressed by John Marshall.

And obviously he heard few kind words for David Randolph's one-time sponsor Jefferson. He wrote home: "I am happy to hear that the same odium is everywhere attached to the name of Jacobin. This is the case even in Democratic Virginia. A *Jacobin* is synonymous with a dishonest, immoral, factious, and disorganizing man." While in the Randolph house Channing had been worried for fear Marshall would not be elected to Congress.

He made no note of the fact that David, while not a horse breeder like his cousin Archibald Randolph, owned Desdemona, a filly of the well-known Dare Devil. In contrast with his own parsimony which left him with clothes inadequate for attendance at a Merry Christmas party in the Randolph house, the spending around him must have seemed vast. He did not, however, note then, as others did later, that the household was not "an economical one." It was left to Channing's abolitionist biographer, writing in 1848, to look back across years to the period of Channing's stay and declare that "Virginia was at this time still in her prosperity, and scarcely beginning to reap the penalty which slavery has since brought in blasted fields, deserted mansions, ruined estates and scattered families."

This Northern statement of later troubles or the expression of a sort of death wish for the Slave South was a prospect in the future, but something of the sort was now at hand for David and Molly Randolph. It dated from the Alien and Sedition trial of Callender which was held in Richmond in 1800. David Randolph undoubtedly confronted this much damning and much damned journalist who had smeared his Federalist idols with something of the same righteous asperity Judge Samuel Chase showed on the bench in his trial.

Callender had fled to America in fear of prosecution for attacks he had made on the British government. Jefferson and other Republicans regarded him as "a man of science fled from persecution." The Virginia Republican leader had been ready to use his talents for invective or calumny against the Federalists. He patronized the writer's work, advanced small sums to him and was suspiciously close to Callender's publication of titillating exposures of an illicit and disreputable amour in which Hamilton had to admit he had been engaged. When Philadelphia became too hot for the writer under the Alien and Sedition Laws he escaped to supposed asylum in Virginia. There, however, his publication, in general approved by Jefferson, of more slanders about President Adams brought him into the court of ferociously Federalistic Judge Chase who had already displayed his partisan venom in Pennsylvania.

Jefferson wrote Governor James Monroe that Callender "should be substantially defended, whether in the first stages by public interference or private contributors." He was defended in fact by lawyers who later served the Jefferson side in a greater trial in Richmond. As defense attorneys, George Hay and William Wirt, however, were outraged by the harsh, contemptuous treatment they received from Chase and of his tyrannical conduct of the case. Later it was charged that David Randolph, at the instruction of Chase, had packed the jury with Federalists. Randolph always denied it. The important fact, however, was that Jefferson believed it.

It could hardly have been a complete surprise to David and Molly therefore when a year later President Jefferson picked David as one whose head should be among the first to roll. Indeed, on March 12, 1801, the President wrote to Molly's brother, Thomas Mann Randolph, saying he knew this would cause him pain. The surprising thing was that circumstances pushed Randolph and Callender into what Jeffersonians regarded then and later as a combination in calumny. Randolph was said to have made difficulties about returning to the journalist the fine Chase had imposed along with a prison sentence on Callender. This Jefferson now ordered removed in his sweeping Presidential decision that the Alien and Sedition Laws were not only tyrannical but unconstitutional. It was suggested that there were irregularities in Randolph's accounts, though no formal charges were made about this. Callender was vindicated—but not satisfied. He wanted as political reward the position of postmaster in Richmond, which he confided to Madison would make it possible for him to marry a lady of his choice. This Jefferson declined to do, Callender charged, because he wanted to disassociate himself from the rough politics in which he had engaged the journalist. Indeed, when Jefferson sent him some money at this time, Callender accused the President of paying him hush money to keep him from disclosing his patron's part in the slander services the journalist had performed.

Now, according to historian Peterson, who in 1970 was Thomas Jefferson Foundation Professor at the University of Virginia, David Randolph and other Federalists became Callender's "partners in libel." A new Federalist weekly, the *Richmond Recorder, or Lady's and Gentleman's Miscellany,* which catered to the taste for scandal, employed Callender. It seems doubtful that David Randolph at this time had money with which to help start a new paper even in Richmond where often sheets suddenly appeared and quickly expired.

Randolph did have, as did everybody else in Virginia, a store of skeletons in the state's closets and in the closets of Monticello in particular. Already, said Peterson, Light-Horse Harry was maliciously reviving the Walker scandal. Also, Peterson declared, the story that Jefferson maintained a quadroon slave as his mistress at Monticello "had titillated Jefferson's enemies in the neighborhood of Monticello for years."

What Callender chiefly did was to rattle old bones. But he did so at such a time and in such a way as to attract great attention in a nation in which there was a ready market for the traduction of Jefferson. Certainly he made the man of Monticello squirm. On July 2, 1802, the President wrote Monroe about the so-called disclosures Callender was making. He was, he wrote, "really mortified at the base ingratitude of Callender. It presents human nature in a hideous form." At the outset the turncoat journalist, as Jefferson said, tried to show him responsible for all the scurrilities in his writings about "genl. Washington, Mr. Adams and others." Jefferson insisted that the payments Callender blandly published had been made to him were only charities to an unfortunate man. Monroe did not think such an explanation would suffice. And Abigail Adams, still smarting under the Callender attacks on her husband, concluded, as she later told Jefferson, that he had now been bitten by a serpent he had "cherished and warmed."

Callender's scandalous chronicling paid off. Jefferson's first major biographer Randall reported that the *Recorder* "which was an obscure paper, scarcely known out of the city, rapidly attained a circulation throughout the United States." Though Callender squealed in delight at his success in revenge, he did not long profit from it. He was soon destitute "in part because of mistreatment by his partner," according to Malone. Also, Malone said, the writer was drinking heavily. On July 17, 1803, his body was found in the muddy fringes of the James River. A coroner's jury, quickly empaneled, held that he drowned while drunk. The *Richmond Examiner*, as a Jefferson organ which had no reason to like Callender, took the view that the unfortunate man, sunk to the depths of misery, killed himself.

If, as Malone said, Callender was shunned in his last days, the David Randolphs in their troubles kept their heads high and were welcomed in the best Richmond society. David's dismissal from office coincided with a recession in 1800–2 resulting from a ruinous fall in tobacco prices. He "had to sell" his horse Desdemona. He got a good price for her from John Tayloe III, who then was breeding horses in partnership with Captain Archie Randolph of Ben Lomond. The $2,500 David got for Desdemona did not slow his financial slide. In August 1802, he offered for sale "sundry lots and tenements" in Richmond. In the same year also he put Moldavia on the market. David and Molly left it in 1804 for a rented house on Cary Street where Molly was planning to open a boardinghouse.

Such troubles in Richmond were far from the generally reported incidents in history. Great events were occurring. In the month in which Callender died Jefferson received word from France of the treaty ceding Louisiana to the United States. Also, greater antagonists were directing their fire at the President. The Supreme Court was reconvened by Chief Justice Marshall in February 1803. Placed first on its calendar was the case Charles Lee had supposedly brought for the obscure Mr. Marbury.

Marshall "backed into" the case in such a way as not to directly challenge the President but to give him a rebuke as to his duties. Such a legal scholar as Edward S. Corwin in his treatment of the Chief Justice in the *Dictionary of American Biography* thought that since Marshall signed and sealed the commision which Marbury—or Lee—was seeking, he should have "by a nicer view of judicial propriety" disqualified himself from sitting on the case at all.

Instead for "the unanimous court," the Federalist jurist held that Marbury was entitled to the remedy he sought but added that the court was without jurisdiction in the case. In this dog-fall or cart-before-the-horse decision, however, he re-emphasized for the court its greatest prerogative—the final right to say what the law is under the Constitution. Jefferson could not contest this position since he had taken a similar view some years before. But the President could and did resent what he regarded as the politics of judges which could fortify what seemed to him to be a Federalist usurpation of ultimate decision.

Soon, indeed, the President showed himself ready to put the judiciary in its place with the weapon of impeachment. Early in May 1803, Judge Chase assailed the Republicans as "our late reformers" in a fierce charge to a Federal grand jury in Baltimore. As soon as Jefferson heard of Chase's Federalist outburst in his judicial robes, he suggested quietly that the House take the steps necessary to the impeachment of the judge. The task fell to John Randolph.

While the behavior of Chase was building Jefferson's political irritation, he was suffering from personal grief. On October 17, 1804, he made a spare note in his Account Book: "This morning between 8. & 9. my dear daughter Maria Eppes died." This prettier of his two daughters had never recovered from the birth of her third child earlier in the year. The child did not survive her long. Another baby had died. Only her boy Francis Wayles Eppes lived to maturity.

Death did not interrupt politics. The winter of 1805, when the Chase case came to trial, was one crowded with drama in the Randolph story. It is not easy to put into order the personal and political events of this period. One solid date was January 29, 1805, when a resolution was introduced authorizing a compromise with "innocent purchasers" of lands in the Yazoo Fraud which John Randolph had observed with such indignation in Georgia as a younger man. The Federal government, to which Georgia had ceded its rights to the millions of acres involved, favored a compromise. Jefferson's Postmaster General, Gideon Granger, with much patronage to distribute, appeared in the Congress as a chief lobbyist for the claimants. While still speaking in this debate in terms of loyalty to the President, Randolph in effect compared this proposal with the speculation in public securities which Jefferson had condemned in Alexander Hamilton.

Though such administration stalwarts as Albert Gallatin, James Madison, and Attorney General Levi Lincoln had approved the compromise, Randolph directed his fury particularly at Postmaster General Granger. That official claimed to speak for "innocent purchasers," many in New England, who had nothing to do with the original fraud. Randolph regarded many of them, including Granger, as far from innocent. Granger was not a very pleasant character. He had been involved in land speculations of a doubtful nature in the West. Also, recently in the President's purposes to dispose of Aaron Burr as a figure of importance in American politics, Granger had played a double-dealing role. Pretending to be a Burrite, he had acted as spy in Burr's councils, reporting regularly to Jefferson. Madison's two principal biographers, Irving Brant and Ralph Ketcham, both wrote of him as engaging in both ingratiation and blackmail. He was involved in a malaprop defense of Dolley Madison and her sister from whispers as to their chastity. Also these biographers wrote that Granger clung to some private papers entrusted to him about Jefferson's affairs as a means of maintaining his place and powers.

How much John Randolph knew about Granger in this business at this time is not known. Later, however, he wrote in his diary: "Gideon P.M.G. holds his office by a *certain* tenure. When a prosecution was commenced *at common law* in Connecticut for a libel upon Mr. J., he wrote to Granger confidentially and entrusted certain papers to him relating to Mrs. W——'s affairs, which the wary Yankee refused to give up. He was alternately threatened and soothed by the P. and his agents, but to no purpose; and, although he is for the best reasons hated by Mr. M——n, and, what is of more moment, by Mrs. M——n, he boasts that he will retain his place under the new P."

Randolph kept his charges against Granger in the Yazoo debate to the "corruption" at issue. He spoke of the Postmaster General as a swindler "goaded by avarice." In his impassioned speeches he still spoke of Jefferson as "the great and good man who now fills, and who (whatever may be the wishes of our opponents) I hope will long fill the Executive Chair." Still the man in the Executive Chair could not have heard with equanimity Randolph's resounding peroration: "What is the spirit against which we now struggle, and which we have vainly endeavored to stifle? A monster generated by fraud, nursed in corruption, that, in grim silence, awaits his prey. It is the spirit of Federalism, that spirit which considers the many as made only for the few; which sees in Government nothing but a job; which is never so true to itself as when false to the nation."

Randolph's language was undoubtedly intemperate. His anger shook his frail frame as he made his prolonged speeches. He was exhausted in the debate when he should have been preparing for his appearance a few days later as the chief House manager in the Chase impeachment trial. He appeared as the representative of the House which was enthusiastic for impeachment. But in the public mind he appeared as the agent of the President. He was not only worn by the long Yazoo debate. Also he was not a trained lawyer in opposition to the array of counsel Chase had secured, which included almost as a matter of course Charles Lee. With Jefferson in the background, this trial again was a sort of Randolph gathering. Chief Justice Marshall, showing in his appearance that he feared he might be next in a succession of impeachment proceedings, took his place as both observer and witness. Among the witnesses for the defense (and their own defense, too) were Marshall's brother William the Richmond court clerk and David Randolph. Of them all Marshall apparently most showed his trepidation. He was no longer, as the trial began, in any such mood of deft defiance as he had shown in the Marbury vs Madison decision. Indeed, to the continuous astonishment of his admirers since, he wrote about this time that he thought the "modern doctrine of impeachment should yield to an appellate jurisdiction in the legislature. A reversal of those legal opinions deemed unsound by the legislature would certainly better comport with the mildness of our character [than] would removal of the Judge who has rendered them unknowing of his fault."

"In other words," wrote Edward S. Corwin, "if Congress would only leave John Marshall in office they might reverse such of his legal opinions as they 'deemed unsound' to their heart's content, and thereby consign both judicial review and the principle of the separation of powers to the scrapheap."

But Chase was not convicted. Marshall's immediate fears of peril to himself and the whole national judiciary were removed. Oddly Jefferson did not seem too perturbed by the outcome. Later he confided to the diarist, Senator William Plumer, whom he would convert to Republicanism, that "impeachment is a farce which will not be tried again." Beveridge thought that the President's feelings "were balanced between grief and glee." The President was, the biographer thought, rather pleased that John Randolph had not gained a personal triumph. Certainly Randolph seemed the chief loser in the case over which it was generally agreed that Aaron Burr, debonair on the eve of his departure from public life, had conducted the trial "with the dignity and impartiality of an angel, but with the rigor of a devil." Many in the company at the Chase trial would meet this gentleman again.

Much has been written about the oratorical frenzy and sometimes erratic behavior of Randolph this winter. Few have related his public performance with an event in his private life soon afterwards at Bizarre. Nancy Randolph later dated the time of the incident by the ages of her nephews, St. George and Tudor Randolph, as 1805. Tudor then had been seriously ill. Randolph himself in a letter from Bizarre on March 17, 1805, two weeks after Congress adjourned, described the illness of the boy whom Nancy said she had "nursed several weeks in a dangerous illness at the hazard of my life."

In bitter contradiction of each other both Nancy and John described the episode later. Nancy recalled to Randolph that soon after Tudor had left "to take the benefit of a change of air, you came into the room one evening, after you had been a long time in your chamber with my sister, and said, addressing yourself to me, 'Nancy, when do you leave this house? The sooner the better for you take as many liberties as if you were in a tavern.'"

She went on in her account which was also an accusation: "On this occasion, as on others, my course was silent submission. I was poor, I was dependent. I knew the house was kept in part at your expense. I could not therefore appeal to my sister. I replied with the humility, suitable to my forlorn condition, 'I will go as soon as I can.' You stalked haughtily from the room, and poor, unprotected 'Nancy' retired to seek the relief of tears."

Randolph's version was in sharp variance to this. After the death of his brother Richard, he wrote Nancy fiercely, she became a virago at Bizarre: "Your quarrels with your own sister, before fierce and angry, now knew no remission. You tried to force her to turn you out of doors that you might have some plausible reason to assign for quitting Bizarre. But, after what my poor brother had been made to suffer, in mind, body and estate, after her own suffering as wife and widow from your machinations, it was not worth while to try to save anything from the wreck of her happiness, and she endured you as well as she could, and you poured on. But your intimacy with one of the slaves, *your 'dear* Billy Ellis,' thus you commenced your epistles to this Othello!, attracted notice. You could stay no longer at Bizarre, you abandoned it under the plea of ill useage. . . ."

In her later letter containing her description of her ejection (or departure) from Bizarre, Nancy also threw light like a lightning thrust on Randolph's life at this time after the collapse of the case against Judge Chase. He had come home to Bizarre, she wrote tauntingly, "complaining of the fatigue of your public labors, but elated with the prospect of a foreign mission." Even as Nancy wrote scornfully of it, his elation then included a wish to take his other nephew, the deaf St. George, to England for treatment.

"As usual," his sister-in-law wrote bitterly, "you rode your new Hobby to the annoyance of all who like me were obliged to listen. Your expected voyage enchanted you so much that you could

not help talking of it even to your deaf nephew: 'Soon, *my boy,*
we shall be sailing over the Atlantic.' But, all at once, you became silent and seemed in deep melancholy. It appeared soon
after that Mr. Jefferson and Mr. Madison, knowing your character, had prudently declined a compliance with your wishes.
A new scene now opened; you became a patriot, double distilled,
and founded your claim to the confidence of new friends on the
breach of that which had been reposed by your old ones."

So Nancy, who cannot be classified as an objective historian,
marked the break with Jefferson which had seemed foreshadowed
in the Yazoo debate. Bruce wrote that Randolph had nothing to
do with the proposal that he be sent to England. Apparently
others, friends of both the President and of Randolph, suggested
this as a means of preventing the break between the two cousins.
Congressman Christopher Clark, a native of Albemarle County,
and "several of his Virginia colleagues" had urged Randolph's appointment. Randolph was not privy to the suggestion when it was
made, Bruce added, "but the fact that it had been made and rejected became known to him subsequently, and must have had a
more or less corrosive effect on a nature so proud and resentful
as his."

Later in commenting on the break with Jefferson, Randolph
himself said wryly and characteristically that it began when he
beat Jefferson at chess. Certainly the triangle of Randolph hostilities in the capital was in being when, by the acquittal of
Chase, Marshall was freed of his fears of his own impeachment
by Jefferson operating through Randolph. Toward each other
Jefferson and Randolph might bide their time but Marshall was
freed from any intimidation. He had other worries.

Charles Lee and William Marbury had lost any title they
hoped to have as judge or justice of the peace. But Marshall
remained concerned about land titles. They were involved in
many cases which came before his high court. Questions of land
titles lay behind the case of Fletcher vs Peck in which he put
a final end to John Randolph's fight against the government
making a compromise with the "innocent purchasers" of the
Yazoo Fraud lands. There, important for judicial history, he held

that the "obligations of contracts" clause in the Constitution stood in the way of a state's repeal of a grant of public lands. He held this to be so even though an earlier legislature's law making the grant had been induced by the notorious bribery and corruption against which Randolph inveighed.

Other land titles much interested Marshall, notably in connection with the Fairfax estate in which he and his brother were deeply involved. In this summer there seemed still some cloud upon these titles. There certainly remained a load of debt on Marshall and his brother in connection with their investment in the Fairfax lands. They owed $31,500 on this purchase and a smaller sum to their brother-in-law Rawleigh Colston whose interest in the speculation they had purchased.

In part these debts induced the Chief Justice to undertake his biography of Washington. He hoped to make at least $50,000 out of the project. Even before he began it, however, Jefferson had thought politics, not profits, impelled him. It was written, Jefferson said, "with a view to electioneering purposes." It turned out to be more ponderous than financially or politically profitable even if it was more than "a party diatribe" as Jefferson described it. Certainly it was an onerous undertaking in Marshall's crowded life. One item added to his resentment over the repeal of the Federalist Judiciary Act was that it required him to spend much time holding court on the circuits. That, as Randolph said, gave him "duties to perform." Also this interrupted the Justice's literary activities. That meant, however, that he would be on the bench in Richmond in a great trial in which once again Randolphs would be dramatically arrayed against each other.

A portent of that greater trial came soon after the close of the year. Then John Randolph, in open revolt, was opposing what he described as the President's furtive plan to get Congress to provide him with funds with which to bribe Napoleon to force Spain to give up Florida to the United States. Randolph also opposed a plan much favored by shipping interests in New England to retaliate on England for impressing American seamen by non-importation of British goods. In a war which might follow Randolph scoffed at American ability to match Britain on the

seas. The old Jacobin now saw Britain's Navy as the only bul-
wark against Napoleon's universal domination. He cried: "Give to
the tiger the properties of the shark, and there is no longer safety
for the beasts of the forests or the fishes of the sea." Tiger and
shark might have been symbols for opposing Randolphs, too. On
a first test, John Randolph's proposal to arm against Spain in the
Southwest rather than to pay off Napoleon was beaten 72 to 58
in the House. But on the non-importation bill he lost 93 to 32.

Mr. Jefferson wrote, "I have never seen a House of Representatives more solidly united in doing what they believed to be the
best for the public interest. There can be no better proof than
the fact that so eminent a leader should at once and almost
unanimously be abandoned."

Evidently Mr. Jefferson felt secure. While this debate was going
on he dismissed as definitely suspect a warning which he received from Marshall's brother-in-law U. S. Attorney Daveiss in
Kentucky. Mystery remains as to why the President had kept this
furious Federalist, appointed by Adams, so long in office. His
relationship to the Chief Justice could hardly have recommended
him to the President. The middle name which Daveiss had
adopted out of devotion to Jefferson's great antagonist Alexander
Hamilton, now dead after his duel with Aaron Burr, certainly
tagged him as no friend of the Democrats.

Long before this time, Democrats in Kentucky must have complained about keeping Daveiss in the desirable Federal job.
There was nothing furtive about his Federalism. It was blatant.
He was associated in politics with Humphrey Marshall, who
was both the Chief Justice's first cousin and brother-in-law. That
name recalled an incident Jefferson always remembered with un-
ease. While he was Secretary of State in 1793 this arrogant
Federalist, who was said to measure his money by the peck,
had exposed and opposed a plot by the French Minister Genêt
to attack Spanish and English territories from the American West.
He had then accused Jefferson's friend, Governor Isaac Shelby,
of complicity. In the ensuing excitement Humphrey Marshall
had defeated for the United States Senate John Breckinridge,
now Jefferson's Attorney General, who had in fact been ready

to back Genêt. Jefferson himself had been too close for political comfort to Genêt's plans at this time. In the Senate, Humphrey Marshall had supported the Jay Treaty and so won mob attentions from his radical Kentucky constituents. The Kentucky Marshalls remained unintimidated anti-Jeffersonians.

From such a background, Daveiss sent Jefferson his warning dated January 10, 1806. It was that Aaron Burr was planning treason in the West and that Breckinridge, the President's old friend and now his Attorney General, and other good Democrats were in on the game. Jefferson must have feared a trick but he did not yet fire this Federalist partisan on his adminitration's payroll. He filed the letter and later damned Daveiss for being premature. Only then, when he was hunting Burr, did he fire this firebrand relation of his Randolph kinsmen in Kentucky.

Chapter XII

FAMILY REUNION

DESERTING or driven from Bizarre, Nancy threw herself, John Randolph wrote, "on the humanity of Capt. and Mrs. Murray (never appealed to in vain), and here you made a bold stroke for a husband—Dr. Meade. Foiled in this game, your advances became so immodest you had to leave Grovebrook. You afterwards took lodgings at Prior's (a public garden), . . ."

In their sharply contradictory biographical treatment of each other, he directly insinuated that the sister-in-law, whom he charged with infanticide, the murder of his brother, and an affair with a slave, had now turned to prostitution. She answered him in bitter indignation: "You say I took lodgings at Prior's, a public garden. It is true Mr. Prior owned a large lot in Richmond, and that there was a public building on it, in which public balls and entertainments were given, and this lot a public garden, but it is equally true that Mr. Prior's dwelling and the enclosure round it were wholly distinct from that garden. In that house, I lodged. My chamber was directly over Mrs. Prior's, a lady of as good birth as Mr. John Randolph and of far more correct principles."

John and Nancy violently disagreed over the description of her room in which he once visited her with a proffer of charity which she rejected. He wrote: "You were at that time fastidiously neat, and so was the apartment. I *now* see *why* the banknote was returned. . . . Your subsequent association with the players—your decline into a very *drab*—I was informed of by a friend in Richmond." She retorted: "You sat on my bedstead, I cannot say bed, for I had none. I was too poor. When weary, my limbs were rested on a blanket, spread over the sacking."

The one certainty seems to be that there was such an amusement center operated by Major John Pryor (correct), a veteran of the Revolution who tried to repair his fortunes by operating a pleasure resort called the Hay Market Garden. Also he had a wife described as "an interesting and strong-minded" young woman. She was the Mrs. Anne Whiting Pryor who a few years later scandalized Richmond by running off with a French émigré schoolteacher, Jean Charles Frémon. She is remembered in history as the mother of General John C. Frémont.

Contrasts were often sharp in the Old Dominion and among no Virginians more than the Randolphs. In the summer of Nancy's depravity or destitution, her youngest sister Virginia (Jenny) was the immaculate center of a scene of the perfect plantation South. Jenny was only nineteen this summer, beautiful and already indicating the brilliance she would later show in her novels and her *Letters on Female Character*. Since the remarriage and death of her father a dozen years before, she had lived most of the time at Monticello or the nearby place of her brother and sister-in-law Thomas Mann and Martha Randolph at Edgehill. Now she was marrying her cousin Wilson Jefferson Cary.

"I take it for granted," Jefferson wrote Martha, "that Virginia's marriage is to take place at Monticello, as we have so much more room there for our friends, and conveniences of other kinds also."

Martha replied, "The marriage will take place at Monticello early in August entirely private except the old Gentleman and Lady and Aunt Carr."

The President, who always managed to be there at this time of the year in order to escape the miasmas of the capital, looked forward to the event. He headed for his little mountain in July despite worries about his embargo which John Randolph had opposed as both provocative and inept. He was troubled, too, about the truculence of Spain in the West which seemed based upon the promises of French support. He was hoping to come to terms with England about its high-handedness on the seas. From

Monticello he wrote his Secretary of State: "We should not permit ourselves to be found off guard and friendless."

Some guards and some fears about friendliness were necessary even in wedding plans at Monticello. Virginia's young man had much to recommend him to Jefferson. Young Cary's mother, "Aunt Carr" to Martha, had been Jean Barbara Carr, the child of the President's sister Martha and his dearest friend Dabney Carr who had died young. Jefferson first laid out the Monticello graveyard for his burying place. Wilson Cary, Wilson Jefferson Cary's father, had died young, too. But his grandfather, Colonel Wilson Miles Cary was robustly alive at seventy-one and vigorously opposed to the policies of President Jefferson. His feeling then was expressed a few years later when he added a codicil to his will leaving John Randolph, then no longer of Bizarre, "five guineas as a mark of my approbation of his manly and patriotic exertions in the Congress in checking the persecuting and partial proceedings of some former administrations."

There was no doubt about what administrations the Colonel was referring to when he wrote his will. He took no pains to conceal his political views at the time of his grandson's wedding. And though, as it turned out, young Wilson Jefferson Cary remained a devoted Jefferson supporter all his days, the master of Monticello may have had some misgivings about ideas which the young man may have imbibed from his grandfather. Furthermore, Wilson Jefferson had studied law in Richmond in the office of Edmund Randolph, who evidently was nourishing resentment about Jefferson's earlier description of him as a "trimmer." Honored and successful in Richmond, Edmund was still scarred by the termination of his Cabinet career in a disgrace fabricated for him because he actually stood strong against Jefferson's enemies in the Cabinet of George Washington. For Washington, Edmund had only resentment. No reverence for the Father of his Country could have impelled him to Federalism. But in gossiping Virginia, he must have known of the slurs about him Jefferson had written even to his in-laws the Nicholases. Certainly he would be a man sensitive about any charges of treason quickly made by any President in power.

Significantly, however, Jefferson and Edmund Randolph shared the affection and respect of George Wythe, the great law teacher and jurist. And in April 1806, the President and Edmund Randolph were involved as Wythe's friends in connection with the tragic murder of the eighty-year-old Chancellor. No Virginian at the time was more respected than Wythe, signer of the Declaration of Independence, great teacher, and Chancellor of Virginia. Richmond reacted in shock when it was learned that he had been poisoned by his great nephew and namesake, George Wythe Sweeney. The trauma was the greater because of circumstances related to it which could only be whispered.

Wythe had been twice married. No child survived either marriage when he was left the widower of his second wife in 1787. Then in his apparently circumspect household Wythe made a slave house servant, Lydia Broadnax, his mistress. She bore him a son, a mulatto boy called Michael Brown. Wythe raised the boy with affection, teaching him Latin and Greek. Wythe not only freed the slave boy but was leaving him a substantial part of his estate. Knowledge of this by his great nephew evidently was the motive for the crime.

Sweeney was a dissolute young man, plagued by petty debts. In the month of the murder he had tried to sell books from Wythe's library, probably to cover gambling losses. Then he forged his granduncle's name on six checks drawn on the Bank of Virginia. In this maze of misbehavior, he put poison in the coffee at the Wythe house. The slave boy died quickly. Lydia escaped. But Wythe, lingering in agony, called in Edmund Randolph to help him write deathbed codicils to his will.

He disinherited Sweeney. He directed: "I give my books and small philosophical apparatus to Thomas Jefferson, President of the United States of America: a legacy considered abstractly perhaps not deserving a place in his museum, but, estimated by my good will to him, the most valuable to him of anything which I have to bestow. . . . to the said Thomas Jefferson's patronage I recommend the freed boy Michael Brown in my testament named, for whose maintenance or other benefit I will the bank stock of the value thereof. . . ."

Jefferson wrote: "I sincerely regret the loss [of the freed boy Michael Brown], not only for the affliction it must have cost Mr. Wythe in his last moments, but also as it has deprived me of an object for attentions which would have gratified me unceasingly with the constant recollection & execution of the wishes of my friend."

Edmund handled the legal details in the case. Despite (or perhaps because of) the fact that Wythe had expressed the wish that Sweeney be not punished beyond disinheritance because "I dread such a stigma being cast upon my name or my sister's," Edmund appeared as the assassin's counsel. Associated with him was the eloquent William Wirt, who soon would appear in opposition to him in a greater case. Interestingly, the case was prosecuted for the state by Philip Norborne Nicholas, Edmund's brother-in-law. Though twice indicted by grand juries, Sweeney was never punished. The crucial witness, Lydia Broadnax, could not as a slave testify. The *Richmond Enquirer* reported: "The unfortunate man then sought refuge in the West; where his career was brought to a premature and miserable close."

At a distance in literary composition, Edmund and Jefferson were also both engaged in a sort of historical debate. In his ready patronage to literary men, Jefferson had encouraged John Daly Burk. This man, like Callender, had fled to Virginia after he had been indicted under the Alien and Sedition Laws for "seditious and libellous" utterances against President Adams. In Virginia he was more circumspect than Callender in political utterances. He expressed his democratic passions in a *History of Virginia.* Jefferson sent him some material which had come to his hands on Bacon's Rebellion. And in the second volume of his work, published in Petersburg in 1805, Burk drew, with the President's approval, the familiar picture of Bacon not as a rebel but as the early Virginia evangel for democracy.

Edmund was already contemplating his never finished history in which he took the opposite view. Chief Justice Marshall now arrayed himself against Jefferson and his writer friend Burk in the first volume of his *Life of Washington,* which the President was to call a "four volume libel." The great Democrat was directing his remarks especially at the Chief Justice's story of the Federalists and the Republicans in the new nation. But Marshall's comment on the colonial conflict offended his design of early history, too.

The Chief Justice dismissed the retrospective democratic enthusiasm. Bacon, he wrote, "treading the path by which ambition marches to power . . . harangued the people on their grievances, increased their irritation against the causes of their disgust, and ascribed the evils with which they thought themselves oppressed to those who governed them, while he professed no other object than their good." Marshall concluded: "Whatever may have been his object, the insurrection produced much misery, and no good to Virginia."

By remarkable coincidence these differences marked the great case in which soon these three Randolphs—Marshall, Jefferson, and Edmund Randolph—along with others, were soon engaged. Ten months after Jefferson had dismissed the warning of District Attorney Daveiss about treason in the West, he raised by proclamation a hue and cry after Aaron Burr. Dismissing any notion that Burr might be engaged in land settlement or, more gloriously, in putting himself in readiness to fight for his democratic country in the event of war with imperial Spain, Jefferson declared that Burr was a worse rebel than Bacon had seemed to Marshall and Edmund Randolph.

Jefferson had been vague in the language he used in launching the manhunt in the West. John Randolph, on January 16, 1807, insisted that he be specific. In a resolution, marking the fully grown hostility between the President and himself, the gaunt Congressman demanded that the President lay before Congress any information he possessed concerning the conspiracies he had mentioned in his proclamation and a recent message to Congress. On January 22, the President replied, naming for the first time Burr, "whose guilt is placed beyond question," in his intent to pull the West away from the Union. However, the President said he had "little . . . to constitute legal and formal evidence."

Randolph moved as no defender of Burr. Nearly two years before he had written of a meeting of Burr and one of his associates in the West that it was "a conjunction of malign planets [which] bodes no good." Two months after his resolution of inquiry, on March 25, 1807, he wrote from Bizarre about the passage of Burr under arrest to trial in Richmond:

"Col. Burr (*quantum mutatus ab illo!*) passed by my door the day before yesterday under a strong guard. . . . His very manner of traveling, although under arrest, was characteristic of the man—enveloped in mystery—and, should he be hanged for treason, I dare say he will 'feel the ruling passion strong in death,' and contrive to make posterity doubt whether he was actually executed, or whether (as was alleged in the case of the Duke of Monmouth) some counterfeit did not suffer in his stead."

Richmond was crowded that summer with witnesses, newspapermen, politicians, and ordinary gawking spectators at the trial which seemed the greatest show in America. No players could match it. Nancy's old landlord, Major Pryor, offered to rent for use as a hotel his Hay Market Garden as a great bargain: "The great concourse of strangers that may be expected to assemble in this city . . . ought to be an object with the persons inclined to rent." Indeed, some of the concourse lived in tents. The heat was terrific. Disease threatened. Influenza was said to be present in "half the houses in town."

In many ways it was also a sort of Randolph family reunion. The most ubiquitous person in town, though not actually present at all, was Jefferson who directed the prosecution from Washington. But to his chagrin the presiding judge was Chief Justice Marshall. Jefferson's leading prosecutor George Hay, though no Randolph, had been appointed U. S. District Attorney by Jefferson after Hay had furiously and publicly lashed at Marshall when the Chief Justice seemed finagling in the Burr-Jefferson tie contest. On the opposite side of the counsel table as senior attorney for Burr was Edmund Randolph, showing already a decline in health and powers which would not long after manifest itself in paralysis. He was ready, however, as was charged, to try to turn the trial of Burr into a trial of Jefferson. Finally, when the grand jury panel had been depleted by challenges, Justice

Marshall summoned John Randolph as a juror and soon appointed him foreman.

By this time the hostility between Jefferson and John Randolph had almost reached the point of bloodletting. The preceding summer the President's son-in-law, Thomas Mann Randolph, Jr., who had been elected to Congress in a close race in 1803, misunderstood some words of his gaunt cousin as an insult to him. Thomas Mann blustering "that he had always thought and always should think that lead and even steel made very proper ingredients in serious quarrels," faced the danger of one or the other in a duel. The affair was adjusted but bitterness lingered. Also in the summer of 1806, John Randolph heard that Jefferson's Postmaster General Granger had been trying to get Creed Taylor, who had launched Randolph on his Congressional career, to become a candidate opposing him.

Jefferson had been surprised at the Federalist sentiment shown in the Richmond district a half dozen years before when Marshall was elected to Congress. He had reason to be chagrined about that now. In noise and numbers in the courtroom and the crowded streets and bars, Republicans ready to see Burr hung dominated the crowds. Chief Justice Marshall himself, said to be fearful again of impeachment, moved carefully, but Republicans said with a predatory tread.

However strong was the mass feeling against Burr, "society" took him to its bosom. He moved elegantly in its company when he was released on bail at first by Marshall. He was petted with presents and visits when he occupied apparently elaborate quarters in the new penitentiary under the care of an amiable guard. Randolphs were involved in patrician partisanship for Burr. The three gentlemen who provided $10,000 bail for the elegant adventurer indicated this. Little is known of Allan Pollock except that he was a merchant in Richmond. Burr's companion in catastrophe, Harman Blennerhassett, wrote during the trial: "Burr will be soon in cash having concluded some financial arrangements with a Mr. Pollock who is very rich." Thomas Taylor was a prominent citizen who an historian of the period said "frequently entertained John Randolph." The third bailor Henry (Harry)

Heth was the gentleman who had as a partner in coal mining Beverley Randolph, a daughter married to Robert Beverley Randolph, and David Meade Randolph as a sort of technical coal mining adviser.

Blennerhassett, more than Burr, left notes about his and Burr's Randolph connections. In August he wrote that he had just received "a tender of friendship" from General Henry Lee. Light-Horse Harry offered "with warmth any services I might stand in need of." He declined, having been warned "to beware in any case of any dealing with him," because he was "a man equally violent in his friendships and his enmities." Blennerhassett only mentioned casually, apparently not much impressed, that Burr had added the General's brother, Charles Lee, to his array of lawyers.

He wrote at some length, however, about Molly Randolph, no longer living at Moldavia, whom he met at the house of John Augustus Chevallie, the French consul and Richmond businessman. Chevallie operated a flour mill with his brother-in-law Joseph Gallego who had purchased Moldavia from the David Randolphs. His Federalism was adequately indicated by the fact that he had been a witness for the defense in Judge Chase's impeachment trial.

Blennerhassett described one visit with Molly at tea at the Chevallies'. She was, he wrote, "a middle-aged lady and very accomplished, of charming manners, and possessing a masculine mind." He went on: "From this lady, the near relation of the President, and whose brother is married to his daughter, I heard more pungent strictures upon Jefferson's head and heart, because they were better founded than I had ever heard before, and she certainly uttered more treason than *my wife* ever dreamed of; for she ridiculed the experiment of a Republic in this country, which the vices and inconsistency of parties and the people had too long been shown to be nothing more than annual series of essays to complete a work ill begun, and which appeared to be nearly worn out before it was half finished. But 'she always was disgusted with the fairest ideas of a modern republic, however she might respect those of antiquity.' And as for the treason, 'she cordially hoped, whenever Burr, or anyone else, again attempted to do anything, the Atlantic States would be comprised in the plan.'"

This conversation which Blennerhassett said came after a day of high winds and much dust seems a little blown and murky. Evidently Molly, however, did not confine her talk to the despised Jefferson. She told Blennerhassett about the visit to Richmond not long before of the Irish poet Thomas Moore "with whom she was highly pleased here." She recited some favorite extracts from his poems. She was, however, "very much mortified by the indiscriminate censure of Virginia, with which he had requited the hospitality and consideration with which he was universally treated in this state—his only two exceptions from his strictures being Wickham and the Chief Justice."

Molly would not have been one of the Richmonders now who were outraged when John Wickham, as social leader and Burr's able defender, gave a dinner at which he put Justice Marshall and defendant Burr in congenial company. In view of her "pungent strictures" it may be wondered whether one of the "favorite extracts" from the poet's work was the recently published verse containing the lines:

> The patriot, fresh from Freedom's councils come,
> Now pleas'd, retires to lash his slaves at home;
> Or woo, some black Aspasia's charms
> And dream of Freedom in his bondmaid's arms.

The trial went interminably on and has been interminably reported. Jefferson's great witness, General James Wilkinson, at last arrived, pompous and strutting but withering, too, under the suspicions, later proven to be true, that he was a paid Spanish agent. Wilkinson barely missed indictment himself. Grand Jury Foreman Randolph wrote condemning the General and sneering at the President whose chief witness against Burr he was:

"W. [Wilkinson] is the most finished scoundrel that ever lived; a ream of paper would not contain all the proofs; but what of that? He is 'the man whom the King delights to honor.'"

In contradiction, as Jefferson felt, of a decision the Chief

Justice had made in an earlier case, Marshall ruled that since Burr was not present at the scene which the government had chosen as the site of treason, he could not be convicted. Actually all the evidence against Burr was either largely hearsay or, as in the case of a cipher letter he wrote to Wilkinson, much doctored. Dramatic as was the trial of such a man as Burr, the event was most significant as a duel between the President and the Chief Justice. Marshall, said one of the government's attorneys, stood between Burr and the gallows—between Burr and Jefferson. Certainly in this great trial there was animosity enough to include the whole company engaged.

Possibly, though loudly damned, Marshall was the victor. Jefferson dared no impeachment proceedings. Marshall's debts on the Fairfax lands now had been paid. He was comfortable on the court. As a Federalist he could now be above and apart from the battling of his cousins inside the Democratic party. It did not concern him that John Randolph was now undertaking to strike at the happiness of the Virginia Dynasty Jefferson was creating by pitting Monroe against Madison in the race for the place as Jefferson's successor.

Writing in the fall to Martha, the President told her: "A Caucus of malcontent members has been held, and an organized opposition to the government arranged, J.R. and J.C. at its head." The editors of *The Family Letters of Thomas Jefferson* properly identified J.R. as John Randolph but erred in thinking J.C. was John C. Calhoun, who did not enter Congress until later. This J.C. was Joseph Clay, a Pennsylvania Congressman and close friend of John Randolph's who worked to prevent the President's friends from removing Randolph as chairman of the Ways and Means Committee.

Jefferson went on: "Their object is to embarrass, avoiding votes of opposition beyond what they think the nation will bear. Their chief mischief will be done by letters of misrepresentations to their constituents; for in neither house, even with the assured aid of the federalists, can they shake the good sense and honest intentions of the mass of real republicans."

He continued with a sigh almost audible in his letter: "But I am tired of a life of contention, and of being the personal object for the hatred of every man, who hates the present state of things. I long to be among you where I know nothing but love and delight, and where instead of being chained to a writing table I would be indulged as others are with the blessings of domestic society, and pursuits of my own choice."

Less than two months later, on January 2, 1808, Martha wrote him from Edgehill to tell him that not all in the society of Virginia for which he sighed were finding the blessings he depicted. Of her husband she reported: "Mr. Randolph has been a fortnight in Richmond setling (sic) David Randolph's affairs. He has not property to pay his debts. Sister Randolph's house servants have been saved by a prior mortgage to an old lady of the name of Stith in Williamsburg who means to leave the debt to *him* at her death, in the meantime the interest must be paid and from what funds it is not easy to say. Sister Randolph has opened a boarding house in Richmond, but she has not a single boarder yet. Her husband has gone to England upon some mercantile scheme with barely money to defray his expenses." David had, indeed, gone to England where he desperately hoped to find capital for his inventions.

Molly's prospects as a boardinghouse keeper were not as bad as Martha feared. But there were other troubles. Jefferson's daughter wrote on in anguish: "The ruin of the family is still extending it self daily. William is ruined. His negroes during his absence remained three days in the dwelling house to save themselves from the sherif. Archy is without a shelter for his family but for her Father's, and Will. Fleming goes constantly armed to keep the sherif off. I ought rather to say *went* for in consequence of the pistol going off in his pocket he is rendered a cripple for life."

Certainly Martha made a catalogue of family woes. William Randolph was another brother of Thomas Mann's who had married Lucy Bolling Randolph, his cousin of course. The saddest fall except for that of David and Molly was the descent to shelterlessness of Archie Randolph. He was always described as the elegant Captain Randolph. One of Nancy's suitors before the scandal at Glenlyvar, he had afterwards married Lucy Burwell. He set himself up at Ben Lomond in Goochland County, which he had purchased from his first cousin Thomas Eston Randolph. There he was recognized as a skilled breeder of thoroughbred horses. In 1804, he and John Tayloe III, rich horse fancier of magnificent Mt. Airy, had owned equal shares in the blind mare Castianira. On May 1, 1805, the great mare bore a colt sired by the famous Diomed. The sleek little creature was originally named Robert Burns, but was to become known as Sir Archie, the most famous racer and sire in Virginia annals. Even then, however, Archie Randolph at thirty-six was in financial trouble. He seemed dogged by bad luck. One of his children died the summer Sir Archie was born. Archie lost his lands and had to move his family to the charitable shelter of his father-in-law, Nathaniel Burwell, at Carter Hall in Frederick County. Sir Archie galloped to fame in other hands.

Possibly even more Lucifer-like was the fall of Light-Horse Harry Lee whose troubles Martha did not mention. Soon after Blennerhassett saw him still magnificently tendering any services at the Burr trial, his mounting debts overtook him. A year before in the grandeur of Stratford, now transformed into a fortress against process servers, his son Robert Edward was born in a high-ceilinged room in which two other Lees, both signers of the Declaration of Independence, had been born in happier days. Harry's second wife, Ann Carter Lee, with this child which she said she had not wanted and four other children, moved from the great house to simple quarters in Alexandria. Fortunately for her, she had a small inheritance which had been guarded from her husband's speculations. Light-Horse Harry went to prison for debt. Still arrogant in insolvency he used his time in prison to write his war memoirs which Jefferson, in resentment of his references to him, described as historical fiction. Lee was composing this work while Martha was writing her father of the troubles of other Randolphs.

Martha's catalogue of misfortunes lengthened. She and her husband hoped very much that the President could get a midshipman's place for Tarleton Fleming, "a grandson of Aunt Fleming and one of a large family of beggared orphans." The young man was, of course, related to the Will Fleming who had shot himself. Thomas Mann's great aunt, Mary Randolph, had married an earlier Tarleton Fleming whose estate was then called Rock Castle. And Richard S. Hackley, who had married Thomas Mann's sister Harriet, much needed to be appointed consul at Cádiz. Mr. Jefferson, whose views about nepotism were well known, managed to make both appointments.

Trouble was not suggested at this time in the migration to Kentucky of Jefferson's sister, Lucy, who had married her first cousin Charles Lilburne Lewis. Her sons, Lilburne and Isham, moved westward with hundreds of other Virginians from the Old Dominion where two centuries of tobacco farming had doomed much of the land to the briars and the brush, the wild turkeys and the deer. With their slaves such men moved to what they hoped was a better chance. Though Jefferson's eldest grandchild, Anne Cary Randolph, had heard that "Aunt Lewis" had a dreadful journey, no one feared then that her sons had carried malignancy as well as slaves west with them.

Neither young Anne Cary Randolph nor any others in the Randolph connection then seemed concerned about the troubles of her homeless aunt of the same name. Indeed, Nancy Randolph's movements in this period are lost in much obscurity. As a woman now about thirty-three years old, she moved North. An unverified tradition has it that she taught school in a small Connecticut town. She was part of the time in Newport and in distress there. Indeed, in that resort, suffering from want and fever, she pocketed both her resentment and her pride to request from John Randolph, as she said later, "not the gift (I would sooner have perished) but the loan" of fifty dollars. She wrote that he did not even reply: "Perhaps, you hoped that the poor forlorn creature you had turned out of doors would, under the pressure of want, and far removed from every friend, be driven to a vicious course, and enable you to justify your barbarity by charges such as you have now invented."

Not all Randolphs were poor. Great estates were maintained. Randolphs still lived decorative lives at Wilton and Chatsworth.

The great house at Cawsons was still occupied. Many of the gentry lived in houses which Jefferson as amateur architect had designed. John Randolph at Bizarre and later at his unpretentious place at Roanoke was multiplying the horses and dogs, which as much as Palladian architecture marked the aristocracy of Virginia. And some Randolphs, who were not ostentatiously rich, like "an old Lady by the name of Stith," were willing to help others. This old lady was Mary Stith, elderly maiden of Williamsburg. She was doubly descended from the Randolphs: Mary, the daughter of the first William of Turkey Island, had married Captain John Stith, and their son William had married his first cousin Judith, daughter of the first Thomas of Tuckahoe. Though blood could sometimes seem like bile among the Randolphs, it was also often thicker than water.

Not all were able to help. Evidently the break between Jefferson and David Meade Randolph had not alienated Thomas Mann from his sister Molly. Martha was ready even in extremity to take Molly and her children to live at Edgehill. Her husband's trials in the family troubles were great, Martha told her father, "but thank heaven he has resisted their solicitations and has had the prudence not to hamper himself by security ships." He was having financial troubles enough of his own at the time. So was Jefferson.

In answer to Martha's description of the family's troubles, he preached a sermon on economy which he always praised even when he himself was most extravagant. Then fearful of his son-in-law's possible imprudence, he added: "I never in my life have been so disappointed as in my expectations that the office I am in would have enabled me from time to time to assist him in his difficulties. So far otherwise has it turned out that I have now the gloomy prospect of retiring from office loaded with serious debts, which will materially affect the tranquility of my retirement."

Even children reported troubles which could not easily be remedied. Fourteen-year-old Ellen Wayles Randolph, whose correspondence with her grandfather was on such mutual interests as the seasons and the flowers, told him sadly at this time: "The

Orange trees do not look well. Davy let the box that had the Geraniums fall out of the cart and break by which means we have lost them."

Also, righteously this granddaughter told the President of the unwillingness of Virginians to sacrifice as reported to her by her Aunt Virginia, now Mrs. Wilson Jefferson Cary: "She says that the embargo has thrown the dissipated inhabitants of Williamsburg in great confusion. The Ladies say they cannot give up tea and coffee and the gentlemen wine."

Despite such dissatisfied personages, Mr. Jefferson easily made Madison his successor, brushing aside John Randolph's efforts to put Monroe ahead. Burr had become "absolutely invisible." Even more invisible then—and too much in history—was David Meade Randolph. He had carried to Burr in Philadelphia after the trial a copy of the pamphlet of the now removed U. S. District Attorney Daveiss in Kentucky. In it this member of the Marshall clan damned Burr, Wilkinson, and Jefferson together. The diatribe did not help Burr or Randolph. David Meade, like Burr, was on his way to desperately penurious exile abroad. Even Burr at one time feared that David, whom he described as "a tall, eager, pale, white-haired man," might kill himself.

One light gleamed in this time so dark for so many Randolphs. Despite Martha's foreboding report, Molly's boardinghouse in Richmond was a great success. She had been sure, the Richmond chronicler Samuel Mordecai wrote, "that those who had, in her prosperity, partaken of her hospitality, would second her when in adversity." An advertisement in the *Virginia Gazette* of Richmond, in March 1808, announced that "Mrs. Randolph has established a BOARDING HOUSE in Cary Street. She has comfortable chambers, and a stable well-supplied for a few horses." More famed than her facilities was her fare. As she presided over it, Rootes, who had named Moldavia, christened her "the Queen." She held her head high enough to wear a crown.

Chapter XIII

"PATCHED AT THE ELBOWS"

MEMBERS of the multiplying Randolph family noted in 1811 that the year was the hundredth anniversary of the death of the first William of Turkey Island. Certainly, however, none of them associated its celebration with the dreadful pyrotechnics which, on December 26, 1811, destroyed the Richmond Theater, killed seventy-three of the state's best people and made another Randolph, a later Peyton, Governor of the state for nine mourning days.

Mortality was not always so dramatic but death took its steady toll of the gentry. Still, more and more infant Randolphs were being brought into the world. One, four years old then, was Robert E. Lee, who had been born while bailiffs were at the door trying to serve papers on his insolvent father. Entering the Virginia world at approximately the same time was Lee's first cousin, Robert Lee Randolph of Haymarket in Clarke County, whose progeny were to include a bishop and a comic song writer. His distinction in the multiplying and intermarrying Randolph family was that as fifth in descent from William I, he had in his veins the united blood streams of five of the seven sons of the first William.

Such combinations could be complicated in terms of both genius and aberration as the lines of the two greatest members of the family at the time, Jefferson and John Randolph, indicated. In a reticence which Jefferson forever maintained, this year 1811 was the time of the greatest blot on his blood. His mother's sister, Mary Randolph, had married Charles Lewis of an apparently impeccable Virginia family. Jefferson's sister Lucy took the Lewises' son, Charles Lilburne Lewis, as her husband. As Jefferson was approaching the end of his term in the Presidency, he expressed the hope that he might visit Lucy and her sons, Isham and Lilburne, on their Kentucky plantation. He noted that he had never visited the West, so much of which he had added to the nation. He never made the trip. Lucy died. And on December 11, 1811, in the midst of a period marked around their plantation by earthquake, a great comet, and floods, her sons committed the murder of one of their slaves in a fashion of classic brutality. Before they could consumate a suicide pact after the discovery of their crime, one of the brothers accidentally killed himself. Soon after, the other escaped from jail. Only tradition followed his trail to report that he died fighting under Andrew Jackson in the Battle of New Orleans.

The news came back to Monticello only in a whisper. Jefferson biographers did not mention this horrid episode which must have scarred the retired philosopher as it marred his line. At the time he was trying to help his grandson by his dead daughter, Mary, young Francis Wayles Eppes, learn Latin grammar or "gramer" as that young man spelled it. The coincidence and the gap in brilliance and aberration was more evident—even spectacled—in the line of John Randolph, now adding "of Roanoke" to his signature.

The lovely, "tawny" Frances Bland Randolph Tucker, who died in 1788, would have been both proud and troubled if she had lived to know about her children and her grandchildren— and probably greatly puzzled, too. She and her first husband, John Randolph of Matoax, cousins in both the Randolph and the Bolling lines, had loved each other very much. She had passed, as she wrote in her prayer book, an "unhappy widowhood" before she took as her second husband the brilliant and high-spirited Bermuda-born St. George Tucker. By her first marriage she had left the trio—Richard, Theodorick, and John. By her second marriage, in addition to two children who died young, she had two sons—Henry St. George Tucker and Nathaniel Beverley Tucker—and a daughter Anne Frances Bland Tucker.

The two broods of Frances Bland seemed to fall apart in fate. The Randolph boys appeared dramatically doomed; the Tucker children were destined to rich, conventional fulfillment. Indeed, God or genetics appeared determined to wipe out the line of the first children she had loved so much.

In 1811 St. George Tucker, who had remarried in his forties, was about to be named Federal judge by Madison after service on the Virginia Supreme Court of Appeals. On a social occasion during the Burr trial he had argued with his wife's cousin, Chief Justice Marshall, insisting upon the right of a state, if it wished, to "recede" from the Union. Already his sons were showing great promise. Henry St. George would follow him as an eminent legal scholar. Nathaniel Beverley, who had no patience with Jeffersonian democracy but firm faith in state sovereignty, was to add to his eminence as a teacher of the law a literary career in which he produced what Edgar Allan Poe thought was the "best American novel." Their sister, as the wife of Judge John Coalter, became the cherished confidante of her strangely lovable, hateable, gentle, and violent, frail, and furious half brother John.

John Randolph needed such affection now that his brothers, Richard and Theodorick, were long dead and in some wise damned. The one lady in his life, Maria Ward, who apparently was once much in love with him, had married his cousin Peyton, son of Edmund. In 1813, even his constituents were ready to leave him. Then Jefferson's son-in-law, John Wayles Eppes, with whom John had come close to the dueling point, took advantage of the unpopularity John had won by his almost one-man opposition to the War of 1812. Some indication of the intensity of such feeling had been shown when John's cousin Light-Horse Harry, defending a Baltimore editor with similar anti-war views, had been maimed for life by a mob. On the same tide of feeling Eppes won in Virginia. It had taken Jefferson three tries to accomplish Randolph's defeat. It was an ejection which would not last. John might be doomed but he was incandescent.

Three years before he had moved from Bizarre to his primitive Roanoke plantation forty miles away in Charlotte County. He wrote then: "*Graces à Dieu*, I make a shift to get along without as many headaches as I have been made to feel by feminine caprice and affection." He carried some feminine fastidiousness with him, however. His godson later wrote that, despite the numbers of horses and dogs he kept, the grounds about his house "were more free from everything that could soil a house than any other place I ever saw; no fowls of any kind were allowed on his premises; nor was a horse permitted to graze in his yard; flies shunned the place."

John withdrew in distaste in other matters. Now he added the words "of Roanoke" to his name to distinguish himself from another John Randolph, a brother of Judith and Nancy. He described this other John as a homeless vagabond of infamous character who had made a murderous assault on him which might have cost him his life. The only cause, the gentleman "of Roanoke" wrote, was that he had been guilty of "the outrage of seeking to collect the sum of twelve pounds due him" for services to the other John's mare by one of his stallions.

"I have every reason to suppose," John of Roanoke stated, "that this fellow with whom I never had any intercourse further than to speak when we met, was instigated, probably hired, (for he is needy and desperate), to commit the deed. I was wholly unarmed, yet he drew a knife upon me, and would have stabbed me, if it had not closed as he struck. He did cut my coat. I gave him the lash, and afterwards the butt end of Leigh's whip, leaving a mark upon him that he will not soon lose."

While Bruce vouches for this incident, evidently the other John, though nicknamed "Possum," was no homeless vagabond. In Randolph genealogies he is listed as *Dr.* John Randolph, so apparently he was a physician. Aged about thirty at the time of this incident, he was married to Judith Lewis of Amelia County. Their son, William Mann Randolph, became the husband of Margaret, daughter of Thomas Jefferson Randolph, the great statesman's favorite grandson. Some of their descendants became leaders in the keeping of Randolph records and traditions.

Childless himself, John of Roanoke often described as his

"sons" St. George and Tudor, the boys of Judith and his brother Richard. With other young members of the family they were often at Roanoke riding and hunting. But, as early as 1805, St. George, at thirteen, had been sent abroad as a deaf-mute who might be aided by Thomas Braidwood in his school for such afflicted children at Hackney near London. The boy, despite his handicap, was a handsome young fellow, black-haired, firm-featured, and with dark piercing eyes. His uncle, still hoping, sent the boy from London to Paris where the Abbé Roche Ambroise Cucurron Sicard offered the therapy he had described in his *Cours d'instruction d'un sourd-muet de naissance*. Apparently young St. George had been helped by treatments in Europe but inadequately. [Others of the Bolling line with similarly afflicted children later brought Braidwood's grandson to teach them in Virginia, only to find him too much addicted to drink to maintain his school.]

Home again, still confused, St. George at twenty-one fell desperately in love. In April 1814 he wrote his uncle, "This country has none the gold rings. I wish you to get one for me in Richmond, if you please." Evidently he thought then that he was about to be married to a cousin whom his mother described as "a very amiable, exemplary girl, but one destitute of every personal charm whatever—I mean Jane Hackley."

Perhaps that was an adequate description of Jane, the daughter of Judith's sister Harriet for whose husband, Richard S. Hackley of New York, Jefferson had secured the post of consul at Cádiz, Spain, in 1808. Jane could have been little more than a child at this time. Her description as lacking charm, however, is surprising. Her sister Harriet, as the wife of Robert E. Lee's friend Andrew Talcott, appears in a portrait by Thomas Sully as one of the most beautiful women of her time.

Plain or pretty, Jane or her parents turned St. George down. Judith wrote of his dark disappointment and a year later John Randolph noted in his diary, "Rec'd Judith's letter, announcing St. George's insanity." Indeed, John soon found the boy a "frantic maniac." Distressing as this was, nothing much had been expected of this boy who was to spend much of the rest of his life in and out of a variety of the primitive mental institutions of the time. But coincident bad news about Tudor, the younger brilliant boy, must have been a terrific blow to the uncle who put all his future hopes in him.

Proud of his progress, John Randolph had sent this boy to Harvard under the escort of his friend Josiah Quincy, the Federalist and "solid man of Boston." Quincy had secured quarters for Tudor in the home of Harvard's president, John Thornton Kirkland. Perhaps such special treatment for a young Virginia Randolph did not help curb and may have increased the boy's extravagances. Yet his professors praised him as "a very smart fellow, very studious and had read almost all the Greek and Latin that was ever written." Suddenly, however, his college career was interrupted. Ironically, as it must have seemed to John—perhaps to Judith—word came from Nancy, for whom there had been no room at Bizarre, that Tudor was very ill at her house near New York.

Nancy was no longer in a position of begging and borrowing but of giving. Her story emerges from wandering obscurity in 1808 when she was staying at the house of "old Mrs. Pollack" in New York City. (Oddly in this same year Aaron Burr, on his way to exile, said goodbye to his daughter Theodosia in the "house of Mrs. Pollock." Spelling being what it was in the letters of the time, the place could have been the same. This landlady could have been kin to Allan Pollock, the Scotch merchant of Richmond who lent Burr money when he was on trial there.) At this inn, Nancy wrote later, giving no intimation of any preliminaries, she was visited by Gouverneur Morris who had known her at Tuckahoe as a child. This sparkling statesman and self-described philanderer was now fifty-six and in retirement on his estate Morrisania. There, according to tradition, he reigned not only over inherited wealth but over jewels, plate, and other valuables he had received from fleeing nobility while he was Minister to France. To Nancy he "expressed a wish that some reduced gentlewoman would undertake to keep his house, as the lower class of house-keepers often provoked servants to a riot in his dwelling."

Nancy demurred for six months, she wrote later, but when he asked her again to come in the housekeeping capacity she "thought it much better to have employment than remain a burden on my friends." Evidently some friends were still true. John of Roanoke wrote that when he "heard of your living with Mr. Morris as his *housekeeper*, I was glad of it as a means of keeping you from worse company and courses. Considering him as a perfect man of the world, who, in courts and cities at home and abroad, had in vain been assailed by female blandishments, the idea of his marrying you never entered my head. Another connection did."

Evidently as expectant heirs, Gouverneur's relatives regarded the matter in the same light. They included David Bayard Ogden, prominent attorney who had been born at Morrisania, the son of Samuel Ogden, Revolutionary iron founder and land speculator, and Euphemia Morris; and Gertrude Meredith, sister of William Morris Meredith, later Secretary of the Treasury, whose mother had been Gertrude Gouverneur Ogden. There was surprise in Virginia and shock in New York when relatives learned that on Christmas Day 1809, Morris married his pretty housekeeper from Tuckahoe and Bizarre. Nancy wrote, "I glory in stating that I was married in a gown patched at the elbows." Now much more seemed patched than her sleeves.

From Philadelphia Gertrude Meredith wrote a petulant protest which brought a firm and gentle reply. Wrote the suave master of Morrisania: "I received your letter, my dear child, and perceive in it two charges; viz, that I have committed a folly in marriage and have acted undutifully in not consulting you. I can only say to the first that I have not yet found cause to repent, and to the second that I hope you will pardon me for violating an obligation of which I was not aprized. . . . If I had married a rich woman of seventy the world might think it wiser than to take one half that age without a farthing, and if the world were to live with my wife, I should certainly have consulted its taste; but as that happens not to be the case, I thought I might, without offending others, endeavor to suit myself, and look rather into the head and heart than into the pocket. Perhaps it would gratify a laudable curiosity to say what I discovered; but that must be omitted, to avoid the charge of partiality—and the rather as the step I have taken gives sufficient evidence of my opinion. When we have the pleasure to see you at Morrisania, it is possible you may approve my choice and you will certainly find that I am, as ever affectionately yours. . . ."

Such family approval was doubtful particularly from David Ogden whose financial affairs needed the propping of inheritances he had expected from his uncle. Indeed, family disapproval grew to dismal disappointment when, on February 9, 1813, Nancy bore a boy named Gouverneur, of course. On the surface there was family adjustment to the situation. Gouverneur's relatives still asked him for financial aids. In Virginia, John Randolph seemed pleased by a letter from Morris making sympathetic suggestions about poor deaf and crazy St. George. He offered Randolph and Judith the hospitality of Morrisania. Randolph replied with his "warmest acknowledgement."

Then, on August 4, 1814, Tudor arrived at Morrisania from Harvard in a phaeton and with a servant. He had been in communication with his aunt there before. She had a special affection for the young man dating back to the days when she had nursed him in illness at Bizarre. One of her laments after leaving Bizarre had been that she was not allowed to see him. She had sent him gifts of money at Harvard. He had borrowed more from her. Now she was distressed to see him evidently very ill—as it turned out with tuberculosis. She put him to bed. On September 25, he had a copious hemorrhage. Morris—at his own expense, of course—called in, to stay for two days, the famous New York physician Dr. David Hosack and a colleague. Only afterwards did John Randolph unintentionally make it appear that in caring for the boy the Morrisses were nursing a viper.

Soon after the boy's arrival Nancy sent word to Judith who hurried North, having borrowed money for the journey from St. George Tucker. In a sense she was homeless now, too, Bizarre having burned to the ground in 1813. John Randolph had learned as early as September 6 that "poor Tudor is ill, very ill, at Mr. Morris' near New York." Still he remained in Richmond until October 6. Already he was making continuous dark poetry about his own ill health. He had had a bad fall in Georgetown not long before. Now on his way northward he was delayed four days in Baltimore by a fall down a steep staircase which left him unconscious at the bottom. However, he reached Morrisania on October 22. From there he wrote a friend, "After various accidents, one of which nearly put an end to my unprosperous life, and confined me nearly a week on the road, I reached this place yesterday. Tudor is better; I have hopes of him, if we can get him to Virginia in his present plight."

John remained at Morrisania only one day. At the time there seemed nothing malignant about his talks with the reviving Tudor who afterwards he made to seem a young monster of ingratitude as a bearer of tales about Nancy's "lewd amours." Actually what happened on this day, like so much else in their lives, was described in bitter contradiction by John and Nancy.

She wrote to him: "When you entered this house and when you left it, you took me in your arms, you pressed me to your bosom, you impressed upon my lips a kiss which I received as a token of friendship from a near relation." Also: "Recollect, Sir, when you rose from the table to leave Morrisania, you put in my husband's hand a note to my sister expressing your willingness that she and her son should pass the winter in his house."

Nothing suggests that this was not true except John's brief visit and speedy departure. On his way into town he suffered another accident when his carriage was driven over a pile of stones in Courtland Street and overturned. He was, he reported, "very seriously injured." He could hobble about only with the help of a stick. During this week Morris and Nancy visited him more than once. Nancy took her small son with her on one visit. Tudor was also well enough to visit his incapacitated uncle.

Yet, in this week following the accident, Randolph composed the letter of dreadful accusation which he addressed to Nancy but sent to her husband. She wrote that "under pretext of consulting Com. Decatur and Mr. Bleecker, you communicated your slanders to them, and then to Mr. Ogden." The order she gave to the names is doubtful. Ogden probably should have come first, not last, and as one inciting scandal, not merely hearing it. Whatever the facts about Randolph's preparation of this malignant missive, his letter remains substantial but incredible:

Greenwich St., October 31, 1814

Dear Madame:

When at my departure from Morrisania, in your sister's presence, I bade you remember the past, I was not apprised of the whole extent of your guilty machinations. I had nevertheless seen and heard enough in the course of my short visit to satisfy me that your own dear experience had availed nothing toward the amendment of your life. . . .

[He went over the whole long, ugly story of his accusations. He quoted Tudor as a witness to the wickedness he alleged. Then rhetorically he demanded:] What did I see? A vampire that, after sucking the best blood of my race, has flitted off to the north, and struck her harpy fangs into an infirm old man. To what condition of being have you reduced him? Have you made him a prisoner in his own house that there may be no witnesses of your lewd amours, or have you driven away his friends and old domestics that there may be no witnesses of his death?

[He closed:] Before this reaches your eye, it will have been perused by him, to whom next to my brother, you are most deeply indebted, and whom, next to him, you have most deeply wronged. If he be not both blind and deaf, he must sooner or later unmask you unless *he too die of cramps* in his *Stomach*. If I were persuaded that his life is safe in your custody, I might forebear from making this communication to him. Repent before it is too late. May I hear of that repentance and never see you more.

John Randolph of Roanoke.

Evidently Morris, though outraged, was not disturbed. He hesitated even to show the letter to Nancy but at last permitted her to pour out her fury in answer. She mocked at "Jack" Randolph calling himself "John Randolph of Roanoke." If he believed these slanders, she demanded, how could he have let his heir whom he hoped to carry on his name be left under the care for three months of "a wretch who had murdered his father

. . . dependent on the character of a negro's concubine?" Her letter was a steady whip of scorn. He was a liar and a hypocrite, a vainglorious boaster who had turned into a base calumniator. She matched Randolph's quotations of Shakespeare. His letter, she said, was "a tale told by an idiot, full of sound and fury, signifying nothing."

Evidently this exchange signified nothing more to Morris than an obscene assault on his wife by her furious cousin. Eighteen months later, he wrote to a friend in England: "I lead a quiet, and more than most of my fellow mortals, a happy life. The woman to whom I am married has much genius, has been well educated, and possesses, with an affectionate temper, industry and love of order."

Nancy herself did not let the matter lapse so serenely. She broadcast copies of the letters to friends and relatives in Virginia. She offered them as material to Randolph's enemies, one of whom was informed by Randolph that if he stuck his nose into the matter he would be expected to answer on the dueling field. Neither of the fierce antagonists apparently suffered then from the exchange. Nancy's life at Morrisania continued on a serene basis untroubled by the visits of ill or evil Randolphs. Gouverneur lived until November 1816, when he died a natural though painful death.

In Virginia Martha Randolph wrote regularly to her father who was rusticating at his Poplar Forest retreat. There admirers and tourists followed him still. One group startled and pleased him. It turned out to be General Andrew Jackson and his party on the way to celebration of his military victories in Washington. Yet, as an old man Jefferson was withdrawing into family affairs which intimately concerned him. Martha had written on March 14, 1816, of the "death of Mrs. Judy Randolph." Four days later she told him that the husband of her daughter, Anne Cary, Charles Lewis Bankhead has "recommenced his habits of drunkenness." Then in the midst of a discussion of tulip and hyacinth bulbs she told him on November 20th: "You will have seen by the papers the death of Gouverneur Morris. His loss will be irreparable to his wife by lessening the *little* consequence that

I am afraid she had, and exposing her unprotected to the persecution of his heirs who have been disappointed by the birth of her child of his large possessions. I wrote her upon the occasion although we had not previously corresponded, but poor creature she is surrounded by enemies and never in more need of the support of her family than at present."

Martha need not have worried about Nancy. Morris had made her both guardian and trustee under his will. No Ogdens or Merediths overwhelmed her. She was able as time went on to say: "Now the ante nuptian contract is the *only* remaining debt; so that I can safely say my noble-minded son's property is unencumbered." Nancy's story was happily ended later when that noble-minded son, turning back to Virginia for a wife, chose Patsey Jefferson Cary. She was the daughter of Nancy's sister Virginia Randolph who had been married to Wilson Jefferson Cary at Monticello in 1805. So once again it was a marriage of first cousins.

In 1815 John Randolph's constituents, with their tobacco caught behind the blockade, had had enough of the war Mr. Jefferson had in a sense initiated and Madison had declared. The gaunt man of Roanoke was sent back to Congress by constituents who approved his increasing Southern and states' rights policies and rejoiced in the forensic entertainment which he provided for them and the country. Much as he was opposed to nationalistic measures, the tariff and the chartering of the second bank of the United States, his greatest concern was still the health of Tudor. He sent the young man abroad, as he had sent St. George, in the hope that he might be benefited by the medicinal springs at Cheltenham in Gloucestershire. Unbenefited by the fashionable spa, Tudor died there. It was significant of his promise that, though he had been forced to give up his studies, Harvard granted him his degree. Randolph placed a stone over Tudor's grave in Cheltenham where, he wrote, "is lodged in the bosom of the earth the treasure of my heart."

Such tragedy was not the lot of all Randolphs, young or old, at this time. In Virginia other young members of the family had worries while St. George and Tudor were moving to long confusion and early death. At sixteen Ellen Wayles Randolph was asked by Jefferson to keep him informed at Poplar Forest about the campaign on the Canadian border where her father had gone as a colonel of infantry. Thomas Mann came home from the service without either glory or injury. His and his family's troubles came from the British blockade which caused him to lose many barrels of flour he had collected on speculation. He needed but did not get a Federal job to save his estate. Still, in 1816, young Ellen was able to go on a pleasure trip to Washington at the beginning of Mr. Madison's last year in the Presidency.

As a young woman of twenty, she was having a good time when she wrote her grandfather in March 1816. She was delighted with $100 which he had sent her and which she was sure would add much to her "moyens de jouissance." Of the forthcoming Presidential election she only remarked that Mrs. Monroe had made herself unpopular by her evident aversion to society. But she added that she could not tell him much about Congress as she "had very little acquaintance with the members."

She was to improve that acquaintance as years went on. She was visiting in Washington again after the election of her father, who could not manage his own affairs, as Governor to manage the affairs of Virginia. He also at the time was vice-president of the Richmond Jockey Club. Surfaces at least were bright. Certainly Ellen in Washington, in the early 1820s, did not seem the representative of a precarious family situation. It was desperate in prospect as early as the year in which her father had been elected Governor. Then the family had learned "that Colonel William Cary Nicholas has been *protested* for a large sum." Jefferson was his endorser on notes for $20,000. In the same letter in which she mentioned this, Martha Randolph noted of the husband of her daughter Anne Cary, "Mr. Bankhead has begun to drink again." When he had been drinking before he had violently assaulted Martha's son, Thomas Jefferson Randolph.

Young Ellen reflected none of the troubles at Monticello and Edgehill in Washington. She attracted much Congressional attention, and particularly that of a diminutive, yellow-haired widower, Senator Martin Van Buren of New York. Van Buren's venerable colleague, Senator Rufus King, wrote his son: "There is here a Miss Randolph, granddaughter of Mr. Jefferson; about whom the young members of Congress collect, and with them V.B.

"She is intelligent and more interesting for her education and literature than for her beauty, or the manners of good society," King added.

As to her manners, King was evidently shocked because at a party attended by Van Buren, Ellen asked the Marine Band to play a currently popular song called "The Yellow-Haired Laddie." The playful raillery of this representative of the younger generation evidently pleased Van Buren. Soon he journeyed to Richmond to visit Ellen's father the Governor. Some contemporary commentators thought the purpose of the trip was to form a new alliance between the "ancient dominion" and the "great state." One of the young New York Senator's correspondents, however, heard that "the object of your journey, was a beautiful & accomplished lady, not distantly related to the Governor of Virginia." A Van Buren biographer wrote that the small Senator, who many thought looked like Aaron Burr, was too busy with politics to think of love. Van Buren's purposes were never easy to determine. John Randolph, as an older member of the House at this time, later said that Van Buren always "rowed to his purposes with muffled oars." Certainly Ellen was more merry than matrimonial in her relations with the New Yorker. Their friendship, however, in part laid the basis for a remarkable Randolph role in the society and politics of the national capital a little later.

While Ellen was not drawn to the New Yorker, like many others of her generation, she did not feel bound to Virginia— certainly not to the intermeshing intermarriages of Randolphs there. Many young people were already leaving, some to make impeccable replicas of old Tidewater plantations in Kentucky, Mississippi, Alabama. Her cousin of Roanoke had already said that the best old areas of Virginia become "yearly more deserted. Deer and wild turkey are nowhere so plentiful in Kentucky as near Williamsburg." Friends and neighbors were leaving Albemarle.

Still, when young Joseph Coolidge, Jr., of Boston, came South

early in 1824, Monticello, despite the mounting debts and decadence about it, must have looked like an invulnerable château.
Coolidge, whose people had come to Massachusetts before Randolphs established themselves in Virginia, had graduated from
Harvard shortly after Tudor had been given his posthumous degree. He had, of course, as rich Brahmin, made the grand tour
of Europe on which he had pleased Lord Byron as "a very pretty
lad . . . only too full of poesy and 'entussymussy.'"

Actually the poet was much flattered by the young man and
in later consideration described him as "intelligent, very handsome . . . a little romantic, but that sits well upon youth." Certainly he must have looked charming to Ellen Randolph who,
at twenty-nine, was almost an old maid by Virginia standards.
He pleased also her grandfather who then knew that he was insolvent beyond the possibility of redemption. Joseph and Ellen
were married, on May 27, 1825, in the drawing room at Monticello
which so soon would be stripped of its elaborate furnishings.

Already Ellen's father, whose political and financial affairs
were finally collapsing, had told young Coolidge he had nothing
to give his daughter. Soon losing his property, quarreling with
his eldest son, and angry with his father-in-law, he withdrew
from Monticello and isolated himself in a sulkiness which seemed
touched by insanity. A friend of Thomas Mann's feared that
"homeless and pennyless" he would "rave as wildly as Lear."
Jefferson with one foot in the grave and the other uplifted to
follow it, as he said, remained to the last the patriarch to whom
his grandchildren turned.

Ellen wrote him from Boston, in August 1825, at the end of a
long wedding journey through New York and New England. She
and Joseph had traversed much the same path which Jefferson
and Madison had followed decades before on a trip which many
Federalists had suspected was made more for politics than pleasure. Ellen now wrote as a mature young woman more aware of
sectional than political differences. Evidently she had been made
both happy and sad by what she had seen.

The wedding journey, she said, had given her an "idea
of prosperity and improvement, such as I fear our Southern States

cannot hope for, whilst the canker of slavery eats into their hearts, and diseases the whole body by this ulcer at the core. When I consider the immense advantages of soil and climate which we possess over these people, it grieves me to think that such great gifts of Nature should have failed to produce anything like the wealth and improvement which the New-Englanders have wrung from the hard bosom of a stubborn and ungrateful land, and amid the gloom and desolation of their wintry skies."

Yet she saw growing there, too, a bane in the industry which more and more Southerners felt was being protected by tariffs to the disadvantage of the agrarian South, regardless of its slavery. She wrote of the land in which she was to be the matriarch of Randolphs in numbers almost equal to those in Virginia: "The manufacturer grows rich, whilst the farmer plods on in comparative poverty." Also, she felt that the liberty of the fields "certainly strikes the imagination more favorably, than the confinement of the large but close, heated, and crowded rooms of a factory; the constant whirl and deafening roar of machinery; and the close, sour and greasy smells emitted by the different ingredients employed in the different processes of manufacturing cotton, and woollen clothes; also, I fancied the farmers and labourers looked more cheerful and healthy than the persons employed in the factories, and their wives and daughters prettier, and neater, than the women and girls I saw before the looms and spinning jennies."

Her grandfather had less than a year to live then. His rheumatism troubled him very much. He had tried the Virginia mineral springs. He had visited the Hot Springs and the Warm Springs; "The sweet springs retain esteem, but in limited cases." He had found no such interesting company as John Randolph did at about the same time when he told his fanciful tale about the siring of the great racer and stud Sir Archie. Of Warm Springs Jefferson reported: "so dull a place, and so distressing an ennui I never before knew." His rheumatism was not relieved. Indeed, the result of his multiple baths in the waters was the development of large boils on his buttocks. He was happy that his university was to grow at Charlottesville but he was distressed, late in

1825, over "the riot we had at the University." With this younger generation he had hoped "to trust very much to the discretion of the Students themselves for their own government." But now he joined in a request to the legislature for "a power to call in the civil authority in the first instance of disorder, and to quell it on the spot by imprisonment and the same legal coercions, provided against disorder generally, committed by other citizens, from whom, at their age, they have no right to distinction."

He told Ellen of this decision for discipline where at first democracy had seemed adequate. He had no doubt that she would find the state of society in New England "more congenial with your mind than the rustic scenes you have left: altho these do not want their points of endearment. . . . One fatal stain deforms what nature had bestowed on us of her fairest gifts."

New England had been "mostly desert" when he saw it before. "Now it is what 34 years of free and good government have made it. It shows how soon the labor of man would make a paradise of the whole earth, were it not for misgovernment, and a division of all his energies from their proper object, the happiness of man, to the selfish interests of kings, nobles and priests."

More and more visitors crowded to Monticello—even to Poplar Forest where he lounged as an old man in faded red pants and rumpled jacket. Some friends on their way from Tidewater to the springs came. "The family en masse" gathered in the summers. Also, despite the efforts of the family to protect him from too much company, an increasing number of pilgrims were coming as to a shrine. He was not unaware of his place in the cult of American patriotism. As a substitute for some of their possessions which had been lost on the way to Massachusetts by sea, he sent the Coolidges the "writing box" on which he had composed the Declaration of Independence. "In a few years," he wrote, Coolidge might "see it carried in the procession of our nation's birthday, as the relics of the saints are in those of the church."

John Randolph, becoming more and more wracked and eccentric, saw that prospect without awe. Soon he would be speaking to his constituents of what he regarded as the decline undergone by Virginia and her people. To their faces he compared sons with fathers to their disparagement. He did not exempt his own clan. "In short," he said, "look at the Lees, Washingtons, Randolphs—what woeful degeneracy." Later he was to direct his scorn more particularly at Jefferson. Then to old wit he added bitterness: "I cannot live in this miserable, undone country, where as the Turks follow their sacred standard, which is a pair of Mahomet's green breeches, we are governed by the old red breeches of that prince of projectors, St. Thomas of Cantingbury; and surely, Becket himself never had more pilgrims at his shrine, than the Saint of Monticello."

Such words could no longer trouble Jefferson who, in one of history's great coincidences, had died on July 4, 1826, the fiftieth birthday of independence. Not in coincidence but as a final item of accumulation of change and loss, the last family letter Jefferson received told him that by summer rains the tobacco hills on some of his land had been entirely swept off "soil and all . . . nothing but the clay is left behind."

Chapter XIV

PETTICOATS AND POLITICIANS

"THE GOVERNMENT of a family bears a Lilliputian resemblance
to the government of a nation."

So Molly Randolph, recently retired from the boardinghouse
business in Richmond, wrote as she prepared the first edition
of her very popular cookbook *The Virginia Housewife*, published in Washington in 1824. And some in this period felt that
her sentence might well have been turned around. Members of
political groups each saw their adversaries as Lilliputians in
charge of government. All seemed unable to govern their own
families when they contained such women (ladies was a con-
tested term) as Floride Calhoun, Peggy O'Neale, and even young,
rigid Emily Donelson. Among them Martha Jefferson Randolph
would become the serene matriarch of her big fatherless brood.

Molly then was not concerned with such difficulties. From
Virginia, where more and more families were moving westward,
she and her husband, David Meade, looking paler and more
elderly than when Burr last saw him penniless in Britain, had
moved instead to the national capital. As one historian put it,
"perhaps because of advancing age," they came at sixty-two and
sixty-six to live with their son William Beverley Randolph (called
Beverley), who had married a Georgetown girl and found a
job in the government. As older members of the family, Molly
and David, like Martha at dilapidating Monticello, felt no lure
for the vast West which Mr. Jefferson had opened and which
some thought was responsible for declining land prices in Vir-

ginia. Some younger members of the family already saw destiny in the distance.

The David Randolphs were beyond adventuring in boarding-house management or European speculations. They preferred settled refuge. At Beverley's house they did not find them-selves among strangers. Long established in the neighborhood, though across the Potomac in their great house Arlington, were their cousins George Washington Parke Custis and his wife who had been Mary Ann Randolph Fitzhugh. Apparently Custis, as more playwright than practical planter, was not a very handy man around the house. He was having trouble with leaks in his mansion. So, while Molly wrote her cookbook, David turned his inventive mind to producing a compound which was used to weatherproof the great columned dwelling.

Even in Virginia, where slaves seemed to be eating more than they could grow on worn lands, the move of the David Randolphs did not appear entirely propitious. There were good things to count. Molly's book was profitably beginning its course through many editions. David was close enough to old haunts to join other Revolutionary officers in regalia at the welcome to Lafayette on his return to the Revolutionary scenes which he could re-member with more pleasure than Mr. Jefferson ever could. But in the year of both the book and the parade, the Randolphs confronted disaster again. Their son, Burwell Starke, who had been made a midshipman under President Madison, fell from the mast of his ship and was seriously crippled.

Molly turned her household talents to nursing and devoted her-self so strenuously to the task that she became, as her injured son said, "a victim of maternal love and duty." She died on Jan-uary 23, 1828, and was buried the next day by the the steps of Arlington, "in a spot marked out by herself." Hers was the first burial in what later became the great national cemetery. A low brick wall, still there, was built by the Custises "to keep the cattle away." Custises also planted the ivy which still grows upon it. David did not long survive her.

Their sons remained to greet other relatives leaving hard times in Virginia. Their arrival was heralded by Mrs. Margaret Bayard

Smith, the chronicler then and for the future of Washington society. Member of an elegant Federalist family, she had married Samuel Harrison Smith, whom Jefferson had brought to Washington, in 1801, to be the editor of his party paper *The National Intelligencer*. Mrs. Smith had become an ardent and instant Jefferson disciple on her first meeting with him, but she did not adopt his democratic attitudes toward society. However, she became the intimate friend of his family. Entertained at Monticello in its great days and more recently when she saw it in advancing ruin, she had hearty welcome for Randolphs coming to Washington. Later in the year of Molly's popular book Mrs. Smith mentioned Burwell as a caller at her house to which repaired so many whom she described as the great and beautiful. Burwell was accompanied by "Mr. Trist, a young gentleman married to a granddaughter of Mr. Jefferson"—to whom Henry Clay had given "an appointment of 14 hundred a year."

This was odd since Nicholas Trist's father-in-law, Thomas Mann Randolph, Jr., had a year before been embroiled in a threatened duel with the Secretary of State. The irascible Thomas Mann, in the summer of 1827, had said that Jefferson had confided in him a preference for Jackson. The pro-Clay *National Intelligencer* countered by saying that it was generally known that Randolph was estranged from Jefferson and could hardly have been given his confidences. Suspecting that Clay had been responsible for this slur, Randolph rushed to Washington determined to challenge Clay. Warned by Randolph's son, Thomas Jefferson Randolph, Clay explained the matter so suavely that the challenger returned home appeased—and confused.

There was no reason to believe, however, that Trist's own acts and his Randolph connections would make him pleasing to Jackson, so soon to take office. Trist himself, working with Thomas Jefferson Randolph on the great President's papers, had declined to supply some quotations from them which would aid Jackson's candidacy. This request had been made by Jackson's campaign managers who were men who did not quickly forget.

In mentioning his call, Mrs. Smith did not elaborate on Trist's political connections. She found him a charming young man but she was saddened by a message which he brought. He gave her a letter from Martha, now a widow, announcing that "from reasons of economy [she] will not remove to this place until next autumn." That would be when the Peggy O'Neale furore became, as Daniel Webster thought, one "producing great political effects, and *may very probably determine who shall be successor to the present chief executive.*"

Trist needed the State Department job. A native of Albemarle County, after abortive study at West Point and travels in the West where his brother had established a Louisiana sugar plantation, he had studied law under the aging Jefferson. Following prolonged courtship, almost as a member of the family he had married Virginia Jefferson Randolph. Mrs. Smith had met him when she had visited Martha at Monticello a few months before. Trist and Martha's dutiful son, Thomas Jefferson Randolph, had been then selling furnishings and lands to meet debts. (They ultimately got $7,000 for the estate, saving only the graveyard. In terms of declining Virginia land prices this apparently was a good deal. Less than a decade later it would sell again for $2,700.)

Other Randolphs had needed jobs in Washington. Before Trist got his position in the State Department, Henry Lee, now called Black-Horse Harry, had held a minor post in the Post Office Department from 1824 to 1826. At that time this ugly but fascinating son of Light-Horse Harry had needed both a place to work and a place to hide. Born at Stratford, twenty years before his brother Robert Edward, he had seemed headed for a successful career as both soldier and politician. He served in the Virginia Assembly and on the Canadian border as a major in the War of 1812. He was married in March 1817 to Anne, the heiress daughter of Daniel McCarty. The McCartys were an old Westmoreland family who had been pew holders with Washington in Pohick Church. To Stratford with Anne came her seventeen-year-old sister Elizabeth. Lee was made her guardian and the three made Stratford again a scene of lavish, exuberant living.

Fortress-like, the mansion was no bastion against disaster. As had happened two generations before, at the formidable house, a beloved child, this time tiny Margaret Lee, fell down the massive stone steps to her death. Her mother was inconsolable. In grief she began to take morphine and became an addict. And day after day, as an historian of the great house wrote, Henry and young Elizabeth were thrown "into a state of the most unguarded intimacy." Something reminiscent of the affair at Glenlyvar occurred. Elizabeth bore a child which, according to Westmoreland tradition, died at birth. The girl's stepfather, Richard Stuart, a prominent Episcopal layman, came and took her home. Also, though Lee fought it, his guardianship of Elizabeth was revoked. She put on mourning and became a recluse. At Stratford insolvency was added to scandal. In 1827, the great estate was sold for $11,000.

In the small job he got in Washington, where he saw little of his relatives, Lee found time as a man of literary talent to write a defense of his father's role in the Revolutionary campaigns in the South which a biographer of General Greene had seemed to belittle. He extended such work later in a book damning Jefferson for his criticisms of his father. Also, in Washington he put his writing ability to more immediate use as a propagandist, first for John C. Calhoun, who already had the Presidential bee in his bonnet. As second-place running mate with Andrew Jackson in 1824, he had been elected Vice-President. But Jackson, when the Presidential choice had been thrown into the House of Representatives, was a victim, his followers shouted, of "bargain and corruption." There, by what John Randolph of Roanoke more poetically called a combination of "the puritan with the blackleg" (John Quincy Adams with Clay), Adams had been made President and Clay became Secretary of State. In the Clay-Randolph duel which followed the gentleman from Roanoke's fierce figure of speech, Randolph took Clay's fire, which sent a bullet through his coat, then discharged his own pistol into the air. Advancing with hand outstretched, he cried, "You owe me a coat, Mr. Clay," to which the Secretary of State happily rejoined, "I am glad the debt is no greater."

Andrew Jackson, into whose service Henry Lee had now gone, would not have let Clay off so easily. Nor did John Randolph's enemies so gallantly spare him. Gaunt and increasingly erratic in his first fifties, the dagger-thrusting orator had been elected to fill an unexpired term in the Senate in 1825, in part because of the withdrawal from the race of his half brother Henry St. George Tucker, who had led in the early balloting. But Randolph had been defeated in 1829 on the grounds that some of his behavior in the Senate indicated that he was either crazy or drunk. Many Virginians who regarded him as the chief protector of Southern rights were infuriated. He was sent back to the House almost by acclamation. But he was tired of the "bear garden" of the House of Representatives. So with the inauguration of Jackson in 1829 he retired from Congressional service and accepted with doubtful wisdom, considering his health, appointment as Minister to Russia. He was unanimously confirmed by the Senate. So he set out, already senile appearing at fifty-seven, carrying with him in his baggage the opium on which he more and more depended. (Incidentally in Washington at this time Mrs. Smith reported opium was cheaper than gin.)

Other Randolphs did not fare so well. Dabney Smith Carr, Jefferson's grand nephew, was confirmed as naval officer of the port of Baltimore by only one vote. Henry Lee was not even that lucky. He had served Jackson well. He wrote pamphlets and newspaper articles for the Tennessean. This called for bare-knucks writing at this time when Jackson's self-consciously superior opponents were stooping to a low level of abuse. They accused the General and his beloved Rachel of adultery based on the fact that by mistake they had been married before her divorce from her insufferable first husband was finally granted.

Living at the Hermitage during the campaign of 1828, Lee was there when Rachel died. He had watched Jackson embittered in grief by the character assassination of his innocent wife. Under such stress Jackson much needed Lee's help. The Virginian was credited with the literary form of Jackson's inaugural address. In gratitude the new President gave him a recess appointment as Consul-General to Algiers. Lee sailed promptly to his post. In March 1830, however, when he came up for confirmation, it was clear that the old scandal at Stratford had not been forgotten. Some of his own kin kept memory of it alive. Every Senator present voted against him.

Washington's ear was acutely attuned to scandal. Ominously Mrs. Smith greeted the year 1829 and introduced into documentation the Peggy O'Neale Eaton affair in the same letter. She wrote of Washington, preparing to say farewell to the elegant Adams administration, as "alive and bustling as New York," and of the brightly lit carriages rolling to the last Levee of the Adams-occupied White House. For the first time, she wrote, there was dancing in the great mansion. But the social gaiety, she said was "assumed." It was a masquerade put on in advance of the arrival of the Jacksonians who, said Justice Joseph Story, constituted "King 'Mob.'" Story often reflected the views of his chief, John Marshall, even some said, in the decision which, without Marshall's participation, removed the last cloud on the titles of the Fairfax lands. He echoed Marshall's view about the rude new democracy. Certainly those who considered themselves as the refined and the well-born, including Mrs. Smith, felt that way about both Mrs. Jackson and Peggy O'Neale Eaton.

Evidently, when Mrs. Smith wrote, she was not aware that in Tennessee two days before Christmas Rachel Jackson, mortified and grieving, had died. The chronicler, who regarded herself as a social paragon and has been so regarded, told of laughing and joking about the President-elect's spelling and Rachel's pipe smoking.

Then she reported: "Tonight Gen'l Eaton, the bosom friend and almost adopted son of Gen'l Jackson, is to be married to a lady whose reputation, her previous connections with him both before and after her husband's death, had totally destroyed. She is the daughter of O'Neal who kept a large tavern and boarding house. She has never been admitted into good society, is very handsome and of not an inspiring character and violent temper. She is, it is said, irresistible and carries whatever point she sets her mind on. The General's personal and political friends are very much disturbed about it; his enemies laugh and divert themselves with the idea of what a suitable lady in waiting Mrs. Eaton will make to Mrs. Jackson and repeat the old adage 'birds of a feather will flock together.'"

One who certainly put them together in his heart and in his hot temper was Jackson. Within the month of his inauguration he was engaged in what seemed almost a military campaign to protect Peggy and—to use a mild word—rebuke those he regarded as her traducers. It is doubtful that he then knew of a conversation which had taken place in the house of his Vice-President Calhoun. In his writing at first the President seemed to suspect as the instigator of the gossip the wily and witty Clay, who was afterwards quoted as referring to Mrs. Eaton in his revision of a classic line: "Age cannot wither nor custom stale her infinite virginity." The mobilization of the feminine crusade against Peggy came from a source devoid of any such levity.

Confident and once beautiful Floride Bonneau Calhoun Calhoun (she was now thirty-five and pregnant with her ninth child) solemnly addressed her husband, the Vice-President:

"I have determined, Mr. Calhoun, not to return Mrs. Eaton's visit."

Calhoun may not then have quite realized the threat to his ambition to succeed Jackson as President in this irretrievable position taken by his wife. Already, of course, he was aware of the competition of Martin Van Buren, who as widower had no wife to direct his social steps. Still in such a matter of morals and social recognition, Calhoun bowed to what he believed to be his wife's prerogative in guarding the sanctity of society against the intrusion of a supposedly bad, brazen woman. Floride, as one with no doubts about her aristocratic authority, regarded the matter as closed.

The old warhorse in the White House certainly did not so regard it. He recalled happy days as a Senator when he lived at the inn of William O'Neale. He remembered the sweet singing of Peggy for the enjoyment of her pious mother. Rachel had approved of the girl. He was now ready to defend her to the death of the last politician—or politician's wife. He had nothing but scorn for such a remark as Mrs. Smith's that the ladies of Washington had taken "a stand, a very noble stand" against visiting one who, they said and repeated, had "left her strait and narrow path."

Peggy had been born in Washington, so she herself said, on December 3, 1799. More objective historians fixed the date as 1796. Her father William O'Neale (the name is variously spelled), soon after the founding of the capital opened an inn—or, as Mrs. Smith said with some superciliousness, "a boarding house." Considering Molly Randolph's experience the words "boarding house" did not at the time necessarily carry a degrading connotation in Richmond—or Washington. Of themselves the words hardly damned the O'Neales. Peggy's mother, Rhoda Howell, was the sister of Richard Howell, popular long-time Governor of New Jersey. (Incidentally this made Peggy a cousin of Varina Howell who would later be First Lady of the Confederacy.)

Many residents of Washington and visitors to it, including prominent personages, admired the pretty O'Neale sisters, Margaret, Mary, and Georgiana. Margaret—or Peggy—was from childhood the beauty of the three. Among others Daniel Webster, who early saw the political implications of the affair, testified to her dark and creamy loveliness. Dolley Madison earlier presented Peggy the prize as the most graceful girl at a fashionable dancing school. Her sisters made appropriate marriages. Georgiana married a clergyman. Mary became the wife of Philip Grymes Randolph, son of Archibald Cary Randolph, famous as the breeder of Sir Archie. Like Martha Randolph, he was a great-grandchild of Isham Randolph of Dungeness.

As an assistant surgeon in the Army he filled the files of the Surgeon General with pleas for transfer from the hot, coastal climate of Florida which he reported was destroying his health. Another Army surgeon reported that he had an "evident predisposition to Phthisis Pulmonalis." One of his last requests in the Army for a furlough was put forward for him on August 2, 1821, by Tennessee Senator John Henry Eaton, who at that point was only Peggy's very dear friend. Philip and Mary

Randolph's older daughter Mary later married one of the many Beverley Randolphs, brother of Mrs. Charles Howard of Baltimore. The younger daughter Henrietta married a Pendleton of Virginia.

From among many beaux, Peggy chose, perhaps not wisely, John Bowie Timberlake of Port Royal, Virginia. His mother's family was connected with the Brockenbrough family, a contemporary member of which was John of Roanoke's great friend, Dr. John Brockenbrough, president of the Bank of Virginia. Dr. Brockenbrough was at this time married to Gabriella, widow of Thomas Mann Randolph, Sr. Later Peggy's daughter, Margaret Timberlake, would marry Gabriella's grandson by her first marriage, John Brockenbrough Randolph.

If Peggy was pert, pretty, and pushy, her troubles were complex. Timberlake, whom she had married when she was very young, was "an Adonis from Virginia" but at least impractical about money matters. Suffering from asthma, both his constitution and his character were weak. As early as 1815 when Peggy was sixteen—or nineteen—he got into trouble about his accounts as a purser in the Navy. He claimed that when the ship on which he was serving was about to be captured by the British, he had thrown his account books overboard. Officials took a dim view of this story. Even Jackson, in his defense of Peggy, wrote that "being considered as a defaulter [Timberlake], could not get public employment." His father-in-law, O'Neale, put him into business as a merchant with unfortunate results. Then O'Neale himself was cheated out of his substance by partners. At this point, Senator Eaton as friend of the family and admirer of Peggy, intervened and rescued O'Neale from bankruptcy. Also he got Timberlake reinstated as a purser and, when the officer went to sea, made himself the guarantor of his accounts.

"God bless his memory!" Peggy wrote later of this benefactor, "for God knows that John H. Eaton had no other reason for his munificence toward my dear father and mother than the promptings of his own generous heart. It was too sublime a deed for that degenerate society. They could not understand how

any living man could do such a thing and not have some low
serpent-like design behind."

Peggy, who was often in the company of Eaton during her
husband's absence at sea, was certainly right in this. Serpent-like
or not, suspicions, even convictions, mounted when Timberlake
killed himself, on April 2, 1828, by cutting his throat while his
ship was at anchor at Port Mahon in the Balearic Islands. Less
than a year later, in what Peggy described as a "brilliant wedding," she and Eaton were married. "All the first people in the
first ward were present," she wrote. The chaplain of the Senate
performed the ceremony. But many, as Mrs. Smith indicated,
stayed superciliously away.

They continued to stay away from the fine house Eaton had
provided for his bride. Cards Peggy left at the houses of her husband's Cabinet colleagues were not returned. Then, to the great
dismay of the angry President, he discovered that the stand
against Peggy had invaded the White House itself. The old
warrior felt suddenly unarmed when a part in the proscription
of Mrs. Eaton was taken by the young woman he had brought
from Tennessee to be his hostess in the Presidential mansion.
Emily Donelson was Rachel's niece. Her ties to Jackson were
made stronger by her marriage to another of Rachel's kin who
bore the President's name, Andrew Jackson Donelson. He was
now serving as Jackson's confidential secretary.

Emily would not be shaken by the old President she loved.
And when Van Buren brought his persuasive gifts to bear upon
her, he found himself talking to an icy wall. That gentleman
who, as Randolph of Roanoke said, always rowed to his object
with muffled oars, made a defter move. In effect he arrayed the
Randolphs against the ladies who had taken their social di-
rective from Floride Calhoun. That would please Jackson and
possibly do mortal political damage to the aspirations of his
political rival, the statesman from South Carolina.

Mrs. Smith had been delighted when Martha Jefferson Randolph moved her big family into a house near Lafayette Square.
She was no more pleased than Van Buren who had come to
know Martha well when he was supposed to be courting her

daughter Ellen, now Mrs. Coolidge of Boston. He appreciated the great position Martha held as her father's daughter. The word "Jefferson" had ceased to be the name of a man and politician and become a synonym for the patriotism of the republic. Also, Van Buren understood the social value of alliance with Martha, who certainly no Calhoun lady or her cohorts could scorn. Historians have made much of Mrs. Calhoun's aristocracy as a Bonneau of South Carolina. The name Bonneau was insignificant by that of Randolph. Indeed, despite a sort of historical sychophancy about Floride, her people were only rich Huguenot merchants and planters, not one of whom ever attained more than local eminence.

So Van Buren went to see Martha. As a great lady of fifty-seven she had little money—indeed, only the interest on $20,000 which the states of Louisiana and South Carolina had given her as Jefferson's daughter. Nicholas and Virginia Trist, into whose house near Lafayette Square she moved, had two babies. Martha brought two other children, the orphaned son and daughter of her dead daughter Anne Cary Randolph Bankhead. With her came six, sometimes seven, of her own children. Three of them were unmarried young ladies, ranging from fifteen-year-old Septimia to her older sisters Mary, twenty-four, and Cornelia, thirty. The last two were already doomed to spinsterhood. They had few chances to mingle in society. Even in Richmond, when their father was Governor, they complained that he brought more politicos than gallant young gentlemen to the rather dismal Governor's mansion. Certainly Martha must have hoped for opportunities for them in the capital. She had sharply disagreed with Bishop William Meade, who condemned such dancing and frivolities as Martha welcomed for her girls. The Bishop was as much a Randolph as possible without being one. His father's first wife had been Elizabeth Randolph of Curles, and his mother Mary Fitzhugh Grymes was the widow of William Randolph of Chatsworth. Soon after this time the Bishop surveyed the decline of Virginia society in the company of David Meade Walke, whose grandmother Jane Randolph, daughter of Richard of Curles, had married the Reverend Anthony Walke.

The land these two pious gentlemen observed had once been the "most flourishing" in Virginia, and "having what is called the best society in Virginia." But the Bishop shook his clerical head: "The social glass, the rich feast, the card-table, the dance, and the horse-race, were freely indulged in. . . . And what has been the result? . . . the bankruptcy and ruin and untimely death of those [who] once formed the gay society."

Though retiring, as Mrs. Smith said, Martha indulged in no such lugubrious prospect. Bankruptcy had already done as much as possible to her. She wanted beaux for her girls—well-to-do ones if possible. Her boys needed opportunities. And in the city which had not ceased to be gay with the departure of John Quincy Adams, the amiable bachelor Van Buren was the Cabinet chief of young Trist. Yes, yes, Martha would be happy to be the guest of honor at Van Buren's gala dinner for the Cabinet officers and their wives, which would, of course, be attended by the lively and beautiful wife of the Secretary of War.

As a chronicler torn between affection and antipathy, Mrs. Smith described the event with great skill in terms of a tribute to Martha: "She has been treated with the greatest attention and respect by all the citizens as well as the officials. When she dined at Mr. V.B.'s he led her first to the table, even before the ladies of the President's family [who apparently on this occasion were present with Peggy], and at the President's house, Gen'l. Jackson led her before the Senator's or Secrs. ladies. And as our system of etiquette is more rigidly observed than it ever was before, Mrs. R. is thus placed at the head of society."

Apparently the dinner was not a complete success so far as its purpose for Peggy went. Evidently, however, it served Van Buren's purpose as the gallant protector of Mrs. Eaton which he made in the President's eyes. The deft, diminutive New York politician wrote: "Thus it resulted that at the second Cabinet dinner of the season to which all the ladies of the family of its members were invited not one of them 'assisted,' and the party being freed of any kind of embarrassment their joy was unconfined. Mrs. Randolph especially manifested the greatest gratification, to the satisfaction of all my guests who reverenced her almost as much as I did."

If the effort did not break the social glacier for Peggy, it pleased Jackson and benefited Van Buren. And it certainly did Martha and her big family no harm. Soon afterwards, not being able to control his niece Emily Donelson, Jackson sent her back to Tennessee. Donelson followed her. And a situation was created which advanced the security of the crowded house where Martha and her big brood lived with her son-in-law and his wife. During Trist's brief stay at West Point he had become a friend of Donelson. Trist's relationship to Jefferson enhanced Jackson's trust in the young man. So Trist moved on loan from Van Buren's State Department into the position of confidential secretary to the President.

Other Randolphs found the Washington scene in these Jackson days congenial, profitable, and pleasant. As little more than a boy, Martha's son George Wythe was given an appointment to West Point. His older brother Meriwether Lewis, not yet ready for civilian appointment, was decorative at White House social functions. Possibly, at that time seeming most fortunate of all was Dr. Philip Grymes Randolph, no longer a complaining assistant surgeon at an unhealthy Army post. Promptly after Eaton was made Secretary of War he removed the old chief clerk and put his brother-in-law Philip in that position which was then the equivalent of the Undersecretary of War in later years. And there were other Randolphs who were hoping for favor. One in the Navy was Robert Beverley Randolph, proud and handsome descendant of Pocahontas in the line down from Richard of Curles. More significantly in the Washington circle, he was the nephew of David Meade Randolph. His father, David's brother Richard, had married Maria Beverley of the great house of Blandfield. The younger Robert Beverley was to marry another Beverley elegantly named Eglantine. He was to discover that what Van Buren called the Eaton Malaria could be a malady from which even a Randolph could suffer.

Eaton, when he named Philip as second in command in the War Department, had told the former occupant of that position that he was not firing him because he had even the "slightest objection" to him. He felt, however, that the chief clerk "should to his principal stand in the relation of a confidential friend." The doctor was soon to have ample opportunity to demonstrate such a tie.

Possibly this close relationship was demonstrated when Eaton soon tried to abolish the position of Surgeon General Joseph Lovell, who had not always been sympathetic to Philip's repeated pleas for transfers and furloughs. Certainly it was shown in crisis when, in the socially quarreling Cabinet, Van Buren, along with Eaton, resigned. That provided the opportunity for the President to reorganize his whole Cabinet by firing, in effect, the anti-Peggy members.

The time had passed in the social feud for deft maneuvers. So Eaton, freed from any restraints of official proprieties, began demanding satisfaction of his former colleagues. Of those whose wives had scorned his wife, his resentment flamed particularly toward Secretary of the Treasury Samuel D. Ingham, whose own wife Eaton said was not above reproach. Philip Randolph was at Eaton's hand in shaping his bristling correspondence. Both had O'Neale wives cheering them on. They and their friends were infuriated when Ingham, on June 18, 1831, wrote Eaton that he "must be a little deranged to imagine that any blustering of yours could induce me to disavow what all the inhabitants of this city know, and perhaps half the people of the United States believe to be true." Two days later Ingham reported in indignation to Eaton: "Yesterday morning your brother-in-law, Dr. Randolph, intruded himself into my room with a threat of personal violence."

The next day, according to a report by Ingham to the President, Eaton, denied satisfaction on the field, attempted to waylay the Secretary of the Treasury on the streets "for the purpose of assassination." Eaton led a heavily armed company against him, Ingham reported. Randolph, he said, was one of them. Another apparently was Major William B. Lewis, Jackson's long-time friend of Tennessee days, now second auditor of the Treasury Department, a resident of the White House and member of the President's Kitchen Cabinet. He was an Eaton brother-in-law, too, having married a sister of the Secretary's first wife. He may also have been related to Randolph as he came from one of Virginia's oldest families. Probably also a member of the supposed posse was Amos Kendall, another Presidential crony and adviser. Eaton and all his alleged companions denied any such ganging up on the Secretary of the Treasury. "Unattended and alone," wrote Eaton, he did endeavor to meet Ingham and to settle their differences. Ingham hid, he sneered.

Perhaps Eaton did not lead any such group, but in her autobiography Peggy wrote that on this day her husband went out "in company with Major Lewis and Dr. Randolph. I kissed him good-bye, not knowing whether he would come back again; but I felt that we had all better be dead than in this misery. During the day my husband did seek for Mr. Ingham and endeavored to find him. But he could not be found in any of the places where it would be natural to seek for him—his boarding house (Mrs. Cochran's on F St.), or his office, or on the passage from one to the other. The next day the miscreant fled from the city and went into that contempt and obscurity which his mean and cowardly nature deserved."

The Randolph connection with the Eaton story did not quite end with the departure from the Washington scene of many of the chief participants in that affair. Indeed, for Robert Beverley Randolph, U.S.N., his almost accidental role in the story was just coming to climax. Peggy wrote about him in great indignation. After Timberlake's suicide, she stated in her autobiography, she would have been left a rich woman if Lieutenant Beverley Randolph had not been appointed his successor as purser. She declared: "This man took the money, mutilated the books, and endeavored to make it appear that Mr. Timberlake was a defaulter to the Government to the amount of twenty thousand dollars."

That was not a universally accepted version of the matter. When Randolph succeeded Timberlake, irregularities were found in the accounts. But a naval court of inquiry acquitted Lieutenant Randolph of any blame. That verdict could hardly have pleased the generous Eaton who was on Timberlake's bond. So the case was reopened by Amos Kendall as Treasury auditor and Eaton friend. At his instigation, four years after Timberlake's death, another inquiry was held in June 1832. Much of the evidence in the record now seems confusing. Certainly there was considerable acrimony at the hearing between Randolph and Kendall. The court's conclusion seemed uncertain as to responsibility for the government's loss—or Eaton's. There was nothing uncertain about the verdict which Andrew Jackson scrawled across the papers on April 8, 1833: "In the opinion of the President, the facts which appear in the case, and the conduct of Lieutenant Randolph throughout the investigation, prove him to be unworthy of the naval service of this Republic, and an unfit associate of those sons of chivalry, integrity and honor, who adorn our navy. The Secretary of the Navy is therefore directed to dismiss Lieutenant Robert B. Randolph from the naval service of the United States."

Randolph certainly believed, as at least one careful student of the matter concluded later, that he had been done a "monumental injustice." Evidently others shared his feelings. He undertook to express them in the most dramatic way. He chose as the occasion a day in the following month. Then the President, who was on his way to dedicate a monument to the mother of George Washington, came by steamer to Alexandria. Soon after the ship docked, Randolph, "late a lieutenant in the navy," came aboard and went directly to the cabin where the President was sitting. Deliberately—almost ceremoniously—taking off his gloves, he attempted to tweak the startled President's nose. In the violent scuffle which ensued with Presidential aides, "friends of Randolph clutched him, and hurried him ashore." A citizen of Alexandria, adding personal caution to public indignation, said to Jackson, "Sir, if you will pardon me, in case I am tried and convicted, I will kill Randolph for this insult to you, in fifteen minutes!" The President declined to make the bargain. No prosecution followed. And Jackson, counting his Randolph friends as well as foes, set out on a triumphal Northern journey with Trist in constant attendance.

Jackson was not forgetting the Randolphs, particularly with Trist by his side and young Meriwether Lewis Randolph who was often in his parlors. Though Trist denied credit for it, Captain Thomas Mann Randolph, U.S.N., was appointed Inspector of the Land Offices of Alabama and Florida. This one of many Thomas Manns was the great-grandson of the original Isham Randolph of Dungeness. His mother had been Jane, daughter of Thomas Mann Randolph of Tuckahoe (1741–93). So he was the cousin of Martha Jefferson and the nephew of her husband. Apparently other Randolphs had already gone to the Deep South and had not found the climate so unhealthful as Dr. Randolph had described it in his complaints.

Indeed, the appointment of a Randolph to the land office position in Alabama and Florida had been made at the urging of Francis Eppes, son of Polly Jefferson who had died so young. He was the grandson who had sent the dying Jefferson the last, discouraging news about his crops. This was only an item in the agrarian troubles of Virginia. In 1826 Francis had written Trist urging a general family move to "Florida, or Kentucky, or Tennessee, or Missouri." He particularly liked "the country between the Chattahoochee and the Suwaney rivers" where land, he said, could be bought for four dollars an acre: "Here lies the road to wealth!" Francis did move to the Tallahassee neighborhood, taking along with him his father-in-law, Thomas Eston Randolph, who, as its last inheritor, had recently sold the run-down Dungeness estate. The road did not turn out to be as rosy as he had expected.

There was nothing new about such proposals for Randolph migration. As long before as 1802, as Jefferson wrote at the time, Thomas Mann Randolph, Jr., "had been allured by the immensely profitable culture of cotton" and "had come to a resolution to go to the Mississippi territory and there purchase lands and establish all his negroes in that culture." Martha had not wanted to go. Jefferson discouraged his son-in-law. So that move was never made. But now Meriwether Lewis Randolph, looking also in the direction so many others had gone, was eager to follow. After many financial difficulties his brother Benjamin Franklin was finishing his education as a doctor. George Wythe had the possibility of becoming a commodore before him though his salary as midshipman was only $319 a year. Only the ill health of James Madison, described as "more industrious than brilliant," foreshadowed his early death. As head of the family, Thomas Jefferson Randolph was already showing the financial acumen which his grandfather lacked. Among them all Meriwether Lewis seemed the shining star and man of adventurous inclination. He looked with determination to the West his grandfather had purchased.

Particular notice was paid to this handsome young man when he served as floor manager at the inaugural ball celebrating Jackson's second inauguration. He was a favorite of the old warrior President who, though Mrs. Smith had described as in his "dotage" two years before, had put an end to Calhoun's threat of "nullification." Against Clay the General had rolled up 219 electoral votes to 49. Now he had rewards for his friends. He had made Eaton first Governor of Florida, then Minister to Spain where Peggy was accepted with the acclaim due her beauty and charm and nobody worried about possible lapses in the past. (His "confidential friend" Dr. Randolph carried dispatches from Jackson to Spain certainly no longer bristling in tone to anybody.) Trist was made consul at Havana to begin a long career as diplomat.

The appointment which must have most pleased Jackson's sentimental old heart, however, was that of Meriwether Lewis Randolph. Emily Donelson was back from Tennessee, no longer at odds with her uncle over social questions. And she brought with her Elizabeth Martin, her niece. Soon there was gossip about Meriwether and Elizabeth but of a happy, warm-hearted kind. She was a true daughter of the Tennessee West which was now much tamed. She had enjoyed training in voice and other ladylike accomplishments at the Nashville Female Academy. Her high-spirited fiancé, however, described her as "Western to the backbone" in a letter to his sister Septimia. He wrote: "A good sized yearling heifer ran across the track & she grabbed her by the tail and swung her clean over the wall, and kept the tail in her hand to brush off flies." Looking a good deal less so wild Western, she married Meriwether in Tennessee in April 1835. As a pre-marital gift Jackson had appointed Meriwether Secretary of the Territory of Arkansas two months before.

Times were looking better for all Randolphs then. Mrs. Smith described Martha and her daughter Mrs. Coolidge on a visit to her house. "Mrs. R. was so handsomely dressed (in general she disregards her toilette) and looked so dignified and well. Mrs. Coolidge looked lovely and elegant." Mrs. Randolph seemed a little taciturn, however. Mrs. Coolidge "conversed with perfect ease and great fluency until dinner, which was not served until five o'clock, when the curtains being drawn and shutters closed, the candles on the table were lit. . . ."

It was a time of taciturnity for Martha. She had burst out with her fears when George Wythe, hardly more than a boy, went into the Navy. Now Meriwether was headed toward the West which she had dreaded so long, remembering her own reluctance about it and perhaps the tragic crime there in which her Aunt Lucy's boys had been involved.

Meriwether was exuberant about his plans. Soon after his wedding he set out eagerly to examine his frontier post. Ever since 1833 he had been trying to borrow money for investment in the West. Now he was in a better position to secure both lands and funds. He made living arrangements for himself and Elizabeth in the new country. Then he returned East securing more funds with which he purchased thousands of acres of the "most desirable" land in the territory. On his return to the West he saw for the first time his son: "I have determined to call him Andrew Jackson. The Pres[iden]t has been my best friend & benefactor and, indeed, we are all indebted to him."

On his return to Arkansas he found the land boom he had

anticipated in progress. He bought more lands and established a plantation with two overseers and a score of slaves brought from Albemarle. With the help of his nephew Thomas Mann Randolph Bankhead he cleared land and began to build a "great house" (though perhaps of logs) on the banks of Terre Noir Creek at its confluence with the Little Missouri. Statehood was in prospect for Arkansas (not attended by any such quarreling as had marked the Missouri Compromise seventeen years before). Everything seemed ready for the re-creation of such a plantation order of the Golden Age as had once existed in Virginia.

Then in the midst of speculation another fever struck him. At twenty-seven, on September 24, 1837, he died of "bilious congestive fever" which would now be diagnosed as a malignant malaria. Betty brought her boy to her father's house near Nashville where he, too, soon died. She married her aunt's widower and Trist's friend, Andrew Jackson Donelson. They had a son named Lewis Randolph Donelson. But in Arkansas the cleared woods ran back over the unmarked grave of Meriwether which was only located by antiquarians more than a century later. His mother had not lived to hear of the death of her boy in the West she dreaded. She died on October 10, 1836, and was buried in the weedy and briar-grown graveyard at Monticello.

Meriwether's fate, wrote a family chronicler, confirmed the prejudice which many of his family including his mother had had about the West. "It discouraged," he wrote, "other members of the family from seeking their fortunes there." Still, others were to go and some would find that the West alone did not hold danger. It existed in far away places and at home in Virginia, too.

Perhaps even sadder than the death of Meriwether had been the fortune of Black-Horse Harry Lee. He had been as exuberant as his young cousin who went West when he arrived in Algiers in 1830. The Senate then had not implacably and unanimously turned him down when he wrote to Emily Donelson in the President's House on January 1, 1830. He told her:

"The Bey of Algiers has given me a fine Lion's skin which is tanned with the hair & the majestic mane, the claws and the teeth, and I mean to send it as a present to the Genl by the first good opportunity. It is said by both Turks and Christians to be the largest ever seen in Algiers and measures 11 feet & 1/2 from the tip of the nose to the end of the tail. I have thought it might be suitable to the heroic and magnanimous character of the Genl. and I should like to see it hung up in the passage at the Hermitage—where I hope the lion of our country will end his days in cheerful ease and tranquility."

Lee was not so to end his days. He was reunited with his injured wife but he never came home again. He became an extravagant admirer of Napoleon, undertook his biography and made a gift to Napoleon's mother of a letter George Washington had written to his father, an item of great pride. Apparently he maintained little contact with his younger brother who was to become a great captain, too, and strangely free from the faults of his line. Still, Black-Horse Harry Lee was not exiled from a Virginia without troubles. Young Robert Edward Lee was on duty at Fortress Monroe, Virginia, in August 1831, when news came from Southampton County not far away that a slave named Nat Turner had, leading a bloody revolt, horribly butchered fifty-five white persons—thirteen men, eighteen women, and twenty-four children. Lee's troops, which were in readiness a short distance away, were not required to put an end to the insurrection. Armed planters did that quickly. A report said that the number of the blacks that were killed in the suppression of the uprising has never been ascertained.

Certainly killed that August was the hope of an end to slavery by manumission, colonization, or any non-violent means, or the creation anywhere of a Golden Age of plantation living based on slavery. And never again was Virginia or any other part of the slave South free from fear. Something of ancient plantation security seemed lost even at such a great, quiet place as Arlington where young Robert Edward had married his cousin Mary Ann Randolph Custis less than two months before black Nat Turner had taken an eclipse and other solar phenomena as signs from heaven that the time to strike had come. Turner was mistaken. Still there were more portents of tragedy than tranquillity in Virginia—and not merely vague omens in the sky.

PART FOUR

Dispersal

Chapter XV

ADVENT OF THE LOCUST

THE LOCUST YEARS seemed descended upon Virginia. Great houses disappeared in flames or slipped from ancient owners into other hands. As the sectional debate mounted over the evils of slavery and the abomination of tariffs, the Golden Age of the plantation appeared to recede further and further into the past. Fire and debt wiped out the monuments of the gentry. The burning of Bizarre had a quality of nemesis about it. But the great, multi-chambered house of Cawsons seemed almost casually to suffer the fate which Bruce wrote had "reduced to ashes so many storied houses in the region of open, screenless fireplaces and careless negro servants." So little notice was taken of Dungeness's disappearance that it can only be conjectured in history that it went up in similar flames.

There was no missing the fate of Stratford and Monticello as they went out of Randolph hands to satisfy clamoring creditors. And, in 1830, Thomas Mann Randolph, the third of that name, sold Tuckahoe. Despite the fact that his stepfather, Dr. John Brockenbrough, was president of the Bank of Virginia (or possibly related to that fact in this time of banking troubles and controversy), this Randolph master of the old house had fallen into financial difficulties. The estate went to Hezekiah Wight, whose first name reflected a non-Anglican nomenclature unknown among Randolphs. This last Randolph holder of the homeplace was not alone in his troubles. In thirteen unlucky years, land values in Virginia had fallen from $206 million in 1817 to $90 million in 1830. Yet, in the 1830s, two great Randolphs died rich.

John Marshall, who spent the last thirty-five years of his life in public office, left, his biographer said, "bank and railroad stock and immense quantities of land," much of it in Randolph County, now West Virginia. Still at the last he was poor in spirit. He was troubled about the Nullification movement in South Carolina with its threat of secession. It recalled the Kentucky and Virginia resolutions his adversary Jefferson had sponsored when they were arrayed against each other. Also as a justice he met a more direct antagonist than Jefferson in Andrew Jackson. In one of those decisions in which Marshall limited state powers under the Federal Constitution, he had declared Georgia laws dispossessing Cherokee Indians as unconstitutional. But the same Jackson who had upheld the Union against Nullification was quoted as saying: "John Marshall has made his decision, now let him enforce it." The Chief Justice saw falling to pieces the Union which he felt had been "prolonged thus far by miracles." Yet his own fame was as secure as that of his cousin Jefferson.

This distaff branch of the Randolph family of Tuckahoe had flourished. Perhaps the Marshalls in Kentucky seemed unnecessarily blunt in the inscription they put upon the tombstone of Mary Randolph Keith Marshall, granddaughter of the first Thomas of Tuckahoe: "She was good, not brilliant, useful, not ornamental, and the mother of 15 children." Not always in such plain fashion, others of her brood as well as the Chief Justice had thrived. Some daughters had married well in Virginia. In Kentucky her daughter Mary was the wife of her cousin Humphrey Marshall, one of the greatest of the state's landowners who local tradition said counted his money by the peck. James Markham Marshall, who joined in the Fairfax land speculation, shared vast land holdings with his children. Only Louis Marshall, among the brothers, showed more eccentricity than acquisitiveness. Physician and teacher, he boasted of many duels during a sojourn in France, had strange ideas of academic discipline, and set the date when he said the world would be destroyed. Yet he served as president of Washington College (later Washington and Lee) until, as a sympathetic biographer reported, he lost the applause of his students and the support of his faculty. Beyond this generation Marshalls showed in a number of individuals the strength of this family line.

Another member of the Randolph tribe showed great financial acumen considering the eccentricity, even derangement, with which he was charged. John Randolph of Roanoke, when he died on May 24, 1833, in a fantastic deathbed scene in Philadelphia, with a whip in one hand and a pen to sign the manumission of a favorite slave in the other, left at least equal wealth. He was possessed of 8,000 acres of land, nearly 400 slaves, a valuable stud of blooded horses, packs of dogs of a variety of breeds. Though he often lacked cash, he had increased the patrimony which years before his stepfather had feared might be lost to British creditors. His farming operations were successful while Jefferson and Thomas Mann Randolph were sinking deeper and deeper into debt.

Often an ill man, he was a voluble hypochondriac always. Though he had changed as he aged from skepticism to almost fanatic religious faith, he had less confidence in the future of his beloved Virginia. He did not accept the doctrine of Nullification, but he had been in the field earlier than Calhoun in defense of the rights of states. His last campaign was for resolutions against Jackson's proclamation condemning the South Carolina move. He had earlier cried: "Asking one of the States to surrender part of her sovereignty is like asking a lady to surrender part of her chastity." He was impatient with the new—even the Jeffersonian —democracy: "I am an aristocrat; I love liberty, I hate equality." But his arrogant disregard of the opinions of others did not reach beyond his death. He left wills and codicils which were to serve as the basis for a decade-long inquest into his life.

In a will made in 1821, he had shown his humanitarian attitude toward slavery by provisions to set his own blacks free and establish them on lands to be purchased for them. Yet even earlier and eternally he had opposed any Federal action about slavery as an infringement of the rights of the states. In 1832, after his return from his unfortunate mission to Russia, however, the kind master became an abusive one, turning even on his beloved body servants. Then he made a new will ordering that his slaves be sold, in effect, "down the river" as the unhappy phrase was. Other questions were involved in the probate of the wills but this matter of the slaves was paramount.

Sentiment against such manumissions was growing throughout the South at this time, inspired by such fears as were stirred by the revolts of Nat Turner and others and by the mounting resentment against Northern abolitionist activities in the South. But those Virginians, named in the first will (notably Bishop Meade) to carry out the provision for the freedom of his slaves, stood firm against the revocation of this grant by the instrument of 1832. The legal question turned, of course, upon Randolph's sanity at the time he drafted the testaments.

Bishop Meade's views on slavery seem quaint a century and a half later. They seemed almost radical in the South of the 1830s and 1840s. Many Virginians, including Randolph and Bishop Meade, had indicated troubled consciences about the institution as members of the American Colonization Society which proposed the return of slaves to Africa. But many other Virginians, as multiplying slaves became a burden on worn lands at home, found the rearing of slaves for market in the Deep South almost the basis for survival or at least for maintaining the old standards of plantation living.

The year before John Randolph of Roanoke died, his cousin Thomas Jefferson Randolph, even in the excited legislative debates following the Nat Turner revolt, expressed his strong distaste for this business as a member of the House of Delegates. He favored the gradual emancipation of slaves but he was particularly concerned about Virginia's traffic in the slave trade. In 1832, he told his fellow legislators that the exportation of slaves for profit from Virginia had averaged 8,500 for the preceding twenty years. He declared: "It is a practice and an increasing practice, in parts of Virginia to rear slaves for market. How can an honorable mind, a patriot and a lover of his country, bear to see this ancient dominion converted into one grand menagerie, where men are to be reared for market, like oxen for the shambles?"

This Thomas Jefferson Randolph was no philosopher like his

grandfather, nor a brilliant and erratic man like his father. He was a practical businessman. The supposedly enlightened philosophic—or religious—view about slavery in Virginia was expressed by Bishop Meade. He was much interested in the spiritual welfare of the slaves and often preached to them. He had liberated his own slaves but later believed that this was a mistaken kindness. Slavery troubled him; he saw its adverse effects upon Virginia, but he was in great measure apologetic for the institution which he believed was a part of God's plan for salvation. The leisure of some provided by slavery had, he said, helped make Virginia "the fruitful nursery of patriots and orators and statesmen." Yet by producing among whites the notion that there was a "disgrace belonging to labour" slavery had created in "many of the sons of Virginia gentlemen idleness and dissipation." Apparently he was not shocked as Thomas Jefferson Randolph was by the export business of slaves from Virginia to the Deep South.

"Already the abundance of the South and West," he said, "is attracting them, as it does their masters, and they leave many parts of Virginia with joy, in the hope of a milder climate, a richer soil, and ampler provisions for their bodily sustenance."

Meade and others, named by John Randolph in his first will to handle the freedom and settlement of his slaves, undertook to prove that when the gaunt, old statesman revoked it, he was insane. Possibly it seemed evidence of aberration that in his last days he cried in a speech at Prince Edward Court House that Virginia had undergone a painful decadence in recent years and scoffed at the younger men before him in comparison with their fathers.

Not all Virginians were prepared to admit the sanity of such pessimism. Better evidence was given that at the time he changed his will excessive use of both liquor and opium had been added to his dementia. He saw devils. He spoke with vulgarity he had never used before. The Prince of Darkness was tempting him with "a beautiful mulattress." He talked much of death. Yet clearly beyond this acute period of mental disturbance he had been keen and clear again when he drafted resolutions in connection with the Nullification controversy, stating his view of Virginia's place in the Federal Union. One of his resolves was prophetic: ". . . that Virginia has never parted with the right to recall the authority so delegated [to the Union] for good and sufficient cause, and to secede from the Confederacy, whenever she shall find the benefits of union exceeded by its evils; union being the means of securing liberty and happiness, and not the end to which these should be sacrificed."

The litigation about the wills dragged on for ten years until February 1845, when the instrument of 1821 freeing the slaves was held to be the "only true last will and testament" of John of Roanoke. Apparently this was a decision shaped in the interest of the two principal but unhappy parties to the suit: the voiceless slaves and the deaf and dumb St. George Randolph, the last, lost heir of Bizarre. The verdict "gave the slaves their freedom and $30,000, [and] secured to St. George Randolph's estate a property valued at more than $50,000." Many Randolph relatives received small parts of the great estate. Some, wrote Constance Cary Harrison, "put these old fragments of Randolph inheritance into souvenir rings and silver tea-sets, to be handed down in memoriam of the unhappy genius, the shooting star of the Randolph galaxy."

The fortune of the slaves was not settled finally by the verdict. Under it, 3,200 acres were purchased for them in Mercer County in western Ohio. No welcome greeted them there. Henry Howe, in *Historical Collections of Ohio*, wrote of the freed blacks:

"These arrived in the summer of 1846 to the number of about 400, but were forcibly prevented from making a settlement by a portion of the inhabitants of the County. Since then, acts of hostility have been commenced against the people of this settlement; and threats of greater held out if they do not abandon their lands and homes."

Apparently not all the ex-slaves were intimidated in this supposedly free state. Some of them at least established themselves in the same county at the village of Montezuma, where their descendants were still living more than a century later.

St. George Randolph was about forty years old at this time and apparently no threat to himself or others. When his insanity had first become evident his mother wrote of the necessity that he be restrained by the slaves. Three years later, in 1817, Henry St. George Tucker went to see the demented boy at an insane asylum to which he had been committed in Philadelphia. He reported that he was surprised to find "his madness of so bad a type." St. George recognized his "Uncle Harry," but Tucker felt that "the moody expression of his countenance" indicated incurable insanity: "He tears everything to tatters that he lays his hands on." Later he was removed to another asylum at Baltimore. Apparently while not recovering his wits, he became a harmless lunatic and was brought to live at the home of his court-appointed guardian, Wyatt Cardwell, at Charlotte Court House, where years before his Uncle John of Roanoke, in opposition to Patrick Henry, had made his first speech. There apparently he was given full liberty of movement. Both rich and crazy, he was a familiar figure in the little town.

Sometimes others in his family seemed far more furious. There was resentment in the Tucker-Randolph family over the dead John's suggestion that his stepfather, St. George Tucker, had shown partiality for his own brood in the handling of the properties left by his twice-married wife. At one point John had refused to take the elder Tucker's hand. Still the younger Tuckers —Henry St. George, Nathaniel Beverley, and Anne Frances (Fanny) Bland Tucker—were devoted to their erratic half brother. His letters, particularly to Fanny, show a lasting, uninterrupted affection. Writing to Henry of his deranged nephew, John had said: "Except in the veins of a maniac, and he too possess'd 'of a deaf and dumb spirit' there [runs] not one drop of my father's blood in any living creature besides myself." Fanny gave him a sort of progeny on his mother's side, however, when her daughter Elizabeth by Judge John Coalter married Randolph's much loved godson and namesake, John Randolph Bryan, son of the Georgia friend of his youth.

Nathaniel Beverley Tucker (1784–1851) seemed particularly the political heir of his half brother. Possibly he was even in advance of him in his states' rights views. As far back as 1820, he had advocated secession from a union marked as he thought by "Yankee industrialism" and "shirt sleeve democracy." In his intense love of Virginia, he idealized much in the institution of slavery—especially those Negroes whom Meade described as "the most amiable race of savages which I believe exists upon the earth." As professor of law at William and Mary, Nathaniel passed on such views to his students. It was as a writer, however, that his influence was most widely felt. His book, *The Partisan Leader,* which Edgar Allan Poe described as "the best American novel," in 1835 expressed the feeling that secession was inevitable and prophetically described the approach of civil war. It was surreptitiously published, suppressed, and yet was used as propaganda for the South and against it. In less combative fashion, his brother Henry St. George Tucker and the descendants of both of them attained eminence in law and politics. Certainly they showed no signs of any such "weak strain" as Eckenrode ascribed to "the Randolphs of Bizarre" whose close kin they all were.

Other Randolphs were angrily engaged in mounting intersectional debate. James Pleasants, son of Anne Randolph, sister of Jefferson's mother, tried to maintain in the quarrel some of the characteristics of his paternal Quaker ancestors. As Governor of Virginia Pleasants, said John Randolph of Roanoke who rather liked him, was "too weak for the plow, and too slow for the turf." He was unable to go along with the more and more militant Democrats of his state but was relatively mild in his opposition.

No Quaker mildness marked his son, John Hampden Pleasants, as a militant Virginia editor. He vigorously opposed Jackson. His Richmond *Whig* became the organ of that party which in general espoused the cause of the propertied and the national unity they cherished. Long after Randolph of Roanoke's death, it was remembered that he described John Pleasants as "the unworthy son of a worthy sire," meaning evidently that he was the Whig son of a Democratic father. The young editor's relationship with Randolph during that statesman's life has been less remembered than a Randolph witticism about it. If true, the story indicates Pleasants's arrogance as well as Randolph's wit. Editor Pleasants, who was twenty-four years younger than Randolph, as the story goes, met the old orator on Pennsylvania Avenue in Washington. Placing himself squarely in front of Randolph, he exclaimed loudly: "I don't get out of the way of puppies!" He drew no expected violence. Stepping aside, Randolph replied: "I always do, pass on."

Possibly prejudice preserved this story. Other collisions were to have less amusing consequences. As a member of "Captain Harrison's troop of horse" he had gone quickly to the scene of the Turner revolt. Apparently, as reporter as well as soldier, he wrote the article in the *Whig* for September 3, 1831, in which shock was expressed over the savageries and cruelties of both the blacks and whites. Of the scene at one house in which the family was massacred, he said that "a bloody and more accursed tragedy was never acted even by the agency of the tomahawk and the scalping knife." But he spoke "with pain" of the "slaughter of many blacks without trial and under circumstances of great barbarity . . . generally by decapitation or shooting."

Pleasants also denounced legislation passed by the General Assembly of 1835–36, in effect, making any advocate of abolition guilty of a felony. Pleasants, wrote Virginius Dabney, "remained a courageous advocate of gradual abolition, despite the drastic change in public opinion during the 1830s." In the hammer and tongs pre-war politics he often found himself arrayed against the Democratic Richmond *Enquirer* edited by the elegant and effective Thomas Ritchie and his sons. Ritchie's sons, less able and more offensive, were operating the *Enquirer* in 1846. Thomas Ritchie, Jr., in the angry debate called Pleasants an abolitionist and a coward. Opposed to dueling, Pleasants, in the face of this ultimate insult, felt that under the circumstances only a challenge would preserve his honor. He called out the younger Ritchie. Thomas P. Abernethy, as historian, wrote that Pleasants appeared at the appointed place "but lightly armed." Then "he advanced to within striking distance of his antagonist, apparently making only a perfunctory attempt to defend himself. He fell with several wounds, but lived for two days." A contemporary journalist reported that "it was plain that he had practically immolated himself upon the altar of public opinion, and had given

his own life, rather than take the life of another." Dabney added
the judgment that "an eloquent voice, which maintained to the
last that slavery should be got rid of, had been silenced." Not all
Randolphs deplored the passing of this member of the tribe.

Many Virginians, however, opposed even the suggestion of
secession, including such an influential person as Bishop Meade,
who vainly hoped that "for the sake of peace and union, crimina-
tions and recriminations would cease." This was a vain hope. At
the end of the decade before the war, out of a white population
of 1,047,299 only 52,128 persons owned slaves; half of these held
one to four, and only 114 individuals owned as many slaves as
John Randolph's will set free. But ownership was no measure
of opinion. Tensions mounted—and bitterness and scorn. When
John C. Frémont ran a strong race as the Presidential candidate
of the new Republican party in 1856, Richmonders recalled that
his mother had run off from the Hay Market Garden, leaving her
husband for a French schoolteacher. So the word bastard could
be said more bitterly and with more confidence in Richmond.

Bitterness had been long and slowly growing. Even when
Francis Eppes was first urging family migration to the West or
Deep South, he had spat out scorn against Yankees and Virginians whom he felt submitted to Yankee ideas. The liberality,
generosity, and patriotism of the Old Dominion he felt were on
the wane.

"The noxious exhalations from the eastern states have poisoned
our atmosphere. Yankee notions and Yankee practices have
wrought a thorough change in the public mind. The maxim
now is to take care of number one; and that too at the expense
of every principle of honour, and generosity, and justice. You
may depend that the settling of this leaden-hearted, copper-
souled race of tin pedlars amongst us has had a great effect in
poisoning the public mind."

But in the same letter he added: "Mind you, I only abuse the
masses;—I never saw a fellow in all my life who gained so much
upon my affections in the same space of time as Jos. Coolidge:
—but it was because he was *entirely* different from any Yankee *I*
ever knew."

Still, in the Randolph family there were increasing tensions. Ties of great affection had been maintained between the family in Virginia and the household of Ellen Wayles Randolph Coolidge in Boston. Before George Wythe Randolph went briefly into the Navy as a midshipman, he had lived with Ellen while going to school at Cambridge. His mother and sisters had often visited at the Coolidge house. But, as the years passed, the Coolidges, young and old, lived in a world vastly wider than Virginia. Ellen and Joseph had spent an adventurous time in the Far East while he was adding to his fortune in the China trade. They spent much time in Europe. Around Ellen slavery seemed an anachronism even if not a curse. Yet strong convictions which she encountered were not wholly strange to her. She had been disturbed about slavery when she wrote her grandfather after her wedding journey northward. Now she seemed almost the center of an elegant abolitionist society. She found herself immediately in the company of the distinguished Bulfinch family. Her mother-in-law was Elizabeth, sister of the architect Charles Bulfinch, who (in a Randolph marrying fashion) had been the cousin of her husband Joseph Coolidge, Sr. Ellen's Joseph went into business with his first cousin Thomas Bulfinch, who proved himself a better writer than businessman. He is best remembered for his books, *The Age of Fable* and *The Age of Chivalry*. The South which cherished chivalry had little liking for Bulfinch. Significantly in this tense time, Bulfinch, though he hated controversy, was a strong supporter of William Lloyd Garrison, militant editor of *The Liberator*, in the anti-slavery movement.

In the 1850s Ellen's children seemed making more and more anti-slavery alliances by marriage with such New England abolitionists as the Dwights, the Gardners, the Appletons, and the Lowells. In a swift succession: Thomas Jefferson Coolidge married Mehitable Sullivan Appleton on November 4, 1852; Ellen Randolph Coolidge married Edmund Dwight on January 24, 1855; and Joseph Randolph Coolidge married Julia Gardner on December 18, 1860. Their Northern ties were fixed.

The Coolidge-Randolph children had in part been educated abroad. Two of the boys, Randolph and Jefferson, attended a

Gymnasium in Dresden. Randolph and Sydney were enrolled in
the Saxon Royal Military Academy there. Jefferson, Randolph,
and Algernon returned for more education at Harvard. Randolph
came to Virginia briefly to engage in railroad building which
was later to occupy so many members of his family. The striking
figure among them, however, who was to become a tragic symbol
of the divisions, North and South, was Sydney, born in 1830
as the twin of Algernon. A family tradition was that, having
exhausted themselves with family first names, Ellen and Joseph
picked these two fancy names at random on the way to the
christening. Genealogists would have been well served if others
had abandoned the repetition of the same family names generation after generation.

Sydney, who was given an honorary A.M. by Harvard in 1857
when he was twenty-seven years old, was a remarkable and must
have been a romantic young man. His adventurous career apparently began when he was twenty-two years old as an astronomer and civil engineer with Commodore Matthew C. Perry in the
famous first expedition to Japan. Walter Muir Whitehill, director
of the Boston Athenaeum, who married a Coolidge, in 1965 described Sydney's crowded youth. Whitehill drew his materials
from the famous Harvard geologist, Nathaniel Southgate Shaler,
who knew Sydney when the young man was an assistant in the
Harvard Observatory. Shaler, wrote Whitehill, "claimed that he
[Sydney] had been a soldier in the Franco-Italian-Austrian war
of 1859, had engineered a Mexican revolution, and, after seeing
a hundred Chinese beheaded, had made anthropological meas-
urements of their corpses!"

Participation in Perry's expedition may have been a favor
granted a promising well-bred young man by a New England
naval officer. The Franco-Italian-Austrian war may have made a
natural appeal to a young man trained in a Royal German military academy. Chinamen, dead or alive, may not have been too
strange to a young New Englander in this day of the China trade.
Engineering a Mexican revolution would seem, however, to have
been an improbable enterprise for a young Yankee. If such an
event did take place, Sydney may very well have been drawn

into the matter by the experiences of his aunt Virginia Randolph's husband Nicholas Trist or his relative Robert E. Lee.

The Mexican War showed the promise of Lee. It had provided both the climax of the career and the final undoing of Trist. Rising as a diplomat he had become what amounted to Assistant Secretary of State under President James K. Polk and Secretary James Buchanan. Then he had been dispatched by Polk to negotiate peace in the Mexican War. He made the peace, but on terms more mild than Polk had come to wish. The President damned Trist but had to accept the treaty. The diplomat justified his action on grounds which seemed strange in a Southerner in view of subsequent events. In a sixty-five-page letter he defended his action on the grounds that a harsher peace would have led the United States into imperialistic conquest inconsistent with all its ideals. The taking of more Mexican territory (to become possible slave states) than his agreement provided would, he declared, be "such an act of aggression against Mexico [as] would give the North grounds for secession to preserve for themselves a portion of the American experiment in democracy." Certainly this concern for preserving the North's anti-slave balance in the American Union seemed strange doctrine for a Southern Democrat. But Trist was one who rejected extreme states' rights ideas and strenuously condemned talk of secession. He was logical even if he seemed an apostate to Virginia when he voted for Abraham Lincoln in 1860.

His relative Sydney Coolidge may have found room for revolution in the confused Mexico which Trist left more intact than Polk wished. Certainly other Randolph connections were looking askance at the declarations of hotheaded Southerners that they meant to maintain slavery even if that meant destroying the Union. That required no reversal of views by Gouverneur Morris whose mother had been the tempestuous Nancy Randolph of Bizarre. His father, the greater Gouverneur, had disapproved of slavery. Now as the master of Morrisania but grandson of lost Tuckahoe, the son took the firm Northern view about slavery and the South. He had not been altered in this by his marriage in 1842 to his first cousin, Patsey Jefferson Cary.

The present Gouverneur, as an old line Whig, had found a most congenial place for himself as an original member of the new Republican party. Approaching fifty as talk of secession grew, he was choleric in his discussion of threatened rebellion. Yet his house was a sort of Virginia Randolph shrine. There were kept the family records. Oddly, as the supposedly erring daughter of the family, Nancy had received the Tuckahoe family Bible (which at long last through the Coolidges was to return to Tuckahoe). Also, Gouverneur, in reverent recollection of his Randolph mother, had provided the funds for the erection of St. Ann's Church on the Morrisania lands. Nancy and old Gouverneur were buried in its grounds which would later become surrounded by the tenements of the Bronx.

Just as there were young Coolidges in Boston, Gouverneur and Patsey Morris had a son, another Gouverneur, born in 1843, who was sharing the excitement of other young Northern men over the dangers to the Union. He was sixteen years old in October 1859 when his distant cousin, Colonel Robert Edward Lee, on leave at Arlington, received orders to hurry to Harpers Ferry. There the militant abolitionist John Brown had seized the United States Arsenal and called for an uprising of the slaves. On a roaring locomotive Lee, in civilian clothes, hurried to the scene.

Such things mattered little to a deaf-and-dumb old man at Charlotte Court House. Autumn was only beginning to mark the hills where St. George Randolph, though imprisoned within himself, had a freedom which had been denied him in the frantic middle years of his life. He had his own riding horse. He read and apparently enjoyed books in English, French, and Latin. His was a peculiar but almost perfect peace preserving the image of the mounted, cultured Cavalier. He was, wrote one who saw him then, a man of venerable appearance, with snow-white hair and a full white beard, but his figure, which was above medium height, was still "erect as a Virginia pine." As he walked, he planted his feet straight forward "like an Indian." His "eyebrows were black, his eyes were dark and piercing, and his features were finely chiseled."

In the perfection of his appearance, the determined movement of his walk, and the madness within him, St. George seemed a perfect symbol of the advance of the old, old dominion of the Randolphs into war. Some faced the prospect with forebodings. Some hailed it with cheers. They were soon to become famous as the rebel yell in the chivalrically described Army of Northern Virginia under the impeccable command of the son and brother of Light-Horse Harry and Black-Horse Harry Lee. Randolphs were ready—and tragically ready—on both sides of the divided American house.

Chapter XVI

THE DIVIDED HOUSE

WHATEVER may have been the facts about the Mexican revolution Sydney Coolidge was said to have engineered, there is no question about the role played by his cousin Edmund Randolph in Latin-American politics. Certainly as Randolphs taking opposite extreme positions in America's divided house these two seemed properly designed in contrast in personality and appearance. Sydney, according to his friend the geologist Shaler, was "a rather small, delicate person, with a delicate pale face, and a large nose adorned with eye-glasses." There was about him almost a "woman's look." He had, however, an "interior of valor."

Edmund, twelve years Sydney's senior, was not only courageous but also looked the lion. Born in 1819, he was given the name of his grandfather, Washington's Attorney General. His father, Peyton, spent an unadventurous life as clerk and chronicler of the Supreme Court of Virginia. His mother was the famous belle Maria Ward, who had rejected the courtship of John Randolph of Roanoke. Educated at William and Mary and the University of Virginia, this Edmund moved in his early twenties to New Orleans. There, perhaps with Randolph pull in Washington, he was appointed clerk of the U. S. District Court. Also, he found as a wife Tarmesia (or Thomassa) Meaux, daughter of a physician with a fine house on Canal Street. Significantly for his future, he acquired knowledge of the Napoleonic Code which was to serve him well in California.

The gold rush of 1849 pulled him West with thousands of

other men, but he did his prospecting, not with pan and shovel, but as lawyer and newspaperman. He had scarcely arrived in California when he was elected to the first legislature to convene under the State constitution. Almost as quickly, he became a member of San Francisco's leading law firm and a partner in newspaper publishing of dramatic William Walker. This diminutive, mild-mannered Tennessean is described in compendiums of American biographies simply as "adventurer." Already Walker's head was filled with visions of a Central American slave empire. Evidently Randolph shared them. After abortive early attempts in Mexico, Walker established himself as President of Nicaragua and secured American recognition of his rule. Randolph went to the tropical and turbulent country to help establish the government of which, it was presumed, he would be chancellor.

Unfortunately for Walker—perhaps for Randolph—the famous filibusterer found himself arrayed not merely against poorly armed Nicaraguans but also the formidable and relentless Commodore Cornelius Vanderbilt. Walker, possibly with the advice of his attorney, had taken the wrong side in a fight between American capitalists. Vanderbilt held, and meant to continue to hold, a company providing isthmian transit for the hordes hurrying to California. Walker died before a firing squad. Randolph then was safely back in San Francisco in a comfortable house on Telegraph Hill with a happy family, some of whom he sent back to Virginia for education in the fashionable school Thomas Jefferson Randolph's spinster daughters maintained at Edgehill.

Nobody was going to push Edmund Randolph around. In 1851, Randolph had boldly, as editor and journalist, opposed the Vigilance Committee which in the name of order had taken the law into its own hands. The committee had shown its readiness for stern dealing by hanging five supposed desperadoes and providing lesser forms of summary justice to others. However, wrote a California historian of this period, Randolph as lawyer devoted to the rights proclaimed by his cousin Jefferson: "publicly and boldly denounced that organization, its leaders, abettors, and sympathizers; and so terrible became his anathemas that a subcommittee from that body was sent to wait upon him." Pointedly the group suggested that he cease his denunciations, "or quit the city." But: "The reply received by the parent committee was such that the request was not renewed, *nor the penalty imposed.*"

The measure of his stature was shown when he stood equal and unawed in the panel of great American lawyers arrayed in the greatest law suit California had known, the United States vs Castillero. It involved the question as to the ownership by the United States or an earlier Mexican claimant of the vastly valuable Alameden (or Almaden) quick silver mine. With Randolph for the government appeared Edwin M. Stanton, soon to become Lincoln's Secretary of War. Opposed to them for Castillero was Reverdy Johnson. He was a former U. S. Attorney General, Senator, and diplomat. He had been prominent in the case in which Dred Scott was held by the U. S. Supreme Court not to be freed by a sojourn in free territory. With Johnson was Judah P. Benjamin, soon to be Secretary of War of the Confederacy, a position in which he would be succeeded by Edmund's cousin George Wythe Randolph. The case was to be a triumph for Edmund who demonstrated the greatest scholarship in California history and knowledge of the Spanish and American law involved in the case. He was to die before the case was finally argued on the basis of a monumental brief he prepared. His wife and friends thought the government was niggardly in the fee it finally paid for the victory he won.

He is less well remembered for his legal and historical learning, however, than for the oratorical fervor which, on a crucial occasion, he displayed. Evidently, though a pioneer in California, he had not lost his Virginia sentiments. He opposed secession and upheld the Union but staunchly defended slavery as the great American debate mounted. Then came Lincoln's call for troops to invade the South. With fury he turned on the President in a speech in Sacramento in July 1861. Then though already an ill man, a California historian wrote that he spoke with "the fury of an inflamed patriot and the frenzy of an inspired prophet." His feverish speech perhaps reflected the tuberculosis of which he, like so many of his family, died. Furiously he took his stand:

"Gentlemen; My thoughts and my heart are not here tonight in this house. Far to the east, in the homes from whence we came, tyranny and usurpation, with arms in its hands, is this night perhaps slaughtering our fathers, our brothers, and our sisters, and outraging them in every conceivable way shocking to the heart of humanity and freedom. To me it seems a waste of time to talk."

But he went on: "For God's sake, gentlemen, tell me of battles fought and won. Tell me of usurpers overthrown, that Missouri is again a free state, no longer crushed under the armed heel of a reckless and odious despot. Tell me that the state of Maryland lives again, and oh, gentlemen, let us read, let us hear at the first moment that not one hostile foot treads the soil of Virginia. If this be rebellion, then I am a rebel. Do you want a traitor, then I am a traitor. For God's sake speed the ball, may the lead go quick to his heart—and may our country be free from this despot usurper, that now claims the name of President of the United States."

Edmund roared his almost Booth-like call for the assassination of Lincoln in the month in which Union and Confederate armies rushed to their first full meeting at Bull Run. Then he went home to his house on Telegraph Hill to die at the age of forty-two. He was spared news which outraged other Randolphs in Virginia. The *Richmond Dispatch* carried the shocking information that Sydney Coolidge in Boston had been commissioned a major in the Union Army. After reading the report Sallie Carter, wife of Dr. Benjamin Franklin Randolph of Round Top plantation in Albemarle, wrote the Virginia family verdict: "A rascal—so much for his Southern feeling and love of Southern kindred!" Similar sentiments existed, if they were not expressed, about Randolph cousins at Morrisania, even about Virginia Randolph Trist who was loyal to her husband who remained loyal to the Union.

In the angry months before secession, Randolphs in Virginia moved headlong or reluctantly to the evidently "irrepressible conflict." The greatest of them in this generation provided the pattern of sad acceptance of what he regarded as his inescapable duty. Colonel Robert E. Lee (or simply R. E. Lee as he signed himself and as Virginians still prefer to call him), had been offered the command of the Union armies. He put the proffer aside. The Union he had loved was not one to be held together with bayonets. He could wield his sword only in defense of his native Virginia. Perhaps this, as his Virginia biographer Freeman said, was "the answer he was born to make."

Yet he did not urge even his sons to follow him. His son William Henry Fitzhugh Lee, called Rooney, had gone to Harvard in the years when the Coolidge boys were there. His classmate, the acid historian Henry Adams, said he had then "the Virginian habit of command." But other schoolmates noted that as he pulled the stroke oar in the Harvard crew he was the best oarsman they had ever seen. Like his West Point-trained brother, George Washington Custis Lee, Rooney had followed his father into the American Army. The father was thinking of both of them when, before war began, he said: "Custis must decide for himself and I shall respect his decision whatever it may be." It was hardly expected then that a youngest son, Robert, would be soon called to arms. They, too, were born to stand by Virginia.

Old and young so born were most others of the Randolph connection—women sometimes more fiercely than the men. John Brown's raid had freed the least hot-headed of them from indecision. At Edgehill, Thomas Jefferson Randolph, once advocate of the elimination of slavery, began to lay in a supply of Navy revolvers. His easygoing brother, Dr. Benjamin Franklin Randolph, in his fifties drilled with a military company in which his son enrolled. The youngest of the brothers, George Wythe Randolph, infuriated at Northerners, who were trying to make a martyr of John Brown, called them "low, half educated Yankees," though some of them were the cultured Boston friends of his sister. His oratory was praised when he presided over an early mass meeting designed to hasten Virginia secession. Strangely, considering his extreme views, he was one of three Virginia commissioners sent to try to secure a Lincoln promise not to threaten to coerce the states which had already seceded. Possibly contributing to the failure of this effort was the fact that Randolph was publicly hailed in Washington as "a poisonous secessionist."

The younger Randolphs hurried to the colors of the new Confederacy. They were at the great First Battle at Bull Run. Constance Cary, Jefferson's great-niece, wrote of her sixteen-year-old brother Clarence, later to join the Navy, there serving as a marker for the artillery. Her cousin Wilson Miles Cary, a Randolph too, began to keep at twenty-three a remarkable diary of his war experiences. Perhaps most dramatic of the younger group was Private Randolph Fairfax, grandson of the Virginia Randolph who had been married at Monticello in 1805, and first cousin of the current Mrs. Gouverneur Morris of Morrisania. At nineteen this young soldier began to write letters home to his mother which became classic in the Confederacy. Certainly one of the gayest, most versatile, and articulate soldiers in the Confederate armies was Innes Randolph, descended from the line of William II of Turkey Island. Entering service as a lieutenant of Engineers at twenty-four, he was to fight through the whole war and come out of it an unrepentant rebel.

Much of the whole history of this war of brothers was made on the battlefield by such young Randolphs as these and the Lees of the tribe including not only the great commander and his sons but also Fitzhugh Lee, their nephew and cousin. The supreme Lee, called "Marse Robert" in the colloquial term of his followers, was welcomed into Confederate service with language, prophetic in part, drawn from words written by his father Light-Horse Harry. The presiding officer at the still sitting secession convention addressed him: "You are at this day among living citizens of Virginia 'first in war.' We pray God most fervently that you may so conduct the operations committed to your charge, that it will soon be said of you, that you are 'first in peace,' and when that time comes you will have earned the still prouder distinction of being 'first in the hearts of your countrymen.'" There was to be no doubt about the last.

That story was to be made on great battlefields, but much of the Randolph record, long neglected, was shaped in the two emotional capitals of the divided nation—Richmond and Boston. Though it had been the seedbed of the abolitionists, the Boston of the Coolidge-Randolphs did not always seem so heroic as the early enlistment of Sydney Coolidge indicated. Sydney's younger brother, Thomas Jefferson Coolidge, who was twenty when the war began, later wrote with no apology of his own role in the war years:

"The war had broken out in '61 and the United States had issued irredeemable currency. History had taught me that the issue would continue because it gave immediate relief, but that the ultimate effect was invariable depreciation, which showed itself in the apparent rise in value of everything that represented real property, I therefore bought freely anything that came under my hand—pepper, coffee, iron, etc.,—and at the end of the first year found myself, owing to having followed general principles, the happy possessor of one hundred thousand dollars. The next year I did as well, and, as I was wise enough to stop when our currency began to improve, I found myself in '63 comfortably off."

That statement by their Boston cousin would have been taken by Virginia Randolphs with the scorn they felt for such "tin pedlar" Yankees as young Francis Eppes had damned long before the war. Certainly it suggested a Boston—even a Boston-indoctrinated Randolph—in complacent contrast to the beleaguered, sometimes almost breadless Richmond full of the horribly wounded which Constance Cary described in her book, *Recollections Grave and Gay.*

As nurses, cooks, bandage makers, seamstresses making old clothes and scraps and pieces serve their wardrobes, ladies helped maintain the courage of Richmond as the Southern citadel. They also were its chroniclers upon whom depends much of the remembrance of life in the besieged city in which the best and the worst of the Confederacy congregated. Ablest among them was Constance, afterwards famous as a novelist and social historian. She was the daughter of Archibald Cary of Carysbrook. "All old-time Virginians," she wrote, "loved to write themselves down as part of their parental estates." Her father's sister had married the contemporary Gouverneur Morris. Constance's mother, herself a heroic wartime nurse, was born Monimia Fairfax, daughter of Thomas, ninth Lord Fairfax who never claimed the title.

In Richmond Constance and other Randolphs maintained an amazingly gay society while they tended the wounded with whom they may have been dancing a few nights before. Hearses rolled close at hand. But in Boston Ellen Randolph Coolidge, with her Sydney in service, was not watching the prices of pepper, coffee, and iron but the casualty lists of Yankee boys so many of whom went away from Boston to die.

The war was closer at hand as well as to the heart in Virginia. After futile efforts with quarreling soldier-politicians in what was soon to be West Virginia, Lee was called to desk duty beside the egotistical and thin-skinned President Jefferson Davis. Perhaps the greatest contribution of Davis to his cause was the unswerving confidence he maintained in Lee. He held to it even in the first days of the war when Lee in the west was called "Evacuating Lee" and, when he prepared Richmond's defenses, "the King of Spades." Also a West Pointer, Davis had exaggerated ideas of his own military genius. When Lee was called from the field to serve as Davis's chief military assistant, the *Charleston Mercury* wrote that the appointment reduced him "from a commanding general to an orderly sergeant." Only at a critical point in the war in May 1862, with the Yankees at the gates of Richmond, was he given command of what he named "The Army of Northern Virginia" in which he displayed both his military genius and his character as a true knight of Virginia's chivalric aspirations. The faults of those two Harrys, his father and his brother, seemed no part of his personality or his tradition.

Still, an item of Randolph tradition marked his move to his magnificent command. He rode to his army on a young horse which he had first seen and admired in West Virginia. The deep-chested, quick-eyed, gray horse with black mane and tail was Traveller who carried him throughout the war. Fairfax Harrison, as an historian of Randolphs and their horses, believed that this great horse had in him the blood of the famous Randolph-bred Sir Archie.

Wars are generally the stories of great commanders. The Battle of Fredericksburg, in December 1862, was certainly not

merely the story of Private Randolph Fairfax. He was only one
of 18,000 men who died in the battle. More important seeming
was his cousin the Reverend Alfred Magill Randolph (later chaplain and bishop). His Fredericksburg church was, to Lee's indignation, destroyed in the battle there by Federal artillery fire. But
before Private Fairfax fell as a member of the "Stonewall Bri-
gade," he had written the beautiful letters from the field to his
mother who had been Mary Randolph Cary. After his death
they were edited by a famed clerical historian, Philip Slaughter,
and 10,000 copies distributed throughout the Confederate Army
at the expense of three of his cousins and greater comrades in
arms, Generals R. E. and Fitzhugh Lee, and James Ewell Brown
Stuart, called Jeb. Later, Slaughter, in speaking of the descendants of William Randolph of Turkey Island, said that this boy
Randolph Fairfax "was (considering the brevity of his career)
morally and physically one of the most beautiful branches of
this remarkable family tree."

That was, of course, only a pious pronouncement. No one could
project the promise of any of the young dead in that war. Another such one of the Randolph line died far from Boston in the
fierce battle near Chickamauga Creek in Tennessee, in September 1863, along with 36,000 other casualties. Another Harvard
man, who had gone into the Confederate Army, described the
death there of Sydney Coolidge. This young Rebel said that he
"was with the force that broke the Federal line where the Six-
teenth Infantry was stationed." As the shattered remnant went
back, he saw Coolidge "standing in his place with the point
of his sword up, making what the soldiers called a 'defy.'" His
old college mate recognized him and "knew that his signal of
no surrender would quickly lead to his being shot." He ran
toward him, apparently hoping to save Coolidge. But before he
reached his friend in the opposing army, he himself fell, desperately wounded. This witness, Leslie Waggener, recovered
and later became president of the University of Texas. What
Sydney Coolidge would have become no one knows. He was certainly interested in more things than the price of pepper, coffee,

and iron, but the description of his end suggests a man readier
for death than surrender.

That was much the mood in Richmond to which the Carys
had come as refugees. At the Fairfax estate, near Alexandria,
Constance had observed the tumult around the First Battle of
Manassas, or Bull Run. Then in Richmond Constance and her
mother were joined by other Carys. Notable among them were
Constance's double first cousins, Hetty and Jennie. Hetty, "as
fearless as she was beautiful," had been ordered out of Baltimore,
to which their family had moved before the war, by Union
authorities. Her crime was that she had played the role of Barbara Fritchie in reverse and flaunted a Confederate flag at passing Union troops. Equally guilty, her sister Jennie had set the
stirring poetry of "Maryland, My Maryland" to the music of an
old song brought to her by Burton Harrison, a young man from
the Deep South who had been a student at Yale.

With Confederate officers as aides, Constance, Hetty, and
Jennie formed the "Cary Invincibles," which added much to the
gaiety of soldiers on leave. They were asked, so Constance wrote,
by a committee of Congress to make the first battle flags of the
Confederacy "after the design finally decided on by them." They
saw much, of course, of their cousin George Wythe Randolph,
who, with the departure to the field of Lee, was the most prominent member of the family in the capital. He was thin, frail,
and dyspeptic. Long ago he had given up with distaste a career
as a naval officer for the law. He had married, in 1852, Mary
Elizabeth Adams Pope, a rich widow. They had moved into a
fine house on fashionable Franklin Street where they maintained
a brilliant salon. Perhaps his wife's wealth helped make it possible
for him to give up the law when his indignation was aroused
by the John Brown raid. He had not limited himself to secessionist
oratory. He organized the "crack" Richmond Howitzers of whose
first company he was captain. Then at forty-three, he saw action
in Virginia's first battle at Big Bethel. Praised and promoted, he
had risen to the rank of general when, early in 1862, Davis, in a
reshuffling of his Cabinet, made him Secretary of War.

The Randolph salon on Franklin Street was revived. Another

chronicler of Richmond in wartime, Mary Boykin Chesnut, wrote that "The men rave over Mrs. Randolph's beauty, call her a magnificent specimen of the finest type of dark-eyed, rich and glowing Southern womanhood. Clean brunette she is, with the reddest lips, the whitest teeth, and glorious eyes." Though older, she seemed almost as lovely as Hetty Cary who was the undisputed beauty of the Confederate capital. Constance Cary, who called Mrs. Randolph "the beautiful Oriental-looking wife of our cousin," helped her give official parties involving a series of charades, the first being "Knighthood." With Jeb Stuart and Fitz Lee joining in the play, the party was a great success.

Stuart, barely thirty, especially seemed the embodiment of "Knighthood" that evening. A descendant of William Randolph II, he was the beau ideal of the Virginia horseman in arms. Always splendidly mounted, in the field he wore a gray cloak lined with red. In his camps there was music and dancing but no drinking under his stern eye. He was a puritan disciplinarian though his cocked hat was crested with a peacock plume. R. E. Lee regarded him and his dashing corps as "the eyes of the army." Certainly in Richmond he must have seemed to the Cary girls too vital a knight to fall as he did in May 1864 in a furious cavalry clash at Yellow Tavern. There he interposed his cavalry between a Union drive and Richmond only ten miles away.

No glory in arms awaited George Wythe Randolph. His wife's salon did not suffice to maintain his spirit in his troubled office. Though his friends and supporters said that he did much to organize and supply the far flung Confederate armies, gradually it became clear to him and everybody else that Jefferson Davis meant to be his own Secretary of War. Word went around that Randolph was "merely a clerk." Perhaps his mistake was that he ceased to be one. Much concerned about the possibility of military disaster in the West, on his own authority he issued an order to a commander in the trans-Mississippi theater to cross the river to aid Confederate forces near Vicksburg, if certain conditions arose. Davis not only countermanded the order but made it clear that the Secretary of War had no discretionary power over strategy or administration. Randolph resigned. Soon afterwards he discovered that he had tuberculosis which made him unfit for renewed service in the field.

Richmond's approval of his course was indicated by his almost immediate election to the city council. He emerged as the city's defender. In that role luck saved him from disaster. On May 3, 1863, when Richmonders heard the news from the pulpits of their churches that Union Cavalry under George Stoneman was advancing in a raid on the city, Randolph organized nine volunteer companies to man the fortifications. The confusion was enormous as the Union force came within five miles of the capital on Monday, May 4. Randolph's volunteers marched to the batteries. There they realized they had forgotten to bring any gunpowder with them. Randolph sent for powder. Then it was discovered that none of the guns had friction primers with which to set off the powder. Fortunately the Yankees withdrew.

No reverent recollections were to be kept of this Randolph. Indeed, Clifford Dowdey, in his history of the Civil War, wrote that as attorney after he resigned as Secretary of War he was unduly active in defending conscript evaders though he had been one of the first advocates of a stringent conscription law and effective in securing its adoption. Dowdey also connected him with another case of some notoriety. Bibles, like everything else, were in short supply in the Confederacy. Episcopalians wanted Prayer Books which did not put "the President of the United States" into their prayers.

A number of clergymen and a Richmond bookseller, John W. Randolph, whose relationship to the family is not clear, engaged to relieve the problem. This bookman dispatched the Reverend J. Steward, a Confederate chaplain, to London through the blockade. On the same mission went a distinguished Richmond Presbyterian minister, the Reverend Moses D. Hoge. On the return run through the Federal fleet some of the religious literature got through, some did not. Apparently some of the religious blockade-runners were intercepted on the basis of a tip by a Union spy, a Mrs. Allen from Cincinnati, who had been given hospitality in the Hoge household. The lady was brought to trial and, as Dowdey put it, Randolph "turned up" as her defender. One version is that she was convicted but later rescued by other Federal operatives.

Dowdey, who evidently had no admiration for Randolph, summed up his recital of Randolph's activities: "Throughout the South the sight of all too many well-placed persons, like Thomas Jefferson's grandson, openly putting their private interests before the country's caused a swelling of that refrain, 'A Rich Man's War and a Poor Man's Fight.'"

Whatever sins he may have committed, George Wythe Randolph was evidently a sick man. Now gray-bearded and with his face a mass of wrinkles, he was examined by professors in the University of Virginia Medical School who diagnosed his illness as "chronic tubercule." With his wife, who no longer looked like the Oriental beauty, they made their way to Wilmington, North Carolina, where they ran the blockade to England via the West Indies. In London, in September 1864, specialists confirmed the diagnosis but concluded that his disease was arrested.

Back home Vicksburg was long lost and New Orleans. Sherman was marching to the sea. Grant was tightening his stranglehold on Richmond and Petersburg where Lee, still gallant in disaster, faced inevitable defeat. The young and beautiful, who were also the brave, still maintained an insistent show of gaiety and confidence to each other. It was two years since the Cary girls in defiant gaiety had organized the "Starvation Club" at the parties of which only amber-hued water from the James River was served. Perhaps the desperate times made love more important. Constance had given her heart to young Burton Harrison whom she had known as a Yale student before the war and who now served President Davis as private secretary. From among many beaux the beautiful Hetty had chosen a handsome West Point graduate, General John Pegram of Richmond.

On the evening of January 19, 1865, as Constance wrote later, "all our little world flocked to St. Paul's Church" to see them married. But Constance remembered that two days before Hetty had brought her bridal veil that Constance and her mother might be the first to see it "tried on her lovely crown of auburn hair."

"As she turned from the mirror to salute us with a charming blush and smile, the mirror fell and was broken to small fragments, an accident afterwards spoken of by the superstitious as one of a strange series of ominous happenings."

That seemed a small bit of destruction in war-torn Richmond. But on the evening of the wedding when Mrs. Jefferson Davis insisted that the Presidential carriage should take them to the church, the horses reared so that they had to abandon the Presidential equipage and take a shabby hack. As Hetty entered the church she accidentally tore her veil. The newly married couple went directly to General Pegram's headquarters near Petersburg, a pleasant farm near Hatcher's Run. Firing nearby did not disturb them. Hetty began fitting up the rooms to her bride's taste. On the night of February 6, Pegram was aroused with the information that the enemy was about to attack. Hetty made coffee. She wound his watch. The next morning when his comrades could summon courage to tell her that he had been killed leading a charge, she knelt beside his body. She put her hand into the breast of his bloody coat and drew out his watch, still ticking.

A cause was dying as well as a brave man. Hetty's brother, Major Wilson Miles Cary, came up from the strangled Confederate camp at Petersburg to Richmond. He wrote in his diary on April 2, 1865:

"I hurried up to Mrs. Pegram's & found Ma and Het. They were to have set off for Baltimore via Flag of Truce boat on Monday Ev'g but for this unexpected turn of affairs. They gave me an account of what took place in church St. Pauls in the morning. In the midst of the sermon and just before Communion Service, a messenger came in and handed Mr. Davis a dispatch. He read it and immediately rose and went out. [Others followed]. . . . finally the minister Mr. Minnegerode rose and read the dispatch of Gen. Lee—viz, that there was no immediate instant danger but that Richmond must be evacuated that night as the enemy at 7 1/2 A.M. had broken through his lines and severed his army. . . .

"I had, however, but little time for conversation and had soon to bid Ma and Het and the Pegrams good bye. Ma went with me to Cons. Cary-Anne Peytons, where I got from my trunk my nice uniform coat intending if I had to be captured or killed to 'go up' in full dress."

He started back to Petersburg but "stopped on the corner of Main and 9th to bid Constance Cary good bye." Back across the river in Chesterfield County where so many of his ancestors had lived he rested in the court of a building to make another diary entry: "Here, one hundred years ago in this very Court Yard, 'Old Iron', Archibald Cary, doubtless had frequently addressed his constituents and counseled their patriotic resistance to the tyrannous impositions of a British monarchy. And here a century later—after four years glorious battling for a continuance of the same rights which his patriotism had been distinguished in establishing in our first Revolution—were now resting in their re-treat before the overwhelming myrmidons of a Republic more despotic and oppressive than its British mother—the shattered army of the Confederacy. Among these wearied troops stood his great great grandson musing on the instability of human affairs. How in so short a period the glorious government framed by our patriotic ancestors should have been converted into a vile mob-ocracy of vile Yankees—pharisaic, bigoted, puritanic, satanic Yankees!!"

His anger was shared. His bitter frustration stirred in the hearts of other men standing at the last for the Confederacy. The less devoted or the more realistic had slipped away in desertion. Not many of those who remained were capable of the greatness in defeat of their general who had in triumph and now in sur-render become the true symbol for Southern chivalry. Sharing his courage but not always his equanimity in disaster were his sons and cousins who had helped build the Southern legend in which all Randolphs shared as Lees and Carys, Burwells, Carters, Harrisons, Fairfaxes, and Pages.

Less well remembered in a war generally told in terms of battles in the field was the great Lee's first cousin, the Confed-erate naval officer Richard Lucian Page, son of Light-Horse Harry's sister. Much earlier than Appomattox, as naval officer turned general, he had had to surrender Mobile to combined land and sea Union attack. Now he was a prisoner of war. He had accepted defeat with the grace of his greater cousin. But another naval officer cousin was less ready to submit. Commodore Thomas Jefferson Page (1808–99), descendant of Sir John and Susanna Beverley Randolph, preferred expatriation to pardon by his conquerors. As a United States naval officer he had a distinguished career involving explorations in many parts of the world. He had made important connections abroad, notably in Argentina and Italy. In the Confederate Navy he was sent abroad late in the war to bring into the South's service a formidable ironclad, the *Stonewall*. Its armament intimidated Union commanders of wooden ships sent to intercept him. But the war's end found him in Havana. He never came home again. He engaged in cattle ranching in the Argentine. Then he moved to Italy where one of his sons became a banker. A daughter married the Count of Spinola. He grew blind as he aged but he presided erectly over a household hospitable to Americans. In addition to his son in Italy, another lived in the Argentine. Still another returned to be a professor at Bryn Mawr. Richmond newspapers gave much space to his obituary when he died in his nineties in October 1899. But his withdrawal from his country was complete. Indeed, in the fullness of expatriation years later, his grandson, George Page, a dark striding man, became a radio propagandist for Mussolini in World War II.

Other exiles were less stubborn. In the dark Southern Easter of 1865, George Wythe Randolph and his wife were in Pau in Southern France, where his London physicians had suggested that he spend the winter. There they learned of the collapse of the Confederacy. They seemed well off compared to their Lee and Cary cousins in Virginia. Apparently they had been able to bring out with them some more dependable wealth than that counted in depreciated Southern currency. But now they lost £500 in the failure of their French bankers, Charles Joyce & Company.

In the summer of 1865, they were joined in Paris by his sister

Ellen Randolph Coolidge and her husband. With them was their
son Thomas Jefferson, who had done so well in pepper, coffee,
and iron. But with them also was the memory of their boy
Sydney, who had died at Chickamauga. Joseph Coolidge was
stiff in his manner at the outset. But George Wythe observed
"a visible thaw" before they parted. Still he was glad to be able
to decline his brother-in-law's offer of financial assistance. When
they met again at Pau in the following winter Mrs. Randolph
felt some twinges of envy for her sister-in-law who had two
servants. In Richmond Mary Elizabeth Randolph had required
six servants. Now she was reduced to one. Also, the one-time fiery
Southern belle was as bitter against the North as her brother-
in-law was about the South. Old ties bound the families together,
however, and Ellen, who was not well herself, wrote home about
her brother: "The dignified submission with which he has borne
ill health, ill fortune, suffering & sorrow has produced a great
impression on all who have seen & know him. He has been treated
uniformly with an amount of respect & consideration which few
people find. Wherever he has been, he has found warm & true
friends & has received the most friendly & flattering attention."

Evidently as George's health failed his heart turned home-
ward. He took the oath of allegiance before a U. S. Consul. He
asked Federal pardon. Mrs. Randolph's fine house in Richmond
was readied for them. He even talked of resuming the practice
of law. But he died on April 3, 1867, at his brother's Edgehill
estate in Albemarle. Ellen Coolidge survived him for nearly a
decade, dying on April 30, 1876, in a fine four-story brownstone
house on Beacon Street overlooking the Charles River.

Other reunions were taking place. Constance Cary wrote, "It
was thought best for us ex-Confederates of both sexes to keep
quietly out of public observation while still the wave of feeling
(enormously increased by the assassination of Lincoln) dashed
high over our reunion with Northern friends." Yet certainly
those friends and relatives were hospitable. She visited first her
cousin Reverend Herbert Norris "who had lost a noble son in the
Union service at Antietam." Then she found sanctuary where

Nancy Randolph in different times and under different circumstances had found it before. Morrisania's mistress now, Mrs. Gouverneur Morris, was her father's sister Patsey Jefferson Cary. She had had a son in the Union Army and, with her girls, was in mourning for President Lincoln when Constance arrived. Morris was "violent in invective against the rebels and all their works." The rest of the family had "to restrain him from jocular remarks of triumph over the conquered South that swelled my heart to bursting." Yet he was sorry when he hurt her and the "dear house" became a second home to her. She was living there when, on November 26, 1867, after a long separation during much of which Burton Harrison had been in prison, they were married in nearby St. Ann's Church.

That wedding scene was in sharp contrast to the picture presented of post-war Virginia and many Randolphs in it. The Lee family had been driven from Arlington early in the war. Now it was becoming a great graveyard where once Molly Randolph had lain alone. General Lee was offered many jobs, most of them by those who wanted to exploit his great name. His name was not for sale. His youngest son, Robert, who had served as a cannoneer in the war, cried: "They are offering my father everything except the one thing he will accept—a place to earn honest bread while engaged in useful labor." The daughters of Thomas Jefferson Randolph, who had been the richest man in Albemarle in 1860, reopened a fashionable girls school. Its revenue, said a family historian, was "indispensable" to the Edgehill household. Other Randolphs bore new burdens and troubles in the overrun Old Dominion.

Those troubles were sharpened in contrast to the marriage of Constance Cary which, as author, she happily described. It constituted rich reunion. The great house of Morrisania was decked and garlanded. Harrison, as recent Federal prisoner, summoned old pre-war Yale comrades, many of whom had served in blue, to stand as his groomsmen. All were gay at the reception in the old Morris mansion. Where Nancy had been married long before in a dress with patched sleeves, Constance, so recently escaped from the straightened circumstances of Richmond in wartime, described her appearance as a bride.

To complete the requirements of a family chronicle (this chiefly for my granddaughters), I will add that the bride wore a gown made by "Caroline Boyer, Faubourg St. Honoré, Paris," of white satin with large pipings of the same, heading frills of blond lace; a full tulle veil and a coronet of orange blossoms; that her bridesmaids appeared in Paris confections of white tarlatan with many skirts, bodices of white satin, and wreaths and bouquets of lilies of the valley; and that the bride's going-away gown, of marron velvet with a toque made of a pheasant's breast crowned with a golden rose and foliage, supported her during the trying ordeal of coming down the stairs into the old panelled hall, between the Marie Antoinette mirrors and tapestries of the Reign of Terror, into a lane of people headed by men joyously singing old Yale ditties as the carriage drove away.

Evidently it would take more than the greatest civil war to end the decorous advance of the Randolphs and their kin.

Chapter XVII

BEYOND REBELLION

NOT ALL Randolphs found reunion so charming and decorative as Constance Cary Harrison did. Nathaniel Beverley Tucker certainly did not. Grandson of St. George Tucker and the Randolph widow Frances Bland, he was a hunted man. At the time of his birth in 1820, his father, Henry St. George Tucker (1780–1848), had served in Congress and soon would become one of the leading jurists and law teachers of Virginia. Though the older Tucker had fought in the War of 1812, he lived a quiet life in Charlottesville enlivened only by an occasional indulgence in the writing of light verse. No such placid existence was in store for his son.

Nathaniel went from the University of Virginia into a variety of activities. He worked on the construction of the James River and Kanawha Canal, a project intended to connect Virginia Tidewater with the Ohio River. He managed one of his family's plantations. During the Mexican War he manufactured munitions in Richmond. His finances, however, were often shaky. He made a business of presenting the claims of others to the Federal government. He edited a newspaper. Then, in 1857, he succeeded Nathaniel Hawthorne as consul in Liverpool. There he made many friends who would be useful to him later when, after brief service in the Confederate Navy, he became a Confederate agent in Europe. His high hopes of securing supplies there were not fulfilled. In 1864, he was sent to Canada on a mission to arrange for an exchange of cotton for other commodities. Also he was supposed to make some kind of secret representations to Northern men of influence. He did make an exchange contract but Appomattox intervened.

He returned to Virginia to discover that he was accused of complicity in the plot to murder Lincoln. A reward of $25,000 was offered for his arrest. In the absence of any evidence the reward was withdrawn in November 1865. But he was tagged by the early suspicion. After unprofitable travels in England, Mexico, and Canada during Reconstruction, he came home in the early 1870s to a life of difficulties, poverty, and illness. He had important friends, however, even among staunch Republicans, and his kin were declining to be held down by adversity.

In more things than resulted from war and its aftermath times had changed for Virginians. Constance indicated that as she moved into the high ranks of New York society as an aristocrat and a writer. She wrote of the books of her grandmother Virginia Randolph Cary: "When I tried to read her books it must be owned that I thought them rather too grave and sermon-like for human nature's daily food." Constance's own books were later to be described as popular but dealing with "rather superficial social life" which made "no lasting impression." Her recollections were better than her novels. She wrote of her Randolph blood "as a slightly menacing inheritance." She had been warned, "Beware, my dear, of eccentricity." She was willing still to confront with zest the new world she found in New York with a successful husband, promising sons, editors waiting for her work, and great houses like those of the Roosevelts, the Fishes, the Rutherfurds, the Belmonts, and the Astors cherishing her society.

Not all Randolph writers welcomed the changed times. Innes Randolph exultantly defied them. His inheritance came down the line from William Randolph II of Turkey Island and his wife Elizabeth Beverley. Their son William married Anne Harrison. In the next generation Peyton Randolph chose Lucy, another Harrison, as his wife. Their boy married Anne Brown Innes. Finally Innes Randolph's parents were James Innes and

Susan Peyton (Armistead) Randolph. That company of ancestors prepared Innes for impregnability.

Evidently his Virginia loyalties were not shaken by his education at Hobart College in New York State and in his father's law office in Washington, D.C. He promptly entered the Confederate Army as a lieutenant of Engineers on the staff of General Richard Stoddert Ewell and served through the war. Afterwards, though still a lawyer in Baltimore, he became at the same time poet, sculptor, music and drama critic. The priceless item of his amazingly versatile career was his hilarious poetic hoot at his conquerors:

> Oh, I'm a good old Rebel,
>   Now that's just what I am;
> For this "fair land of Freedom"
>   I do not care a damn.
> I'm glad I fit against it—
>   I only wish we'd won,
> And I don't want no pardon
>   For anything I've done.
>
> I hates the Constitution,
>   This Great Republic, too;
> I hates the Freedmen's Bureau
>   In uniforms of blue.
> I hates the nasty eagle,
>   With all its brag and fuss;
> The lyin', thievin' Yankees,
>   I hate 'em wuss and wuss.
>
>   ❋   ❋   ❋   ❋   ❋
>
> Three hundred thousand Yankees
>   Is stiff in Southern dust;
> We got three hundred thousand
>   Before they conquered us;
> They died of Southern fever,
>   And Southern steel and shot,
> I wish it was three million
>   Instead of what we got!

I can't take up my musket
And fight 'em now no more;
But I ain't a-goin' to love 'em,
Now that is certain sure.
And I don't want no pardon
For what I was and am;
I won't be reconstructed,
And I don't give a damn.

Innes's poem was not designed to be persuasive to Yankees. Another of Randolph kin, however, succeeded in making the old hated South of slavery a delectable land even in the eyes of some who had most bitterly fought it. Thomas Nelson Page carried in his veins the blood of the Burwells, Nelsons, Pendletons, Wickhams, Carters, Lees—and Randolphs. He lived through the war as a boy not yet in his teens whose father was an artillery officer in the Army of Northern Virginia. He came in contact with Robert E. Lee when he attended Washington College while the great commander was president. He studied law, but, in 1884 when he was thirty-one, the editors of the *Century Magazine* in New York published his story *Marse Chan*. Thomas Wentworth Higginson of Boston, violent abolitionist who had led a Negro regiment during the war, read the story about the death of a slaveowner—and wept tears of sympathy and appreciation. Others in the North were ready to accept Page's picture of the South under slavery. It was, this skilled, sentimental Virginian wrote, "for all its faults . . . the purest, sweetest life ever lived," which "made men noble, gentle and brave, and women, tender, pure and true."

Rose-tinted or not, Page's retrospect met the emotional needs of Virginians including other Randolphs who were not finding the new Virginia easy or beautiful. They needed sustenance and were ready to seek it elsewhere. One such was Isham Randolph, son of Dr. Robert Carter Randolph of New Market. Isham had only come to his seventeenth birthday at the time of Appomattox, but his brother Archie had been surgeon of the 1st Virginia Cavalry.

Isham wrote later: "The valley of Virginia is a good land today, but, Oh, it was a good land and fair to look upon in the days of my boyhood, before the War Cloud burst in '61 and the lightnings thereof scarred and rent the fair scene; before the forests were felled to keep the opposing armies warm; before Sheridan swept it with the torch. . . ." He drew an idyllic scene of his father's slaves at work with the sweep of their cradles harvesting the surging wheat. In midafternoons, he wrote, his father brought each worker a jigger of whisky and later provided them with kegs of home brewed beer. Isham came to manhood in changed time. At twenty he got work as an axeman in surveys for the Winchester and Strasburg Railroad, "a B & O enterprise." Conscious of himself as a Randolph he wrote of the sweating labor.

"It is hard," he said, "to be a nigger and an Irishman in the day time and try to be a gentleman at night."

From the limited opportunity of Virginia, he moved to Illinois in 1870, working on location surveys for the Chicago division of the B & O. There a gentleman rather questioned his credentials. Randolph had declined a drink he offered him.

"What? A Randolph and a Virginian and you don't drink whisky?"

He had other qualifications worthy of any Randolph. By 1885 he had come to eminence in his profession as a builder of railroads, terminals, freight facilities and in Chicago as consulting engineer for the Union Stock Yards of the sprawling hog capital of the world. Then in June 1893, dealing with tough and sometimes crooked politicians, as chief engineer of the Sanitary District of Chicago, he supervised the construction of the Chicago Drainage Canal which changed the direction of the Chicago River so that its waters poured into the Mississippi instead of Lake Michigan.

This was the largest canal in the world until the completion of the Panama Canal. Naturally, he was called by Theodore Roosevelt to the board planning that canal across this isthmus where Isham's cousin Edmund Randolph and William Walker had played for high stakes long before. The Panama Canal as finally built was constructed along lines which Isham Randolph and a minority of this board primarily proposed. He went on planning more canals, big drainage programs, dams, hydroelectric plants across a long life.

It would be interesting to know whether in the active years his trail crossed that of his slightly younger cousin Epes Randolph. Both married Taylors from Virginia. Born in 1856, Epes, the son of William Eston Randolph and his wife Sarah Lavonia Epes, also went into the sweaty labor of railroad building at twenty. Leaving Virginia, he advanced rapidly and soon became a chief assistant of Collis P. Huntington in the building of the Southern Pacific Railroad. Later he worked in a similar trusted capacity with Huntington's successor Edward Henry Harriman.

Epes Randolph's greatest achievement was the rescue of the Imperial Valley of California from destruction by the Colorado River. Control of that recurrently flooding stream became an acute problem which threatened the clients, the interests, and the properties of the Southern Pacific. Harriman assigned Randolph to the seemingly impossible task of controlling the turbulent and destructive river threatening the valley into which thousands of settlers had poured. Despite several failures he worked undaunted. Success finally attended the tremendous business he organized of dumping vast quantities of rock into the stream faster than the river could sweep them away.

When Epes Randolph made this fight against the river he had already been suffering for nearly a decade from tuberculosis. Still, the great railroad builders Huntington and Harriman found him a man after their own hearts. In turn, though Theodore Roosevelt and others sometimes regarded the two magnates as predatory plutocrats, Randolph regarded Huntington and Harriman as public benefactors. He had little sympathy for Federal proposals to check such men in their railroad construction and railroad combinations. Those who regarded themselves as reformers, he thought were troublemakers.

That view was not wholly shared back home in Virginia.

To some there the railroads and the corporations often seemed almost as hostile as uniformed Yankees had once been. Randolphs divided as conservatives and radicals. John Randolph Tucker, brother of the Confederate agent, clung to his states' rights principles which he declined to believe had been wiped out in the war during which he served as Attorney General of Virginia. He stuck to them when he appeared as attorney for Jefferson Davis. He described himself when he went to Congress in 1875 as a Democrat: "an old-fashioned, strict-constructionist, state-rights logician." He spoke of tariffs as a perversion of the taxing power which could amount to robbery or fraud. But along with conservatives he was a so-called "sound money man." Possibly reunion was emphasized again in 1892 when he was elected president of the American Bar Association. Some who elected him, however, were aghast when he appeared before the U. S. Supreme Court for the Chicago anarchists involved in the Haymarket riot of 1886.

"I do not defend anarchy," he said, "I defend the Constitution."

Despite his efforts the anarchists were hanged. Sometimes he felt that the Constitution had suffered a similar fate. He retired from Congress in 1887 to become law professor at Washington and Lee University. The Randolph succession was maintained with his son Henry St. George Tucker taking his Congressional seat. The son seemed advancing beyond the liberalism of his father. He advocated the popular election of Senators. Attacking the control of legislative bodies by great corporations, he declared that "the successful manipulation of railroads and stock boards are often regarded as the most essential of Senatorial equipments." He refused to endorse the platform pledge of the Democrats in 1896 for the coinage of silver at 16 to 1. He voted for William Jennings Bryan, but, at the Democratic State Convention in 1896, he almost alone spoke for gold-standard Grover Cleveland. He declared: "I am not going to stand before a crowd of Virginia Democrats and blackguard a man that you elected."

Some of his relatives were ready to do just that. The landed gentry in Virginia was finding itself in the same hole as less aristocratic farmers in the West. They believed that free silver and inflation might pull them out. The troubled farmers had begun organizing in conservative fashion in 1885. In a Richmond meeting, an aristocrat of the ancient Randolph line, Colonel Robert Beverley of Blandfield, had been chosen president of the Farmers' Assembly. Its leaders planned to operate within the Democratic party. Less conservative farmers and/or planters were restive. In 1888, a Virginia branch of the more radical Farmers' Alliance was organized with 30,000 members, most of them mad at Cleveland, corporations, hard money, and railroads. The Alliance has been made to seem in history a sort of rube uprising. However, Major Mann Page ("than whom," wrote Virginius Dabney, himself of Randolph lineage, "there was no more aristocratic Virginian") became president. His fellow patrician and Randolph kinsman, Colonel Randolph Harrison, became editor of the Alliance's official and furious organ.

These gentlemen welcomed to Virginia such an Alliance leader as "Sockless Jerry" Simpson of Kansas. In 1892, the new Alliance-related Populist party nominated James B. Weaver, a Union veteran of Ohio, for President and James J. Field, a one-legged Virginia Confederate veteran for Vice-President. Much was made by their supporters of this evidence of Northern-Southern unity. That made no appeal to conservatives in Richmond. At a rally there in October, Weaver was denied rooms in a leading hotel. The Howitzers' band broke a contract to make music for the rally. Some eggs were thrown at the visitors. On the platform with Weaver at the rally was the strident-voiced Mary Ellen Lease of Kansas, famous for her cry that the time had come to raise less corn and more hell. The patrician Mann Page presided with unshaken dignity.

Despite defections the Democratic Cleveland carried the state easily. The Populist ticket got only 12,190 votes, though historians suggest vote frauds may have reduced its total. In the gubernatorial race next year the Populists nominated Edmund Randolph Cocke, descendant of the earlier Edmund Randolph who was Washington's Attorney General. His family had entertained General and Mrs. Robert E. Lee at their plantation for several weeks after Appomattox. His Democratic opponent, Charles T. O'Ferrall, beat him by fifty thousand votes.

Radical enthusiasm, however, had grown in Virginia in 1896 when William Jennings Bryan in Chicago made the Populist panacea "free silver" the first issue of the Democratic party. Then Joseph Bryan (no kin to the national candidate) at the other extreme from his cousins who had gone earlier to the Populists, as publisher of the Richmond *Times* helped organize the "Gold Democrats" or "Gold Bugs" as they were called. He was the great grandson of Frances Bland by her marriage to St. George Tucker. Frances's granddaughter had married John Randolph Bryan, no kin but the godson and namesake of John Randolph of Roanoke. Joseph's reverence for the Randolph connection was indicated in December 1879 when, with his father, he disinterred the remains of Randolph of Roanoke and moved them to Hollywood Cemetery in Richmond.

Joseph Bryan was in no funereal mood in the 1896 campaign. His *Times* described William Jennings Bryan's "Cross of Gold" speech as a "studied piece of sophomorical rodomontade." The platform on which Bryan ran "abounded in nonsense and anarchy in equal proportions." Bolting with Joseph Bryan was another Randolph, Beverley Bland Munford, prominent Richmond attorney, whose Randolph line reached back as did Bryan's to Elizabeth, daughter of William Randolph I of Turkey Island. To the angry loyal Democrats they seemed like the Federalists of generations before.

Quieter Randolphs were at work in these years. Sarah Nicholas Randolph, tall, gray-eyed daughter of Thomas Jefferson Randolph, taught with her sisters in the school for young ladies they established at impoverished Edgehill. Then moving to Baltimore, Sarah operated schools for the rest of her life. Her teaching alone did not fill her career. She wrote in reverent remembrance *The Domestic Life of Thomas Jefferson*. She added a life of Stonewall Jackson and an article on her grandmother in *Worthy Women of Our First Century*, published in 1877. More enduringly she worked to monument the past in stone

for both the North and the South. She led in the movement to
erect a bronze figure of Robert E. Lee mounted on Traveller in
Richmond. Later she was consulted by the designers of the
monument in New York to Lee's great, last antagonist, Ulysses
S. Grant.

George Washington Custis Lee, who had emerged from the
war as a major general, labored wisely as his father's successor
as president of Washington and Lee University which had been
a frail little institution at the war's end. There was little violence
in the politics of W. H. F. (Rooney) Lee, though he was elected
to Congress three times. He was the president of the Virginia
State Agricultural Society before farmers and planters moved
into more aggressive farm organizations. Bishop Alfred Magill
Randolph became "the silver-tongued orator of the house of
bishops." His sermons were less resounding than the speeches of
William Jennings Bryan which won that great politician a similar
description. Twice Bishop Randolph, as a symbol of Episcopal
unity, was invited to make the opening address at Pan-Anglican
Conferences at Lambeth Palace in London. Still, said a biographer, despite his deep consecration there was nothing puritanical
about him (as there seems to have been about his predecessor
Bishop Meade). He was "a genial, witty social companion." He
was only one of the Randolph line who added ecclesiastical
eminence to brilliance in the forum and the field. Among the
descendants of Elizabeth Randolph Bland were not only the
Gothic figures of Bizarre but also such impeccable princes of
the church as Bishops Beverley Dandridge Tucker (Sr., and Jr.),
Henry St. George Tucker, and Robert Atkinson Gibson.

Such men of the cloth indicated the easy ability of Randolphs
down their long line to communicate with the people of their
generations. Jefferson, whose voice could hardly be heard across
a room, matched with his pen the arresting, strident oratory of
John Randolph of Roanoke. John Marshall resounded in solemnly
announced judicial decisions. Robert E. Lee's great commands
to battle carried no more insistent message than his counsel to his
fellows in defeat to put down the gun and pick up the plow, to

bless Virginia with their devotion and their hands. Some Randolphs communicated best with the very drama of their lives.

Such a Randolph was the greater Lee's nephew Fitzhugh Lee. His promise had not seemed great at the beginning. In a class of forty-nine at West Point in 1856, he graduated forty-fifth. Still in the Civil War he emerged as one of the greatest dozen cavalry officers ever born in America. He was late in surrender. When his uncle's army was surrounded at Appomattox, he and some of his troopers rode off to Farmville, near the old site of Bizarre. There they capitulated two days later than the commander of the Army of Northern Virginia did.

As a paroled prisoner of war, Fitzhugh spent some time in Richmond. Then he went off as a man who had been a soldier all his life to engage in farming. Later he said: "I had been accustomed all my life to draw corn from the quartermaster, and found it rather hard to draw it from the obstinate soil, *but I did it!*" He did more than that. As popular planter with a fine war record and a great name (sometimes when he was accused of exploiting that name he said he wished it was Smith) he led a rejuvenated Democratic party to victory in 1885. Celebrating the redemption of the state, ladies and gentlemen danced all night in the 1st Regiment Armory in Richmond while two brass bands played. As Governor, Lee was no such Bourbon as his enemies charged such an aristocrat would be. He supported schools and worked to improve agriculture. During his administration a Boston post of the Grand Army of the Republic (perhaps containing the ghost of Sydney Coolidge) was welcomed in Richmond by the former Confederate cavalry general.

Popular and successful as he was, when Lee ran for the Senate in 1893, according to Dabney, railroad money was used to line up votes to elect a more corporate-minded candidate in the legislature. Unfortunately, soon thereafter he became a leader in a highly speculative real estate promotion at the village of Glasgow near Lexington. Lee became president of the company which induced investors from as far away as England to buy lots. He announced with pride that among them were the

Duke and Duchess of Marlborough. The Duke was making other better investments in America at the time—notably a wife who was Consuelo Vanderbilt. Though Lee apparently believed that the investments were sound, the boom collapsed. Neither a large hotel nor a power plant built in great expectations were ever operated. Industry failed to materialize.

Fitzhugh Lee was now a man who had surrendered in war, been defeated in politics, and deflated in business. Possibly as escape he sought and secured appointment in 1896 as U. S. Consul General in Havana. He retained his office there while back home great newspapers of the yellow press were clamoring for what was later called "a splendid little war" with Spain. The calmness, tact, and firmness which he displayed in this difficult position raised him to high national visibility. His return to Washington on April 12, 1898 (two months after the battleship *Maine* was blown up in Havana harbor) took on the proportions of a personal triumph. Less than a month later the former Confederate general, still only sixty-two, was commissioned Major General of Volunteers and assigned to the VII Army Corps which was expected to be the chief combat-force in the assault on Cuba. The fall of Santiago made its operations unnecessary, but Lee took his command to Cuba, established headquarters near Havana, and was charged with the re-establishment of order. He retired on May 2, 1901, as a brigadier general in the Army of the United States.

A new task awaited him in Virginia. No one better than this Randolph-Lee, who had been a general both in the armies of the Confederacy and the reunited Union, was better fitted for it. He assumed a chief role in planning for the Jamestown Exposition of 1907, which would commemorate the first settlement of the English on the Virginia shore. Now bearded, florid, broad-shouldered, he seemed, as the great horseman he still was, a perfect figure for the Virginia of the three centuries. Sadly he did not live to see the exposition he had planned. He died on April 28, 1905. Almost automatically Virginia made the inevitable choice of another Randolph, Henry St. George Tucker, to succeed him. The Randolph blood and the Virginia story were inseparable. Indeed, from Sewell's Point, where the exposition stood overlooking Hampton Roads, the American story ran with the tide up the James River to Turkey Island and forever beyond it.

Chapter XVIII

TALLYHO!

A RANDOLPH is a Randolph forever.

The tenacity to its bloodline is not reduced for many who bear other names. This is true even though, despite inter-marriages, the blood has been much diluted. Its mixture with other great and obscure families has altered the original strains of William and Mary Isham Randolph of Turkey Island. Some of the mixtures have brought diverse results. One member of the family, Fairfax Harrison, after his studies of Randolph humans and Randolph horses, concluded: "What an inscrutable thing is character." He rather questioned whether the marriage of Peter Jefferson to Jane Randolph had been so successful a cross as the later mingling of sturdy frontier stock with the imaginative Randolph-Bland-Tucker line. Yet others felt that Frances Bland, who mothered the Tucker stock, had in her earlier marriage to a Randolph cousin produced a malign strain. How can heredity be confidently counted when such a flashing failure as Light-Horse Harry Lee produced in two sons the almost unanimously rejected Black-Horse Harry Lee and the South's immaculate *beau sabreur* Robert Edward Lee? The geneticists and the genealogists have much still to learn and explain.

The genealogists much complain that Jefferson by his philosophy of equality made it politically unfashionable to put much store by the keeping of family records. One suggested that interest in family trees only began to quicken in Virginia when stories, sometimes fantastically fabricated for profit, suggested that Virginians might, with the help of the fabricators, become heirs to great properties in England. If the supposed heirs were hoaxed, eagerness for acquisition encouraged the tracing of ancestry. Certainly family lines early became important in the rule by the "web of kinship" in Colonial Virginia and afterwards, too.

Without confidently supplying the reasons for it, geneticists confront the fact that the Randolphs, disregarding some Will Wimbles, have produced a mighty American clan. The more enthusiastic among them may count the qualities assigned to such families by the sometimes rash Governor Henry A. Wise, fiery advocate of the Confederacy, in his *Seven Decades of the Union*. Virginia, he wrote specifically mentioning the Randolphs, "was settled by a race, or rather stock, of families the like of which will rarely be seen again—so manly, so refined, so intelligent, so spirited, proud, self-reliant, independent, strong, so fresh and so free." Much earlier Governor Alexander Spotswood had given such families the attributes of haughtiness, hypocrisy and malice. Certainly they were acquisitive, often extravagant. A chief Randolph characteristic was the readiness for the honors, the work and the duty of public service. And it was no accident that generations of Virginians and Americans eagerly called them to their service.

Randolphs believed in the virtue of the Randolph blood. Not even the greatest civil war could diminish their devotion to the family and the scenes of its development. Undoubtedly such devotion was responsible for a visit to Virginia, in June 1865, of Dr. Algernon Coolidge, whose twin brother had fallen at Chickamauga. In the war Algernon had served as assistant surgeon in the Hospital Service of the United States. On this trip he was accompanied by the historian Francis Parkman, already famous as the author of *The Oregon Trail*. From Parkman Coolidge had learned of the importance of family and public papers, many of which had been neglected in Virginia or destroyed in the war. Also, according to a family historian, he came to Richmond and Charlottesville "to see how his uncles, aunts, and cousins had fared during the war." On this trip were acquired the great collection of Virginia and Confederate documents and imprints now in the Boston Athenaeum. Other Randolph-Coolidges, notably the great scholar and builder of Harvard's Widener Library, Archibald Cary Coolidge, and the rich Thomas Jefferson Coolidges, father and son, added to the collection of Randolph family manuscripts now in Massachusetts.

On his visit to Charlottesville, Dr. Algernon Coolidge must have become aware of the dilapidated condition of Monticello. Even then the desire to rescue it from oblivion was aroused. Efforts to purchase Monticello were unavailing, but in 1898 Tuckahoe, where Jefferson had spent his earliest years, was sold for debt. Joseph Randolph Coolidge bought it in. Joseph's son Harold maintained a special interest in the place. It was held until his death in 1934, when it was sold out of the family again but to people who have kept it reverently. Indeed, as an "unrestored" but guarded plantation house above the James River, it seems to keep the Randolph background more intact than some other Randolph places bearing a sort of curator touch.

Randolph relatives in Albemarle and elsewhere guarded the often despoiled Monticello graveyard which still belonged to them. They organized a society of Jefferson's descendants who maintained public interest in the much neglected estate. Then in 1923, almost a century after the great man's death, the Thomas Jefferson Memorial Association was organized which was able to purchase the mansion and its grounds for half a million dollars. Now thousands daily drive to vast parking areas below the house and listen to ladies guiding them on tours through it. It is immaculately maintained but lacks the clutter which must have marked it when Jefferson as insatiable collector was filling it with everything from busts and books to seedlings and mastadon bones.

Other Randolph monuments remain. Colonial Williamsburg almost stage sets the scene on which so much of the Randolph drama was originally played. The Rockefeller rerun is excellent but somehow lacks the dust and sweat, and the mixture of slaves and statesmen, manure and tobacco juice which marked the original production of history. Dignity and beauty are well preserved at Blandfield which in this century was still occupied by Randolph descendants. Edgehill still stands on the grounds where Randolphs were happy and impoverished by turns in the past. There are other old places full of Randolph memories, even sometimes inhabited still by Randolph ghosts. Progress almost wiped out two of them, as fires and armies did others. The land needs of a great chemical company complex threatened Ampthill on the south bank and Wilton on the north bank of the James below Richmond. In danger of demolition the National Society of the Colonial Dames of America acquired Wilton, took it gently down in 1933 and rebuilt it in Richmond. Similarly earlier, Ampthill was removed to Richmond where today it is occupied by Tennant Bryan, media magnate, who as late as 1971 wrote that "there is probably not a drop of Randolph blood in my veins." Actually, of course, his ancestress was Elizabeth Randolph, daughter of William I of Turkey Island. Her niece Mary, daughter of Richard of Curles, presided over Ampthill as the wife of Archibald Cary. Even moved to Richmond Ampthill may contain her ghost ready to haunt this Bryan for his lack of attention to his household gods.

Most Randolphs remember, but their virtue in this century is that they do not have to look back to old houses and old deeds for their eminence. In his lifetime Fairfax Harrison wrote of another Archibald Cary, a great-grandson of the one who bred the famous Sir Archie. In Northern Virginia he was maintaining the thoroughbred tradition of his sires. Sedulously he preserved the bloodline of that great race horse and stud. Annually he sent Sir Archie's progeny to the yearling sales at Saratoga Springs. The hoofbeats of mounted Randolphs sounded long after that. In the 1970s, in the same Northern Virginia country, horses and hounds still abounded. At Middleburg, *The Chronicle of the Horse*, official organ of the Masters of Foxhounds Association of America, had as editor Alexander Mackay-Smith. He may be the perfect example of the Randolphs who never could quite leave Virginia. His own thoroughbred pedigree runs back in the Randolph line through Joseph Coolidge of Boston and

Ellen Wayles Randolph of Monticello and Edgehill. In his horsy journal Mackay-Smith listed as the master of the nearby Piedmont Fox Hounds Mrs. Archibald Cary Randolph of Oakley Farm, near Upperville. This Hunt, established in 1840, has on its button crossed brushes based upon the legend of the presence in this Piedmont country of a fox with two brushes that only runs on the full of the moon and has never been killed. Randolph hunters galloping in scarlet and old-gold colors seem approximately as immortal.

From this same country had come the engineer Isham Randolph. His son, Colonel Robert Isham Randolph, engineer too, and active promoter of river development was a colorful figure in Chicago in the years between the First and Second World Wars. In a life of varied activities he became the leading authority on Randolph genealogy. No cloistered scholar however, in 1933, he was director of the Century of Progress Exposition which made the best efforts of his Virginia cousins at the Jamestown Exposition pallid in comparison. More dramatically this Colonel Randolph, as the president of the Chicago Association of Commerce, also headed, though without rope and pistol, a vigilante type organization of rich Chicagoans called the Secret Six. The Colonel claimed for his group much of the credit for the prison-end to the rackets career of Al Capone. Some thought the Colonel exaggerated his role in that much hailed contribution to that era of gangsters, gin, and jazz.

There can be no doubt about another Randolph contribution to this time of prohibited gaiety and almost promiscuous gang gunfire. Captain Alfred Pace Randolph was a graduate of Annapolis and the Harvard Business School who gave his country serious service through World War II. But as a young officer he kept the light touch. Not exactly in the Anglican tradition of his grandfather Bishop Alfred Magill Randolph, the young officer added his own song to the light verses so many Randolphs wrote for their relaxation from great affairs. Perhaps his work did not qualify him for full association in letters with his ancestor, Thomas, the poet Ben Jonson called "son." Still, his generation gaily sang the lyrics of his song. Arranged for play on the ukulele it ran or skipped along like this:

> How could Red Riding Hood
> Have been so very good
> And still keep the wolf from the door?
> Father and mother she had none
> Where in the world did the money come from?
> Please let me ask it
> Who'd fill her basket?
> The story books never tell.
>
> They say that she found a wolf in granny's bed
> A big sun-bonnet pulled over his head,
> But you know and I know what she found instead.
> How could Red Riding Hood
> Have been so very good
> And still keep the wolf from the door?

Randolphs in the future may find more suitable for framing, as more conventional figures in a gallery of ancestors, four others in the Randolph line in this century—two gentlemen and two ladies. The ladies are better remembered. They were more decorative. Regarding them, it is not difficult to understand that procreation among the Randolphs was not merely a process designed to provide charts for genealogists. Nancy and Irene were the two most famous of the beautiful Langhorne sisters. Their father, Chiswell Dabney Langhorne, counted his ancestry back through Randolph marriages with Dabneys and Prices six generations to the marriage of William Randolph II and Elizabeth Beverley.

Chiswell Dabney Langhorne was one of the innumerable Randolphs and other Virginians who were, they said, ruined by *the* war. But he possessed in ruin a gentlemanly avocation. His daughter Nancy reported that "He told us that after the Civil War he played poker and was so good at it he thought people would get suspicious." In addition, like others of his kin, he turned to railroad building as a man with a special skill in handling black Virginia labor which found that freedom was not entirely composed of jubilee. With the fortune he so acquired he purchased Mirador in Albemarle County—a house complete with all the stage properties of Southern aristocracy: pillared porch, marble hall, curving staircase.

From that house surrounded by its stables, Irene first emerged to adulation. Virginius Dabney presented as a not to be neglected episode in Virginia history Irene's appearance at the much refurbished White Sulphur Springs in 1889. A regally beautiful girl of sixteen, she sent "palpitations through the ranks of eager young men." Undoubtedly many stout Virginia hearts were torn when she chose as her husband, in 1895, a Massachusetts Yankee artist named Charles Dana Gibson. She not only became his wife but his model for "the Gibson girl," who in hundreds of pictures became the American model for what the good, beautiful, erect young woman of this land should be.

In many of these pictures Gibson portrayed his lady as scornful of decadent European aristocrats on the hunt for rich and beautiful American girls. Irene's sister Nancy did not seem quite her opposite. Still, after a first unhappy experience, the man she married was a member of the British peerage though his father was an American Astor who some Britons felt had as an American expatriate bought his British title. Nancy Astor depended on no title for her place in England and the world. She was remembered in Virginia as a famous horsewoman whose vocabulary sometimes seemed shockingly derived from the stables. Famed as the first woman member of the Parliament of Britain from which her Randolph ancestors had come so long before, she was alternately regarded as a paragon and a pest. Feminist, prohibitionist, Christian Scientist, she lived to become a character of international controversy when, as hostess at the great estate Cliveden on the Thames, she seemed to some an active appeaser of the dictators before World War II. Gay, courageous, vital, she would not have deigned to defend her own aristocracy. But in the new, moneyed American aristocracy of her husband she gave play to her wit. To Grace Vanderbilt she was reported to have said: "The Astors skinned skunks a hundred years before the Vanderbilts worked ferries." Of her Virginia tradition she found it necessary to say only: "Everything of importance happened to me in Virginia."

Of the two gentlemen, Fairfax Harrison, though born in New York and educated at Yale, shared such a feeling about Virginia. With an estate—or farm, as he preferred to call it—close to horse breeding neighbors in Northern Virginia, he lived a life of amazing diversity. He combined in one crowded life careers as railroad president, historian, farmer, and classical scholar. Both energetic and precise, he published his books privately and anonymously lest, as he wrote, he be troubled by ladies anxious to prove ancestral ties adequate for membership in the Colonial Dames. Occasionally a trifle stiffly impatient, he wrote a long letter dismissing his New York tailor for keeping him waiting for a fitting.

In Chicago, where Isham Randolph had turned a river around, he was scornful of the society of some of the pretentious rich. Also there, when he walked through the turmoil of its crowded streets, he found it "extraordinary that we are a great nation when such mobs choose our magistrates." From such turmoil, as a too modest scholar he found release and intellectual stimulation in translating and publishing *Roman Farm Management: The Treaties of Cato and Varro*. Yet, he served that "great nation" in World War I as chairman of the Railroads' War Board aggressively urging the companies to unify their efforts. He had little patience with the Democratic doctrine of states' rights: "a strong centralization of power in the hands of the Government at Washington is the only effective way to deal with the industrial problems which today face the American people." He felt that he had escaped the political strangulation of men of Southern sentiments in the Democratic party when he voted for Warren Harding in 1920.

Strangely, Harrison's views both coincided and sharply differed from those of his relative Thomas Jefferson Coolidge, Jr. (1893-1959). Both revered their ancestors. This Boston great-great-grandson of Jefferson described himself as a "very old-fashioned liberal." In his case that was a long, long way from left wing. A perfect Boston Brahmin in this century, his mother was an Amory and his grandmother an Appleton. A Harvard man, of course, he played varsity football and graduated magna cum laude. He was related to Boston's most solid and proper financial and philanthropic institutions, including the Old Colony Trust, the First National Bank of Boston, art museums which his family had endowed, the Peter Bent Brigham Hospital, and the United Fruit Company.

In a climax of his career he confronted another Harvard man of a great American family—Franklin Delano Roosevelt. Though Roosevelt had had Coolidge's great uncle, the historian and library builder Archibald Cary Coolidge, as his adviser, he did not graduate magna cum laude but was handsomely evident in the Harvard Yard as a young man of many extra curricular activities. While he was to seem to some a traitor to his and Coolidge's class, he honored great names and admired great riches. In 1934 he named Coolidge Undersecretary of the Treasury. That was an experiment bound to fail. Coolidge, like his ancestor Jefferson whom Roosevelt admired as the founder of his party, believed in the decentralization of government and strict limitation of government spending. Inevitably the exuberant Roosevelt and a disillusioned Coolidge parted company in 1936. The latter went back to Boston to write the almost plaintively titled book *Why Centralize Government?* But Roosevelt that year carried both Massachusetts and Virginia and all but two of the other states. In this rushing disregard of his question Coolidge did not lose his composure. Randolphs had often been greatest in defeat. Coolidge walked proudly out of history, but his steps took him often to the small mountain in Virginia where he presided as president of the Monticello Association. The world could still be seen in proper perspective from there.

Other Randolphs were moving with him in that period when America was advancing from Depression to War. They served as lawyers, professors, writers, diplomats, doctors, ministers, scientists, a famed naval architect, a noted psychiatrist, still soldiers and politicians, too. They guarded—and guard—the lares and the penates, not disturbed because there are some mere Will Wimbles among them. Even these last are useful as items by which to measure the greatest eminence of other men and women who still bless their land and add glory to its story.

The race-horse breed still runs with mane and tail flying in the race down the course of a land which still needs its stamina and speed.

Tallyho!

SOURCES AND ACKNOWLEDGMENTS

FINISHING a book about the Randolphs as almost certainly the first family of America, a man feels much as he might have felt if, as a stranger, he had sought his way through the boxwood labyrinth at Tuckahoe and, after bafflement in blind and twisting green alleys, found his way to the end.

Certainly the story makes a maze of intermingled, often inter-married men and women, wearing similar names in successive genera-tions. Even some Randolphs have been lost in their "web of kinship." There long remained conflict, even among those who kept the records of the family tree and all its branches, as to whether the wife of the first Thomas of Tuckahoe was a Churchill or a Fleming. Genealogical authorities have clung for nearly three centuries to an incorrect death date for William Randolph I despite contemporary evidence in the diary of William Byrd. Some authorities are suspect. Even such a one as Wassell Randolph has sometimes been flippantly described as Wassell, the Fossil. Still confronting the maze of kinship and the dangers of writing about it, I bespeak charity for others as I know I may need it myself. Considering the number of John Randolphs in the family it is no wonder that one of them added "of Roanoke" to his name. There were three Thomas Mann Randolphs living at one time. Lees and Carys have had the same addiction to name duplica-tions. And the confusion grew as the family multiplied.

Certainly the great family descended from William and Mary Isham Randolph, "the Adam and Eve of Virginia," has proliferated in approximately ten generations. Only their big brood is included in this book. It should be mentioned, however, that there are other Randolph lines of distinction even if they did not produce the giants—notably the Randolph family of New Jersey and the other Virginia

Randolphs descended from William's uncle Henry. Some of the Turkey Island line were childless but the stone over the grave of Thomas Jefferson Randolph and Jane Hollins Nicholas in the Monticello cemetery was erected by their twelve children. Big families bulged big houses. And Randolphs have scattered in restlessness, pioneering, marriage, and exile. Thomas Jefferson, for instance, has more descendants in New England than in Virginia.

Having crossed the trail of many Randolphs in other books, my fascination and curiosity led me to write this one. My long time friend and aid in research, Margaret Price, of the North Carolina State Library, was a little appalled by my temerity as a North Carolina democrat writing of Virginia aristocrats. She went to work gathering materials all the same, and steadily enriched my resources until she died in 1971. This book is a small shaft erected in her memory.

Despite her warning, Virginians seemed hospitable to my enterprise. John Melville Jennings, the debonair director of the Virginia Historical Society, saw no invasion in my entry into the historical realm over which he presides. Wryly he remarked that it did not seem strange to him that a North Carolinian writing history had to cross the border into the Old Dominion. Some Randolphs apparently welcomed my poking into their family preserve. Very helpful among them were Ethel Hunter Anderson, Ursula Harrison Baird, Lucy Tunstall Randolph Hottel, Angus Menzies, McDonald Wellford, Dr. Angus Randolph, Mrs. A. C. Randolph, George Green Shackelford, and Olivia Taylor. Other very helpful Virginians were: James A. Bear, Jr., Joseph Bryan, III, Tennant Bryan, Virginius Dabney, Alonzo T. Dill, Clifford Dowdey, Carey McConnaughey, J. G. Mizell, David Y. Paschall, and Elie Weeks.

Randolph related materials are as scattered as the family. Curators in various libraries and archives have generously given me aid. I thank particularly Edmund Berkeley, Jr., of the University of Virginia Library; Julian P. Boyd, editor of The Papers of Thomas Jefferson; Jane Carson and Burke Davis of Colonial Williamsburg; Richard Dillon, of the Sutro Library in San Francisco; Clark A. Elliott, of the archives division of the Harvard University Library; John L. Ferguson, of the Arkansas History Commission; Henry Grunder, of the Earl Gregg Swem Library at William and Mary; John O. Gustafson, of the National Archives and Records Service; Lila Hawes, of the Georgia Historical Society; James J. Heslin, of the Historical Society of New York City; Vice Admiral Edwin B. Hooper, director of Naval History;

John Melville Jennings, of the Virginia Historical Society; Louis C. Jones, of the Historical Association of New York State; I. T. Littleton, of the D. H. Hill Library at North Carolina State University; Jerrold Orne, of the University of North Carolina Library at Chapel Hill; Conrad Weitzel, of the Ohio Historical Society; and Walter Muir Whitehill, of the Boston Athenaeum.

Others who gave me aid and comfort in writing the book include: Elizabeth Boatwright Coker, Landon and Katherine Derby, Claytor W. Graham, Jr., Lodwick Hartley, William and Marianne Highberger, Francis C. and Ethel Hunter, Edith Inglesby, George London, Joseph T. Murtagh, Francis Paschal, Hugh B. Patterson, James Patton, Jet Ragsdale, Richardene Ramsay, George Rogers, Jr.

As always this is as much the book of my wife Lucy as it is my own. To her I say my thanks for researching, editing, typing, and above all —for patience.

Finally I am grateful to the authors and editors, living and dead, of the following books and papers which made possible this story:

Abernethy, Thomas Perkins. *Western Lands and the American Revolution,* New York, 1937.

Adams, Charles Francis, editor. *Letters of Mrs. Adams, the Wife of John Adams,* 2 vols., Boston, 1841.

Adams, Henry. *John Randolph,* 11th edition, Boston, 1888.

———. *History of the United States During the Administration of Thomas Jefferson* and *History of the United States During the Administration of James Madison,* 4 vols., edited by Henry Steele Commager, New York, 1930.

Adams, James Truslow. *The Living Jefferson,* New York, 1936.

Addison, Joseph. *The Spectator,* No. 108.

Agar, Herbert. *The People's Choice,* Boston, 1936.

American Guide Series. *New York,* New York, 1940.

   Virginia, New York, 1940.

   Washington: City and Capital, Washington, D.C., 1937.

   Washington, D.C.: A Guide to the Nation's Capital, New York, 1942.

Anburey, Thomas. *Travels Through the Interior Parts of America,* 2 vols., Boston & New York, 1923.

Anderson, Jefferson Randolph. "Tuckahoe and the Tuckahoe Randolphs," *1970 Annual Report of the Monticello Association,* Charlottesville, 1971.

Anderson, Sterling P., Jr. *Virginia Cavalcade,* "'Queen Molly' and the Virginia House Wife," Vol. XX, Number 4, Richmond, Spring 1971.

Appleton's Cyclopedia of American Biography, New York, 1888.

Archives, Harvard University Library. Photocopies from the fortieth anniversary report of the class of 1858.

   Photocopies from the fiftieth anniversary report of the class of 1850.

Arkansas Gazette. Photostats re Meriwether Lewis Randolph, Jan.–Feb. 1956.

Armes, Ethel. *Stratford Hall: The Great House of the Lees,* Richmond, 1936.

The Atlantic Monthly. "An Old Virginia Correspondence," Vol. LXXXIV, Boston, 1899.

Axelrad, Jacob. *Patrick Henry—The Voice of Freedom,* New York, 1947.

Bagby, George William. *The Old Virginia Gentleman and other Sketches,* New York, 1910.

Ballagh, James Curtis, editor. *The Letters of Richard Henry Lee,* Vol. I, 1762–1778, New York, 1911.

Barzman, Sol. *The First Ladies,* New York, 1970.

Bassett, John Spencer, editor. *Correspondence of Andrew Jackson,* Vol. 4, Washington, D.C., 1929.

——. *The Writings of "Colonel William Byrd of Westover in Virginia Esqr.",* New York, 1901.

Baugh, A. C., et al. *A Literary History of England,* New York and London, 1948.

Bear, James A., Jr., editor. *Jefferson at Monticello,* Charlottesville, 1967. (paperback)

Bergh, Albert Ellery, editor. *The Writings of Thomas Jefferson,* Definitive Edition, Thomas Jefferson Memorial Association, 20 vols. in 10, Washington, D.C., 1907.

Betts, Edwin Morris and Bear, James A., Jr., editors. *The Family Letters of Thomas Jefferson,* Columbia, Mo., 1966.

Beveridge, Albert J. *The Life of John Marshall,* 4 vols., Boston, 1916.

Beverley, Robert. *The History and Present State of Virginia,* edited by Louis B. Wright, Chapel Hill, 1947.

Biddle, Francis. *A Casual Past,* New York, 1961.

——. "Scandal at Bizarre," *American Heritage,* XII, 5, August 1961.

Biographical Dictionary of the American Congress 1774–1949, Washington, D.C., 1950.

Blanchard, Elizabeth Amis Cameron and Wellman, Manly Wade. *The Life and Times of Sir Archie—The Story of America's Greatest Thoroughbred 1805–1833,* Chapel Hill, 1958.

Bowers, Claude G. *The Party Battles of the Jackson Period,* Boston, 1922.

——. *The Tragic Era,* Boston, 1929.

——. *Jefferson in Power—The Death Struggle of the Federalists,* Boston, 1936.

Boyd, Julian P. *The Murder of George Wythe,* Philadelphia, 1949.

——. *Between the Spur and the Bridle,* New York, 1968.

——. *The Spirit of Christmas at Monticello,* New York, 1964.

——, editor. *The Papers of Thomas Jefferson,* Princeton University Press, 1950 forward.

Boyd, Thomas. *Light-Horse Harry Lee,* New York, 1931.

Brady, Joseph P. *The Trial of Aaron Burr,* New York, 1913.

Brant, Irving. *James Madison—*
  Vol. I, *The Virginia Revolutionist 1751–1780,* Indianapolis, 1941.
  Vol. II, *The Nationalist 1780–1787,* Indianapolis, 1948.
  Vol. III, *Father of the Constitution, 1787–1800,* Indianapolis, 1950.
  Vol. IV, *Secretary of State 1800–1809,* Indianapolis, 1953.
  Vol. V, *The President 1809–1812,* Indianapolis, 1956.
  Vol. VI, *Commander in Chief 1812–1836,* Indianapolis, 1961.
Brewster, Lawrence Fay. "Summer Migrations and Resorts of South Carolina Low-Country Planters," *Historical Papers of the Trinity College Historical Society,* Series XXVI, Duke U. Press, 1947.
Brock, Robert A. *Pocahontas, Alias Matoaka and Her Descendants,* Richmond, 1887.
Brooks, Jerome E. *The Mighty Leaf—Tobacco Through the Centuries,* Boston, 1952.
Brooks, Van Wyck. *The World of Washington Irving,* New York, 1944.
Brown, Everett Somerville, editor. *William Plumer's Memorandum of Proceedings in the United States Senate, 1803–1807,* New York, 1923.
Bruce, Philip Alexander. *The Virginia Plutarch,* 2 vols., Chapel Hill, 1929.
Bruce, William Cabell. *John Randolph of Roanoke,* 2 vols., New York, 1922.
Burke, John Daly. *The History of Virginia from its First Settlement to the Present Day,* 4 vols., Petersburg, 1860.
Burke, Pauline Wilcox. *Emily Donelson of Tennessee,* 2 vols., Richmond, 1941.
Burnaby, Andrew. *Travels Through the Middle Settlements in North America in the Years 1759 and 1760,* reprinted from the third edition of 1798 with introduction and notes by Rufus Rockwell Wilson, New York, 1904.
Burt, Nathaniel. *First Families,* Boston, 1970.
Caldwell, Mary French. *General Jackson's Lady,* Nashville, 1936.
The Cambridge History of American Literature, edited by W. P. Trent et al., New York, 1921.
Campbell, T. Beverly. *Virginia Oddities,* Richmond, 1933.
Carter, Hodding. *The Angry Scar,* New York, 1959.
Channing, William Henry, editor. *Memoir of William Ellery Channing,* Vol. I, Boston, 1848.
Chesnut, Mary Boykin. *A Diary from Dixie,* New York, 1905.
Chastellux, Marquis de, revised translation and notes by Howard C. Rice, Jr. *Travels in North America in the Years 1780, 1781, and 1782,* 2 vols., Chapel Hill for Williamsburg, 1936.
Coit, Margaret L. *John C. Calhoun—American Portrait,* Boston, 1950.
Coleman, J. Winston, Jr. *Slavery Times in Kentucky,* Chapel Hill, 1940.
Collis, Maurice. *Nancy Astor: An Informal Biography,* New York, 1960.
Connecticut Historical Society, Walcott Collection. Photostats letters re Theodorick Bland, Jr.
Conway, Moncure Daniel. *Omitted Chapters of History—Disclosed in the Life of Edmund Randolph,* New York, 1888.

Crandall, Margaret Lyle. *Confederate Imprints—A Check List Based Principally on the Collection of the Boston Athenaeum*, Boston, 1955.

Craven, Avery. *Edmund Ruffin, Southerner*, New York, 1932.

Cresson, W. P. *James Monroe*, Chapel Hill, 1946.

Dabney, Richard Heath. *John Randolph*, Chicago, 1898.

Dabney, Virginius. *Virginia—The New Dominion*, New York, 1971.

Davis, Matthew L., editor. *The Private Journal of Aaron Burr*, 2 vols., New York, 1838.

———. *Memoirs of Aaron Burr*, 2 vols., New York, 1838.

Department of the Navy, Naval History. Photostat of Lt. Robert B. Randolph's naval service record.

Dictionary of American Biography.

Dowdey, Clifford. *The Land They Fought For: The Story of the South as the Confederacy 1832–1865*, New York, 1955.

———. *The Great Plantation: A Profile of Berkeley Hundred and Plantation Virginia from Jamestown to Appomattox*, Berkeley Plantation, Charles City, Va., 1957.

———. *The Virginia Dynasties—The Emergence of "King" Carter and the Golden Age*, Boston, 1969.

Dumbauld, Edward. *Thomas Jefferson—American Tourist*, Norman, Okla., 1946.

Eaton, Margaret. *The Autobiography of Peggy Eaton—with a preface by Charles F. Deems*, New York, 1932.

Eckenrode, H. J. *The Randolphs: The Story of a Virginia Family*, Indianapolis, 1946.

Encyclopedia Britannica, 11th edition and 1967 edition.

Fishwick, Marshall W. *Virginia: A New Look at the Old Dominion*, New York, 1959.

Fiske, John. *Old Virginia and Her Neighbors*, 2 vols., Boston, 1897.

Freeman, Douglas Southall. *George Washington—A Biography*, 4 vols., New York, 1949.

———. *R. E. Lee—A Biography*, 4 vols., New York, 1935.

Gaines, William H., Jr. *Thomas Mann Randolph—Jefferson's Son-in-Law*, Baton Rouge, La., 1966.

Garland, Hugh A. *The Life of John Randolph of Roanoke*, 13th edition, New York, 1860.

Glenn, Thomas Allen, using passages by Kate Mason Rowland. *Some Colonial Mansions—and Those Who Lived in Them*, Philadelphia, undated.

Goochland County Historical Society Magazine, Vol. 3, No. 1, Spring 1971.

Hallum, John. *Biographical and Pictorial History of Arkansas*, Vol. I., Albany, 1887.

Hamlin, Talbot. *Benjamin Henry Latrobe*, New York, 1955.

Hanna, Dr. W. *Memoirs of Dr. Chalmers*, New York, 1850.

Harrell, Isaac Samuel. *Loyalism in Virginia—Chapters in the Economic History of the Revolution*, Duke U. Press, 1926.

Harrison, Mrs. Burton. *Recollections Grave and Gay*, New York, 1911.

Harrison, Fairfax. *The Virginia Carys—An Essay in Genealogy*, privately printed, The Devinne Press, New York, 1919.

——. *The Randolph Stud*, privately printed, Richmond, 1930.

——. *The Equine F.F.Vs.—A study of the evidence for the English horses imported into Virginia before the Revolution*, privately printed, Richmond, 1928. Copyright 1928 by Fairfax Harrison. [Name of author does not appear on title page of these 3 vols.]

——. *A History of the Legal Development of the Railroad System of the Southern Railroad Company*, Washington, 1901.

——. "The Proprietors of the Northern Neck," *The Virginia Magazine of History and Biography*, Chapter Four, Vol. XXXIII, No. 4, October 1925.

——. *A Selection of the Letters of Fairfax Harrison*, Copyright Francis Burton Harrison, 1944, Charlottesville, Va.

Heitman, Francis B. *Historical Register and Dictionary of the United States Army, From its Organization, September 29, 1789, to March 2, 1903*, Vol. I., Washington, 1903.

Hendrick, Burton J. *The Lees of Virginia*, Boston, 1935.

Hinke, William J., editor & translator. "Report of the Journey of Francis Louis Michel from Berne, Switzerland, to Virginia, October 2, (1) 1701–December 1, 1702," *The Virginia Magazine of History and Biography*, Part II, Vol. XXIV, No. 2, April 1916.

Hirst, Francis W. *Life and Letters of Thomas Jefferson*, New York, 1926.

Hoge, Peyton Harrison. *Moses Drury Hoge: Life and Letters*, Richmond, 1899.

James, Marquis. *Andrew Jackson—Portrait of a President*, Indianapolis, 1937.

Johnson, Gerald W. *Randolph of Roanoke—A Political Fantastic*, New York, 1929.

Johnson, Robert Underwood and Buel, Clarence Clough, editors. *Battles and Leaders of the Civil War*, 4 vols., New York, 1887–88.

Jones, Hugh, edited by Morton, Richard. *Present State of Virginia*, Chapel Hill, 1956.

Jordan, Winthrop D. *White Over Black—American Attitudes Toward the Negro, 1550–1812*, Chapel Hill, 1968.

Karsner, David. *Andrew Jackson—The Gentle Savage*, New York, 1929.

Ketcham, Ralph. *James Madison—A Biography*, New York, 1971.

Kimball, Marie. *Jefferson: The Road to Glory 1743–1776*, New York, 1943.

——. *Jefferson War and Peace 1776–1784*, New York, 1947.

Latrobe, Benjamin Henry. *The Journal of Latrobe*, New York, 1905.

Lee, Henry. *Memoirs of the War in the Southern Department of the United States*, by Henry Lee, Lieutenant-Colonel Commander of the Partesan Legion During the American War—a new edition, with revisions, and a biography of the author by Robert E. Lee, New York, 1869.

Lee, E. J. *Lee of Virginia 1642–1892*, Philadelphia, 1895.

The Lees of Virginia, published by The Society of the Lees of Virginia, 1967.

Library of Congress. Photostat letter from David Meade Randolph to Thomas Jefferson, 1/10/1804.

Library of Southern Literature, ed. E. A. Aldermann and Joel Chandler Harris, New Orleans, Atlanta, Dallas, Martin & Hoyt, 1910.

Lutz, Francis Earle. *Chesterfield—An Old Virginia County,* Richmond, 1954.

Lynch, Denis Tilden. *An Epoch and a Man—Martin Van Buren and His Times,* New York, 1929.

Maddex, Jack P., Jr. *The Virginia Conservatives 1861–1879—A Study in Reconstruction Politics,* Chapel Hill, 1970.

Malone, Dumas. *Jefferson and His Time—*
Vol. One, *Jefferson the Virginian,* Boston, 1948.
Vol. Two, *Jefferson and the Rights of Man,* Boston, 1951.
Vol. Three, *Jefferson and the Ordeal of Liberty,* Boston, 1962.
Vol. Four, *Jefferson the President—First Term 1801–1805,* Boston, 1970.

Materials on Fairfax Harrison, provided by William F. Geeslin, asst. v-pres. Southern Railway System.

May, Alma. *The Negro and Mercer County,* unpublished thesis, 1968, University of Dayton (Story of experience of the emancipated slaves of John Randolph of Roanoke).

Mays, David John. *Edmund Pendleton 1721–1803—A Biography,* Vol. I, Harvard U. Press, 1952.

——, editor. *The Letters and Papers of Edmund Pendleton 1734–1803,* 2 vols. U. Va. Press (for the Virginia Historical Society) Charlottesville, 1967.

Meade, Bishop William. *Old Churches Ministers and Families of Virginia,* 2 vols., reprinted Genealogical Publishing Co., Baltimore, 1966.

Minnigerode, Meade. *Some American Ladies,* New York, 1926.

Mordecai, Samuel. *Virginia, Especially Richmond, in By-gone Days,* Richmond, 1860.

Morgan, George. *The True Patrick Henry,* Philadelphia, 1907.

Morton, Louis. *Robert Carter of Nomini Hall—A Virginia Tobacco Planter of the Eighteenth Century,* Williamsburg, 1941.

Morton, Richard L. *Colonial Virginia Vol. II. Westward Expansion and Prelude to Revolution 1710–1763,* UNC Press, 1960.

Mott, Frank Luther. *American Journalism,* New York, 1956.

National Archives. Records of the Adjutant General's Office, Medical Officers Personnel Files, Phillip G. Randolph, 1826–28.

——. Microfilm of the Record of the inquiry into the case of Lieutenant Robert B. Randolph and President Jackson's decision to dismiss him from the Navy.

The National Cyclopaedia of American Biography, New York, 1926.

Nelligan, Murray H. *Old Arlington,* U. S. Dept. of the Interior, National Capital Parks, Washington, D.C., 1958.

Nevins, Allan, editor. *The Diary of John Quincy Adams 1794–1845,* New York, London, Toronto, 1928.

Nock, Albert J. *Jefferson*, New York, 1926.

Norfleet, Fillmore. *Saint-Mémin in Virginia: Portraits and Biographies*, Richmond, 1942.

Oberholtzer, Ellis Paxton. *Robert Morris—Patriot and Financier*, New York, 1903.

Padover, Saul K., editor. *Thomas Jefferson and the National Capital*, Washington, D.C., 1946.

Page, Richard Channing Moore. *Genealogy of the Page Family in Virginia*, New York, 1893.

Page, Thomas Nelson. *Bred in the Bone*, New York, 1904.

——. *In Ole Virginia*, New York, 1887.

——. *The Old South*, New York, 1892.

Parton, James. *The Life of Andrew Jackson in Three Volumes*, New York, 1860.

——. *The Life of Thomas Jefferson*, Boston, 1899.

Paxton, William M. *The Marshall Family, or A Genealogical Chart of the Descendants of John Marshall and Elizabeth Markham*, Cincinnati, 1895.

Peterson, Merrill D. *Thomas Jefferson & the new nation—A Biography*, New York, 1970.

——. *The Jefferson Image in the American Mind*, New York, 1960.

Phillips, Ulrich Bonnell. *American Negro Slavery*, Gloucester, Mass., 1959. (First printed in 1918.)

Phisterer, Frederick. *New York in the War of the Rebellion, 1861–1865*, 2nd ed., Albany, Weed Parsons Co., 1890.

Pleasants, Lucy Lee. *Old Virginia Days and Ways*, Menasha, Wis., 1916.

Pollack, Queena. *Peggy Eaton, Democracy's Mistress*, New York, 1931.

Prominent Families of New York, The Historical Company, New York, 1897.

Randall, Henry S. *Life of Thomas Jefferson*, 3 vols., New York, 1858.

Randolph, Alfred Pace. "How Could Red Riding Hood," copy of song undated.

Randolph, Edmund. *Vindication of Mr. Randolph's Resignation*, Philadelphia, 1795.

——, edited with an introduction by Arthur H. Shaffer. *History of Virginia*, U. Va. Press, 1970.

Randolph, Innes. *Poems*, Williams & Wilkins Co., Baltimore, 1898.

Randolph, Isham. *Gleanings from a Harvest of Memories*, privately printed by E. W. Stephens, Columbia, Mo., 1937.

Randolph, John. *Randolph Family of Virginia*, (pamphlet).

Randolph, Mary. *The Virginia Housewife*, Washington, D.C., 1824.

Randolph, Robert Isham. Scrapbook in possession of Dr. Angus Randolph, Winston-Salem, N.C.

——. *The Randolphs of Virginia*, Chicago, 1936.

Randolph, Roberta Lee. *The First Randolphs of Virginia*, Public Affairs Press, Washington, D.C., 1961. (paperback)

Randolph, Sarah N. *The Domestic Life of Thomas Jefferson*, New York, 1871.

Randolph, Wassell. *Henry Randolph I (1623–1673) of Henrico County, Virginia, and His Descendants*, Memphis, Tenn., 1952.

——. *William Randolph I of Turkey Island, Henrico County, Virginia and His Immediate Descendants*, Memphis, 1949.

Reniers, Percival. *The Springs of Virginia*, Chapel Hill, 1941.

Report of the Adjutant General [N.Y. State]. Registers of the 5th and 6th Artillery [N.Y.] in the War of the Rebellion for the year 1896.

Reports of the Trials of Colonel Aaron Burr for Treason and for a Misdemeanor, taken in shorthand by David Robertson, 2 vols., Philadelphia, 1808.

Rive, Alfred. "A Brief History of Regulation and Taxation of Tobacco in England," *William and Mary College Quarterly Historical Magazine*, Second Installment, Vol. IX, No. 2, April 1929.

Rivers of America Series. Gutheim, Frederick, *The Potomac*, New York, 1949.

——. Niles, Blair, *The James: From Iron Gate to Sea*, New York, 1945.

——. Waters, Frank, *The Colorado*, New York, 1946.

——. Hansen, Harry, *The Chicago*, New York, 1942.

Robert, Joseph C. *The Story of Tobacco in America*, New York, 1952.

Rochefoucauld-Liancourt, Duc de la. *Travels Through the United States of North America*, 4 vols., London, 1799.

Rogers, George C., Jr. *The History of Georgetown County, South Carolina*, USC Press, 1970.

Rothert, Otto A. "The Tragedy of the Lewis Brothers," *The Filson Club Historical Quarterly*, vol. 10, No. 4, Louisville, Ky., October 1936.

Rutland, Robert A., editor. *The Papers of George Mason 1725–1792*, 3 vols., Chapel Hill, 1970.

Safford, William H. *The Blennerhassett Papers—Embodying the Private Journal of Harman Blennerhassett*, Cincinnati, 1864.

——. *The Life of Harman Blennerhassett*, Chillicothe, Ohio, 1850.

Savage, Henry, Jr. *Lost Heritage*, New York, 1970.

Schachner, Nathan. *Aaron Burr*, New York, 1961. (paperback)

——. *Alexander Hamilton*, New York, 1961. (paperback)

——. *Thomas Jefferson*, 2 vols. in 1, New York, 1964.

Scharf, J. Thomas. *History of Westchester County, New York*, Philadelphia, 1886.

Schlesinger, Arthur M., Jr. *The Age of Jackson*, Boston, 1945. (paperback)

Seaton, William Winston. *A Biographical Sketch*, Boston, 1871.

Seitz, Don C. *Famous American Duels*, New York, 1929.

Shackelford, George Green, editor. *Collected Papers to Commemorate Fifty Years of the Monticello Association of the Descendants of Thomas Jefferson*, Princeton, N.J., 1965.

Shaler, Nathaniel Southgate. *The Autobiography of Nathaniel Southgate Shaler*, Boston and New York, 1909.

Shuck, Oscar T. *Bench and Bar in California*, San Francisco, 1888.

——, editor. *Representative and Leading Men of the Pacific*, San Francisco, 1870.

Smedes, Susan D. *Memorials of a Southern Planter*, New York, 1965.

Smith, Margaret Bayard. *The First Forty Years of Washington Society*, New York, 1965.

Stanard, Mary Newton. *Richmond, Its People and Its Story*, Philadelphia, 1923.

———. *The Story of Virginia's First Century*, Philadelphia, 1928.

Stone, Irving. *Men to Match My Mountains—The Opening of the Far West, 1840–1900*, New York, 1956.

Sutro Library. Photostats re Edmund Randolph of California.

Swem, E. G. *Virginia Historical Index in Two Volumes*, Vol. Two L–Z, Roanoke, Va., 1936.

———. "Some Notes on the Four Forms of the Oldest Building of William and Mary College," *William and Mary College Quarterly Historical Magazine*, Vol. VIII, Second Series, No. 4, October 1928.

Swiggett, Howard. *The Extraordinary Mr. Morris*, New York, 1952.

Sydnor, Charles S. *Gentlemen Freeholders—Political Practices in Washington's Virginia*, Chapel Hill, 1952.

The Negro in Virginia, compiled by workers of the Writers' Program of W.P.A. in Virginia, New York, 1940.

Thomas, Emory M. *The Confederate State of Richmond: A Biography of the Capital*, Austin, Texas, 1971.

Thomason, John W., Jr. *Jeb Stuart*, New York, 1930.

Tinkham, George H. *California Men and Events—Time 1769–1890*, Stockton, Cal., 1915.

Torrence, Clayton, editor. *The Edward Pleasants Valentine Papers, Abstracts of Records in the local and general Archives of Virginia*, Richmond, 1927.

Town Topics, New York, Thursday February 18, 1897. Obituary of Gouverneur Morris.

Trent, W. P. *The American Historical Review*, "The Case of Josiah Philips," Vol. I, October 1895 to July 1896, New York, 1896.

Trudell, Clyde F. *Colonial Yorktown*, Old Greenwich, Conn., 1971.

Tyler's Quarterly Historical and Genealogical Magazine, "Bland Seats on the South Side of the James—Jordan's Point, Farmingdale, Cawsons," by Magdalen Bland Temple, Vol. XXIV, No. 2, October 1942.

Vandiver, Frank E. *Their Tattered Flags*, New York, 1970.

The Virginia Historical Society. *An Occasional Bulletin*, "Isham Randolph: Jefferson's Grandfather," Number 22, April 1971.

The Virginia Magazine of History and Biography.
  "Culpeper's Report on Virginia in 1683," Vol. III, No. 3, January 1896.
  "Virginia Council Journals, 1726–1753," Vol. XXXII, No. 1, January 1924, and Vol. XXXII, No. 2, April 1924.
  "Narrative of Bacon's Rebellion," Vol. IV, No. 2, October 1896.
  "The Randolph Manuscript," Vol. XXII, No. 4, October 1914.
  "Virginia Council Journals, 1726–1753," Vol. XXXII, No. 1, January 1924.

"Edmund Randolph's Essay on the Revolutionary History of Virginia, 1774–1782," (continued) Vol. XLIV, December 31, 1936.

"Descendants of John Stith and Mary Randolph," by Armistead C. Gordon, Vol. VIII, No. 1, July 1900.

"Some Side-Lights on Early Virginia Coal Mining," by Howard N. Eavenson, Vol. L, December 31, 1942.

"The Causes of Bacon's Rebellion," by Warren L. Billings (La. State U.) Vol. 78, No. 4, October 1970.

Von Riedesel, Baroness, a revised translation with introduction and note by Marvin L. Brown, Jr., with the assistance of Marta Huth. *Baroness Von Riedesel and the American Revolution—Journal and Correspondence of a Tour of Duty, 1776–1783*, Chapel Hill for Williamsburg, 1965.

Walz, Jay and Audrey. *The Bizarre Sisters*, New York, 1950.

Washburn, Wilcomb E. *The Governor and the Rebel: A History of Bacon's Rebellion in Virginia*, Chapel Hill, 1957.

Waterman, Thomas Tileston. *The Mansions of Virginia 1706–1776*, Chapel Hill, 1945.

Weeks, Elie. *Dungeness*, unpublished manuscript.

Wellman, Paul I. *The House Divides*, New York, 1966.

Wertenbaker, Thomas J. *Patrician and Plebeian in Virginia*, New York, 1959.

Whitehill, Walter Muir. *Boston and the Civil War*, Boston, 1963.

William and Mary College Quarterly Historical Magazine.

"Williamsburg—The Old Colonial Capital," Vol. XVI, No. 1, July 1907.

"Letters of Major Thomas Rowland, C.S.A. From North Carolina, 1861 and 1862," Vol. XXV, No. 2, October 1916.

"Werowocomoco," Vol. X, No. 1, July 1901.

"Randolph Family," Report of Isaac G. Bates. Communicated by Miss M. Randolph, Ruxton, Baltimore County, Maryland, Vol. XXI, No. 1, July 1912.

"Virginia Patents," by A. J. Morrison, Vol. II, Second Series, No. 3, July 1922.

"Randolph Family," by W. G. Stanard, Vols. VII & VIII, 1899 and 1900.

Williams, John Rogers, editor. *Philip Vickers Fithian—Journal and Letters 1767–1774*, Princeton, 1900.

Wilstach, Paul. *Tidewater Virginia*, Indianapolis, 1929.

——. *Potomac Landings*, Indianapolis, 1921.

Wiltse, Charles Maurice. *The Jeffersonian Tradition in American Democracy*, Chapel Hill, 1935.

Wise, Henry A. *Seven Decades of the Union*, Philadelphia, 1872.

Wister, Mrs. O. J., and Irwin, Miss Agnes, editors. *Worthy Women of Our First Century*, Philadelphia, 1877.

Woods, Edgar. *Albemarle County in Virginia*, Bridgewater, Va., 1932.

Wright, Louis B. *The First Gentlemen of Virginia—Intellectual Qualities of the Early Colonial Ruling Class,* San Marino, Cal., 1940.

——, editor. *Letters of Robert Carter—1720–1727—The Commercial Interests of a Virginia Gentleman,* The Huntington Library, 1940.

—— and Tinling, Marion, editors. *The Secret Diary of William Byrd of Westover 1709–1712,* Richmond, 1941.

——. *William Byrd of Virginia—The London Diary (1717–1721) and Other Writings,* New York, 1958.

INDEX